WHAT IS THE

Good Life?

WHAT IS THE

Good Life?

Luc Ferry

~ ~ ~ ~ ~

TRANSLATED BY
LYDIA G. COCHRANE

THE UNIVERSITY OF CHICAGO PRESS
CHICAGO

LUC FERRY has taught at the Sorbonne and
at the University of Caen. He is the former Minister of Education
and Youth in the French government. Ferry is the author
or coauthor of eight previous books published by the Press, including
most recently *The New Ecological Order* and *Man Made God.*

LYDIA G. COCHRANE has translated several books
from French and Italian for the University of Chicago Press,
including Alan Boreau's *The Lord's First Night*
and Renzo Dubbin's *Geography of the Gaze.*

Originally published as *Qu'est-ce qu'une vie réussie?,*
© Éditions Grasset & Fasquelle, 2002.

The University of Chicago Press, Chicago 60637
© 2005 by The University of Chicago
All rights reserved. Published 2005
Printed in the United States of America
14 13 12 11 10 09 08 07 06 05   1 2 3 4 5
ISBN: 0-226-24453-9 (cloth)

LIBRARY OF CONGRESS
CATALOGING-IN-PUBLICATION DATA

Ferry, Luc.
[Qu'est-ce qu'une vie réussie? English]
What is the good life? / Luc Ferry ; translated by Lydia G. Cochrane.
p. cm.
Includes bibliographical references and index.
ISBN 0-226-24453-9 (cloth : alk. paper)
1. Conduct of life. 2. Success. I. Title.
BJ1612.F4713 2005
170—dc22   2004020135

⊗ The paper used in this publication meets
the minimum requirements of the American National
Standard for Information Sciences—Permanence of Paper
for Printed Library Materials, ANSI Z39.48-1992.

To Marie-Caroline, "Matao," my wife,
for whom this book was written

~ ~ ~ ~ ~

CONTENTS

PROLOGUE

Our Daydreams:
Success, Ennui, & Envy

I

~ ~ ~ ~ ~

PART I

*Creating the Good Life:
Metamorphoses of the Ideal*

CHAPTER I

Beyond Morality, After Religion

The New Age of the Question

17

CHAPTER 2

The Meaning of the Question
& the Slow Humanization
of the Responses

29

~ ~ ~ ~ ~

PART II

*The Nietzschean Moment:
The Good Life as the Most Intense Life*

CHAPTER 3

On Transcendence as Supreme Illusion

*The Twilight of the Idols, or How to Philosophize
with a Hammer: The End of the World,
the Death of God, & the Death of Man*

49

CHAPTER 4

The Foundations & Arguments
of Nietzschean Materialism

60

CHAPTER 5

The Wisdom of Nietzsche, or
The Three Criteria of the Good Life

*Truth in Art, Intensity in the Grand Style,
Eternity in the Instant*

78

CHAPTER 6

After Nietzsche

*Four Versions of Life after the Death of God:
Daily Life, the Bohemian Life, the Life of Enterprise,
or Life Freed from Alienation*

103

~ ~ ~ ~ ~

PART III

*The Wisdom of the Ancients:
Life in Harmony with the Cosmic Order*

CHAPTER 7

Greek Wisdom, or The First Image
of a Lay Spirituality

The Secularization of Salvation

135

CHAPTER 8

The "Cosmologico-Ethical"

*Power and the Charms of Moralities
Inscribed in the Cosmos*

153

CHAPTER 9

An Ideal-Type of Ancient Wisdom

The Case of Stoicism

164

~ ~ ~ ~ ~

PART IV

*The Here & Now
Enchanted by the Beyond*

CHAPTER 10

Death Finally Conquered by Immortality

Philosophy Replaced by Religion

185

CHAPTER 11

The Renascence of Lay Philosophy
& the Humanization of the Good Life

213

~ ~ ~ ~ ~

PART V

*A Humanism of the Man-God:
The Good Life as a Life
in Harmony with the Human Condition*

CHAPTER 12

Materialism, Religion, & Humanism

249

CHAPTER 13

A New Approach to the Question of Happiness

271

~ ~ ~ ~ ~

NOTES

289

INDEX

311

Our Daydreams:
Success, Ennui, & Envy

Je m'présente, je m'appelle Henri,
J'voudrais bien réussir ma vie, être aimé,
Être beau, gagner de l'argent,
Puis surtout être intelligent,
Mais pour tout ça faudrait que j'bosse à plein temps . . .

Daniel Balavoine

In a brief lecture that he published in 1908, "Creative Writers and Day-Dreaming," Sigmund Freud ventured an interpretation of the significance of an aspect of our psychic life that might at first sight seem simply anecdotal, the "daydreams" and "castles in Spain" that our imagination sometimes constructs to compensate for the frustrations inflicted on us by real life. These little scenarios of ordinary revery are usually cast in the three dimensions of time: acknowledging the poverty of the present, they plunge into the past for materials for a skillful reconstruction that traces the contours of a more successful future. To illustrate his theme, Freud invites us to reflect on the following fable, clearly invented for the occasion:

> Let us take the case of a poor orphan boy to whom you have given the address of some employer where he may perhaps find a job. On his way there he may indulge in a day-dream appropriate to the situation from which it arises. The content of his phantasy will perhaps be something like this. He is given a job, finds favour with his new employer, makes himself indispensable in the business, is taken into his employer's family, marries the charming young daughter of

the house, and then himself becomes a director of the business, first as his employer's partner and then as his successor. In this phantasy, the dreamer has regained what he possessed in his happy child-hood—the protecting house, the loving parents and the first objects of his affectionate feelings. You will see from this example the way in which the wish makes use of an occasion in the present to con-struct, on the pattern of the past, a picture of the future.[1]

The brief anecdote is a bit thin, as Freud cheerfully admits. He was neither a writer nor a poet, and his example is little more than a composite picture. The reveries that he credits to the young of his epoch seem decidedly con-ventional today, but with a bit of goodwill we understand perfectly what he means. When we add a personal correction here and there or make a few adjustments for current conventions, it is hard not to see ourselves in the anecdote. Whether we admit it or not, at one time or another, and often well past adolescence, we all give in to fantasies like the one Freud re-counts. The success of certain films or novels (which even make up a liter-ary genre of their own) makes it unnecessary to insist on the point. Yet, as Freud so rightly notes, a strange and deep-seated feeling of shame is at-tached to admitting to such reveries.

We would rather own up to our least pardonable faults than publicly re-veal our secret fantasies, even though everything tells us that they are com-mon, if not universal. They correspond to criteria of an astonishing banal-ity and fall under a typology so elementary as to be easily sketched. There are, first, dreams of *possession,* the model for which is La Fontaine's Per-rette, the milkmaid who dreams about what she will do with the proceeds when she has sold her jar of milk, then drops the jar, spilling both her milk and her dreams.[2] If only we could win the lottery, inherit a fortune from a long-lost uncle, or something similar, we too would buy cows, pigs, and chickens—or rather a car, a boat, or a house in the country, at the seashore, or in the mountains—and perhaps even remember to give a little (not too much, though) to brothers and sisters, to Aunt Nina, and to charitable in-stitutions. Next in order come fantasies of *rectification.* If courage failed us during an altercation, if we could not produce a telling retort in a dispute, if our wit dried up in a conversation, or if our behavior was less than ster-ling, the daydream provides an impeccable restoration of what we so sorely lacked in reality. A third category involves the ideal of *seduction.* Here we are at last endowed with sublime qualities; we are a virtuoso musician flaw-lessly playing an instrument on which up to now we have produced only agonizing squeaks; we are champions at a sport we were about to give up in disgust; we display to others hitherto unsuspected virtues of intelligence and beauty, including (carrying irony to a new height) a modesty, even a humility, that attracts universal admiration and makes our many talents shine all the brighter. If we add *erotic* dreams, both sexual and amorous, a category that includes "true love" and its complement of Prince Charmings and *femmes fatales,* we will have just about covered our imaginative capabilities in the realm of "social success." Why, then, are we so ashamed to admit to such aspirations?

For some "good reasons"—by which one generally means the worst reasons—which are not lacking in interest. First because the daydream, as we well know, is to a large extent infantile. As we can see on a daily basis, children are quick to use their imaginations for fantasizing: they continually invent marvelous worlds for themselves, working with great concentration and investing immense amounts of affect in them. Here, as Freud stresses, the contrary of play is reality, not seriousness. We need to add, however, that children have an excuse for daydreams that adults have unfortunately lost: they play at being "grown-ups"—doctors, pilots, train engineers, or race-car drivers—or they acquire the lofty status of parents of their teddy bears and dolls. When they do so, we gladly judge their behavior "appropriate"—that is, in conformity with their status as children, given that is their destiny to "grow up." This privilege is in large part withheld from us.

In an adult the infantilism of the daydream combines with an egocentrism, even an egotism, that it is considered unseemly to display in public. One of the most consistent and obvious traits of our fantasies is that we invariably appear in them as the Hero, the center of the tale and the focus of all eyes, the unstoppable person who succeeds in everything and stands firm through the most terrible trials. Once again, many literary works directly echo the daydream: at the chapter's end, Rouletabille, Gaston Leroux's detective hero, lies at the bottom of the river, bound by heavy, solidly padlocked chains. This does not worry us, however, because we know that the next episode will begin, "When Rouletabille climbed back up on the riverbank . . ." Reality is of course less friendly to our beloved Self.

A third characteristic of this psychic activity contributes even more subtly to discrediting all disclosure. To have a need to fantasize is to concede, be it only by implication, unhappiness in a real world that characteristically resists our desires. We know from experience that letting it be known that we belong to the unenvied and unenviable category of the "frustrated" is not well received. This is also why—last but not least—day-dreaming in certain cases is taken as an early symptom of insanity. If losing contact with reality is a prime sign of mental instability, constructing castles in Spain, particularly when it becomes an exuberant and invasive activity in an adult, is taken as behavior on the edge of neurosis.

Psychology textbooks offer students a well-known definition of the difference between neurosis and psychosis: the psychotic individual, they tell us, has acquired the unshakable conviction that two and two make five. Anyone who attempts to persuade this person otherwise is a trickster out to do harm. The psychotic has lost contact with reality. The neurotic is equally persuaded that two and two make five *but, unlike the psychotic, is immensely bothered by it.* The neurotic still has a relation with reality, if only through anxiety. An anecdote (invented, I think, by a German author) says the same thing in the form of a joke, and it is not entirely by chance that it borrows from the model of the daydream: the neurotic constructs castles in Spain; the psychotic lives in them (a decidedly more unfortunate state of affairs); the psychiatrist pockets the rent!

Are we about to give in to madness? Is it possible that, urged to think in fantasy terms about making a success of our lives, we are teetering on the brink of psychosis? Some might consider this an idle question. It might be said that interrogations regarding the "good life," which can be attested in the grandiose history of philosophy since ancient Greek times, are too serious to be approached lightly or in such a blatantly "psychologizing" manner. I would agree. I would have given up my pursuit of the topic if these few thoughts of Freudian inspiration did not seem to parallel one of the deepest and most philosophical traits of our time: the confusion between what the Ancients—to return to them—called the "good life" and mere "social success"; between true wisdom and the "cult of performance"[3] for its own sake in a narcissistic and unlimited concentration on power, money, and recognition. Rousseau, who showed little love for the modern world that was taking shape before his eyes, claimed that individuals' unhappiness came from the fact that they are alone when they are with others and with others when they are alone.[4] They are isolated because they are resolutely engaged in universal competition; they are close to one another because, remembering the inevitable frustrations engendered by the needs of competition, they bathe in the compensations of the daydream. The remark is profound.

We also need to understand why simple "success"—success reduced to pure performance, to power for its own sake, independent of the praiseworthy objective that it might allow us to attain—has so often become the ultimate goal of our thoughts and aspirations, even though, as is true of daydreams and for analogous reasons, we are somewhat ashamed to admit it. It might be said, not without reason, that this is not true of everyone; that the wise manage to be content with what they have; that there are other values than social success. Yes, of course, and we shall return to the topic throughout the present volume. But we must not underestimate the formidable meanders of our unconscious. Giving up infantile ideals revealed by the presence of daydreams can also mean ceding to the ideologies of renunciation, which are just as dubious and suspect in their genre as the ideologies of "success." Once again, the great La Fontaine said it all: the fable of Perrette finds a response in the fable of the fox and the luscious grapes that he judges "too green" and "good for louts" when they prove desperately inaccessible.[5]

Let us admit it: the contemporary world, for reasons that should not be eluded, incites us to daydreams at every turn. Its impressive train of stars and spangles, its culture of servility in face of the powerful, and its immoderate love of money tend to present daydreams as a *model* for life. In or out, up or down, in top form or broken down, winner or loser: everything combines today to make success—success for its own sake—an absolute ideal in all imaginable domains. Sports, the arts, the sciences, politics, business, love—everything is included, with no distinction of rank or hierarchy of values. As with the great television show portrayed in Federico Fellini's film *Ginger e Fred,* as long as the performance takes place, it *must* arouse admiration and figure as a success in the record books. It hardly matters whether the performer is a vagrant or a doctor, a football player or a musician. The imperative of success begins to look like a new way of finding fault with individuals: "losers" remain anonymous.

After all, the idea of "success" seems highly contestable. Is it not inadequate, even fallacious, as a standard for evaluating an existence as a whole? Is it not both naïve and mistaken to insist on thinking about life in terms of a category better suited for a year-end exam than for the development of a good life? Isn't it enormously pretentious to think that we can make a success of our lives in the same way that we successfully produce a soufflé or a *boeuf en daube,* especially when we consider all the things in our existence that do not depend upon us, but rather on the hazards of birth, the pure contingency of events, or the blind strokes of fortune and misfortune? Do we not grant too much of a starring role to our unhappy ego, or to a free will that plays only a bit part in the drama? The fact remains, though, that illusions of social "success" and the fantasies surrounding the myth of the self-made man and the gildings of power are so forceful today that they seem to occupy all available space, to the point of obscuring the horizon. Under cover of inviting us freely to action and to self-fulfillment, is not the ideal of "success," to which both our daydreams and the contemporary cult of performance give so much weight and set at such a high price, fast taking shape as a new tyranny?

Some may think, fatalistically, that the search for success is one of the fundamental aspects of the human condition, an essential and eternal characteristic that has always been present in the history of societies. Nothing is less certain, however. We need to be wary of anachronisms and received ideas: they risk impeding any comprehension of what is perhaps exceptional in our current situation. It is that situation that we need to take into account in order to understand how the question of the good life is posed today in terms that are just as problematic as they are novel.

The Good Life or the Successful Life? The Eclipse of Transcendence and the Condition of Modern Man

For centuries, and at the very least since the birth of philosophy in classical antiquity, to pose the question of the "good life" has been primarily a search for a transcendent principle—some entity exterior to and superior to humanity—that would permit human beings to appreciate the value of their singular existence. To evaluate the success or failure of a human life, to know whether that life had been worth living and whether it was "saved" or not, required a suprahuman criterion, a sublime unit of measurement in the name of which a more or less objective judgment could be made here on earth. As time passed, great visions of the world dominated humanity, even though such visions were certainly forged by humanity itself. Ideas such as that of a harmonious cosmic order within which each individual must find his or her proper place, or that of a benevolent God whose love would guide all human life, provided the basis for convictions that not only linked human beings to each other but also attached them to commanding values and ends that were, in their eyes, far superior to pure performance.

Closer to us in time, but in a consciously materialistic perspective, reference to principles that transcend the individual and to the religious problematic of salvation still predominated in the human world. That attitude persisted even within revolutionary ideologies that perhaps preserved the essence of faith: by conforming one's life—sacrificing it if need be—to an ideal, one could retain the conviction of being "saved" (in the literal sense) by final access to eternity. Beyond their rivalry, Don Camillo and Peppone, the feisty parish priest and the Communist mayor of the small town in Giovanni Guareschi's *Little World of Don Camillo,* could still walk the streets together. It is of course not by chance that some trace of that earthly faith should find naïve expression whenever death, by shattering the destiny of a great hero, posed the question of the ultimate meaning of his life. When Stalin died, *France Nouvelle,* the major weekly newspaper of the French Communist party, printed a front-page story written in terms that seem stupefying today but that perfectly convey the religious (even fundamentalist) nature of political belief:

> The heart of Stalin, the illustrious companion in arms and the prestigious perpetuator of Lenin, the leader, the friend, and the brother of the workers of all lands, has ceased to beat. But Stalinism lives; it is *immortal.* The sublime name of the brilliant master of world communism will shine with a flaming clarity throughout the centuries and will always be pronounced with love by a grateful humanity. To Stalin we will forever remain faithful. Communists will strive to merit, by their untiring devotion to the *sacred cause* of the working class . . . the honorable title of Stalinists. *Eternal* glory to the great Stalin, whose magisterial and *imperishable* scholarly works will aid us in gathering together the majority of the people [emphasis mine].[6]

Even today, the Cuban national anthem displays a last vestige of this religion without gods when it extends the hope of salvation to simple citizens, on the condition that they sacrifice their individual destiny to a higher cause, "because to die for the country is to live."

Even though all this is close to us in time, it has an oddly archaic ring to it. It suggests the discourse of integralism, even of mystical delirium, more than any political analysis worthy of the name. Europe has quite clearly entered into a new era of thoroughgoing secularity (or, if preferred, of radical materialism) in which for many people nothing seems truly "superhuman." "Man" has become the alpha and omega of human existence, and the transcendences of times gone by—the Cosmos or God, but also the Homeland or the Revolution—seem illusory, if not dogmatic and death-inducing. Some of course keep the faith, but they are in decreasing numbers, and for all the rest, death is henceforth without any "why," without appeal, and without a "beyond"—which is why our societies tend irresistibly to hide death from view.

As a first approximation, one might say that what best characterizes the present day (at least in the Western democracies),[7] is the conviction—joyous or nostalgic according to circumstances—that whether a life is a success or a failure will no longer be evaluated by any standard of transcendence. One highly important consequence is that, as Nietzsche understood (and he was the first and most powerful thinker of modern times in this regard), it is *within real life,* without leaving the sphere of actual human experience or fleeing toward some superior principle, that we judge an existence as more or less "successful" and "enviable," more or less rich and intense, more or less worthy of having been lived, or, to the contrary, mediocre and impoverished. Beyond a doubt, given these conditions, the first response to our interrogation regarding the good life reflects the logic of the waking dream: if there is no more transcendence, why should we not cultivate performance for performance's sake, success for the sake of success, the successful life rather than the good life, lived in the here and now rather than in a "beyond" that has become decidedly hypothetical?

Heidegger permits us to understand this change—which we might call "world-historical," to speak like Hegel, given that it has nothing anecdotal or transitory about it—in a new light, above and beyond conventional discourse on "the disenchantment of the world," the "end of ideologies," or the "disappearance of utopias." It is a change worth taking the time to comprehend and meditate.

The Cult of Performance, the World of Technology, and the Liquidation of the Question of Meaning

In his "Overcoming Metaphysics" Heidegger outlines the stages through which the contemporary world took a new path that gave primacy over all other possible aims in life to the will to power[8] and, by that token, dissociated the love of power from the superior ends that it was more or less called upon to serve in past times. This is what Heidegger calls, quite understandably, the world of *Technik.* Technology is in fact "instrumental" reason par excellence; a consideration of means as such, whatever the objectives. In this sense, one can say, for example, that a "good medical technician" (who may or may not be a good doctor) is someone who can just as easily cure a person as put a person to death. Technology, from this point of view, is thus power as such; power for its own sake, over and above any consideration of the legitimacy of its aims. What Heidegger demonstrates is that the birth of a world in which technology rules supposes a rupture not only with the traditional conceptions of science, properly speaking (which cannot be reduced to a mere instrument), but also with conceptions of the ends of human life, notably as they appear in the political realm.

Let us briefly review the stages of this process. With the emergence of modern science, symbolized (rightly or wrongly) by the name of Descartes, there arose a project for the domination of the physical world that until then had been inconceivable and that allowed us to become, in Descartes' famous formula, "the masters and possessors of nature."[9] To be more precise, however, we should add that this domination takes two forms.

It operates, first, on a *theoretical* or intellectual level as simple knowledge of things. With the appearance of modern physics (that is, of "mechanism"), nature, probably for the first time in the history of humanity, ceased to be perceived as a mysterious being, a "Great Living Creature" endowed with "occult qualities" and animated by invisible and supernatural forces that could be penetrated and to some extent channeled only by means of alchemy, religion, or magic. In this sense and despite his scientific errors, Descartes was indeed the inventor of modern rationalism. By positing that nothing in the universe changes without a reason (the principle of inertia), he did away with both the ancient cosmology that had emerged from the physics of Aristotle and the animism of the Middle Ages. If nature is losing its opacity and its mystery, it is because, from that time on, the scientist has been thinking of it and all its parts as being in conformity (by law, if not in fact, given that science is a never-ending pursuit) with his own mind. Modern science appears with the conviction that the opacity of the physical world is neither definitive nor inscribed in reality itself: it is simply the reflection of an ignorance whose boundaries can, in principle, be pushed back indefinitely.

A *practical* domination of nature corresponds to this mastery of the universe by theory (mathematical, physical, biological, etc.) in a dichotomy similar to that of will and understanding, the two essential attributes of human subjectivity. Seen as raw material, stripped of all inherent value and all meaning, nature becomes a vast reservoir of objects that humans can use as they please with a view to achieving happiness. The whole world belongs to them; everything in it becomes a means for the ends of a subjectivity with a virtually unlimited power to consume. In short, if the universe is calculable and predictable on the theoretical level, on the practical level it is manipulable and open to merciless exploitation.

This "dominating" vision of the world, which peaked in the Enlightenment and became widespread in the nineteenth century, was not yet the "world of technology" properly speaking—that is, it was not yet a world in which a consideration of ends totally disappears to the profit of a consideration of means. In the context of seventeenth- and eighteenth-century rationalism, the project of scientific mastery of the natural world, and then of the social world, still had an emancipatory aim: in principle, it was still subject to the realization of certain ends that appeared infinitely superior to it. If the point was to "appropriate" the universe, it was not out of pure fascination with human power, nor was it in order to enjoy power as such, but rather to attain such objectives as "liberty" and "happiness." This is what the Enlightenment philosophers called "Progress." Moreover, it was in relation to those higher ends that the development of the sciences seemed the vector of *civilization*. Whether or not this vision of the virtues of reason was illusory or not is beside the point here. What matters is that it was still clearly connected to objectives external to itself, and, in that sense, it could not be reduced to a purely instrumental or technical reason.

What was to characterize the technological world, on the other hand—a world wholly given over to instrumental reason as opposed to an "objective" reason that determines ends—is that production, efficiency, and performance are all that count in it. To be more precise, its only objective (to the extent that one can still speak of an objective) is that of the intensification of means as such. Thus, for example, a globalized liberal economy functions on the basis of a principle of competition that prohibits people from ever stopping to consider the end results of an incessant augmentation of productive forces. One must—whatever happens, whatever the cost—develop in order to develop, advance or perish, and no one can really tell whether development for its own sake—that is, as an increase in instrumental power—procures more happiness and liberty than was true in the past. Today's ecologists have their doubts. The romantics had theirs in an earlier epoch.

In this new perspective, the world resembles a gyroscope that simply has to keep turning, independent of any purpose, or it will topple over. Movement has become of the essence. Let us pursue this analogy for a moment. In the economy of global competition, progress is assimilated to a biological need: an enterprise that failed to compare itself with others so as to keep moving forward would soon be fated to disappear. In other words: as with the gyroscope, evolution can no longer be described confidently as progress, for the good and simple reason that when it is stripped of a purpose (not to say of a brain), there is no longer an external criterion by which it can be evaluated. Henceforth it is dependent on efficient causes, not on final causes. This leads to the impression that where the world is heading escapes us, just as it escapes our political representatives, even our economic leaders and scientists. This in turn produces a feeling of *dispossession* that at times seizes individuals when they contemplate the spectacle of a globalization that seems to betray the most elementary promises of democracy, which state that by putting an end to the societies of the ancien régime, we would finally be able to play a role in working out our own destinies and making our own history.

Quite comprehensibly, this technological perspective encourages (and even renders obligatory) a veritable cult of performance for its own sake, thus shattering the old logic of meaning in favor of an exclusive use of the logic of competition. The historical processes that affect our daily lives, which are mechanically induced and elude the control of nation-states more and more each day, are developing at a speed that is undoubtedly accelerating but, above all, is subject to no visible purpose. In this perspective, *to live, to survive,* and *to succeed* become terms that are, in the final analysis, synonymous: no matter what the "good life" might have meant in past times, it is now forced to give way to the "successful life"—or to a failed life. As a consequence, aside from absolute failure, which shockingly becomes the mere inability to adapt to the general movement, the principal menace burdening existence (aside from the fact that it comes to an end) resides in insignificance, banality, and ennui. The exponential growth of the phenomenon of envy is one of the surest signs of this. Here, too, La Fontaine's fox and his Perrette are two of a kind. Here is why.

Ennui and Envy

Technology, in the strong sense given above, is the height of ennui. This is not the fault of the objects or the machines engendered by a sometimes fecund, even inspired, technological intelligence. Nor are we referring to technical activity or its products when we speak of ennui. What I have in mind is rather the infinite logic, guided by no higher ends, of the world of technology. It is the radical and essential uselessness of what is called (probably by antiphrasis) "utility." Tools are, by definition, useful. We use a screwdriver, pliers, and a hammer to construct bookshelves, for example. But why bookshelves? To put our books on, of course. But why put them there? To avoid having cumbersome stacks about us, to find a book more easily, and so forth. But why, to pursue the question, should we need to find the book again? So that, so that, so that . . . This means that the chain of utility is, by definition, endless,[10] and it is always by positing *values superior*

to it that we put an end to it—for example, by affirming that reading and
the knowledge that it procures are *good in themselves* rather than merely
being means to other objectives. The logic of utility, like that of the daydream, is the logic of childhood, which is always asking "why" about
things, and to which the answer, sooner or later, is a dogmatic but necessary "that's the way it is," because that is indeed the way it is. But this is
also, and perhaps above all, the logic of consumption—of shopping—
which also knows no other limit than that of our means. Consumption is
similar to the daydream of possession in that once we have purchased the
calf, the cow, and the chickens (at least in our imaginations), there is nothing left to do but come back down to earth. The dream inevitably collapses,
and Perrette falls down with it. Not, as one might think at first sight, because realization of the dream is impossible, but, quite to the contrary, because we know that in the final analysis it would not bring us exactly what
we hoped from it. Nothing is worse than failure, unless it is success when it
is less than total. Nothing is more dangerous than realizing our fantasies.
They are not true desires, wishes capable of opening up real possibilities in
our lives (of the sort that perhaps should be realized), but indications of an
essential frustration that inevitably engenders in us the absurd logic of consumption and a senseless surrender to the universe of merchandise and all
its fetishes.

Is this remark reliant on luxury? Is it an attitude of the affluent? Perhaps
in part, but less than might be thought, because the domination of con-
sumeristic imperatives weighs on us all, wherever we stand on the scale of
goods and wealth. It produces approximately the same effects everywhere,
as witnessed by the uniformity with which the cruel pangs of envy afflict all
levels of modern societies.[11]

It is true that jealousy and envy are passions as old as the world. They
are already at work in the Bible, for example in the hatred that Cain bears
his brother Abel. Still, the competitive society has raised the phenomenon
to new heights. It even gives the phenomenon new meaning, as Tocqueville clearly saw in relation to the world of the aristocracy. That world was
based on the idea of a *natural hierarchy* of human beings and on the conviction that, since social classes were inscribed in the nature of things, a
proper civic order should display, as it were, "everyone in his place," the best
at the top and the rest ranged in order below them. For centuries, no one
appears to have challenged that conviction, especially since it seemed guaranteed by God himself. All more or less gracefully accepted their fate: it is
unthinkable to revolt against the dictates of nature, which include both so-

cial hierarchy and the rain and the cold. As soon as the basic equality of humankind is affirmed, however, and as soon as the principle of privilege is abolished and human beings of all origins can claim access (at least by right) to all positions in society in accordance with their works or their merit—as promised by the French Revolution and the Declaration of the Rights of Man and Citizen—things take a quite different turn. "If I am my neighbor's equal, why should he have more than me?" So goes the discourse of envy in democratic societies. For the same reason, envy is directed largely to our neighbors, to those in the same conditions as ourselves and who share our social profile. The more the givens are identical at the outset, the more the differences at the point of arrival appear "unjust." People search endlessly for reasons—immoral ones, of course—to "explain" the unjust and unmerited success of others, in an attempt to *reduce* their insupportable worth as much as possible.

There is more, however. Beyond the jealousy that has always been there—that of Cain toward Abel—and even beyond the "democratic envy" described above, there is what might be called a "superior" form of resentment. This is, of course, an unworthy sentiment, and one that morality rightly reproves. But we must not fool ourselves: if the view of the "success" of others at times affects us so strongly (even though, as with the daydream, we experience a certain shame when we acknowledge it), it is not so much because of the moral failing of covetousness (we tell children, "Never mind what other people have on their plates!") as it is because of an irrepressible metaphysical sentiment of making a false step on the road to salvation. In a universe deserted by transcendence and a world henceforth with no "beyond," the phenomenon of envy dissimulates something that runs deeper than what morality sees in it, and others' success seems to us factual proof that we are about to botch our own career, with no chance of recourse or reparation. If there is no "elsewhere," true life does not reside there: we must seek it here and now, not in a too-hypothetical future. In this perspective, the success of others is a sign that we too might have a richer, more intense, and more exalting life. Jealousy is no longer as focused on visible signs of election as it was in the universe of believers described by Max Weber; rather, given that God is dead, jealousy sends us back negatively to signs of perdition and to definitive and purely earthly failures. If there is no longer a catch-up session, it is here and now that we must be happy, and we must find ourselves "where it's happening." That we are not there is clearly demonstrated by others' success. If hell and heaven do not exist, the downturns in our fortunes lose the painful but eminent—and at times fertile—status of *trials* in an itinerary that unfailingly leads to the great beyond. The *redemptive* virtues of suffering and unhappiness are reduced to nearly zero. At most, they give us "experience," in the sense of the technical adage that what doesn't kill us makes us stronger. Those who have known "success" give others the cruel feeling that "real life" may not be "elsewhere" for everyone. Envy is directed to what the old religious (and lay) ethical systems saw as the lowliest, most insignificant, and most material aspects of existence. And slander, soon raised to the level of a literary genre, is used to reveal the disloyal and vicious strategies of the happy few, a nasty gruel that we, at least, will refuse to eat. Our only option, in this case, is to await maturity, bow to events, and permit the natural course of biological existence to calm the tumult of such infantile passions.

Has inquiry into the meaning of life become definitively outmoded in a universe in which everything combines to turn the most radical immanence of reality, just as it is, into the inviolate rule of human existence? Has the ancient question of the "good life" disappeared, another victim of the technological world? What is certain, at the very least, is that the question is posed differently, and it is that difference that the present volume intends to explore. As a first approximation, our inquiry today must be situated along the only two axes that will truly enable us to define its new meaning. First, we will need to understand how the question of the good life pertains to a sphere of philosophical thought situated beyond morality and religion. Second, we will need to measure in what sense that same question appears in a radically new light at the end of its long history, in the course of which human beings have claimed to have gradually been freeing themselves from the tutelage of the great cosmological, religious, and even secular transcendences.

PART I

Creating the Good Life: Metamorphoses of the Ideal

I believe that in philosophy it is unnecessary to invent
new words and technical terms. . . . Quite the contrary:
that technicization is the great danger of university philosophy,
and it is what distances it from things.

E. M. Cioran, *Œuvres*

You choose to mention, as a just criticism, the lack of popular
appeal in my work, a criticism that can in fact be made
of every philosophical writing, if it is not to conceal
what is probably nonsense under a haze of apparent cleverness.

Immanuel Kant,
letter to Christian Garve (7 August 1783)

CHAPTER I

Beyond Morality, After Religion

~ ~ ~ ~ ~

The New Age of the Question

In *The Angel and the Octopus,* Simon Leys shares with his reader his disappointment with contemporary philosophical works.[1] An eminent specialist in Chinese calligraphy, Leys had long been looking forward to the publication of a certain work on his favorite topic, and he bought the book as soon as it was published. After several attempts to read it, however, he was so discouraged by the weight of the conceptual apparatus that he gave up. At this point he recounts how his failure brought to mind an anecdote of Elie Wiesel's: A rabbi has to attend a marriage in a nearby village. He hires a carriage to take him there, and the coachman takes him on with no hesitation. At the first rise in the road, however, he politely asks the rabbi to get down and help him push the carriage, because his horse is old and tired and hasn't the strength to pull it by himself. The rabbi, a helpful man, agrees, and with his assistance they arrive at his destination, but very late. Disappointed but still wise, he tries to give a meaning to this unexpected turn of events, and he says to the coachman, "I can understand why you came: you needed to earn your payment. I can understand why I came: I needed to attend a ceremony. But I cannot understand why we brought a horse along."

Philosophical works in place of the old horse? The lesson is a harsh one. I am not sure that it is always unjust. At the least, it invites us to be clear about how philosophy will be examined here. Philosophy today is all too often reduced to a "discourse on"; a commentary with little connection to the prime aspiration of "love of wisdom" that its etymology reveals. When it originated among the Greeks, however, philosophy was seen as an intellectual activity inseparable from an attitude toward life. Its ultimate concern was the "good life," and "How should one live?" was its most pressing question. Even when it digressed into highly sophisticated speculations on physics, mathematics, or logic, the ultimate aim of philosophy was to procure a "practicable" (in the literal sense of the term) response that would provide real guidance in the conduct of life.

It was by reconnecting with that tradition that André Comte-Sponville defined philosophy as "thinking one's life and living one's thoughts." The formula not only is well turned but states clearly the necessary integration of reflection and life. I happily adopt it as my own, on the condition, however, of adding a complement that seems to me decisive. The life that we are called upon to think, and the thought that is ours to live when we adopt a philosophical attitude, are neither everyday life nor everyday thought, but rather life and thought inasmuch as they are conscious of being *mortal.* As the Greeks were acutely aware, it is because we are destined to die and we know it, because we will lose those who are dear to us, because banality constantly threatens daily life, that the question of the "good life"—of what is truly worthwhile in this existence and not in another—deserves to be posed. It is also why all the great philosophies have wrestled with the question. Shocking as it might seem today, those great philosophies have, perhaps always, been linked to the problematic of *salvation.*

It might be objected that assigning a saving dimension to philosophy in this manner is to risk confusing philosophy and theology. What is more, by associating philosophy too closely with the theme of finitude and the drawbacks it entails (boredom, banality, ignorance, evil, sickness, suffering, death, etc.), do we not risk turning it into an equally inappropriate therapeutics? In this perspective, how can we be fair to the philosophies of language, the sciences, morality, law, politics, and more, the rise of which so strongly affected the twentieth century? Is the epigram "To philosophize is to learn how to die" too dated to still be applicable to contemporary thought, which—we should not forget—has concentrated as never before on "deconstructing" the illusions of metaphysics and religion?

Perhaps. But this would be to misunderstand what I mean here by "salvation," which in no way presupposes the existence of a realm beyond real life that is the dwelling place of gods capable of offering the means to that salvation. Put bluntly, the difference between religion and philosophy in this regard can be stated thus: religion offers the promise that we *will be saved;* philosophy invites us *to save ourselves.* Humility and pride, faith and reason, heteronomy and autonomy: this short list of contrasting pairs barely hints at the breadth of the abyss that separates the two attitudes or the ties that unite them. It is clear that religion cannot be reduced to heteronomy, nor can modern individualism be reduced to autonomy.[2] Faith can also be a free act, a deliberate response, willingly assumed, to a call that, even if it emanates from the Most High, nonetheless leaves the human being full *responsibility.* As for the liberty of the Moderns, everything indicates that it does not exclude determination from without, beginning with the influence of the social and historical unconscious. The very existence of psychoanalysis and sociology, to say nothing of biology, bears ceaseless witness to such determination. Still, the more the world becomes disenchanted, the less it is inhabited by the gods, and the more legitimate it seems to have to save oneself by one's own efforts rather than wait for the Savior. In this connection, even the most materialist philosophies, from Spinoza to Nietzsche, have been unable to forego some sort of relationship to "beatitude" or an "eternal recurrence"—in short, to what *transcends* the sphere of daily life. How, in fact, are we to respond to the inquiry regarding the good life if there is nothing that is *absolutely* worth being lived? On the other hand, how can we admit an absolute without falling back into a religious problematic? This is the whole question.

In order to define that question better, let us for a minute imagine that Mephistopheles comes to see us and, as he did to the aging Faust, offers us everything—absolutely everything—that one could possibly hope for in the way of earthly success. Let us also suppose that he does so, like any demon worthy of the name, in exchange for our "soul" or whatever we might, rightly or wrongly, call by that name, such as moral or spiritual conviction, political loyalties, affective or other attachments. Is it then certain that when he tries to carry off that "soul" he encounters no escape clause in the contract, no proviso? It is possible, and the hypothesis deserves to be taken seriously. It's not a sure thing, however. I know some people who I think would say, perhaps even without hesitation, that he would not succeed. Why so? By which I mean, in the name of what? Although the proposition might seem simplistic, perhaps even trivial, and one might easily find other ways to state it, it seems to me truly profound. It urges us to ask ourselves about the status of what seems to us "non-negotiable" and in that sense absolute, in the age of the purely terrestrial, an era when the will to power prevails, where the relative seems the only horizon of our universe. Can one do without thought of this sort in a meditation on the good life? I think not. I am not even sure that Nietzsche believed it possible. He seems to have held many things as "non-negotiable" and by no means relative or indifferent. But let us consider the inverse hypothesis for a moment: that the question of the good life can be imagined without respect to any of the visages — whatever they may be — of the absolute. If that were the case, how could one avoid ceding to the cult of means, of the calculable, of pure performance, of the negotiable — in short, of what used to be called "merchandise," the empire of entertainment and consumption? Is that really what we want to hold sacred in the name of the desacralization of everything?

When we pose the question of the good life — the "successful" life — we place ourselves in that perspective. This is why the great philosophies have been unable to do without a relation to the absolute, even if in an agnostic or anti-religious sense. We are speaking of a genuine absolute, not of half measures, compromises, or subterfuges. There is an Arab proverb that puts it well: A man who has never risked losing everything is a poor man. It is a sign that he has never had an opportunity to test his relation to what is absolutely worthwhile, and not just relatively so, following the dictates of the times. It is not by chance that Nietzsche (to return to him), although the great adversary of metaphysico-religious illusions, placed his whole thought under the sign of eternity. His doctrine of eternal recurrence had no other aim than that of distinguishing, even in the most ordinary human experiences, between those that do not merit being relived and others that we might want to recur an infinite number of times. Thus Nietzsche, who liked to describe himself as resembling the Antichrist, cultivated a relation to the infinite, the absolute, and eternity.

I am not saying that the question is closed — far from it — or that it is easy to think about. Only that it deserves full consideration. It is the question that will be the guiding thread to this inquiry. In this sense, the opposite of the philosopher is not the manual laborer, as might be implied if we speak of "intellectuals," but the tourist, the person who sees the world exclusively as a playground, just a collection of places in which to exercise his will to power and liberate his infinite aptitudes for consumption. The conviction that animates the present book is perhaps naïve, but at least it has the merit of being clear: entertainment is one of the greatest pleasures on this earth, but it is not the alpha and omega of our existence. Leaving aside all moralization, it's impossible to rid ourselves of the feeling that we can't just stop there. Why? For what reasons? That is the whole question, and it seems to me that today the question is posed in new terms, beyond morality and religion.

The Contemporary Status of the Question: Beyond Morality and Religion

Investigation of the good life did not frighten the Ancients. As if by enchantment—or out of disenchantment—such investigation seems to have deserted the pages of contemporary thought. The very question seems immodest, beyond the scope of a disillusioned politics, inaccessible to the positive sciences by its very nature, but just as prohibited to a philosophy that is often reduced to "reflections" on historical, political, or scientific realities that always elude its grasp. It is as if even in the best of circumstances the ancient question of the good life no longer has any pertinence outside the subjective and intimate dimension of the private sphere.

Perhaps contrary to appearances, this notion is not an invitation to pessimistic rumination. It does not aim at surreptitious legitimation of the logic of the "step backward" or any rehabilitation of past and outmoded figures of thought in face of some sort of decline of the West—a return to the Greeks, to the wisdoms of the East, to the ancien régime, to a virgin nature, to the Republican Idea, to messianic utopias, or to who knows what. Whatever its powers of seduction, such an attitude always cedes to facility in the end: it is easier to sacrifice to the nostalgia of a paradise lost than to think about what is, for us, here and now. In *La sagesse des modernes,* André Comte-Sponville and I suggested a direction in which we believed contemporary philosophy needs to expand, "*after religion* and *beyond morality.*"[3] Despite some basic disagreements, we agreed on this crucial point. The formula has given rise to some misunderstandings, but it still seems to me as pertinent as ever. Since I would like to situate the current volume within the sphere of thought delimited by that formula, I need to explain it more fully than I did previously.

To begin with "beyond morality." Certain critics have chosen to see that statement as a "renunciation of ethics," a sudden conversion to "immoralism," and a shift in attitude all the more surprising—we are told with scholarly gravity—because each of us had written several works devoted to moral and political philosophy. False naïveté? Genuine misunderstanding? I have no idea. The fact remains that the "beyond" in question obviously has nothing in common with a *rejection* that would, incidentally, be both futile and inappropriate. The phrase was intended to announce, not a "strategic retreat," but a new route for reflection, one that each of us had, in his own way, sketched out in the very works that the same critics wrongly forced into the mold of "moralistic" works.

It seemed to us obvious that morality is quite simply *insufficient* to the conduct of life and that it fails to exhaust all the possible points of view toward existence. Many others have said as much before us, beginning with the giants: Spinoza, to be sure, but Kant himself, in his writings on art and religion, not to mention Hegel and his constant effort to reach beyond the principles of a formal morality toward a broader doctrine of ethical custom. Today, however, at the heart of a resolutely secular world, that insufficiency seemed to us to be taking on a new dimension. Clearly, venturing "beyond morality" could no longer mean (at least for us) turning toward the consolations of art or religion. If the "good life" is indeed situated in this ethical "beyond,"[4] how are we to understand it or to measure the challenges it puts before us today? This is the first thing to be examined.

One might quite simply define the moral sphere, at least in its modern form—let's say, since the appearance in the eighteenth century of great secular visions of the world—as a set of values expressed by precepts or imperatives that invite us to the minimum of *respect for others* without which a peaceful life in common is impossible. What our societies marked by the ideal of democracy and the rights of man oblige us to consider in the figure of the other, if only through the civics courses provided to children, is (to the limits of the possible) man's dignity and his right to *liberty* and *happiness*. It is hardly an exaggeration to say that our formal values here are almost entirely circumscribed by the familiar dictum that "my liberty stops where that of others begins." This, after all, is the primary axiom of that "respect for others" without which no peaceful coexistence is possible. It also explains the relative simplicity of the rules of the democratic ethic: Do not treat others as a means, but always as an end as well. This implies not using others instrumentally, as an object or a thing—for example, as a pack animal, or as a source of organs that I can buy and set aside for myself or my family. It also implies leaving others free to think their own thoughts; to hold opinions that differ from mine or religious or philosophical beliefs that I do not share; to seek well-being as they see fit, provided that no one is harmed; and so forth.

One might also show how the less formal imperatives of solidarity, even of fraternity, are virtually included in these minimal requirements of a modern humanism. It is not by chance that the first declarations of the rights of man raised the questions of charity and public assistance. All this may seem simple, or at least familiar territory, and there is little need to be a historian of philosophy to form a concrete idea of it: we all know those founding texts of our republics, which can rightly be considered charters of common morality. They are, so to speak, the popular and public equivalent of the great philosophical treatises in which, beginning in the eighteenth century, utilitarian philosophers in Great Britain, Kant and his German followers, and even the republicans in France gave abstract and conceptual expression to the fundamental principles of respect for others.

What seems to me essential is that such great moral visions, focused on a respect for the liberty and well-being of others, be considered indispensable, as anyone claiming to be a democrat can hardly doubt. In their absence, all-out war looms on the horizon. They thus appear as the *necessary condition* of the peaceful common life that democratic societies attempt to engender. It is equally clear that such visions do not constitute a *sufficient condition* of that life. Far from it. Respect for others in no way prejudges the actual, concrete nature of the relations with others that alone confer meaning and worth to commerce among people. This is why one can legitimately state that morality does not "suffice," but rather indicates, as it were in itself, a need to go beyond morality.

To be persuaded of this, reflect for a moment on the following tale. Imagine that we had a magic wand that would make everyone living in the world today observe perfectly and on a daily basis the ideal of respect of others as stated in humanist principles. Each individual would thus fully take into account the dignity of all and the equal right of all to the two fundamental goods of liberty and the pursuit of happiness. It is hard to imagine the tremendous upheavals and the incomparable revolution that such an attitude would introduce into our behaviors. There would be no more war, no massacres, no genocide, no crimes against humanity, no "clash of civilizations," no racism, no xenophobia, no rape, no theft, no domination, no exclusion; and repressive and punitive institutions such as armies, police, the judicial system, and prisons could disappear. This shows that morality is indeed something; it also shows the extent to which it is necessary to life in common and how far we are from realizing it, even approximately. To be sure, it does not mean that all conflict would disappear if the ideal became reality. Divergences of interest or viewpoints would of course remain, among the faithful of the various religions, among the partisans of divergent political views, between the rich and the poor, and so forth. To take an even simpler example, there is no easy way to reconcile the interests of the ecologist who loves the forest and wants to preserve its life and its natural beauty, the hunter who wants to be able to track game in that same forest, the driver who perceives it as a terrain for off-road sport, and the ordinary citizen who wants to be able to walk in it freely. At the least, however, we can hope that they might use peaceful means to seek an agreement that reflects both the general interest and a respect for individuals.

Still—and here I have to weigh each one of my words—none (I really mean none) of our most profound existential problems would be resolved if this came to pass. Nothing, even in a perfect realization of the most sublime morality, would prevent us from aging; from witnessing, powerless, the appearance of wrinkles and white hair; from falling sick, dying, and seeing our loved ones die; from worrying about the outcome of our children's education or from struggling to achieve what we want for them. Even if we were saints, nothing would guarantee us a fulfilled emotional life. Literature is full of examples that demonstrate that the logic of ethics and the logic of love in our lives are governed by different principles. It is safe to assert that none of the existential questions depicted in the greatest works of fiction is connected with morality, which means that if morality authorizes a peaceful life in common, it still, in and of itself, does not give any meaning or even any aim or direction to that life. Moreover, setting aside the more tragic aspects of existence, the simple struggle against boredom and banality that constantly threaten daily life would in no way be facilitated by the incarnation of a moral perfection. Some even think that opposite would be true.

Let us pursue the matter. The insufficiency of morality quite obviously extends to the spheres of law and politics as well. It is often said that politics today has become insipid; that imagination no longer inhabits a power that, for the most part, is content to assure the management of current affairs in a globalized economy, at times with competence and probity, but never with genius. At this point, some adopt a nostalgic tone to stress the contrast between today's gray monotony and the joyous utopias of a still-recent past. To do so is to quickly forget that such a contrast in itself—verifiable though it is—neither justifies nor explains anything. When revolutionary discourses declared, with childlike seriousness, that "everything is politics," they were at best making a silly statement and, even more surely, expressing a totalitarian fantasy. Although politics obviously cannot be reduced to morality, given that it must take into account the divergent individual or collective interests that I mentioned above, it also excludes—and for similar reasons—considerations regarding the human condition itself. To imagine, as utopias used to do, that in a classless society without exploitation there would be no more folly or frustration, no existential drama or unrequited passion, also derives from the logic of totalitarian illusions.

Does this mean that politics is no longer of interest? By no means, and even quite to the contrary. It merely gives a more accurate measure of its indispensable scope. There is no "individualistic retreat into oneself" in our statement, no invitation to let down one's guard against injustice, no suggestion that we accept some unworthy "withdrawal" into the private sphere. To point out the limitations of politics is not to declare politics insignificant or useless any more than pointing out the limits of morality is an invitation to immorality. It is, quite simply, to have done with a totalitarian/revolutionary imagery. It is to state the very opposite of what was being proclaimed so happily thirty years ago and to insist that politics too possesses a "beyond," that the question of the good life supposes politics but cannot be reduced to politics.

This leads us to the religious part of "after religion and beyond morality." In past times, metaphysics and religion were charged with filling the empty space beyond morality and with responding to the questioning, both quotidian and ultimate, of individuals. They spoke to individuals about the contradictions that inevitably set the attachments of love against the denials of separation and death. They endowed education with a larger purpose and claimed to provide profound insights into sickness and suffering, labor and entertainment, the various ages of life, and the links between generations. One might say, with militant atheists, that religion performed this task poorly, ideologically, and fallaciously, and that its aim was either false consolation or repression. But at least it did its job, and even if we adopt a reductive image of religion, even if we denounce its message as the "opium of the people," "nihilism," or an "obsessional neurosis" on humanity's part, we cannot deny that it fulfilled a unique function and that, by its mere presence, it put its stamp on an entire category of questions. Nothing indicates that the thinkers who are the most eager to deconstruct the figures of metaphysics and religion and proclaim the "twilight of their idols" have been able to do without them entirely. Perhaps philosophers have treated religion and metaphysics differently, as we shall see, but to claim that they can do without them reflects a strange naïveté. Deconstructing a question is but a new way of taking it into account.

How, then, are we to understand that "after"? Are not believers sufficiently numerous to make such an assertion an act of arrogance rather than a statement of fact? It has been suggested that religion has been "surpassed." What are we to think, then, of the undeniable reality of the "World Youth Days" organized by the Roman Catholic church, when a million young people gathered in Paris and nearly two million in Rome, not to speak of the rising tide of Islam in Africa, the Middle East, and elsewhere? Even if we concede that the number of Christians has diminished in the last fifty years—at least in Europe—is not this quantitative reduction (which, incidentally, seems to have leveled off today) in large measure compensated by a rise in the "quality" of individual belief? Not long ago people went to Mass on Sunday out of pure habit, out of respect for family tradition more than conviction. But today, when such practices are no longer obligatory, are they not valued even more?

Perhaps, and even probably. These objections are just. The fact remains, though, that we have in many ways "come out of" the traditional figures of religion, and this is true from at least three viewpoints that are of inestimable importance for the question with which we are dealing here.

First, as no one can deny, Europeans have become emancipated from the various figures of the "theologico-political." This is clear to any observer: whereas law in past civilizations drew its legitimacy from being rooted in a universe that was (or was taken to be) outside humanity—the universe of cosmology or theology—democratic law is declared to be created solely by and for humankind. That is not only the most profound significance of France's great Declaration of the Rights of Man and Citizen, but also, on the institutional level, the reason for the creation of parliaments. In Islamic republics the legitimacy of the governing authorities is still derived from a religious source (men can marry four wives because it is so stated in the Koran), but democratic law is secular and declares itself to be *constructed* on the basis of the will, the interests, and the reason of human beings, who are thus the *genii* of the law.

There is a second aspect of the public decline of religion. No matter how many believers there are or how many attend gatherings that those believers can freely organize within a secular society, faith remains a *private matter*, with respect not only to the sources of law, but also to the imperatives of the state. This does not mean that faith has become "confidential" but simply that in matters of faith the modern state is neutral and recommends, prohibits, and imposes nothing. Even if 99 percent of the population of France were to profess the most fervent Catholicism, this would still hold true. The "privatization" of religion is a question not of quantity but of status: religion is the affair of private persons, not of the juridical or political authorities, and that is that.

A third discontinuity also contributes, more secretively but more decisively, to the need to pose the question of the good life outside the framework imposed by traditional religions. The ideal of democratic thought is consubstantial with a rejection of arguments from authority. Whether one embraces or deplores the notion, the contemporary mind finds it intolerable to accept an opinion because it is imposed from the outside by a superior institution. We rebel against both the magistrates and the party lines. On this level, it matters little, ultimately, whether individuals are religious believers or not. According to the opinion polls, a scant 8 percent of Catholics follow papal recommendations to the letter. Moreover, those people quite possibly do so out of personal conviction, because they agree with the recommendations, not just because they emanate from the head of the church. For the rest, what is left of the messages of the supreme authority, at least in this world? Perhaps less than it seems. I obviously have no absolute certitude in this connection, and it is always dangerous to claim to read people's hearts or know their gut reactions. Still, I can say, because I followed the event closely, that the million young people who came to the Champ-de-Mars to drink in the pope's words were probably not all ardent readers of St. Thomas Aquinas. I'm even afraid that many of them were more familiar with the writings of Paul Coelho than with the encyclicals of John Paul II, and that sentimentality or emotional outbursts speak to them more directly than the overly rational and arcane intricacies of "participated theonomy." When the pope, not without a certain intellectual courage, published his encyclical letter *Faith and Reason,* a work of Thomist inspiration that presents an apology of philosophical and scientific rationality for its ability to reach the verities of the faith unassisted, he was certainly taking the opposite course from his own listening public regarding widespread irrationalism.[5]

A rejection of arguments from authority, then. But after all, many believers will say, why not? What does that have to do with a supposed decline in religiosity? Is not religion too a matter of inner conviction and personal conscience?

The connection is quite direct, however. This is because the Cartesian ideal of "thinking for oneself" and of systematic and *a priori* doubt regarding everything that we receive from outside ourselves, either by education and upbringing or from tradition or any other authoritative source, enters into direct conflict with the religious concept of revelation. This does not mean that the believer experiences personal faith as *imposed* or as a figure of "heteronomy." He or she certainly lives faith as the result of serious reflection, I willingly grant. Still, in a deeper sense, the believer must *also* recognize that faith cannot be reduced to a mere psychological sentiment, that it draws its origins from a radical alterity, and that it occurs more through a gratuitous gift of God than by means of an intellectual process of demonstration. If the old syllogisms that claim to prove the existence of God were sufficient by themselves, there would be no need to be a *believer* in the religious sense of the word. One would *know* God, and that would be that. Who cannot perceive the abyss that separates the attitude of humility appropriate to the acceptance of revelation and the Cartesian pride that intends to submit all received ideas to the critical examination of a sovereign self?

For all of these reasons—and also for the believers, given that they are no longer alone in the world—we need to pose the question of the successful life, placing it outside the framework of morality and religion.

CHAPTER 2

The Meaning of the Question & the Slow Humanization of the Responses

What, then, is a good life?

The question urges us to suspend for a moment all that is mechanical and unreflective in the course of existence. It invites us—an exercise extremely rare in ordinary times—to take a more global view; to become spectators of ourselves, if only fleetingly. The simple fact of posing the question implies a kind of secret hope that we could in some fashion take things into our own hands and change the course of fate. The minute we pose the question, however, we encounter an objection so obvious that it seems to undermine all desire to continue the adventure even before it is launched: the question may be a good one (or at least an amusing one), but it calls for individual responses, responses so subjective that they would discourage *a priori* investigation. There can be no common model, no collective criterion, that permits approaching the question with even a minimum of objectivity. Is it not self-evident that each individual is the sole judge of himself and of the meaning and worth of his life? This means that viewpoints vary enormously, producing an almost infinite diversity of perspectives on life. For some, success is above all a personal affair linked to a spirit of conquest. It is invested in seeking celebrity and wealth and in winning love. For others, however, it may just as easily take the form of altruism, committed involvement in a collective project, or support of a great cause thought to be in the general interest. A seemingly more modest choice may lead some to situate success in the private sphere, in the values of love, friendship, the family or—why not?—in an ideal of total emancipation, an aspiration to be free of others, but also of one's own demons, or even in an attempt to strive, throughout one's existence, to become "perfect" or to "outdo" oneself in fashioning a life like a work of art. All of these responses (and others as well), diverse or contradictory as they may be, are in essence acceptable. One could even make a mixed bouquet, choosing bits from one response or another. Does that fact disqualify the question and sap it of its interest?

This objection draws its force from an individualistic atmosphere so pervasive that its certitudes have become second nature for us. It should not necessarily, however, be trusted unreservedly or without reflection. If what is intended is just to recall that today no model of success is imposed on us *in an authoritarian manner*, that each one of us is free to lead life as he or she pleases and to seek happiness wherever it lies, the objection is well taken. Does this mean, however, that society suggests no ready-made attitudes to the sovereign individuals, fully conscious and masters of ourselves, that we are henceforth supposed to be? I doubt it. Above all, are we to assume that no "common sense," no agreement on the grand visions of the world, lurks behind choices supposed to be "subjective"? That can hardly be the case. In reality, individualistic sentiment is much more the result of a long history than of consciously made, deliberately undertaken philosophical choice. To put this in perspective but also to situate more precisely the new significance that our question takes on today, we need to review that history briefly. Its two most salient traits are the humanization of the responses brought to the question of the good life and a gradual retreat of all forms of transcendence. How have we come to the strange equation according to which henceforth—after the cosmologies, after the religions and the utopias—the well-lived life must be thought of without reference to principles external to and superior to humanity? In the interest of a better understanding of the intellectual origins of this state of affairs, I shall propose and discuss four fundamental moments, four types of response, that preceded the current age.

1. The "Cosmological" Moment, or Objectivized Transcendence

Most ancient Greek thinkers situated the question of the good life in relation to the overall order of the world, to the cosmos considered in its totality,[1] and

not exclusively in relation to subjectivity or to the ideal of personal fulfillment or individual free will, as we tend to do today. Plato and Aristotle, but
also the Stoics, took it for granted that a well-lived life supposed an awareness of belonging within an order of reality *external to* and *superior to* each
one of us. Not only were human beings not considered to be the authors and
creators of this cosmos, but they shared the feeling of being only an infinitely
small part of it; of belonging to a totality of which they were by no means
"masters and possessors," but one that instead surrounded them and utterly
surpassed them. They were not called upon to *invent* the meaning of their
life within the universe, but rather, and more modestly, to *discover* it. This,
moreover, is an attitude that still speaks to us: we find traces of it in certain
currents of contemporary ecological thought, and even in certain aspects of
Eastern traditions such as Tibetan Buddhism. In these modes of thought,
the philosophical life is an absolutely indispensable condition for a successful
life, which is organized along three major axes implying three major tasks,
the first theoretical, the second practical, and the third spiritual.

Theōria: **Beginning with the "Contemplation of Things Divine."** For the
earliest philosophers, the prime task was to comprehend the organization
of the cosmos and to *contemplate* it by means of the intelligence: without
such knowledge, how could one find his rightful place—or, as Aristotle
put it, his "natural place"—in that cosmos? This implies one of the possible etymologies of the word *theōria*, literally *theion orao*, "I see the divine,"
which for the Greeks meant not one particular god or another, but the just
and beautiful ordering of the world within which the individual is called to
find his place. Just as each organ and every part of a living organism has its
proper place and function, not to be confused with any other, so too every
being, human beings included, was supposed to possess a specific location
within the Great Whole. That harmonious, just, and beautiful order, which
was external to humans and superior to them, thus comported something
of the divine that needed to be understood as such. This led to the importance, in the eyes of the ancient philosophers, of speculative disciplines
such as mathematics, physics, and logic, but also of sciences of observation
such as zoology, physiology, and anatomy, which reveal the marvelous
structure of a reality that is not neutral or indifferent but, to the contrary,
organized and ordered. Despite its supreme importance, this theoretical
task was not an end in itself.

Praxis: **"Wisdom Exercises."** After theoretical intelligence alone, there
came the second phase of the demands of practical wisdom. Once the nat-

ural order of the world had been identified, individuals were called to their ultimate vocation, which was to seek and, if possible, find their rightful place within that order. This next step required going beyond contemplation and discourse to action: it required an *adjustment* to the order of the world that had been revealed in its "divine" dimension of justice, harmony, and transcendence of the human. Thus one must learn the concrete lesson of living "according to nature" rather than by artificial social conventions. The many anecdotes about the teachings of the Greek schools still bear the trace of these practical demands. The Cynics are reported to have accosted their contemporaries in public places and market squares, shocking them with some instance of scandalous behavior or provoking them with an apt sarcastic remark (the name "Cynic" in fact implicitly compares them to dogs who root around, nip people, and sniff indiscreetly). Crates of Thebes, the founding father of the Stoic school, also the master of Zeno of Citium, declared that because he had decided to live "according to nature," he had nothing to hide and therefore made love in public with his wife Hipparchia. In a similar spirit, Diogenes invited his pupils to go about the city of Athens dragging a herring on a string, a habit that invariably attracted the predictable sort of jibes, which they were expected to turn to advantage. The first step in learning to live "according to nature" was to rid oneself of the burden of social conventions. In the same spirit but in a more serious vein (though this point is debatable), the Greek philosophers developed a number of "wisdom exercises" aimed not only at reaching beyond "What will people say?" but also at broadening the individual mind, which is always egocentric and limited, to the dimensions of the cosmos.[2] This helps us to understand—to pick one example—the famous Stoic distinction between things that depend on us and those that do not, but also the *practical* injunction to which that distinction guides those desirous of achieving happiness and wisdom: take care of the primary things and let the secondary things take care of themselves. To repeat a metaphor that is at times used to describe Stoicism: theoretical truth—the idea that there is an order in the world, a cosmic rationality according to which certain realities depend upon us and others do not—can be likened to the master beam of an edifice within which practice commands us to dwell.

Whatever its importance—and it is crucial—moral activity is not the ultimate goal of philosophy any more than theory is. To state this differently: if we are called to contemplation and told to put the results of our contemplation into practice, it is with a goal that is superior to both of these. The objective is nothing less than achieving salvation by one's own forces. It is not a question of *being saved*, but of *saving oneself* from the greatest of all the ills that weigh on humanity, fear of death. Philosophy, which is inseparable from the thought of finitude, thus culminates in a "soteriology," a doctrine of salvation, or, if preferred, a form of spirituality without God that is situated not only beyond theory but beyond moral praxis itself.

Soteriology, or The First Secularization of the Idea of Salvation. Plato, Aristotle, and (perhaps even to a greater extent) the Stoics kept declaring, quite explicitly, that the anxieties connected with human finitude—the representation of death, to put it more simply—are the foundation of *all* philosophical activity. Thus, for example, according to the *Discourses*, Epictetus said to his disciples: "Will you, then, realize that this epitome of all the ills that befall man, of his ignoble spirit, and his cowardice, is not death, but it is rather the fear of death? Against this fear, then, I would have you discipline yourself, toward this let all your reasoning tend, your exercises, your reading; and then you will know that this is the only way in which men achieve freedom."[3] I shall return to this injunction and the question of the "wisdom exercises" in part 3. For the moment let it suffice to note that Epictetus stresses the effects of existential anxiety. According to him, it is responsible for *all* of our defects and ills, which is why combating it must be the end of *all* our thoughts and *all* consequent philosophical practices. If we believe this assertion (and why not do so, since the statement is so often reiterated?), existential anxiety is the alpha and omega of a philosophy that, far from being simple discourse, is intended to lead us firmly toward wisdom and, by that token, toward the good life. If we must adjust to and attach ourselves (inasmuch as this is humanly possible) to the master beam of the cosmic edifice that *theōria* reveals, it is in order to gain access to "salvation"—and the word is not too strong, because, the Stoics tell us, it is solitude, ennui, and even suffering and death that such a "joining in" can spare us. Unlike Christianity, Stoicism did not see this adherence as facilitating access to personal immortality; rather, as in Buddhism, it liberates its adherents from all fear connected with the sentiment of finitude. The moment the wise man understands that the vicissitudes of existence depend not on him but on an order of a world that is in other ways harmonious, the moment he has determined to want what happens rather than to try to change the course of what escapes his control, he also knows not only how vain it is to complain but, above all, how in a more subtle and more profound sense he is himself divine, because he is an integral part of the eternal cosmos with which he aspires to perfect reconciliation. The order of the world, man, and man's salvation: once the three terms of the problem are articulated harmoniously, it is possible to accede to a truly successful life.

2. The Theological Moment, or Transcendence Personified

The question of the good life is resolved in the name of a totally different conception of transcendence once the representation of the divine is no longer seen as immanent to the order of the world but as embodied in the figure of a personal God placed at the origin of the universe, thus situated outside it. Now the question is no longer to find one's natural place within the organic structure of reality, but rather to place oneself under the benevolent eyes of an other, the Most High, and to conform to the laws that the pure and gratuitous love of such a power was inspired to offer humankind. Despite radical differences between the two responses, however, they are at base analogous. Even when faith replaces knowledge and revelation takes over from reason, the first need is to achieve access to a principle external to and superior to humanity, then, on the basis of that conversion, to find practical ways to conform to the divine verities that such a principle requires. The master beam of the edifice has changed, to be sure, but there is still a transcendent reality to which love of wisdom and the desire to achieve salvation recommends that we adjust our sights, as far as it is possible, in this world. It is at this cost and this cost alone that we will be able to vanquish the only challenge worthy of the name, that of finitude. It is also in this perspective that profound reflection on the temptations of the devil developed within Christian theology. Contrary to the set of popular images often purveyed by a church whose authority was threatened, the devil is not an entity that operates on the moral plane to lead us away from the straight and narrow path by appealing to the weakness of the flesh; he works instead on the spiritual plane, where he does everything possible to *separate* us (*dia-bolos*) from the vertical connection to God that is our only means of salvation from desolation and death.

The great Greek cosmologies have often been presented as less "religious" than Judeo-Christian monotheism with the argument that since the Greeks saw the divine order of the world as perfectly immanent, they had no need to refer to any "beyond" in the religious sense of the term. Christian transcendence is usually contrasted with Greek immanence in this connection. The inverse reading is possible: one might even rightly sustain that personalization of the divine—notably in Christianity, which, unlike Judaism, puts the personalized God on the world stage, incarnate in human form—constitutes an initial form of the secularization of transcendent principles. Is not personalizing—even humanizing—the divine in the final analysis a way to bring it closer to us more surely than the principles of cosmic order could ever do? If God created man in his own image, are God and man not ultimately closer to one another than the mind and nature could ever be?

The great cosmological and theological responses are thus linked by an invisible thread, often dissimulated in the name of differences that are, in fact, considerable and that do separate them. To the question of the successful life they both bring responses based on theoretical recognition of a principle, cosmic or divine, that transcends humanity. For both sorts of response, wisdom resides in an attempt—which can take a lifetime—to reconcile oneself with that principle. Salvation—understood in both cases as perhaps a very different but nonetheless ultimate response to the challenges of human finitude—depends upon the "success" of that attempt. If I find my place within the order of the world and manage to become a truly integral part of it, if I succeed in living in obedience to and love of God to the point of becoming one with him, then I will in some fashion accede to eternity, or at least I will be liberated from caring about transient things of this world that do not depend on me.

There is another decisive element that must be taken into account in this picture, to which I shall attempt later to supply the missing colors. In this cosmological or theological optic, not only does the aspiration to wisdom manage to deliver the human being from the torments inflicted by our mortal condition, but in doing so and in this very earthly life, it offers him a place within the community of men. The sage and the saint—it may be objected—are rather solitary figures, at times even martyrs. Admittedly. But for the common run of mortals, it is not only existence in face of death or after death that is organized by a quest for wisdom, but also, and more particularly, life in common with others in the here and now. As is known, one of the possible etymologies of the word "religion" indicates that humans are "tied," bound together within the harmonious order of the universe and in the love of God, forming an *ecclesia* that is both an assembly and a community. Outside of this community lies desolation and the realm of the ephemeral. Today some criticize "communitarian" movements—religious ones in particular, if "religious communitarianism" is not a tautology. These critics may have good reasons, but we should remember that similar movements have enabled humanity to live in society for thousands of years. This, moreover, is why cosmology and religion could claim to take the place of politics, taking that term in its strongest sense.

If modern humanism—or the secularization of the world that is another name for it—consists in the fact that individuals have emancipated themselves from these communities; if it resides in a constant propensity, in its attempt to achieve the most complete autonomy possible, to reject all the forms of transcendence on which these communities were founded, how can we still respond to the question of the good life? Where can we find that master beam to which we must adjust for our salvation if humanity is henceforth left alone, face to face with itself? And at this point, if individuals have lost all that ties them together, is humanity not threatened with an irremediable atomization?

3. The Utopian Moment, or Transcendence Contested

In order to respond to this sort of objection, messianic utopias had to be transformed into veritable religions of terrestrial salvation. In the absence of cosmic or religious principles, it is humanity itself that becomes sacralized, to the point of acceding, in its turn, to the status of a transcendent principle. The operation is by no means unthinkable: after all, no one can deny that humanity, in a global sense, is superior to each one of the individuals who constitute it, in the same way that the general interest should, in principle, prevail over particular interests. From scientism in the style of Jules Verne to nineteenth-century patriotism and the communism of Karl Marx, the great secular utopias have had the merit of attempting the impossible—that is, of reconciling immanence and transcendence, the human and the divine, without departing from the framework of humanity itself. This project, even aside from the failures and, at times, the catastrophes that resulted from it, managed to irritate believers and, in the long run, the most resolute of atheists as well.

Christian thinkers, Kierkegaard first among them, attempted to set limits to the secular utopias by observing that the salvation of the individual, in spite of all efforts, cannot be equated with the salvation of humanity. Even if the individual were to devote himself to a sublime and generous cause in the conviction that it was imbued with an ideal infinitely superior to him, the fact remains that, outside of the religious perspective, there is no transcendence that is valid after death, hence no veritable salvation. Individual human beings can always fool themselves and their conscience, but sooner or later they must face the truth that in the long run they will suffer and die as particular beings—no one can die in their place—and, given this *personal* death, the cause of humanity risks eventually seeming an abstraction that, for all its beauty, is desperately empty. Human beings can never save *themselves.* They must be saved *by an other,* and even though devotion to a humanist cause can arouse sympathy on the moral level, it is nonetheless illusory on the spiritual plane.

True atheists, beginning with Nietzsche, could only perceive the passion for "great designs" supposedly superior to the individual, or even to life itself, as an ultimate ruse on the part of religious nihilism; a way of continuing to deny life in the name of a cause purported to be superior to it; a manner of sacrificing, again and again, the world here and now to a "beyond," the perceptible to the intelligible.

These two opposed but ultimately convergent forms of criticism produced their effects. I am not certain (far from it!) that they are always accurate, nor that all forms of humanism are incompatible with new representations of transcendence. Nor am I certain that one can totally do without a relationship to the collective or the political. Marx's thinking, in spite of its baleful fate, was grandiose in that it invited us to situate the accomplishment of the self within our relation to others. But, cost what it may, once the wine had been drawn, it had to be drunk to the dregs: the corrosive logic of secularization and disenchantment with the world was carried to its conclusion. This is what happened during the latter half of the nineteenth century, in a development that Nietzsche's thinking, more than that of any others, captured with true genius.

4. The Materialist Moment, or Transcendence Abolished

If cosmologies are no longer popular, if "God is dead," utopias are defunct, and the great schemes have been abandoned, where are we now to find the master beam to which the history of "conceptions of the world" has always, in one way or another, invited humans to adjust? The secular universe seems to leave no room for this question. Nonetheless, it has an irreplaceable merit: like no other question before it, it invites us to lucidity. If I were forced to give a definition of the twentieth century, I would say that it was the era of all the deconstructions, the first century to put to work Nietzsche's injunction that henceforth philosophizing must be done "with a hammer." Nietzsche's self-appointed task was to shatter the idols of metaphysics and religion and to deflate their bloated notions and consoling illusions like so many balloons. Whatever his critics might say, there is no place for nostalgia here: those who regret the age of the joyous utopias need to be reminded they were largely murderous and destructive of liberty. We also need to remind those who deplore the disenchantment of the world and the diminished role of religions that—at least in their traditional forms—religions still continue, even today, to be at the origin of almost all the wars and conflicts that bloody our planet.

The question of the good life, nonetheless, seems more than problematical in a world without transcendence, to the point that the only plausible response bequeathed by our twentieth century appears to be a purely *formal* one, indifferent to any content. It can be summed up in one word: *intensity*. In a universe of globalized consumerism, making a success of one's life seems no longer connected with any cosmic, religious, or utopian principle but simply with the will to power—that is, with a maximal intensification of one's own existence. In the absence of any referent external to or superior to the individual, the good life is a life lived to the full, a life in which one is both "really oneself" (what else is there to rely on, and what other end might we envisage?) and fully invested in one's chosen activities, *whatever they may be*. Whether one is a singer, someone engaged in scientific research, a captain of industry, or a soccer player, the essential thing is to "succeed" in that domain, to "shine" in it.

Nietzsche was quite clearly and par excellence the author of this "earthly" and disillusioned response. Not that he treated the topic superficially; quite to the contrary, he gave it depth and its letters of nobility. But unlike any of his predecessors, he drew the final consequences of the decline of transcendent principles. He was the first to have the audacity to say that, in the absence of such principles, nothing mattered but the intensity of life, whatever the content to which it might be directed. "My doctrine teaches this," he wrote in a crucial text that should be read in this spirit: "He whose supreme joy is in effort, let him strive! He who likes repose above all, let him rest! He who likes to submit, obey, and follow, let him obey! But *let him know well where his preference lies,* and not recoil before *any means!*"[4] It is Nietzsche who predicted, in a flash of incomparable lucidity, the extent to which for us Moderns, after the era of cosmologies and religions, an intensification of the will to power was soon to become the sole aim of existence. And it is also Nietzsche who forged the philosophic concept—somewhat monstrous but highly pertinent to an understanding of our times—of a finality at last totally immanent in reality. The "choices" that he evokes in this passage from his unfinished work—effort and repose, obedience and flight—are not transcendent ideas, but forms of life that coincide perfectly with the impulses inherent in all of us.

The Present Epoch, or The Two Possible Faces
of Contemporary Humanism: Materialist Humanism
or the Humanism of the Man-God

Beginning with Nietzsche and his radical philosophical materialism, we have two possible options that, it seems to me, best characterize the space occupied by contemporary philosophy, at least when it still takes the time to treat questions of wisdom or the good life.

One can of course take the task of "deconstruction" inaugurated by Nietzschean genealogy and carry it to its logical extreme. In the aim of doing away with "illusions" of transcendence, one can even extend and improve the instruments of "suspicion"; here psychoanalysis, sociology, and, perhaps even more, contemporary biology have powerful contributions to offer. Religions and, more generally, all the visions of the world that tend to admit principles superior to and external to humanity are vigorously denounced in the name of the demands of a materialism that aims at revealing, behind values reputed to be transcendent, the very real "modes of production" that have engendered them in the commonest fashion. From the rights of man to the summits of art, from altruism to mother love, nothing, in principle, resists these new reductionisms. Their task, which seems infinite, can occupy a lifetime, the whole question being to know whether the wisdom that should correspond to it—a wisdom of radical immanence—is truly "tenable."

Some philosophers, notably those who follow in the wake of the great materialist philosophies of Spinoza and Nietzsche, think it is indeed tenable. They are, in this sense, philosophers of their times. In conformity with their epoch, they want once and for all, in the name of lucidity and liberty, to have done with the "idols" of metaphysics and religion, as well as with the prophetic or messianic politics of yesteryear—in short, with illusions of transcendence in all their forms. Not only are they unafraid of disenchantment; they are happy with it. It is, so to speak, the condition of liberty, the preliminary to an "innocence of becoming" and to a resolute acceptance of reality that is the sole human verity. Let me be clear: the sentiment that animates such thinkers is in no way common or banal. They do no limit themselves—as was so long the case—to the negative contention that political and religious fundamentalisms brought bloody conflict to the twentieth century. They also affirm, more positively and more profoundly, that there is no happiness worthy of the name outside the reality principle; that all happiness that is ultimately *real* must pass under that principle, and that such lucidity bears a high price, because it requires nothing less than the death of the idols of the past. In this manner, they seek to forge the conditions of an authentic "materialist wisdom," a conception of existence stripped of the trappings of a consoling religiosity. As we shall see in what follows, if I cannot share their conclusions, I cannot help but understand how such an aspiration originates. It bears witness to an intellectual courage that those who love truth can only admire. It possesses a certain grandeur, at times even a certain beauty. To me, at least, it seems futile to contrast that aspiration to a hypothetical "need" for God, for ideals, for hope, and so forth, supposedly immanent in human nature. This is because a "need" of that sort—if we admit that it exists—is the principal objection to the convictions that it claims to undergird: Is it not because we are afraid to die, to be separated from those we love, that we have "invented" belief in a life after death? Is it not in order to give meaning to our lives that we have forged the idea of a perfect society, pure, transparent, without exploitation or domination, that would imply the revolutionary moment? The least we can say is that this is a more than legitimate conjecture. So we should interrogate this stance on the terrain of materialism and in the name of the highest demand for lucidity. To repeat: Is a wisdom of radical immanence tenable? Do not misunderstand me: I am not asking whether this philosophical option is "comfortable" or whether human beings can live agreeably with neither divinity nor utopia, with neither hope nor transcendence, but rather whether such a thing is quite simply thinkable in terms of truth. Let me put it baldly: I believe that no materialist has ever succeeded in thinking his own thoughts, and none has been able to pursue to the limit the consequences of his own principles, without surreptitiously reinstating unavowed (and for him unavowable) transcendences. All such thinkers, as I shall attempt to demonstrate, beginning with the two most imposing pioneers, Spinoza and Nietzsche, have had to make up their minds, sooner or later and for basic reasons, to stealthily reintroduce hope, the universal, the transcendent, and the eternal, not to mention the mystical. This is what prevents me—and I am not a believer—from being a simple materialist.

I think one can also choose another route, setting aside an enterprise in which one risks a triumph without glory by winning too often without peril. After all, nothing proves the invincible pertinence of contemporary materialism, even when it is taken at its highest level, and nothing proves that new sorts of transcendence are inconceivable outside the status of illusion that has always been assigned to them. Even though we have henceforth entered into the orbit of humanism, there is nothing to preclude our continuing—whatever we might think—to perceive truth, justice, beauty, and even love in a perhaps radically new manner but still as values that we *discover rather than produce or invent ourselves.* Indeed, in many ways these values seem just as "sacred" as they were in olden times, as if the divine, although it has descended from heaven to earth and has become humanized, has nonetheless remained present in them. To be sure, we no longer sacralize the cosmos, God, the homeland, or the revolution, as was once the case, but in compensation it is plain that humanity (or rather, the individuals that humanity comprises) conserves for us a value comparable to that of the former figures of transcendence. This is what I have called a "humanism of the man-god," and it is this hypothesis that I intend to explore and test in the present work. If it turns out to have its share of truth, the entire question of the good life will obviously be modified.

Still, the present essay is no more the work of an old-style spiritualist than that of a modern materialist. It seeks no ultimate response to the question it is pursuing—not in a cosmology, not in a theology, and not in an artificial reactivation of defunct utopias. Nor does it cede—as might have seemed necessary—to the sirens of materialism. The conviction that animates it is that although we have not yet taken its measure, we in the West are experiencing today a mutation unlike any other; an upheaval so unexpected that the ready-made philosophies of the twentieth century are no longer adequate to define it. It is not the end of utopias that is the major event of our age, as those nostalgic for revolution assert. It is not the "disenchantment of the world" that is its specific trait, nor the deconstruction of idols, but rather the world's re-enchantment. The novelty here resides in the appearance of new figures of transcendence, no longer situated upstream from humanity, but downstream from it; no longer looming over humanity like a radical "elsewhere," but taking root at its heart. Curiously, in order to be inscribed henceforth on the horizon of humanity and no longer founded on nature or divinity, the values of truth, goodness, beauty, and love have lost nothing—whatever might be said—of their "sacred" character. Although they have, so to speak, been uprooted, these values continue (admittedly, in a new manner) to animate a large part of our existence. This, I suggest, requires new ways of thinking today. In order to perceive this revolution in the status of the vital values and to evaluate the ways in which it leads to a new handling of the ancient question of the good life, we need to situate ourselves in a postmaterialism that is still searching for its name, and within the boundaries of a thought that has learned the lessons of world disenchantment and has pondered the critical power of the deconstructive ideologies of the last century but is not satisfied by them.

A Note on the Organization of This Volume

I shall begin, not wishing to defer entry into the meat of my subject and in the interest of stating clearly what is involved in reflection on the good life, with the "Nietzschean moment," the moment that forms a link between the ancient world and contemporary challenges. This is not to be confused with Nietzsche's thought alone, given that it includes the emergence, at the dawn of the twentieth century, of the philosophies of radical immanence that based their rejection of all forms of transcendence on an uncompromising materialism. The interest of an analysis of this sort is to see how, beyond its deconstructive aspects, it will nonetheless (although in a disillusioned perspective) offer a response to the question of the good life. The rich and interesting problematic of the "intensity" of existence will be fully dealt with here, but also, beyond that problematic and extending it, the emergence of typically modern modes of existence as nineteenth-century imagery has bequeathed them to us. Daily life and the bohemian life (as opposed to that of the philistines) and the life of enterprise will appear as the first offspring of world disenchantment.

Next, turning back from modern times to the origins of philosophy in Greece, we shall attempt to understand, in the light of a few crucial examples, notably those of Stoicism and Christianity, how responses to the question of the good life came to be organized on the basis of a consideration of principles transcending the human species. It seems to me necessary and useful to examine the messages of the past. Not out of a taste for history, nor in order to sketch the archaeology of the present age, but because the responses of those ages are, in many ways, possibilities that remain open. Many continue to think that, all things considered, the "wisdom of the Ancients" is as good as that of the Moderns, and even if I cannot share their views (for reasons that will be clear), I am persuaded that those grand visions of the world still have something to say to us, and that what might be called "secularized" versions of them still exist. It is as if we in the secular world had found that the religious or cosmological responses have a second face, different from the ones they had in their original versions but inherited from them. For example, I can read the great Stoic texts, the Gospel According to John, or the messages of Tibetan Buddhism, and love them without being a Stoic, a Christian, or a Buddhist. Without forcing the analogy, one can say, in a similar vein, that contemporary ecological thought reactivates (at times without realizing it) certain aspects of the ancient cosmologies, or that modern materialism maintains privileged connections with Stoicism and even with certain discliplines of Eastern wisdom, or that humanitarian sensibility is in part the heir of Christianity, and so forth. One could cite multiple examples that suggest the extent to which the idea of the tabula rasa is, here and elsewhere, foolish and silly—perhaps silly more than foolish. One of the most interesting aspects of the study of ancient wisdom traditions—even outside their intrinsic interest—is the way it reveals how profoundly philosophy, throughout its history, has succeeded in forging for itself a status of rivalry with religion as it sought a secular doctrine of salvation, a "soteriology" without God.

But also—and this will be the object of the last part of the present volume—we need to confront the question of what comes *after.* In spite of the radical individualism and the disenchantment of the modern world, and in spite of Nietzsche's declarations about the death of God and the obligation to be at all costs "terrestrial," and although I myself am an agnostic and have no illusions concerning the aberrations of classical metaphysics, I do not think that we have finished with transcendence, or with the problematics of beatitude and salvation. My conviction, which I will attempt to articulate, is that, on the contrary, we must learn to recognize their new, postindividualistic visages and begin to link them with the ancient quests for wisdom. This supposes that we can at last describe two apparently contradictory facts. The first records the secularization and humanization of the responses to the great questions. In the move from the transcendence of the cosmic order to that of a personal God, we have already come closer to man, but when we move from the great humanist causes to the individual will to power, it is transcendence itself, in all its forms, that seems to have evaporated. Still, the question of the good life continues, even at the heart of the most radical materialism, to show signs of new forms of a relation to the absolute and to salvation. In spite of all the deconstructions, and in spite of our attachments to the ideal of individual autonomy, we have to concede, at the end of the road, *that it is not we who invent the values to which we constantly refer, not only within the order of truth but also within that of ethics, politics, and even, no matter what relativist commonplaces might say, that of aesthetics and love.* Nothing indicates with certainty that Nietzsche's dictum that there are no facts but only interpretations is not, in the final analysis and with all due respect, an easy way out masked by a philosophical project that is profound but untenable. Once again, we need to dig a bit deeper.

But neither can we behave, within this itinerary that extends from the Greeks to the most secularized versions of modern atheism and perhaps beyond, as if the most recent position were always the best one. We have had enough of the Hegelian representations of history as a gigantic game of chutes and ladders: the journey on which I invite my reader would have no interest if it did not rest on the certainty that there is something admirable and vibrant, even today, in all the grand responses to the question, including the oldest of them. Thus the present work will end with a reflection on the meaning of this new relationship to the multiplicity of philosophies, avoiding both skepticism and dogmatism. Discussion will be articulated around the two following questions.

1. **The Origin of a Plurality of Responses.** If humanity is one, how are we to comprehend the plurality of responses to so crucial a matter? The astonishment implied in this question may seem outrageous or absurd, according to one's mood. It is nonetheless perfectly legitimate from a philosophical point of view. One would be tempted, of course, to respond by pointing to history and stating the obvious: if human beings have given so many responses to the question of the good life, it is because the contexts in which they formulated those responses were infinitely different from each other. This historicist answer, however, may not suffice or may come up a bit short to be totally satisfactory today. This is because, first, the great responses identified as belonging to the past are still quite present among us, to the point that labeling them as archaic is in itself contestable. Note, for example, the current interest in the ancient wisdom traditions of both East and West, and also in the great spiritual and religious messages. Second, plurality is still with us (even if we remain within the sphere of contemporary thought), just as much as it was in the past and perhaps even more. Never has philosophy been as shattered as it is today; never before have we bathed in a "postmodern" atmosphere where, as if in an immense menu of thought, a full range of attitudes and syncretisms is available to the individual. Hence the need to ask how we are to explain this plurality or, at the very least, if we limit the scope of our question, how we are to think about it.

2. **The Status of the Plurality of Responses in a World That Claims to Be Democratic.** It is no longer a question of why, or even of how, but of what's to be done. Can we still be content, as the teachings of philosophy so often invite us, to take our pick in a spirit of total eclecticism? Two classic attitudes have acquired a certain legitimacy in face of the enigma of plurality. First, in the Hegelian manner, one can seek an overall synthesis, a harmonious integration of all points of view, at the cost of distorting the opposing positions, forcing them to fit the mold of intellectual assimilation and its demands. Or one can display a fine tolerance in the name of the democratic ideal that claims always to accept the Other and to respect multiculturalism in all its forms. I believe neither in the dogmatism of uniformity nor in the skepticism of difference. It seems to me instead that an authentic comprehension of the other—I mean the true other, with whom no basic agreement seems possible and with whom no intellectual affinity exists—does not take the road of integration and assimilation or of a pseudo-tolerance. The latter too often comes close to indifference, which, as is well known, is one of the faces of scorn. The democratic ideal thus invites us to think of plurality outside of the classic schemata. This is a challenge that will occupy us at the end of our investigation of the many approaches to the meaning of the good life.

PART II

The Nietzschean Moment:
The Good Life
as the Most Intense Life

On Transcendence as Supreme Illusion

~ ~ ~ ~ ~

The Twilight of the Idols,
or How to Philosophize with a Hammer:
The End of the World, the Death of God,
& the Death of Man

Before reading or rereading Nietzsche, before meditating once more on his message about the possible visages of human life after the "death of God," I invite the reader to suspend all biases for a moment and to shake off the images of Nietzsche that surround his work like a high wall and impede access to it: Nietzsche the "irrationalist," Nietzsche as politically suspect, as a poet of genius but insane, as a writer whose stylistic fulgurations fail to conceal a lack of the coherence indispensable to any authentic philosophy. Not that such labels and the questions they raise are necessarily illegitimate.[1] It is a fact that Nietzsche ceaselessly denounces the inanity of humanist values, of the rights of man, and of democratic equality and that he slashes at the "idols" of religion (but at those of science as well), asserting that "what must first be proved is worth little" and manifesting his aversion to the "will to truth." In many ways, however, the perspective that he opens onto our world remains one of the most lucid and most profound that exist. It is not impossible that he remains *the* thinker of modern times, the only one who drank the wine down to the dregs, who dared to draw all the conclusions of a disenchantment that leaves no way out and offers no consolation. On this point we must take him seriously and follow him into the abyss to which his "genealogy" of transcendent values leads. We will find there at least an alternative to what he held to be the illusions of "the meaning of life"—those baubles to which humans cling so as to escape despair over their mortal status. May the reader unfamiliar with his works be reassured: I agree with Nietzsche that his thought, difficult as it is at times, is never inaccessible. It is firmer, more rigorous, not to say more luminous, than many discourses garbed in the prestige of bright rationality.

Thus Nietzsche offers an alternative to existences guided by "superior" values and a new and radically disillusioned vision of the "good life." This, and nothing less than this, is what his "materialism" promises.[2] Let us admit it: for those who no longer inhabit the great cosmologies, for those who have deserted religious beliefs or renounced the utopias of a messianic politics, and for those who are unsatisfied with the ideals of a morality of the rights of man, the detour is worth taking. They will not be disappointed. If we ignore some weaknesses linked to the culture of an epoch that was about to give birth to the worst catastrophes humanity has known, Nietzsche's thought has something grandiose about it: it was the first (though not the only) system of thought to take up the challenges of a "human, all too human" existence; of life finally liberated from the mirages of a faith in some sort of superior "ideal." It is a philosophy, no longer of heaven, but of the earth, as Nietzsche proclaims in his typical (that is, irreligious) language in a passage from *Thus Spoke Zarathustra:* "I beseech you, my brothers, *remain faithful to the earth,* and do not believe those who speak to you of otherworldly hopes! Poison-mixers are they, whether they know it or not. Despisers of life are they, decaying and poisoned themselves, of whom the earth is weary: so let them go. Once the sin against God was the greatest sin; but God died, and these sinners died with him. To sin against the earth is now the most dreadful thing, and to esteem the entrails of the unknowable higher than the meaning of the earth."[3] It is worth noting at the start, so we do not forget it, that after the death of God, the possibility of dreadful and even sacrilegious crimes seems to remain, a sign (and we shall return to the topic) that the "twilight of the idols"—that is, the death of all transcendent ideals—is not the end of the story, and that the eclipse of the religious hints at the existence, if not of a new spirituality, at least of another logic of meaning, albeit a terrestrial rather than a celestial one. It may well be that the collapse of representations of the successful life cast in terms of "the beyond" heralds a new dawn.

The fact remains that the deconstruction of illusions, philosophizing "with a hammer," is the first and most urgent task of thought. Nietzsche does not go into details. Each step of the stairway leading from the highest figures of transcendence down to the most human ones is crumbling. The Greek cosmos has vanished in thin air; the great God of monotheistic religions is reduced to nothing; the principles of a secular humanism are laid low. And it is on that tabula rasa, that finally leveled ground, that we must now learn to stand.

Let the reader see what it is like before venturing onto this terrain. What remains of the great Greek cosmologies? Nothing, absolutely nothing, Nietzsche tells us, except a vague memory of the determination to find, cost what it may, the "meaning of life," to postulate, against all evidence, a finality in becoming, as if the entire universe were so well arranged that we could attain beatitude simply by situating ourselves within it: "Some sort of unity, some form of 'monism': this faith suffices to give man a deep feeling of standing in the context of, and being dependent on, some whole that is infinitely superior to him, and he sees himself as a mode of the deity. . . . But behold, there is no such universal!" This forces us to admit two upsetting facts: "Becoming has no goal," and "underneath all becoming there is no grand unity in which the individual could immerse himself completely as in an element of supreme value."[4]

Following the example of the Stoics, we would like the world to have a meaning; to be organized, harmonious, and good; to have a natural place for us established within it for all eternity, where we would find a warm and comforting niche. But the world is not like that: "And do you know what 'the world' is to me? Shall I show it to you in my mirror? This world: a monster of energy, without beginning, without end; a firm, iron magnitude of force . . . a sea of forces flowing and rushing together, eternally changing, eternally flooding back."[5] Another part of this picture is modern science, with which Nietzsche had a complex love-hate relationship: love when science "deconstructs" idols and disenchants the world;[6] hatred when it reinforces those same idols by its belief in a realm of rationality. The idea of a unique and harmonious universe is falsehood par excellence. Not only is the real marked with the stamp of the infinite, but there are "*infinite interpretations*" and an infinite variety of points of view. This was a dizzying verity, according to Nietzsche, but an undeniable one. No restoration of the ancient universe could any longer be attempted: "Once more the great horror seizes us—but who would desire forthwith to deify once more *this* monster of an unknown world in the old fashion? . . . Ah! There are too many *ungodly* possibilities of interpretation comprised in this unknown, too much devilment, stupidity, and folly of interpretation."[7]

Cosmology, which tended *desperately* toward harmony, is thus merely a human "projection" (and Nietzsche's use of the term predates Freud); simply a way to take our desires for realities and to procure a semblance of power over a senseless, multiform, and chaotic matter that escapes our grasp: "All these values are, psychologically considered, the results of certain perspectives of utility, designed to maintain and increase human constructs of domination—and they have been falsely *projected* into the essence of things. What we find here is still the *hyperbolic naïveté* of man: positing himself as the meaning and measure of the value of things."[8]

Exit the good life as the ancients understood it.

Under these conditions, what was an eventual recourse to God worth? The will to put oneself, after the "end of the world," into the hands of a supreme being, a purveyor of love, hope, and meaning, is yet another form of the desire for the absolute, just as vain and fallacious as its predecessor. It goes without saying that Nietzsche was not the first thinker to attempt a radical critique of religion. Many did so before him, beginning with Epicurus and Lucretius, to say nothing of the materialists of the Enlightenment. Contrary to one current opinion, Nietzsche did not even invent the theme of the "death of God." It appears in various forms in David Hume, Adam Smith, and Benjamin Constant.[9] Nietzsche gave it a new meaning, however, by inserting it within a perspective that was both historical (it appears as the typically modern end point of a long history) and genealogical (it is also the result of a deconstruction of the "projections" hidden in the supposed "need for spirituality").

What, in fact, does the phrase mean? It is obviously not to be taken literally. God cannot die: in order to do so he would first have to have existed! But even if we admit the hypothesis of the existence of God, the infinity, eternity, and all-powerfulness that are his natural attributes would have protected him against all forms of disappearance. The paradox—too obvious to insist on—nonetheless contains a deeper meaning: if, from the atheist's point of view, humans have created God and not the contrary, it is also humans who undo what they have made. This deconstructive logic is valid not only for one divinity or another, one particular religion or another, but for all idols, whatever they may be—that is to say, for all the projections or human creations that aim to give meaning to life by referring to transcendent values.

Thus Nietzsche does not denounce "religious superstition" in the name of any substitute ideology; he does not confront God waving the banner of an "other truth" that is more consoling because more lucid, such as the truths of the Enlightenment, of progress, of science, or of socialism. Rather, it is the notion of "ideal" as such that he intends to demolish, once and for all. This explains his intimate conviction that he is the first real critic *of all religiosity in general* and his feeling that this audacious move, despite its apparent precedents, is as yet imperceptible, even to the great majority of those who call themselves atheists but nonetheless continue to believe in other, substitute, idols.

> The most important of recent events—that "God is dead," that the belief in the Christian God has become unworthy of belief—already begins to cast its first shadows over Europe. To the few at least whose eye, whose *suspecting* glance, is strong enough and subtle enough for this drama, some sun seems to have set. . . . In the main, however, one may say that the event itself is far too great, too remote, too much beyond most people's power of apprehension, for one to suppose that so much as the report of it could have *reached* them; not to speak of many who already knew *what* had taken place, and what must all collapse now that this belief had been undermined,—because so much was built upon it, so much rested on it, and had become one with it: for example, our entire European morality.[10]

Indeed, more than a century had to pass before people began to understand some of the reasons for which the "death of God" was an event exclusive to the Christian world, thus above all a European phenomenon, and to evaluate its consequences for what seemed to be the totally secular character of morality and politics. This is because the "religions of terrestrial salvation"—scientism, patriotism, anarchism, communism, and, more generally, all the "new" figures of the *human ideal*—were also to be swept away by the shock wave of the eclipse of the divine. There is a notable paradox here: at first, "progressive" ideologies counted on prospering on the ruins of a religion that they had at times done much to undermine. This was shortsighted thinking and a failure to understand that beyond any *particular* spirituality—here Christianity—spirituality in general was going to be affected. Hence the "death of God" ineluctably presaged—for anyone able to see and to understand—the "death of man."

After the fall of cosmological and theological principles, to claim to reendow life with meaning by relying on "ideals" rooted in the human species was, in effect and in spite of appearances, to maintain intact the structure of religion. From this point of view, scientism, a faith in progress, but in equal measure nationalism and revolutionary ideals, are simply descriptions of various facets of the new modern religions. As Gilles Deleuze writes, commenting on Nietzsche, "Has one killed God when one has put man in his place and retained what is essential—that is, the place? The only change is this: instead of being burdened from outside, man himself takes up the weights and puts them on his back. . . . Values can change; man can put himself in the place of God; progress, happiness, and utility can replace the true, the good, or the divine; but the essential does not change—that is, the perspectives or the evaluations on which those values, old or new, depend."[11] In other words, for a materialist who values consistency, the figures of transcendence—whether they are ancient (cosmological; theological) or modern (founded on man; "humanist")—in the name of which anyone claims to give meaning to life, remain *religious by their very nature*, which means that the death of God changes nothing whatever of their essence. In the eyes of the deconstructing philosopher (or, as Nietzsche says, the "genealogist"), there is still "nihilism" here, the will to evaluate existence in the name of a "beyond" that secretly continues to animate a desperate aspiration for meaning and a desire for the absolute.

We need to understand what, in fact, nihilism is in order to see how an ultimately radical, authentically materialist critique of all the illusions of transcendence *in general* operates. At its deepest level, nihilism resembles the religious attitude itself in its effort—cost what it may—to invent values that are transcendent and superior to life, in the name of which, as if in recompense, one can ultimately evaluate life and declare it more or less good or bad, more or less a failure or a success, more or less worthy of salvation. This is where guilt begins, not to mention the Fall. While existence may be "innocent" (like that of Adam and Eve before the apple) and unfold in a paradisiac serenity, and while thought—as is often the case with artists—may be affirmative and creative, the "theoretical" and spiritualist invention of transcendence comes along and spoils everything. It matters little, in this connection, whether the supreme principle is that of a cosmos, a god, or a human ideal. Once more Deleuze's commentary is pertinent: in all instances, "instead of the unity of an active life and an affirmative thought, one sees thought take on the task of evaluating life, of contrasting it to values claimed to be superior and judging it by those values, of limiting it, of condemning it. In so doing, thought turns negative, we see life

depreciated, ceasing to be active, reducing itself to its weakest forms, morbid forms compatible only with the so-called superior values."[12] Here we
see how Nietzsche, far from restricting his critique to the Christian religion or established monotheisms, like the materialists of his day, attacks
spirituality in general and under all of its forms, on occasion including
atheist forms.

The enemy is transcendence as such, whatever its dogmatic content.
Still, we sense that Nietzsche is not content to "critique," that he does not
neglect the question of the good life, that between the lines his denunciation of traditional values suggests other values. How can one stigmatize
"the weakest forms" of life, lives sapped by guilt, without appealing—perhaps in counterpoint and in a new manner, still to be invented—to other
forms of life that are stronger, less sickly, less culpable? In pursuing these
questions, we shall find the secret to Nietzsche's response to the guiding
question of this book.

For the moment I shall limit my remarks to an evaluation of the effects
of that critique. According to the line of reasoning I have just outlined, if it
is transcendence in general, spirituality as such, that turns out to be "nihilist"—in the sense that it negates life because it is invented uniquely in
order to judge and condemn life—it follows that the victory of modern
humanism (and, indeed, of ordinary atheism) over the ancient cosmological or theological visions bodes no good. It is the notion of the ideal, not its
particular contents, that raises problems, and one cannot "judge" that notion or adopt an attitude of reprobation or "moral" condemnation toward
it, as it seems to incite us to do. Doing so would be to fall into the trap of
the forces of "reaction." If the attitude that judges life in the name of an external criterion, if the thought that opposes the ideal to the real, is the poison par excellence, we need to do everything possible to be wary of it and
to avoid a return to that baleful logic. This explains Nietzsche's odd phras-
ing in his maxims attacking the ideal: "I do not refute ideals, I merely put
on gloves before them"; and "The ideal is not refuted—it *freezes* to
death."[13] This is the best way to annihilate the warmth that is supposed to
animate the hope of believers of all stripes.

Of course, this also explains the pervasive aversion that Nietzsche displays toward modern values and the new religions of terrestrial salvation. It
explains his hatred of science when it is "common" (claiming to be valid for
all, since "nothing is more democratic than logic") or "anti-aesthetic"
(when it denounces the sensible in the name of an intelligible truth), as
well as his constant criticism of all the incarnations of modern "progres-

sivism" and his denunciations of socialism, the republican idea, the parity between men and women, bosses and workers, slaves and free men, and of democracy and the "poison of the doctrine of equal rights for all."[14] It is useless to belabor the point: there are hundreds of pages in Nietzsche's works on these all-too-familiar topics, and except by sinking into a new revisionism we cannot make them disappear. But here, too, although the motifs in these passages may be problematic, they are neither trivial nor brutally "fascist," and when we deconstruct them, do we not discern, between the lines, if not other ideals, at least new alternatives? That is what Nietzsche himself at times suggests; in *Beyond Good and Evil* he states: "We have a different faith; to us the democratic movement is not only a form of the decay of political organization but a form of the decay, namely the diminution, of man, making him mediocre and lowering his value. Where, then, must *we* reach with our hopes? Toward *new philosophers;* there is no choice."[15] There can be little doubt, despite the plural, that when Nietzsche refers to "new philosophers," he is referring to himself. But what faith, what hope, what philosophy is he announcing here? This is the question to which we shall have to return in order to grasp *his* response and *his* message regarding the successful life. At any rate, we can perhaps better understand the extent to which, as Deleuze puts it,

> the death of God is a great, noisy event, but not a sufficient one. For "nihilism" continues, barely changing form. Not so long ago nihilism meant depreciation, negation of life in the name of superior values. And now: negation of those superior values, replacement by human values (morality replaces religion; utility, progress, and history itself replace the divine values). Nothing has changed, because it is the same reactive life, the same slavery, that triumphed in the shadow of the divine values, and that triumphs now by human values. It is the same bearer, the same donkey who was still burdened with the weight of the divine relics, for which he answered to God, but now takes on himself, in self-responsibility.[16]

Modern man, reputed to be free and autonomous, has perhaps gained little over ancient man. Instead of being slave to a radical alterity, he has become his own slave, that's all.

To get to the bottom of the question, we need a better understanding of this apparently odd but actually quite limpid formula about nihilism: that the passion for judging life that makes us invent transcendent values is the passion of a "donkey," a beast of burden who enjoys carrying a load and who, when others fail to take on the task, opts to burden himself. This is where the invisible strands uniting the will to judge and the advent of guilt are woven together; this is the origin of the spider webs that deprive existence of lightness and innocence and render it so heavy, so burdensome, and so difficult for the "moralists," even when they appear to be irreligious.

For the moment, let us leave aside the (perfectly legitimate) question of how far it is desirable, or even possible, to do without morality. This said, it is hard to see how—even in Nietzsche's terms—human existence could not have had dealings, from time to time, with some of those supposed "heavinesses," when they are linked, not so much to values themselves (as if one took on such burdens *only* out of masochistic pleasure), as to a minimum consideration of others from which it is not always sublime to free oneself.

Here as elsewhere, we should keep to what is essential in this introduction to Nietzsche's deconstruction of the idols of transcendence. If the "deification of man" that followed the death of God in the nineteenth century retained the essential elements of the structure of religion, one need hardly be a seer to predict that it will suffer the same baleful fate.[17] After the death of God, the "death of man"—that is, of humanist and "progressive" ideals—is inevitable. Michel Foucault has never hidden the fact that he borrowed the theme from Nietzsche. But Nietzsche's own formulation of the theme is not lacking in interest, given that it is connected to the conviction that the collapse of the last illusions of transcendence leaves us in a world that is *finally* tragic and absurd: "Man a little, eccentric animal, which—fortunately—has its day: all on earth a mere moment, an incident, an exception without consequences, something of no importance to the general character of the earth; the earth itself, like every star, a hiatus between two nothingnesses, an event without plan, reason, will, self-consciousness, the worst kind of necessity, *stupid* necessity."[18]

In every way, what Nietzsche added to the thought of the earlier materialists was a rigorous, implacable exploration of the most profound consequences of this twilight, at long last, of *all* idols, beginning with the ones having to do with the meaning of life. Nietzsche was correct in stating that, in the absence of all reference to any transcendence, even human transcendence, the very question is meaningless: "We have invested things with ends and values; therefore we have in us an enormous fund of latent forces: but by comparing values it appears that contradictory things have been accounted valuable, that *many* tables of values have existed (thus nothing is valuable 'in itself')."[19] This is what ordinary atheists, the "progressives" who still believe in Man, have not wanted to admit. To be sure, they killed God, but their audacity stopped halfway. They retreated before the frightening consequences of a deconstruction taken to the limit that would ultimately have made clear "the absurdity of everything that happens": "Moral explication has become defunct, along with religious interpretation, but superficial minds do not know it. The more irreligious they are, the more they cling instinctively, hanging on by their teeth, to moral judgments. Schopenhauer, who was an atheist, cursed anyone who strips the universe of its moral significance."[20]

There is fear of an absence of meaning here, to be sure, but also a refusal to follow to its ultimate conclusion the genealogical conviction, deconstructive par excellence, that the famous transcendences that bear meaning are mere subjective projections aimed at supporting life: "Our values are *interpretations introduced by us* into things. Could there be a signification in the in-itself? Is not all signification a *relative* signification, a perspective?"[21] But in order to arrive at that conclusion, must one not have the courage to concede, finally, that the value of life cannot be measured by a criterion external to it, that the only value worth anything is life itself, and that its dimension, its evaluation, is radically immanent to it, residing uniquely in its degree of *intensity*? "There is nothing to life that has value, except the degree of power—assuming that life itself is the will to power."[22] But in order to admit this, one would first have had to wield the hammer without pity or restraint and to accept the idea that, after the end of the world and the death of God, the belief in Man expressed by the ideals of modern morality and politics had not the least chance of survival.

Let us accept this notion, if only as a hypothesis, for the pleasure of following Nietzsche and pursuing to the end a radical way of thinking about the disenchantment of the world. After what has been said, the two questions that we must ask him should be obvious.

The first relates to the legitimacy of his deconstruction of idols and the premises on which that deconstruction is founded. Contrary to the image that Nietzsche perhaps wanted to give of himself, which, in the final analysis, may have served him less well than he thought, his philosophy is much more argumentative, much more rational, that it seems at first sight. What I have termed his "materialism"—that is, his all-out critique of cosmic, religious, and human transcendence—is in no way impressionistic or fragmentary. To the contrary, it forms a sort of "system" whose overall coherence we must attempt to reveal.[23] As we shall see, this critique is worth investigating, given that its point of arrival is nothing less than the meaning—or lack of meaning—of human life.

Once we have portrayed his deconstructive perspective, we need to re-trace Nietzsche's more "positive" side (if one can call it that) in the "trans-mutation" of values. We need to interrogate Nietzsche, not on the unfath-omable silliness of his predecessors in philosophy, a topic on which he is inexhaustible, but rather on the nature and—why not?—the pertinence of his own conception of the good life and on the exact meaning of what seems to be his criterion of intensity, which promises, quite simply, to open a new perspective of life to humanity. Beyond a doubt, there is a Nietz-schean "wisdom." The problem is that henceforth, in distinguishing the successful life from the "failed" life, that wisdom can no longer rely on any criterion external to life. How, then, can we distinguish between the good life and other forms of existence? How can we escape from this world without leaving the "earth"? That is the whole question.

CHAPTER 4

The Foundations & Arguments of Nietzschean Materialism

Like any intellectually honest thinker, Nietzsche would certainly have conceded, without the least difficulty, that true materialism—in the sense in which the term has been used in the preceding chapters—is first and foremost a "reductionism," a determination to reduce the mirages of transcendence to the processes that so naturally invite us to deceive ourselves. In the preface to *Ecce Homo*, one of the few among his works to take the form of personal confession, he defined his philosophical attitude in terms that leave little doubt about this point:

> The last thing *I* should promise would be to "improve" mankind. No new idols are erected by me; let the old ones learn what feet of clay mean. *Overthrowing "idols"* (my word for "ideals")—that comes closer to being part of my craft. One has deprived reality of its value, its meaning, its truthfulness, to precisely the extent to which one has mendaciously invented the ideal world. The "true world" and the "apparent world"—that means: the mendaciously invented world and reality. The *lie* of the ideal has so far been the curse on reality; on account of it, mankind itself has become mendacious and false

down to its most fundamental instincts—to the point of worshiping the *opposite* values of those which alone would guarantee its health, its future, the lofty *right* to its future.[1]

To measure the scope of this hunt for "idols" and to perceive just how much more radical it is than all previous conceptions of materialism, we need first to discuss the nature of the "true reality" that Nietzsche opposes to the fictions of the ideal. In other words, we need to begin with Nietzsche's "ontology" and with his definition of a "materiality" that is thoroughly "terrestrial" in the name of which his genealogy operates and to which it reduces fallacious impulses in the direction of the "supernatural." If idols stand for a false reality—one might say, an unreal reality—where are we to situate true reality? Nietzsche's response to that question leaves not the shadow of a doubt: "The innermost essence of being" is none other than "Life."[2] The notion requires explication, however.

The Real Is Life: "Active" Forces and "Reactive" Forces

As we have already seen, Nietzsche saw the world—both organic and inorganic—as a vast field of energy, a tissue of forces, instincts, and impulses whose infinite and chaotic multiplicity cannot be reduced to unity. At the heart of this chaos, which he calls "Life," Nietzsche distinguishes two quite distinct orders, two overall types of force, the "reactive" and the "active." It might be said that the first of these take as their model, on the intellectual plane, the "will to truth," and, on the political level, the democratic ideal. The second type, to the contrary, comes into play essentially in art, and its natural sphere is aristocracy. Our first task is to try to comprehend what is hidden behind these somewhat massive typologies, beginning with an analysis of the "reactive" forces.

To hazard a first approximation, these are the forces that can only be deployed in the world and produce their full effects in it by repressing, annihilating, or mutilating other forces. In other words, they can be posited only as opposing; they derive from the logic of the "no" rather than from that of the "yes"; of the "against" rather than the "for." If we move from an abstract, still unsatisfactory description to their living incarnations, we might say that these reactive forces are best expressed in philosophy and science, the two great representatives of the "will to truth."

The model that Nietzsche has in mind is that of the Platonic dialogues, where we see a central personage (usually Socrates) exchanging remarks with interlocutors of varying degrees of goodwill and naïveté. The exchange is an unequal one, however: Socrates occupies a place in them that is always set a bit off-center; his attitude is *ironic*. His role is essentially negative—*reactive*. He never makes a risky statement, never exposes himself, and seldom proposes anything positive. Rather, his efforts are focused—following his famous maieutic method—on placing his interlocutor in difficulty and leading him into self-contradiction. It is by refuting supposedly false opinions that the dialogue progresses and attempts ultimately to arrive at a truth. This means that truth is proposed *against* the commonplaces that it opposes, just as something that "holds together" stands opposed to something that does not. Truth never appears *directly or immediately* but always indirectly, mediated by a refutation of the forces of illusion, error, and falsehood.

This description of the will to truth in terms of "reaction" against something other than itself remains in large part viable today. In many ways, in fact, contemporary science continues to follow a procedure modeled on the Platonic dialogues. This is, at least, what leading epistemologists tell us: the most important scientific discoveries do not fall from the skies like a ripe fruit dropping from the tree of knowledge; rather, they emerge—to speak like Gaston Bachelard—in *polemics*, in rupture with the naïve representations of common consciousness and in reaction to earlier, erroneous scientific theories.

It is not only in a combat against error that supposedly true knowledge emerges, but also, more generally, in distancing itself from the sensory world as a whole. Philosophy and science share a claim to accede to *ideal* truths, to *intelligible entities* that cannot be touched or seen, to notions that in no way belong to the corporeal universe. So it is against that universe that they attempt to operate, for the senses, as is known, constantly deceive us. To offer a simple example: if we restrict our observation to sense data alone, water is capable of appearing to us under multiple, quite different, and even *contradictory* forms of reality—boiling water, rain, snow, ice—whereas it is always *in truth* one and the same essence. This is why we need to know how to rise above the level of sense experience and even think *against it* if we want to grasp the "idea of water" or, as we would say today, the level of abstraction proper to a scientific formula such as "H_2O." This is also why we must turn toward the intelligible world, as the myth of the cave invites us, if we want to accede to truly philosophical concepts but also, by the same token, to the laws of a science increasingly derived from pure intelligence.

From the point of view of the will to truth, it is thus a good idea to reject all forces dependent on falsehood and illusion, as well as all impulses that depend too exclusively on sense perception and the body. *In short, we need to be leery of everything—oddly enough—that is essential to art.* And of course what Nietzsche suspects is that behind that "reaction" there lies hidden a dimension quite different from a simple desire for truth. Perhaps this is already an ethical option, a prejudice in favor of "the beyond" over the "here and now," as suggested in an ironic interpolation that he himself takes the trouble to stress in a passage from *Twilight of the Idols:* "These senses, which are so immoral in other ways too, deceive us concerning the *true* world. Moral: let us free ourselves from the deception of the senses, from becoming, from history, from lies. . . . And above all, away with the body, this wretched *idée fixe* of the senses, disfigured by all the fallacies of logic, refuted, even impossible, although it is impudent enough to behave as if it were real!"[3]

On the reactive side, then, we find the will to truth in all its forms, a purpose hostile to the impulses at play in the world of the senses, but also a temptation that is, strictly speaking, *democratic* and that Nietzsche never ceases to deride. The truths that science claims to attain are among those, in fact, that supposedly apply to everyone, in all times and all places. They tend, in other words, to *universality,* which means—and Nietzsche's diagnosis leaves little room for debate—that science is "common" and "plebeian." That is, moreover, just what scholars, who are often republicans, love so much about science: it is addressed to the powerful and the weak, the rich and the poor, the people and the princes. This explains Nietzsche's insistence on the "popular" origins of Socrates, the inventor of philosophy and the first promoter of reactive forces directed toward the ideal of the true. It also explains the equivalence that Nietzsche establishes, in the chapter on "the problem of Socrates" in *Twilight of the Idols,* between the democratic world and a rejection of art; between the Socratic will to truth and the ugliness—which was legendary—of the hero of Plato's dialogues, which signaled the end of an aristocratic world still full of its own "distinction" and "authority."

In origin, Socrates belonged to the lowest class: Socrates was plebs. We know, we can still see for ourselves, how ugly he was. . . . Was Socrates a Greek at all? Ugliness is often enough the expression of a development that has been crossed, *thwarted* by crossing. . . . With Socrates, Greek taste changes in favor of dialectics. What really happened there? Above all, a *noble* taste is thus vanquished; with dialectics the plebs come to the top. . . . What must first be proved is worth little. Wherever authority still forms part of good bearing, where one does not give reasons but commands, the dialectician is a kind of buffoon: one laughs at him, one does not take him seriously. Socrates was the buffoon who *got himself taken seriously.*[4]

It is difficult today to ignore the unpleasant aspects of a discourse such as this. All of the ingredients of a fascist ideology seem intertwined in it: the cult of beauty and "distinction" from which the "populace" is, by nature, excluded; an apology of life that turns toward vitalism; a classification of individuals according to their social origins that equates the common people with ugliness; doubts regarding a person's belonging to an admired nation (here the Greeks); painful suspicions about a possible hybridization that supposedly explains some sort of decadence: nothing is missing. Without pausing over this first impression, however, let us attempt to ascertain, in as far as possible, the deeper meaning of these statements. To do so, we will have to enrich our reflection and take into account those active forces that we have left aside for the moment. I have already suggested that, unlike the reactive forces, the active ones could find a place in the world and deploy their full effects there without having to mutilate or repress other forces. If, once again, we move from abstract discourse to real incarnations of this typology, it is in art that these forces find their natural life space. Just as there is a secret connection between reaction, the search for truth, democracy, universalist morality, and a rejection of the world of the senses in favor of the intelligible world, so too there is an Ariadne's thread linking art, aristocracy, the cult of the perceptible or corporeal world, and the active forces.

Artists are, above all, persons who present *values without discussion;* who open perspectives of life for us without needing to demonstrate the legitimacy of what they propose, and even less to prove it by refuting other works that preceded their own. Like the aristocrat, whom the artist resembles in this as in other ways, the genius *commands without arguing against anyone or anything.* Obviously, we can enjoy Bach and Debussy or Rembrandt and Manet without demanding that anyone even dream of having to choose one of them to the exclusion of the other. Where truth is concerned, however, sooner or later a choice cannot be avoided. Copernicus was right and Ptolemy was wrong; Newton's physics is surely truer than that of Descartes. Truth can only be established by pushing aside the errors that litter the history of science. The history of art, to the contrary, is the locus of a possible coexistence of even the most different sorts of works. Not, of course, that tensions and quarrels are absent from the world of art. Quite the contrary. It is just that aesthetic conflicts are never decided in terms of "wrong" and "right"; they always leave open—at least after the fact—the possibility that their protagonists will enjoy equal admiration.

This is perhaps why, since the dawn of philosophy in Greece, two types of discourse, two conceptions of the use of words, have always stood opposed. On one side is the Socratic and reactive model that seeks truth by means of dialogue and, in the interest of achieving that end, combats the various faces of ignorance and bad faith. On the other side is Sophistic discourse, which by no means aims at truth but rather attempts to seduce, to persuade, to produce an almost physical effect on an audience, whose adherence it strives to win by rhetorical power alone. The first discourse is that of philosophy and science; in it language is an instrument in the service of a reality higher than itself, the intelligible and democratic Truth that, sooner or later, everyone will accept. The second is the discourse of art and poetry: here words are no longer simply means but ends in themselves; they have value in and of themselves the moment they produce their aesthetic effects—that is, if one believes etymology, their *sensible* effects—on those capable of receiving them. One of the tactics used by Socrates in his oratory jousts with the Sophists perfectly illustrates this opposition of the reactive and the active. After a dazzling performance by a great rhetorician—say, Gorgias or Protagoras—and before a public still charmed by the poems superbly presented by these artists of the spoken word, Socrates feigns incomprehension. Better yet, he deliberately arrives late, after the spectacle has ended, which gives him an excellent pretext for asking the Sophist to *summarize* his thoughts, to formulate, *if possible briefly*, the essential content of his discourse. This is like reducing a lovers' conversation to its "rational nucleus"; it is like asking Baudelaire or Rimbaud to summarize one of their poems: "L'Albatros"? A sea fowl that has trouble taking flight. "Le Bateau ivre"? A boat in trouble. Socrates has no difficulty making points: as soon as his adversary makes the mistake of taking him up on his game, he is lost, because where art is concerned, it is obviously not the truth content that is important but the magic of emotions, which does poorly in the test of the summary, a reductive exercise par excellence. We see here what Nietzsche means when he speaks of the "ugliness" of Socrates and when he associates that ugliness with the democratic ideology, or, somewhat later in the same text, when he stigmatizes the "*sarcasm of the rachitic*" in someone who takes pleasure in brandishing "the knife-thrusts of his syllogisms" against his interlocutors.[5] This is less a deployment of pre-fascist formulas than an expression of an aversion to the will to truth, at least in its traditional rationalistic and reactive forms.

A Thought of "Absolute" Immanence

The real is thus life, and life is a chaotic fabric of active and reactive forces. Fine. But what are we to conclude from this that will help our investigation of the meaning and the legitimacy of Nietzsche's critique of the various faces of transcendence? First and foremost: the forms that sometimes emerge from this chaos, which seem, because of their relative stability, *to detach themselves from it* and to acquire an *autonomy,* an externality, even a *superiority,* are *in fact not external to it at all; rather, they are merely a result of the very multiplicity of the forces of origins.* They are both totally and wholly *immanent* within the real, within life. Taking this view we may better understand in what sense the illusions of transcendence constitute the ultimate form of human error.

A metaphor will perhaps lead to a more concrete grasp of this. We know today—it is one of the principal tenets of modern science—that a world *without forces* would also be a world *without forms.* Let us consider, for example, the spherical aspect of the planets or, closer to our daily experience, the globular shape of a drop of morning dew on a tree leaf. These things warmed the hearts and inspired the minds of the Ancients, who still lived in an enchanted world. Modern physics tells us, however, that there is no miracle here; no "transcendence" of some cosmic or divine order need be sought in order to explain this seeming formal perfection. The spherical shape is obtained whenever the forces involved act in an identical manner, from all spatial directions, at the same time. Something similar occurs when a glass blower uses a tube to transform hot, shapeless, raw material into a harmonious globe. But now imagine that the glass bubble begins to harden and becomes detached from the tube that formed it. Let us also suppose it to be endowed with a tiny bit of consciousness, a smidgen of intelligence. It too would probably think that it was in some way "autonomized"; that it had acquired an existence independent of its previous support. It might even go so far as to attribute value to its fine round form, and at that point—why not?—it might sketch out a spherical morality, an aesthetics of roundness, a metaphysics of the circular, denouncing the ugliness and perversity of points, peaks, and sharp angles. A pure and simple emanation of vital forces, it would soon set itself up as a judge, as if it could compare and evaluate, *from the outside,* from a *superior and transcendent* point of view, the various aspects of living things. It would believe itself victorious over chaos, and perhaps, in that very victory, elect among all the other forms, chosen by a God who protects and guides it. Until a small shock annihilates it and brings it back both to greater modesty and to the chaos from which it escaped, but only for an instant and only in thought.

Applying the metaphor, removing it from physics alone, and relating it to the whole extent of the forms or modes of life that we may encounter or adopt during the course of our existence, we might say that the authentic philosopher, according to Nietzsche, is one who perceives the infinite variety in the processes that enable us to believe (illusorily) that we transcend life's reality and attain autonomy. The philosopher's task of disenchantment is thus dual: he must first wield the hammer, break the bubbles, deconstruct the idols, and show that the illusions of transcendence are in reality merely a product rigorously immanent in the forces that underlie them. Next, he must investigate the status of his own "deconstructive" discourse or, to use Nietzsche's term, his "genealogist's" discourse (and now we can see why), in particular regarding the question of knowing what "truth" he can claim to use, now that he has rejected the classic authority figures and now that truth is no longer founded on transcendence.

All Judgments on Life Are Only a Symptom of Our Vital States

Regarding the first of these tasks, Nietzsche's thought again displays the merit of coherence: his most consistent thesis is that, in the absence of a viewpoint external to life and superior to it, no judgment on existence in general makes the least sense, except as an illusion, as a pure symptom expressing a certain state of the vital forces of the person judging:

> Judgments, judgments of value, concerning life, for it or against it, can, in the end, never be true: they have value only as symptoms, they are worthy of consideration only as symptoms; in themselves such judgments are stupidities. One must by all means stretch out one's fingers and make the attempt to grasp this amazing finesse, *that the value of life cannot be estimated.* Not by the living, for they are an interested party, even a bone of contention, and not judges; not by the dead, for a different reason. For a philosopher to see a problem in the value of life is thus an objection to him, a question mark concerning his wisdom, an un-wisdom.[6]

For the great deconstructor that the genealogist is, not only can there be no "objective" or, in the root sense of the term, "disinterested" value judgment—that is, one independent of the interests of the person making it, which already supposes the collapse of the classic concepts of law and morality—but, for the same reasons, there also can be no "subject-in-itself" that is free and autonomous, and nor can there be any "facts-in-themselves" that are objective and absolutely true.

This abysmal consequence merits meditation. In the perspective of an authentic materialism—in this case, that of a generalized vitalism—such entities cannot be other than expressions or, to put it better, "reflections," of the "raw material" that is life and of which we ourselves, as living creatures immersed in the world, are but aleatory fragments. Similarly, we can never be autonomous individuals, transcending the real at the heart of which we live, but only products of history, thoroughly immanent to that reality; similarly, and in contrast to what the positivists and the scientists proclaim, there is no such thing as a state of "fact-in-itself." Scientists are quick to say, "The facts speak for themselves!" when they want to set aside an objection or even just express how they feel about the constraint of "objective truth." But the "facts" to which scientists claim to submit themselves, as if to an inviolable and incontestable given, are never—at least from a deeper level of reflection—anything but the fluctuating product of a history of life in general and of the forces that compose it at any particular instant.

Nietzsche attacks the illusions of a "free" subject who claims to rise above or transcend nature and history so as to *judge* them on a moral, political, or even an aesthetic plane, just as much as he does the scientific prejudices that nourish the illusion of an objective thought "in conformity with facts." In order to deconstruct these first steps toward the affirmation of a transcendence, it suffices to relate these illusions to the *unconscious* forces that unwittingly engender them. In this sense, Nietzsche's thought takes the form of a "philosophy of suspicion" (even before the appearance of psychoanalysis) that denounces the elucubrations of the infinitely small part of us that is conscious thought in the name of depth psychology.

The Discovery of the Unconscious, or the End of the Illusions of the Free Subject, Superior to the Forces of Nature

The revelation of a dimension of the unconscious in psychic life thus plays a crucial role in Nietzsche's argument. This is why, in the highly interesting section 357 of *Die fröhliche Wissenschaft* (*Joyful Wisdom*), headed "The Old

Problem: What is German?" Nietzsche (and one instance does not imply a habit) presents an apology for a rationalist thinker, Leibniz, whom he credits with having shown how "our inner world is far richer, ampler, and more concealed" than had been thought.[7] What Leibniz had *profoundly* cast into question, in Nietzsche's eyes, was the supposed "evidences" of Cartesian philosophy and, in particular, the primacy of consciousness in the name of which the "inner" life should be identified with clear and distinct thought. Leibniz may have been the first to introduce into modern philosophy the concept of the unconscious with his famous "minute perceptions" that, by virtue of the principle of continuity, necessarily precede the appearance of full consciousness. The reasoning that leads Leibniz to this discovery is relatively simple. It can be summarized thus: when, for example, I wake from a profound sleep, I pass, in the broad sense, "from the unconscious to the conscious." If we apply the principle of continuity, which states that nature makes no leaps, we will have to admit that this passage does not take place "all at once" but progressively. Let us not forget that Leibniz had just discovered the infinitesimal calculus that permitted him to add infinitely small quantities known in mathematics as "integrals." It is thus by an accumulation of an infinite number of infinitesimal degrees of consciousness that I pass from the unconscious to the conscious state and not, as Descartes would have it, with no transition. This seems a simple affirmation, but Nietzsche found it astonishing because it implied, even at this early stage, recognition of an unconscious psychic life that connects a zero degree of consciousness (the state of deep sleep) with an nth degree of consciousness (the waking state). Thus, according to Nietzsche, Leibniz was to discover "the incomparable idea that proved him right, not only against Descartes, but against everyone who had philosophized until him, according to which consciousness is a simple *accident* of representation, *not* its necessary, essential attribute, so that what we call consciousness constitutes only a state (and perhaps even a sick state) of our spiritual world, not—far from it—that world itself."[8]

With the hypothesis of the unconscious, it is thus the fiction of a transparent subject, master of itself, that is shaken, because (as Nietzsche explains) we must at last resolve to consider consciousness only an epiphenomenon of life, not life itself. The consciousness of the "I" (the ego, or the subject) no longer appears as anything but "the last trait added to the organism when it already functions perfectly; it is almost superfluous." As a result, if the illusion of the unity of the self still possesses any sort of truth, it cannot be on the level of consciousness, as the entire Platonic and Cartesian philosophical tradition naïvely believed: "If I have some unity in me, it surely does not consist in my conscious self." What I am conscious of is never anything but a "terminal phenomenon" whose causes are unknown to me but reside in what Nietzsche calls "the wisdom of the organism"—that is, the living being. Genealogy literally dissolves this "fetishism" of the subject; it bursts the bubble: the "I" is just a "creation": "Even 'the subject' is such a created entity, a 'thing' like all others; a simplification with the object of defining the force which posits, invents, thinks, as distinct from all individual positing, inventing, thinking as such."[9] We believe that with the "I" we are exhibiting a real faculty, but that faculty is actually nothing, or, more accurately, it is only the concretion, the reification, of an activity that never exists except as a particular activity.

The conscious and supposedly sovereign self does not in any way transcend living reality. Quite to the contrary, like a little cork floating on the ocean of the vital forces, it is merely one infinitely small expression, one emanation among an infinity of other possible expressions. *Therefore it can neither judge life nor make choices outside of life;* consequently it cannot be held "responsible" for actions that one might claim to impute to it if it were a transcendent entity in relation to the world. Throughout his works Nietzsche insists that the notion of free will—the claim of the conscious subject to being the author of its thoughts and actions and its aspiration to "responsibility"—is an absurdity. It is clear that such a concept would imply, once again, the old and contradictory idea of the "cause of oneself"; that it would involve the thesis according to which the "I," the *cogito,* must be considered a "substance," along with the unique and ultimate substratum of decisions rooted in it. "The desire for 'freedom of the will' in the superlative metaphysical sense, which still holds sway, unfortunately, in the minds of the half-educated; the desire to bear the entire and ultimate responsibility for one's actions oneself, and to absolve God, the world, ancestors, chance, and society, involves nothing less than to be precisely this *causa sui.*" That notion is quite simply aberrant, however: "The *causa sui* is the best self-contradiction that has been conceived so far, it is a sort of rape and perversion of logic." It serves, "with more than Münchhausen's audacity, to pull oneself up into existence by the hair, out of the swamps of nothingness."[10]

An aphorism in *Beyond Good and Evil* enables us to define more precisely how this critique of free will implies a radical denunciation of man's claims to install himself as actor and transcendent judge of nature and history. Nietzsche questions the "superstitions of logicians" that consist (always the same faith in grammar!) in connecting a verb to a subject. Against that superstition, we must assert "that a thought comes when 'it' wishes, not when 'I' wish, so that it is a falsification of the facts of the case to say that the subject 'I' is the condition of the predicate 'think.' *It* thinks [*es denkt*]; but that this 'it' is precisely the famous old 'ego' is, to put it mildly, only a supposition, an assertion, and assuredly not an 'immediate certainty.'" Here Nietzschean genealogy, as is its custom, takes the form of what one might call, borrowing from the vocabulary of Marx, a "defetishization" of the "hypostasis" that is the illusion of the self. To be "fetishist" is to believe in the existence of something that has been produced as though it had fallen from the skies, forgetting the activity of production that engendered it. This is the very mechanism that leads to the illusion of transcendence. We believe, for example, that we are the authors of our ideas, values, and choices, whereas in truth they are part of a history, a social milieu, a culture, and a nation, within which they have been shaped unbeknownst to the subject. In a similar vein, Nietzsche declares about the illusion of the free subject, "One infers here according to the grammatical habit: 'Thinking is an activity; every activity requires an agent; consequently . . .'" Not only must we learn to rid ourselves of such simplistic forms of reasoning and put an end to the fiction of the free subject, but we must also rid ourselves of the idea of "something" that thinks: "One has even gone too far with this 'it thinks'—even the 'it' contains an *interpretation* of the process, and does not belong to the process itself. . . . Perhaps some day we shall accustom ourselves, including the logicians, to get along without the little 'it' (which is all that is left of the honest little old ego)."[11]

Nietzsche's deconstruction of metaphysical subjectivity is so radical that it seems nearly impossible to formulate: one might be tempted to replace the formula "I think" with "it is thinking in me,"[12] but that would be to risk constant confusion between "it" and an autonomous "substratum" that Nietzsche invites us to get rid of. What is important here is to understand—at least in principle and admitting that such a philosophical position is tenable—that this would amount to saying that neither "objectivity" nor "subjectivity" exists, and that there is, in the final analysis, no objective judgment on earth, because there is, at base, nothing but interpretations without *interpretans* or *interpretandum*—with neither an interpreting subject nor an interpreted object—which would mean that the end of the "subject-in-itself" also signals the end of the "object-in-itself" so dear to scientist ideologies.

The End of the Object-in-Itself: "There are no facts, only interpretations"

The eradication of the subject is thus accompanied in Nietzsche by the inevitable disappearance of the object, as is suggested, following a subtle line of argument, in a decisive fragment of the *Will to Power.*[13] To begin with, it is clear that the liquidation of the subject/substance (of a supposedly clear, autonomous, and responsible consciousness) leads to thinking about the world as an interwoven fabric of interpretations irreducible to any sort of unity, given that they lack any stable substratum. Strictly speaking, then, "One may not ask: 'who then interprets?' for it is interpretation itself, as a form of the will to power, that exists (not as a 'being' but as a process, a becoming) insofar as it is an affect." And if interpretation alone constitutes the basis of what is, it is not only the subject that is an illusion and an effect of fetishism, but also the idea that there might exist objective facts— "facts-in-themselves"—independent of interpretation: "A 'thing-in-itself' just as perverse as a 'sense-in-itself.' . . . There are no 'facts-in-themselves.'" Just as it is vain to seek a "subject" of an interpretation and it is imperative to give up asking, "who then interprets?" at least in the sense in which that "who" would refer to a sovereign being, so it is imperative to abandon "the question 'what is that?'" because that question, similarly, "is an imposition of meaning from some other viewpoint." Hence "at the bottom of it there always lies 'What is that for *me?*' (for us, for all that lives, etc.)." The parenthesis that Nietzsche inserts here is intended to make us comprehend that the "I" is henceforth not to be understood as the metaphysical subject, identical to itself in the transparency of its consciousness, but rather as a shattered subject, one interpretive force among others, a pure point of view: "In short: the essence of a thing is only an *opinion* about the 'thing.' Or rather: 'it is considered' is the real 'it is,' the sole 'this is.'"

In other words, as Nietzsche himself states, if there are no facts but only interpretations, it is because (as he declares in *Twilight of the Idols*): "Judgments, judgments of value . . . have value only as symptoms,"[14] or, as a fragment in *The Will to Power* puts it, "all evaluation is made from a definite perspective; that of the preservation of the individual, a community, a race, a state, a church, a faith, a culture." We simply forget that "valuation is always from a perspective"—that is, in the proper sense of the term, relative to the person who bears such judgments. In short, there are no "things-in-themselves," no "absolute knowledge,"[15] because the multiplicity of points of view turns out to be irreducible.[16] Nietzsche concludes: "Our values are interpreted *into* things"; "Is meaning not necessarily relative meaning and perspective?"[17]

Infinite Genealogy, or Philosophizing with a Hammer

A reader unfamiliar with Nietzsche's works may already have had some difficulty grasping exactly what is at stake and what is the precise scope of Nietzsche's combined critique of subjectivity and objectivity. Similarly, the connections between Nietzsche's critique and what interests us here — a radical, authentically materialist critique of the multiple faces of transcendence — might seem somewhat tenuous. A brief comparison with other "philosophies of suspicion" — those of Marx and Freud — may furnish the necessary enlightenment.

At first glance, one might say that the principal function of critical thought is basically the same in Marx, Nietzsche, and Freud. As many others before me have noted, all three of these authors relativize, even denounce, the illusions of a so-called autonomous and sovereign consciousness and reconnect them to the unconscious realities that have fashioned and engendered them. What is needed is to move back from the conscious to the unconscious, from the determined to the determinant, from an illusory autonomy to a real heteronomy, from the reified "product" to the "mode of production," from the final result that, like our glass bubble, believes itself "independent" to the process of which it is merely the induced effect. Whether we are speaking of the bourgeois "ideologies" that Marx attacked, the "idols" of metaphysics that Nietzsche ridiculed, or the neurotic symptoms that Freud analyzed, the operation is basically the same. To be sure, critical thinking operates from different perspectives and is defined in different terms, but whether we speak of a "critique of ideologies" with Marx, a "genealogy of idols" with Nietzsche, or "depth psychology" with Freud, the point is to have done with the illusions of a humanity that strives to transcend the "material reality" (history, life, impulses) within which it is wholly immersed.

One crucial difference, however, distinguishes Nietzsche's intellectual attitude from those of Marx and Freud, and it is a difference that will permit us finally to comprehend to what extent Nietzsche's materialism (and, by the same token, his critique of the illusions of transcendence) is infinitely more radical than that of his two fellow philosophers of suspicion. Marx and Freud, whatever has been said about them, were still largely heirs of the Enlightenment. That is, their claim to truth, and to greater truth than all the theories that preceded their own, was still inscribed within the framework of a *scientific*, even a rationalist, purpose. They hesitate to abandon reason when they think about the irrational; instead, they apply reason to what is or seems totally different from it: there is a logic of ideologies and their production, just as there is a logic in the emergence of the lapsus, dreams, or neurotic or psychotic pathologies. Although the truths that they discover are at times—in their eyes as well as our own—astonishing, even revolutionary (and I cast no doubt on that here), Marx and Freud both remain convinced that they are founding a new science: the science of history and economics for Marx; the science of the life of the psyche for Freud. A nonpositivist science, perhaps, but one nonetheless attached to the revelation of a truth that sooner or later must carry the day and win general acceptance. Although they revolutionized sociology and medicine, Marx and Freud remained a sociologist and a physician. Between ideology and science, as Louis Althusser has rightly remarked, there remains an indisputable "epistemological break."

For reasons discernible in what has already been discussed, Nietzschean genealogy is, by necessity, completely different. His critique of science and, more generally, of all the figures of the will to truth as a typical emanation of the reactive forces does not permit him to resume, one might say to the "second power," a position—no matter how sophisticated or how novel it might be—as a "scientist" or a "savant." Deconstruction of scientific truth cannot, without flagrant contradiction, turn around and receive the status of scientific truth.

Here, too, a comparison with the other philosophies of suspicion, notably with psychoanalysis, can throw light on the question. A "good psychiatrist"—at least in principle—is someone who has himself gone through psychoanalysis. He must—admitting the hypothesis that such a formula makes sense—have sufficiently "brought to the surface" his own history and its relations with his unconscious before he can treat others. He is said to be a subject "supposed to know," and the interpretations that he gives of the various symptoms perceived in his patients must, as far as possible, possess a certain relation to what is "true." Moreover, in order to reveal the "truth of others," or at least to understand a part of that truth, he must, also to the limits of the possible, have revealed something of himself to himself. What can be read between the lines in a conviction of the sort (although it is rarely explicit) is, once more, that there is a connection between the idea that an experienced psychiatrist possesses a certain autonomy of subjectivity (within himself) and the idea of objectivity (attributed to his interpretations). In other words, there is a conjecture that the psychoanalyst has indeed become, thanks to his own analysis, a subject, if not perfectly free and sovereign, at least a bit more liberated and aware of himself than his own patients are. As a result, the interpretations that he formulates, although perhaps not claiming to be "the absolute truth," none-theless show signs of approaching that aim.

Nietzsche's perspective is much more radical. To recall: when Nietzsche states that there are no facts but only interpretations, he adds, as we have seen, that there is, properly speaking, neither a "subject" who interprets nor an "object" to be interpreted. The formula may seem to be poetic license, a figure of style, and, at the limit, even absurd. Let me say this clearly: it is in no way absurd. This is what it means: the genealogist, like the psychoana-lyst (or the critic of ideologies), is indeed the person who interprets beliefs, idols, and illusions (of transcendence)—in short and in general, *symp-toms*—by relating them, as has already been suggested, to the unconscious processes that have engendered them. But, unlike the psychoanalyst (at least, the non-Nietzschean psychoanalyst,[18] or one who thinks his disci-pline is to some extent a science!), the genealogist fully admits the idea that his interpretation is itself wholly produced by his own unconscious, that it is but a reflection, with no superior verity, of his own vital forces, that those forces can never be reduced to the awareness that he might have of them; thus they elude his grasp, just as they elude the grasp of those he claims to be interpreting. Under these conditions, which are inevitably those of Nietzschean genealogy, by reason of its antiscientific presuppositions, the interpretation of the genealogist cannot have—at least not as a first ap-proximation[19]—any *scientific* claim to truth. To the contrary: as a product of the unconscious forces that invest the genealogist just as much as they do those whose illusions he combats, this interpretation is in turn open to interpretation by another genealogist, whose interpretations are again open to interpretation, in a process that can be repeated ad infinitum.

So the metaphysical claim to judge the world from the here and now as if we could look down on it from on high and free ourselves from the vital forces that make us what we are—or, better, free ourselves from our-selves—is a vicious circle. To understand this vicious circle is also to un-derstand that no philosophical pronouncements, Nietzsche's included, can escape history (or escape life as historicity); that there is not, in any sense whatever, a "metalanguage" of truth hovering over reality. As Nietzsche puts it in *Twilight of the Idols:* "A condemnation of life by the living remains in the end a mere symptom of a certain kind of life."[20] Thus our evalua-tions, our viewpoints, our interpretations of the world can never be founded on any sort of reference to a knowledge that is, properly speaking, *absolute* (not relative to the historicity of life). It is of course in this sense that we should understand the passage in Nietzsche's *Joyful Wisdom* headed

"Our New 'Infinite,'" which states: "The world, on the contrary, has once more become infinite to us: in so far we cannot dismiss the possibility that it *contains infinite interpretations*,"[21] none of which can result in the illusion of being an ultimate truth. Under these conditions, in fact, there can be no objectivity; to borrow the terminology of another domain, there can be no signified, but only the signifier, or, as Michel Foucault states in a commentary on Nietzsche, "If the interpretation can never come to an end, this is simply because there is nothing to interpret . . . for at base everything is already interpretation." I might add, repeating a previous point, an interpretation that is itself is open to infinite reinterpretation.

At this point the authentic philosopher becomes one with the genealogist—that is, in the most radical sense, one who perceives that behind evaluations there is no foundation but an abyss; behind the underlying worlds themselves there are other underlying worlds, always inaccessible because they have no existence in themselves except as hypostases of an interpretation that is itself forever elusive. Foucault rightly insists: "Genealogy does not oppose itself to history as the lofty and profound gaze of the philosopher might compare to the molelike perspective of the scholar; on the contrary, it rejects the metahistorical deployment of ideal significations." He adds that the genealogist "needs history to dispel the chimera of the origin,"[22] which of course leads to the liquidation of all the ancient figures of transcendence: the cosmos; God; man; scientific laws; moral, juridical, or political values; and so forth. The genealogist, who stands alone, outside the "herd," thus has the agonizing task of confronting the abyss: "The hermit . . . will doubt whether a philosopher could *possibly* have 'ultimate and real' opinions, whether behind every one of his caves there is not, must not be, another deeper cave—a more comprehensive, stranger, richer world beyond the surface, an abysmally deep ground behind every ground, under every attempt to furnish 'grounds.' Every philosophy is a foreground philosophy—that is a hermit's judgment. . . . Every philosophy also *conceals* a philosophy; every opinion is also a hide-out, every world is a mask."[23] The hermit's cave is no longer Plato's cave.

In modern philosophy skeptical relativism and the belief that it is impossible to arrive at objective truth had always taken the form of a "subjectivism": if it was impossible to achieve objectivity, it was precisely because the subjectivity of the individual was, so to speak, firm enough to preclude any hope of finding acceptable criteria for objectivity (for beauty, truth,

morality, etc.). There is nothing of the sort in Nietzsche. His skepticism—
if the term is still appropriate—takes the form of a perspectivism without
subject or object; a hermeneutics. Or, at the limit (but a limit that must be
respected), there is only interpretation as such, with no hope of a scientific
truth independent of any notion of either a subject who might interpret or
an interpreted object.

Even if we admit that Nietzsche saw clearly, and that we must never
again think of ourselves as responsible authors of our actions, or ever again
pass judgment on any level—moral, political, or scientific—as if our ap-
preciations could lay claim to some sort of objectivity, what conclusion
should we reach regarding the conduct of our lives? And is not the word
"conduct" already superfluous? What can it mean in a Nietzschean perspective, if not the return of a highly illusory claim to a new mastery?
Should the genealogist not pursue an ultimate conclusion, stopping at lucidity, pure and simple, or at a simple, hard-won disenchantment? And is it
not, under such conditions, totally vain to seek anything like a "wisdom of
Nietzsche" or a response to the question of the good life? This is what we
still need to examine.

The Wisdom of Nietzsche, or The Three Criteria of the Good Life

~ ~ ~ ~ ~

Truth in Art, Intensity in the Grand Style,
Eternity in the Instant

It is often said of Nietzsche that he died "mad." So much solitude, so much loftiness of vision and lucidity are supposed to have led him to insanity. Some have even embraced this mythology of madness, often associated with genius according to a commonplace inherited from romanticism.[1] One danger here is forgetting to read Nietzsche himself. In *Ecce Homo* he goes so far as to entitle the first chapter "Why I Am So Wise" and to end the same chapter with praise of Buddhism. The fact that Nietzsche spent his life denouncing idols, that he carried on a radical critique of the great categories inherited from Greek wisdom—the *theōria* that aims at truth, the *praxis* that tends to moral rectitude, the *soteriology* that promises us that we will be saved one day—should not deceive us about the meaning of his philosophy: the same person who deconstructs also reorganizes the oldest topics and reinvests them with meaning, albeit in a novel, somewhat off-center manner. Nietzsche always thought that authentic knowledge—what he called *die fröhliche Wissenschaft* ("joyous wisdom," the "gay science")—mocked the false only in the name of higher verities, and that true morality made fun of morality only in order to arrive at a way of thinking *differently* about the value and meaning of existence, not to do away with such questions. This is why, despite appearances, it may be possible to discern a "wisdom of Nietzsche," to perceive in him a response to the question of the good life, and even, as we shall see, to present that response by following the three guiding threads of all philosophy[2]—*theōria, praxis,* and soteriology—provided that we keep in mind the shifts and breaks that he constantly introduces into them.

1. Theōria: *The Avatars of the Will to Truth; Art as a Condition of the Highest Knowledge*

It is a fact: Nietzschean genealogy can be distinguished from the investigations of Marx and even Freud in that it gives up any claim to base its legitimacy on science. Does this necessarily mean that Nietzsche was a skeptic; that he abandons all reference to truth and perhaps even to a more joyous and higher form of knowledge? Certainly not. The preface to *Ecce Homo* even invites us quite explicitly to think the contrary:

> Those who can breathe the air of my writings know that it is an air of the heights, a *strong* air. . . . Philosophy, as I have so far understood and lived it, means voluntarily living among ice and high mountains. . . . How much truth does a spirit *endure,* how much does it dare? More and more that became for me the real measure of value. Error (faith in the ideal) is not blindness, error is *cowardice.* . . . Every attainment, any step forward in knowledge, *follows* from courage, from hardness against oneself, from cleanliness in relation to oneself. . . . What one has forbidden so far as a matter of principle is—has always been—truth alone.[3]

This is a particularly interesting passage. Not only does it clearly state that the primary aim of philosophy, as Nietzsche himself conceived it, is a search for truth, and for a truth that is even "higher" than the one with which philosophers and savants had been satisfied up to then. But also it is beyond doubt that he associates that search with an ethical demand for courage, the rejection of cowardice, and intellectual honesty. Furthermore, he makes this ethical demand the ultimate criterion, not just one criterion among others. We find ourselves here at the opposite pole from the skepticism and immoralism that his deconstruction of idols might at times have made us think were his ultimate aim. Was Nietzsche inconsistent? Is there not a contradiction, even a flagrant one, between the genealogy of the will to truth as the highest expression of the reactive forces and a revaluation, after all, of truth as the primary goal of an authentic philosophy? Nietzsche thought he had defeated Platonism and its opposition of a false world of the senses to a true world of the intelligible. But in the final analysis, is he not returning to that view surreptitiously, in a manner both unavowed and unavowable? The question is more complex than it seems. Initially, at least, this contradiction—and one has to recognize from the start that it is a bit too obvious to have escaped notice by a mind as fine as Nietzsche's—is resolved, partly if not totally, when we distinguish between two types of truth (and, as a corollary, two types of error). The first of these is an ordinary (one might say, traditional) truth, the one that philosophy and science seek in the world of the ideal, somewhere beyond the sensible world, and that expresses the reactive forces of nihilism. The second is a truth that is hidden, secret, even forbidden; it is a truth—if one can believe Nietzsche—that can be revealed only in an approach less reactive than that of philosophy and science: an artistic approach. This hypothesis should suggest two questions. To put them simply: Why is "ideal" truth (logical, rational, scientific truth) "false"? And why is "sensible," aesthetic truth "truer"?

The answer is obvious if one has grasped the logic of Nietzschean materialism. What is false in the "ideal" truth is precisely its claim to transcendence and to objectivity; its aspiration to place itself above the vital forces that have wholly produced it—in short, in its implicit will to detach itself from space and time, from nature and history, and in its claim to have value for everyone and to have done with relativism and perspectivism. In contrast, what is true in "aesthetic truth," as revealed by the artist, is the fact (difficult to grasp and perhaps still more difficult to admit) that, as an exact opposite of the first sort of truth, it presents itself *explicitly* as merely a point of view, as a perspective, as an emanation of life rather than a break with life. Art is true because it makes no claim to truth; because it is thus adequate to the real; because it accepts its relativity as a product, while never forgetting the productive activity that has engendered it. There is no hypostasis in art, and no fetishism. A fragment in *The Will to Power* states: "The will to appearance, to illusion, to deception, to becoming and change" that is expressed clearly and as such in the creative activity "here counts as more profound, primeval, 'metaphysical' than the will to truth, to reality, to mere appearance." It is in this sense that art, which is anti-Platonic in essence, "is *worth more* than truth" and is a more direct, more adequate expression of life and of the will to power that constitutes "the innermost essence of being."[4]

It is by this *very perfect equation*, of course, that art acquires the status of truth, by analogy, so to speak, with highly classical definitions of the true as conformity between discourse and reality. "The only possible life: in art. Otherwise, one turns away from life," as Nietzsche has already stated in *The Birth of Tragedy*.[5] Thus one senses that the genealogical deconstruction of *theōria* does not eliminate all notion of truth, that there may be a more profound truth than that of ideas—more real, one might say, than the truth that animates philosophical or scientific rationalism. This is a truth that art alone can satisfy, just as, at that same level, only the senses stop lying to us "in that they show us becoming, disappearance, and change."

If what Nietzsche states in one of his most famous aphorisms, "My philosophy is an inverted Platonism," is true, we need to evaluate the consequences of this inversion as regards the foundation (or the refounding) of a thought that rejects the classical visions of truth as reactive but nonetheless claims to arrive at higher and more authentic forms of knowledge in and by means of art. A partial response is offered in *Twilight of the Idols* in the chapter entitled "How the 'True World' Finally Became a Fable." Here Nietzsche undertakes to show how the "true world" (that is, the intelligible world) that Platonism opposes to the "apparent world" (that is, the sensible world) turns out, at the end of a long history that ends with Zarathustra, to be itself illusion par excellence. Citing his own deconstruction of Platonism, Nietzsche signs the death warrant of the Platonic "intelligible world": "The 'true' world—an idea which is no longer good for anything, not even obligating—an idea which has become useless and superfluous—*consequently*, a refuted idea: let us abolish it! (Bright day, breakfast; return of *bon sens* and cheerfulness; Plato's embarrassed blush; pandemonium of all free spirits.)"[6]

At the end of this road, however, wallowing in the sensible is out of the question, as if the aim of emancipating it from the intelligible world must necessarily lead to sacralizing it. Nor does this imply any reevaluation of the concept of appearance in its classical definition, for it is obvious that the abolition of one of the terms in the pair formed by appearance and truth modifies the meaning of the other. What is needed, then, is to *suppress the very idea that anything like appearance might exist:* "The true world—we have abolished. What world has remained? The apparent one perhaps? But no! *With the true world we have also abolished the apparent one.*"[7] By this we see that art, defined by Plato as the locus of a reprehensible presentation of appearance, can now escape the accusation of being nontruth. Not only, in fact, does art no longer spring from illusion—not, at least, in the reductive, depreciative sense of the term in the entire philosophical tradition after Plato—but it can even claim to lead us to a truer truth, one more adequate to life than the ideal and rational truth that classical metaphysics opposed to the sensible and to appearance. It is thus a question of assigning to art a function of knowledge, a vocation for translating a reality more real than that of the philosophers—a reality that is no longer rational, harmonious, and Euclidian, but illogical, chaotic, distorted, and non-Euclidian. It is in this perspective that Nietzsche develops the theme of the "*artist*-philosopher" or the "dancer-philosopher": in order to grasp the "true truth"; in order to be *in sync with life* (to use a modern expression), thought must no longer claim to rise above or transcend life but, following the model of aesthetics, must accept becoming what might be called a "friendly" expression of life.

The question of criteria, and in a more general sense the question of truth, is thus reintroduced into and by means of aesthetics. The paradox inherent in such a statement is obvious: Nietzsche constantly asserts that art "is *worth more* than truth" and that "we possess *art* lest we *perish of the truth.*" How could he go back to the classical philosophers and make beauty a presentation of the true in the realm of the senses? As I have already suggested, this is possible only at the cost, not of a pure and simple abandonment of all need for knowledge, but of a revolution in the definition of a higher verity situated "among ice and high mountains." Truth may no longer be defined by "right representation." Nonetheless, it resides in a certain type of agreement, between "evaluation" and the real.[8] To make the paradox explicit: it is because art is "false" (it does not claim to rise above the relativism of life) that it is true. This occurs in at least two ways.

First, because art presents itself "honestly" as an interpretation, because it does not claim to be more than it is—because it renounces any claim to an absolute truth, but rather knows that it is totally *relative* to the forces that compose the real—it accords with the perspective nature of existence and with that "finally true truth" that states that all of our judgments are only symptoms and evaluations. As Gilles Deleuze writes, commenting on a famous formula of Nietzsche's: "Art is the highest power of falsehood, it magnifies the 'world as error,' it sanctifies the lie; the will to deception is turned into a superior ideal." Truth may thus take on a new meaning. Truth is appearance. Truth signifies the effectuation of power, elevation to the highest power. "In Nietzsche, 'we the artists' = 'we the seekers after knowledge or truth' = 'we the inventors of new possibilities of life.'"[9] One could hardly state better, however, that the classical ideal of art as an expression of truth has not completely disappeared in Nietzsche. This means that we need to look further than Deleuze does here. At closer examination, in fact, the definition of the veracious has not totally changed, and the Nietzschean "revolution" in Platonism brings us back, at least in part, to his point of departure: if art is true, it is—in spite of all and whatever the terms used—because it is *in some fashion in conformity* with the real, indeed, because it is *much more adequate* to life than the falsehood that has been designated, since Plato, under the name of truth. Deleuze rightly asserts that, for Nietzsche, the artist is a seeker of truth: he is even, and more particularly, a seeker after the "true truth"; only the artist, while lying, does not lie (just as the senses cannot lie). This is why, in the final analysis, the "true" philosopher must make himself into an artist as well. In asserting this, furthermore, we rehabilitate a large portion of the classical definitions of the truth as perfect equivalence.

Consequently, not only is art given a "foundation" for explicitly presenting itself as a mere interpretation or evaluation, but by playing on appearances, producing illusion, and relating its productions to the artist's vital forces, it shows itself to be infinitely truer than any other activity, beginning with "ordinary" intellectual activity such as that of the philosopher or the scientist who have been unable to become "artists" in their turn. All of Nietzsche's interpreters have noted the nonanecdotal, philosophical nature of his aphoristic style. Many have seen in it a "subversion" of the idea of truth, a sort of revolt against the "systematicity" inscribed in the grammar and syntax of traditional philosophical writing. One might have better reason to argue, it seems to me, that on a higher level this is a quite classical concession to the idea of truth. Of course, on first sight, "understood formally, an aphorism is present as a *fragment;* it is the form of pluralist thought"—not, of course, in the "liberal" and democratic sense of the term, but because the "openness" of fragmented writing is presumed to contrast to the "closed" nature of the "system" that is understood as the point of arrival of rationalism. The aphorism is thus the most appropriate artistic form of philosophy. Deleuze adds, "Only the aphorism is capable of articulating sense, the aphorism is interpretation and the art of interpreting."[10] Perhaps. But the subversion is far from being as complete as one might imagine, and in many ways the aphoristic form is also an indication of a conformity to tradition paradoxically greater than ever: in his attempt to find an adequate translation of the chaos and multiplicity of being-as-Life in the chaos and multiplicity of his writing, Nietzsche comes a good deal closer to expressing the concept of truth as equivalence to the real than to denying it.

Thus, although Nietzsche operates *on one level* to subvert the idea of *theōria,* he continues to assign a primordial meaning to it. To be sure, the first mission of philosophy no longer to arrive at a clear vision of suprasensuous "ideas"; it no longer limits itself to the contemplation of a cosmic order that, as we have seen, Nietzsche had denounced as illusory. It is nonetheless secretly animated by a formidable will to truth, a will to a truth stronger than all previous ones. Provided that such a superior truth ceases to claim any superiority or transcendence in relation to "the innermost essence of being" or in relation to the multiplicity of vital forces—provided, that is, that it follows the model of art and presents itself as a perspective, an evaluation—then it can safely remain the ultimate end of philosophic knowledge.

Subversion, then, but also continuity. We will find these again, and in equal quantity, in the second task of philosophy, which is no longer theoretical but practical or ethical. This is the philosophy that, as we have seen, stigmatizes lack of courage or "cowardice"; that aims at "cleanliness toward oneself," as if denunciation of all the moral visions of the past had the sole aim of clearing the way for a "transmutation of all values" and, by that token, for something that would have to be called a "new ethics."

2. Praxis: *The Grand Style, or The Spiritualization of Impulses; Intensity as a Criterion of the Good Life*

There is of course a paradox involved in any attempt to trace the outline of a moral thought in Nietzsche. Even without solid familiarity with his works, everyone knows that he is always defined as the "immoralist" par excellence and that he constantly attacks charity, compassion, and altruism *in all their forms,* whether Christian or other. Pronouncements in this vein abound; Nietzsche denounces *all* moral visions of the world, not just one or several among them, as symptoms of "the very *instinct of decadence*" or as an "idiosyncracy of degenerates,"[11] as displaying a will to deny life that originates solely in the pathological weakness of their authors. Nietzsche's targets even include the earliest humanitarian impulses of the modern age, in which of course he detects a weak, stale odor of Christianity: "This universal love of men is in practice the *preference* for the suffering, underprivileged, degenerate. . . . The species requires that the ill-constituted, weak, degenerate, perish."[12] Moreover, when Nietzsche offers an ethics of his own—for example, when he improvises a "morality for physicians" in *Twilight of the Idols*—this is what he produces: "The sick man is a parasite of society. In a certain state it is indecent to live longer. To go on vegetating in cowardly dependence on physicians and machinations, after the meaning of life, the right to life, has been lost, that ought to prompt a profound contempt in society. The physicians, in turn, would have to be the mediators of this contempt—not prescriptions, but every day a new dose of nausea with their patients."[13] A pretty program, indeed, for the deontology of a new genre. At times, Nietzsche's passion for attacking charity and his taste for catastrophe turns to sheer delirium: those close to him reported that he could hardly contain his joy on learning that an earthquake had destroyed some houses in Nice (a city that he nonetheless liked to visit), deploring only that the disaster was less serious than was first thought. Happily for him, he soon made up for his disappointment when he learned that a volcanic eruption had ravaged the island of Java: "Two hundred thousand beings annihilated at one blow," he writes to Paul Lanzky, "That's magnificent! . . . What we need is a radical destruction of Nice and the Niçois."[14]

Nietzsche—and this is a euphemism—was no altruist, either in his philosophy or, as we can see, in his life. As André Comte-Sponville contends, furnishing a large number of explicit quotations to back up each one of his charges:

Nietzsche is one of the rare philosophers, the only one perhaps (unless one considers Sade to be a philosopher!) who at the same time, and nearly systematically, advocated force against law, violence or cruelty against gentleness, war against peace; who defended egoism, who considered the instincts to be higher than reason and intoxication or the passions higher than serenity, nutritional rules higher than philosophy and hygiene higher than morality; who preferred Pontius Pilate to Christ or to Saint John, Cesare Borgia (a "man of prey"; a "kind of superhuman"!) to Giordano Bruno and Napoleon to Rousseau; who claimed there are "neither moral nor immoral actions" (while declaring himself "the friend of the evil" and the adversary of the "good"!); who justified castes, eugenics, racism, and slavery; who openly advocated or celebrated barbarity, contempt for the greater number, the oppression of the weak, and the extermination of the sick—and all this, as we know, a century after the French Revolution, and while keeping up statements about women and about democracy that are, though less absolutely exceptional, no less distressing.[15]

Under these conditions, isn't it a bit much to speak of a "morality of Nietzsche"? What could he possibly have to offer on the topic? If life is a mere fabric of blind, anxiety-ridden forces; if our value judgments are never more than emanations of those forces, at times decadent but always lacking any sort of meaning other than the purely symptomatic, why should we expect even the slightest ethical consideration from Nietzsche?

It is true that on occasion some rather simplistic young followers of Nietzsche have been seduced by a hypothesis. Restricting themselves to the following reasoning, they state: If some of the many vital forces (the reactive ones) are detestable and repressive, whereas others (the active ones) are admirable and emancipating, should we not simply annihilate the first to the benefit of the second? Should we not simply declare that all norms, as such, are repressive; that to forbid is forbidden; that bourgeois morality is merely an invention of the clergy—thus liberating the impulses that come into play in art, in the body, and in sensibility? Some have believed this, and some seem to believe it still. In the violent debates that shook France in 1968, some were reading Nietzsche in this sense—that is, as a man in revolt, an anarchist, an apostle of sexual liberation, the emancipation of the body, and more.

Although Nietzsche resists comprehension, we need only read him to see that such a hypothesis is not only inaccurate but precisely the opposite of everything that he himself believed. He constantly states, loud and clear, that he is anything but an anarchist. One example among many is this passage from *Twilight of the Idols:* "When the anarchist, as the mouthpiece of the declining strata of society, demands with a fine indignation what is 'right,' 'justice,' and 'equal rights,' he is merely under the pressure of his own uncultured state, which cannot comprehend the real reason for his suffering—what it is that he is poor in: life. A causal instinct asserts itself in him; it must be somebody's fault that he is in a bad way. Also, the 'fine indignation' itself soothes him; it is a pleasure for all wretched devils to scold: it gives a slight but intoxicating sense of power."[16] One can certainly take issue with Nietzsche's analysis, although it is not as inadequate as it seems. But one cannot dress Nietzsche in the libertarian passion and juvenile cries of indignation of a May '68 that he would probably have considered an perfect emanation of the "herd" ideology. The question is of course open to debate, and in Nietzsche's absence, it is easy to put forward any hypothesis. What one cannot do, in any event, is deny his explicitly stated aversion to all forms of revolutionary ideology, be they socialist, communist, or anarchist.

Nor is there any doubt that the very idea of "sexual liberation" horrified him. He considered it a given that a true artist or a writer worthy of the name must strive not to squander his sexual energies. According to a theme that Nietzsche develops to satiety in his famous aphorisms on the "physiology" of art and the artist, "chastity is merely the economy of an artist." The artist must practice chastity without fail, for "the force that one expends in artistic conception is the same as that expended in the sexual act."[17] What is more, Nietzsche cannot find words harsh enough to launch against the tidal wave of passions that he regards as characteristic of modern life after the baleful emergence of romanticism.

If we want to understand Nietzsche as well as just read him, however, we need to add this: It is evident that *any "ethical" attitude that consisted in rejecting a portion of the vital forces, even one that corresponds to the reactive forces, to the benefit of another aspect of life, even one of the most "active," would itself sink,* ipso facto, *into the most patent reaction!* This assertion, moreover, is not only a direct consequence of Nietzsche's definition of the reactive forces as mutilating and castrating; it is also his most explicit and most constant thesis. A crucial (and, for once, limpid) passage from *Human, All Too Human* bears witness to this: "Supposing someone is as much in love with the plastic arts or music as he is enraptured by the spirit of science," being thus seduced by both the active and the reactive aspects of these forces, "and he regards it as impossible to resolve this contradiction by annihilating the one and giving the other free rein, the only thing for him to do is to turn himself into so large a hall of culture that both powers can be accommodated within it, even if at opposite ends, while between them there reside mediating powers with the strength and authority to settle any contention that might break out." It is this reconciliation that Nietzsche sees as characteristic of all "greatness," a term of capital importance for him. It is the sign of the "grand cultural architecture" within which the vital forces, finally *harmonized and hierarchized,* attain both the greatest *intensity* and the most perfect elegance. Thus in every great civilization, on the scale of individuals or of cultures, the purpose of that grand architecture "has been to effect a harmony and concord between contending powers through the agency of an overwhelming assemblage of the other powers, but without the need to suppress them or clap them in irons."[18]

One possible response to the question of Nietzsche's morality would be this: The good life is a life that is *the most intense because the most harmonious;* it is the most elegant life (in the sense that a mathematical demonstration is called elegant because it contains no useless detours and wastes no energy). *That is to say, it is the life in which the vital forces, instead of contradicting each other, tearing each other apart, fighting each other, hence blocking or exhausting each other (and here Nietzsche is approaching Freud), begin to cooperate, albeit giving primacy to some forces—the active ones, of course—rather than others—the reactive forces.*

Thus on the moral plane, parallel to the aesthetization of knowledge, we encounter the "grand style." On this point at least, Nietzsche's thought is perfectly clear, and his definition of greatness in all of his mature works, is unfailingly univocal. As a fragment in *The Will to Power* explains, "the greatness of an artist cannot be measured by the 'beautiful feelings' he arouses"; rather, it resides in the "grand style"—that is, in the artist's ability to "become master of the chaos one is; to compel one's chaos to become form: to become logical, simple, unambiguous, mathematics. *Law*—that is the grand ambition here."[19] To state my point clearly: the only people who will be surprised by these texts are those who commit the mistake—as inane as it is frequent—of seeing in Nietzsche's thought some sort of anarchism or a theory anticipating contemporary libertarian movements. Nothing could be more false, and an apology for "mathematical" rigor and the cult of clear and rigorous reason also find a place within the multiple forces of life. To repeat the reason for this one last time: if we admit that the "reactive" forces are those that cannot be deployed without denying other forces, we must agree that a critique of Platonism and, more generally, of moral rationalism in all its forms, justified as it may have been in Nietzsche's eyes, cannot lead to the pure and simple elimination of rationality. Such an eradication would, in fact, itself be reactive. If we want to arrive at the "greatness" that is the sign of a successful expression of the vital forces, those forces must be put into a hierarchy so as to put an end to their mutual mutilation—and in that hierarchy rationality, too, has its place.

Nothing should be excluded, then, and in the conflict between reason and the passions, to choose the second to the detriment of the first risks descending into stupidity: "All passions have a phase when they are merely disastrous, when they drag down their victim with the weight of stupidity—and a later, very much later phase when they wed the spirit, when they 'spiritualize' themselves."[20] As surprising as it might seem to libertarian readers of Nietzsche, he does indeed make a moral criterion of that "spiritualization"; it is what enables us to accede to the "grand style" by permitting us to domesticate the reactive forces rather than rejecting them "stupidly," including all that we gain by integrating that "internal enemy," thus weakening it rather than banishing it. This is why "another triumph is our spiritualization of *hostility*. It consists in a profound appreciation of the value of having enemies. . . . We immoralists and Antichristians find our advantage in this, that the church exists. . . . The same is true of power politics. A new creation in particular—the new *Reich*, for example—needs enemies more than friends: in opposition alone does it *feel* itself necessary, in opposition alone does it *become* necessary. Our attitude to the 'internal enemy' is no different: here too we have spiritualized hostility; here we have come to appreciate its value."[21] Nietzsche does not hesitate to assert clearly that the "continuance of the Christian ideal is one of the most desirable things there are,"[22] because it offers us, by the confrontation that it authorizes, an extremely sure means for becoming greater.

It is that "greatness" that constitutes the alpha and omega of "Nietzschean morality" and that must be our guide in our search for a good life. The reason for this gradually becomes clear: only greatness will permit us to integrate all the forces within us; only greatness authorizes us, by the same token, to lead a more *intense* life—that is, a life richer in diversity—but also a more powerful life because more harmonious. Harmony here not only is a condition of comfort and sweetness, although it is that too, but also, by helping us to avoid exhausting conflicts and amputations that weaken us, it is a condition of the highest degree of power.

If a concrete image of "grand style" is wanted, it helps to think of what we must do when we work at a sport or a difficult art—and almost all sports and arts are difficult—to achieve perfection. Think, for example, of the movement of the bow over the strings of a violin or, more simply, of a good backhand or a swift serve in tennis. When we watch the trajectory of a ball hit by a champion, that act seems simplicity itself, something of a literally disconcerting facility. With no apparent effort, with limpid fluidity, the ball is sent off at an astonishing speed. This is because the champion integrates perfectly the forces in play in this movement. They cooperate in perfect harmony, with no contrary effort, no wasted energy, no "reaction" in the sense in which Nietzsche uses the term. As a consequence, we see an admirable reconciliation of beauty and power similar to what can also be observed among the young when they are endowed with talent. The opposite is true with age: someone who starts to play tennis too late will have strokes that are irreversibly chaotic, unintegrated, and pinched. They not only will have lost their elegance, but will also lack power, and for the simple reason that the forces involved, instead of cooperating, are working against each other, mutilating and blocking each other, with the result that the inelegance of the act is its very powerlessness.

The good life as the most intense life? A life that would take as its model the "successful gesture," one that contains the greatest diversity with the aim of attaining, in harmony, the greatest power, with no laboriousness, no waste of energy: that is basically Nietzsche's moral vision, the vision in the name of which he denounces all the "reactive" moralities that, since Socrates, have urged that life be fought against, diminished. To reach a better understanding of this ethical aspiration, which is, in effect, new, it may be useful to compare it with what it is not; to see exactly how it opposes, almost term for term, not only Christianity, but Platonism before it and romanticism after it.

Opposing the grand style, then, are all the forms of activity, aesthetic or other, that, because they are incapable of attaining the self-mastery required by the hierarchy of the instincts, give free rein to the flood of passions—that is, to reaction, given that such flood is always a symptom of the reciprocal mutilation of forces. That mutilation defines ugliness. Nietzsche reiterates this point and states it quite clearly, provided that his basic postulates are understood: "Ugliness signifies the decadence of a type, contradiction and lack of co-ordination between the inner desires—signifies a decline in organizing strength, in 'will,' to speak psychologically."[23] In the sphere of philosophy it is Platonism that furnishes the prototype of reaction, but it is useful to understand exactly how Nietzsche symmetrically opposes it to the "grand style." His method lies in the "cure" that Socrates, the prototype of those whom Nietzsche calls "philosopher-physicians" in *Twilight of the Idols*, proposes in his discussion of the problem of "the instincts . . . in anarchy."[24]

Just what is the problem? Quite simply, the history of the appearance, in fourth-century B.C. Greece, of a morality that, through Socrates and then through Christianity, has lasted to our own day. Nietzsche describes that difficult but clearly promising birth as occurring in four major stages. These can be briefly summarized as follows.

The first stage was that of the innocence of the "great Hellenes," aristocrats who had not yet enough culpability to pose philosophical questions concerning human existence but, like artists, were happy simply to command. Questioning was unknown to them, as were resentment and a bad conscience. Theirs was perhaps a paradise lost, but a paradise in which the brutality of still "animal" passions, as yet inaccessible to spirituality (which, as we have seen, consists in joining with the enemy), unfortunately ruined their chances of survival.

The second stage was that of *decadence;* the time of the birth of the first philosophical interrogations, as witnessed by the appearance of Sophism. This was the age of the "fall," a time when life was no longer taken for granted and was beginning to prompt questions; the time of the appearance of the "anarchy of the instincts"—those inner conflicts without which humans would probably never have been led to raise questions about their fate, the meaning of their lives, or the nature of truth, justice, and beauty. It was decadence because humankind had lost its primal innocence, because any questioning can only be a sign of anxiety, hence of a reactive state of the vital forces. Contradictory impulses—and they must have been contradictory in order for the *symptom* that is philosophic questioning to appear—are also forces that mutilate each other, diminishing the overall sum of our energy and our joy in living.

The third stage is that of the cure: this exhausting inner struggle called for a reaction; a remedy had to be found. As Nietzsche explains at length in *Twilight of the Idols,* it was at this point in history that Socrates intervened and invented the "true world"—that is, an ideal universe in the name of which real life may be judged and criticized. On the deepest level, Socrates was putting an end to "the anarchy of the instincts" that appears the minute one leaves the aristocratic universe of tradition, when questioning, investigation, and doubt come to replace authority, command, and the will that posits indisputable values. But the Socratic "cure," the therapy that Nietzsche sees as furnishing the prototype of all morality for the next two thousand years, was a veritable catastrophe: it consisted in "castration," pure and simple; in the suppression of all the instincts (that is, of the sensible world) in the name of a "truth" of the intelligible. The Socratic cure settled the problem, perhaps, but by eradicating all of its terms. Do impulses oppose each other? Very well, let us do away with them; let us invent the intelligible world and deny the sensible world completely, thus settling all questions once and for all. Socrates is the philosopher who combats reaction with reaction, who pushes to its limit the logic of weakening, of eradicating the forces—the mortal logic of nihilism.

The gulf between the Socratic cure and the grand style is clear here. Both approaches have to resolve the same basic problem: that of anarchy, the pathological rending apart of the instincts. Here, too, we are close to Freud, who sees psychic conflict as the origin of all illness, and illness itself as an impotence, an inability to "act and enjoy," to repeat a formula that has been cited thousands of times. For Nietzsche, however, the true solution would have consisted, not in annihilating all the sensible, active forces in the name of other forces (the reactive forces; those of the supposed world of the intelligible), but rather in placing those active forces in a hierarchy and harmonizing them, as they are harmonized in the elegant, strong motions of the sports champion or the virtuoso musician. As Nietzsche significantly states, at base Socrates lacked mastery.

Something similar occurred, on the other end of the historical trail, with the strong emotions of romanticism. In the domain of art, the romantic stance seems — and for like reasons — the summit of the reactive: passions were so unleashed in romanticism that they could not but contradict each other. That is why the romantic hero is always suffering, unhappy, torn, pale, and sick to the point of a death that occurs, ideally, by the age of forty. Just as Nietzsche invites us to combine the forces of logic, mathematical reason, and intellectual rigor instead of "stupidly" rejecting them, so he infinitely prefers classicism, Greek or French, to romanticism: he wonders "whether behind the antithesis classic and romantic there does not lie hidden the antithesis active and reactive?" By its opposition to the reactive, classicism seems the perfect incarnation of the grand style, because " to be classical, one must possess *all* the strong, seemingly contradictory gifts and desires — but in such a way that they go together beneath one yoke." Thus "a quantum of coldness, lucidity, hardness is part of all 'classical' taste: logic above all" — as, for example, in the "three unities" — because one must at all costs guard against sentimentality. According to a theme constant in Nietzsche, the "logical simplification" inherent in the classics is the best approximation to the "great" creation of hierarchy, as is explicitly suggested in another fragment in *The Will to Power:* "'Becoming more beautiful' is a consequence of *enhanced* strength. Becoming more beautiful as the expression of a *victorious* will, of increased co-ordination, of a harmonizing of all the strong desires, of an infallibly perpendicular equilibrium. Logical and geometrical simplification is a consequence of the enhancement of strength."[25]

We are obviously far from the image of Nietzsche as an apologist for any "liberation of mores" or any volcanic emancipation of the passions against a supposedly dry reason. Nietzsche states, quite to the contrary: "We are enemies of sentimental emotions!" The artist worthy of the name is one who cultivates "hatred for feeling, heart, spirit, hatred for the manifold, uncertain, rambling, for imitations."[26] Similarly, Nietzsche contrasts Victor Hugo to Corneille, rehabilitating the latter as one of the "poets who belong to an aristocratic civilization . . . who made it a point of honor to *submit* their perhaps still vigorous senses *to a concept* [Nietzsche's emphasis], and to impose the law of a refined and clear intellectuality on the brutal claims of the colors, sounds, and forms—in doing which they were, as it seems to me, in the tradition of the great Greeks."[27] The triumph of the classics, both Greek and French, thus consists in victoriously combating what Nietzsche significantly calls "that sensual rabble" that elicits the admiration of "modern" (that is, romantic) painters and musicians.

In short, in this morality of grandeur, it is intensity that has primacy; the will to power carries the day against all other considerations: "There is nothing to life that has value except the degree of power!"[28] This does not mean that there is no such thing as value. Quite the contrary. We also need to comprehend, as is clear in Nietzsche's critiques of the Socratic cure and of romanticism, that genuine intensity has nothing in common with unleashed passions or the emancipation of bodies: it resides in the harmonious and classical integration of the vital forces; in the serenity, the calm, but also the lightness that oppose Mozart and Schubert to Schumann and Wagner. Like one skilled in the martial arts, the man of the grand style moves in elegance, at a thousand leagues from anything that seems laborious. He does not perspire, and if he moves mountains, it is serenely, without apparent effort. Just as true knowledge and joyful wisdom laugh at theory and the will to truth in the name of a higher truth, Nietzsche's immoralism mocks morality only in the name of another ethics. The same is true of his doctrine of salvation.

3. *Soteriology:* Amor fati, *the Eternal Recurrence, or Salvation by Instants of Eternity*

But have we not gone a bit too far this time? How can we claim to discern in the Antichrist himself the early fruits of a doctrine of beatitude, a thought focused on salvation? Did Nietzsche not energetically oppose this very notion when he presented all soteriology as a thoroughgoing (albeit unavowed) expression of nihilism and of the negation of life in the name of the beyond? Certainly, no one willingly admits to being a nihilist: "Of course, one does not say 'nothingness' but 'beyond,' or 'God,' or '*true* life,' or Nirvana, salvation, blessedness." Still, "this innocent rhetoric from the realm of religious-moral idiosyncrasy appears much less innocent as soon as we realize which tendency it is that here shrouds itself here in sublime words: *hostility against life.*" To seek salvation in a God or in some other figure of transcendence put in his place is to use "God as the declaration of war against life, against nature, against the will to live!" God is "the formula for every slander against 'this world,' for every lie about the 'beyond'!"[29] Perhaps.

Does this mean, however, that Nietzsche believes all aspiration to beatitude should be swept aside? That is most unlikely, as witnessed by his fraternal admiration for Spinoza, his companion in a quest for an *atheist soteriology*.[30] As with Spinoza, eternity (which should carefully be distinguished from the Christian idea of immortality) occupies a decisive place in Nietzsche's thought. He even considered his doctrine of eternal recurrence, which he barely had the time to formulate before illness prevented him from perfecting it, to be his most original, his true contribution to the history of thought. He constantly compared that doctrine to a religion, asserting both that it "contained more than all the religions that have taught men to scorn life as ephemeral and to look toward *another* life." Moreover, the doctrine of the eternal recurrence was itself to become "*the religion* of the most sublime, the freest, the most serene souls"[31] and "the highest form of affirmation that can ever be attained." Nietzsche even proposes, quite explicitly, to put "in place of 'metaphysics' and religion, the theory of eternal recurrence."[32]

Unless we suppose that Nietzsche used the term lightly, which is highly improbable, we need to ask ourselves why he applied it to what he himself considered the most original aspect of his thought. As is known, his *Thus Spoke Zarathustra* borrows much of its style from the Gospels, and he ceaselessly parodied that style, even in his announcement of the "good news" of eternal recurrence and in the novel figure of love that he calls *amor fati*, an unreserved adherence to fate. Nor is it by chance that he defines that *amor fati*, in a very significant fragment published posthumously, as "the highest state a philosopher can attain."[33] This means that the deconstruction of transcendence is not an end in itself, that one must pursue the question further, and that "joyful wisdom" and the "grand style" do not exhaust the task of philosophy. At this point in his thought, Nietzsche attempts to respond at last to the question of the "good life," as an atheist, certainly, and, it goes without saying, without reference to any "beyond," but nonetheless in the form of a doctrine of salvation, a soteriology all the more interesting for being fully situated in our own age of disenchantment and lucidity.

What does the thought of the eternal recurrence teach us, then? What does it have to say to us today? Basically this: if there is no transcendence and no possible flight into a beyond—be it, after the death of God, a "humanized" beyond—in the form of a moral ideal or a sacrificial politics ("humanity," "justice," the homeland, the revolution, etc.), *it is within the here and now, on this earth, in this life, that we must learn to discern what is worthwhile being lived and what deserves to perish.* It is here and now that we must learn to separate forms of life that are unfulfilled, mediocre, reactive, and weak, from the forms of life that are intense, grandiose, courageous, and rich in diversity. As Gilles Deleuze saw with perfect clarity, Nietzsche's doctrine of the eternal recurrence furnishes us, quite simply, with a *criterion of selection.* Let us reread the famous 1881 fragment in which Nietzsche formulates his thought within the framework of a categorical imperative:

> If, in everything that you want to do, you begin by asking yourself: "Is it certain that I want to do this an infinite number of times?" this will be for you the most solid sort of center of gravity. . . . My doctrine teaches this: "Live so that you must *want* to live again, that is the duty—for you will live again in any event! He whose supreme joy is in effort, let him strive! He who likes repose above all, let him rest! He who likes to submit, obey, and follow, let him obey! But *let him know well where his preference lies,* and not recoil before *any means!* It is a question of *eternity!*" This doctrine is gentle towards those who have no faith in it. It has neither hell nor threats. He who has no faith will feel within himself only a *fugitive* life.[34]

Here we perceive the meaning of the doctrine of eternal recurrence. It is not a description of how the world works, nor a "return to the Ancients" as has at times naïvely been thought, nor a prediction. It is at base nothing but a *criterion of evaluation,* a *principle of selection* of the *instants* that are worth living. Thanks to this doctrine we can interrogate our existence in order to flee pretense and half measures—all the acts of cowardice that would lead, according to Nietzsche, to wanting a thing fleetingly, as a concession; all those moments of existence in which we abandon ourselves to the facility of an *exception* without really wanting it. The true life is living in such way that regrets and remorse—or their very idea—have no meaning. Who, indeed, could seriously want the mediocre instants of life—all those anxieties, all those useless bouts of anger, all those inadmissable weaknesses, those lies, acts of cowardice, and little compromises—to recur eternally? But also, how many instants in our lives would stand up to scrutiny if we applied the criterion of eternal recurrence honestly and rigorously? A few moments of joy, perhaps, of love, lucidity, and, above all, serenity. But we lack the sense of the eternal needed to achieve that goal. This is where Nietzsche's doctrine can indeed claim to take the place of the defunct religions: even in the absence of God, *eternity* remains, and in order to achieve it, we must—as Nietzsche oddly declares—have *faith*.

The crux of the matter, of course, is to know just what faith and what eternity. How are we to understand them? What concrete significance are we to give to them if, as is evident, they are not what they are in Christianity or any other monotheistic religion? Similarly, if we want to grasp Nietzsche's message about the good life, about those instants that are really worth desiring, to the point of hoping for their eternal return, we also have to be clear about what selection is involved, what our choice is, given that an inadmissible and unavowed resurgence of a free will that Nietzsche has so clearly rejected is out of the question. Nor can he invite us to a selection that would retroactively eliminate certain moments of reality in order to keep others: this would imply sinking back into a reactive attitude. But let us go still farther: Why, exactly, should we—at all costs, having reached forms of knowledge higher than all those known up to now, having put into practice in our life the demands of the grand style—why should we now rise to a superior, quasi-religious degree that would permit us to enter into a highly problematic eternity? It is clear that Nietzsche invites us to do so, and that he even sees such a state as a finally perfected figure of love: "Oh, how should I not lust after eternity and after the nuptial ring of rings, the ring of recurrence? Never yet have I found the woman from whom I wanted children, unless it be this woman whom I love: for I love you, O eternity. *For I love you, O eternity!*"[35] But, after all, even if such an eternity without any divinity or any "beyond" makes any sense, why would it be so desirable? Why, in the final analysis, would it be preferable to the fleeting life that will be the fate "only" of those who are incapable of rising to the demands of the eternal? And from what point of view are we to place ourselves to *assign value*, without evident contradiction with the deconstruction of all eternal values, to the *sacralization* of a dimension of time that seems too timeless to be honest? Why is it absolutely necessary that a critique of truth reintroduce truth; that the critique of values rehabilitate values; that a denunciation of the religious in all its forms culminate in a new faith? Can we not (as we are invited to do today in the novels of Michel Houellebecq) be satisfied, *without the involvement of any state of the soul,* with reality as it is—in other words, with being human, not *too* human, but *solely* human, essentially glaucous, rather miserable, and disenchanted? Why, if one is truly a materialist, not be one to the end? Why this *surrepti-*

tious need to reenchant the world, this aspiration to rediscover criteria that would permit us once more—and there is no doubt that Nietzsche, more than any other philosopher, never denied himself this activity—to scorn, to continue to judge the world and our neighbor?

Finding an answer is difficult, perhaps impossible. That quest is the aim of the present volume. But if we remain with Nietzsche, it is here, without a doubt, that he gives evidence of still belonging to the philosophical tradition, that he connects once more to the profound intuition proper to the ancient wisdom traditions[36]—the intuition that the desire for eternity, salvation, and true love converge in an authentic relation to the instant, to the pure present, finally rid of the illusions and the heavy burdens of both the future and the past. The successful life, the good life, is one that manages to live the instant with no condemnation or exclusion, in absolute lightness, no longer feeling that there is any difference between the present and eternity.

We have seen that this theme was essential to Stoic wisdom and also to Buddhist wisdom. Nietzsche rediscovers it, if that is the right word, by his own means, following his own train of thought, as manifested in this magnificent passage from *Ecce Homo:* "My formula for greatness in a human being is *amor fati:* to want nothing to be different, not forward, not backward, not in all eternity. Not merely to bear what is necessary, still less to conceal it—all idealism is mendaciousness in the face of what is necessary—but to *love it.*"[37] To want nothing but what is! This formula may seem strange coming from Nietzsche. Does not this surrender to reality go contrary to the spirit of revolt that animates his entire thought, and even contrary to the principle of *selection* that it asserts, at the same time, in the doctrine of eternal recurrence? Still, the two demands must be maintained, as Nietzsche forcefully insists, for example in this fragment from *The Will to Power:* "Such an experimental philosophy as I live anticipates experimentally even the possibilities of the most fundamental nihilism. . . . It wants rather to cross over to the opposite of this—to a Dionysian affirmation of the world as it is, without subtraction, exception, or selection—it wants the eternal circulation:—the same things, the same logic and illogic of entanglements. The highest state a philosopher can attain: to stand in a Dionysian relationship to existence—my formula for this is *amor fati.* It is part of this state to perceive not merely the necessity of those sides of existence hitherto denied, but their desirability."[38]

The contradiction is troubling: the criterion of the eternal recurrence invites us to make a choice, a selection of the unique instants whose infinite repetition we might desire, whereas *amor fati,* which accepts fate, must, by definition, reject all triage, all exception; it must take in everything and comprehend everything within one and the same love of the real. How can these two theses be reconciled? Perhaps by admitting, quite simply, that a love of fate operates only after the application of the very selective requirements of the eternal recurrence: if we lived according to that criterion of eternity, if we found ourselves finally within the grand style and the highest intensity, everything would seem good to us. The low blows of fate would have no more existence than the happy times: it is the real in its totality that we could finally live as if it were, at every instant, eternity itself. This is true for a reason that Buddhists and Stoics, well before Nietzsche, had already understood: if everything is necessary, if we understand that the real can in truth be reduced to the present, then the past and the future will finally lose their inexhaustible capacity to make us feel guilt and will persuade us that we might have been able—and consequently should have been able—to do *otherwise*. This is an attitude of remorse, nostalgia, and regret, but also of doubts and hesitations regarding a future that always leads to inner turmoil, to the opposition of the self to itself, hence to the victory of reaction, given that our vital forces at that point are in conflict with each other.

If the doctrine of the eternal recurrence inevitably leads to that of the *amor fati*, the latter in turn culminates in the ideal of a total elimination of culpability, in an affirmation of what Nietzsche calls the "innocence of becoming": "For how long now have I attempted to prove to myself the total *innocence* of becoming! . . . And all that for what reason? Was it not to procure for myself the sentiment of my complete irresponsibility, to escape all praise and all blame?"[39] For it is thus and only thus that we can finally be *saved*. From what? As always, from fear. By what? As always, by serenity, This is why, in all simplicity, "we . . . desire to restore innocence to becoming. . . . There is no being that could be held responsible for the fact that anyone exists at all, that anyone is thus and thus, that anyone was born in certain circumstances, in a certain environment.—It is a tremendous restorative that such a being is lacking. . . . There is no place, no purpose, no meaning, on which we can shift the responsibility for our being, for our being thus and thus. . . . And, to say it again, this is a tremendous restorative; this constitutes the innocence of all existence."[40]

Perhaps unlike the Stoics, Nietzsche did not think that the world is harmonious and rational. The transcendence of the cosmos is abolished. But like the Stoics, he invites us to live in the moment; to save ourselves without anyone's help by liking everything that is; to flee the distinction between happy and unhappy events; above all, to free ourselves from the anxieties that the temporality of free will fatally introduces in us, including the remorse associated with an indeterminate vision of the past ("I should have done differently") or hesitations about the future ("Shouldn't I make a different choice?"). It is by freeing ourselves from this insidious dual visage of the reactive forces (to repeat, all anxiety is by definition reactive), by freeing ourselves from the burdens of the past and the future, that we attain serenity and eternity, here and now, *because there is nothing else*, because there is no longer anything to introduce culpability and to relativize present existence.

Truth in art, intensity in the grand style, eternity in love of the world as it is: these are Nietzsche's criteria for a good life, finally rid of the illusions of transcendence. His is thus a radical immanentism, and one might object that it raises a good many questions. I shall mention only three, to which I intend to return in part 5 of this work; since they are inherent in all forms of materialism, they seem to me to mortgage its overall coherence.

The first of these questions regards the status of free will and the responsibilities it implies. How can one do without free will, if only on the level of the choice that we could (or should?) make of an "affirmative" and "innocent" life rather than a negative and culpable one? The passage in *The Will to Power* in which Nietzsche presents the imperative formula of the eternal recurrence as a selection of instants begins with a consideration of a preliminary objection: "'But if everything is determined, how can I dispose of my acts?' Thought and belief are a weight that burdens you, as much as and more than any other weight. You say that the nourishment, the site, the air, the society transform you and condition you? Well, your opinions do so even more, for they are what determine you in the choice of what you eat, your dwelling place, your air, your society. If you assimilate this of all thoughts, it will transform you." One might think it was Epictetus or Marcus Aurelius speaking! It is as if, the world being necessary and independent of our will, there still remained a margin of liberty *in thought;* as if our opinions could *depend upon us* more than the weather does, or falling bodies. But isn't this, precisely, a reintroduction, par excellence, of free will? Is it not a way of asserting that we can change ourselves without help, can freely affect our mental dispositions, and are thus responsible for attaining or failing to attain a successful life?

Amor fati: to regret a bit less, hope a bit less, love the real as it is a bit more, and, if possible, love it wholly! This is the constant message of materialism. That is fine. I understand the serenity, relief, and "comfort," as

Nietzsche says, that inhabit the innocence of becoming. But do we really need all this deconstruction of the idols in order to get back to Spinoza and Zeno? And to return to the very difficulties that they had already encountered? The injunction is of course valid only for the more ignoble aspects of reality: to invite us to love reality when it is lovable would, in fact, make no sense because it goes without saying. If we must assent to everything, if we cannot just "take it or leave it" but must accept everything, how can we avoid falling back on what Clément Rosset so rightly called "the hangman's argument" (in the interest of rejecting it, however): torturers exist, they are undeniably a part of the real, and therefore to love the real as it is implies also loving torturers! Rosset, who is a Nietzschean and a Spinozan, considers the objection banal and derisory. On the first point, he is right: the argument, I agree, is trivial. But on the second? Cannot a proposition be both banal and true? How are we to respond to this? As Theodor Adorno asked, after Auschwitz, can we still invite people to be reconciled with *the world as it is,* with a "yes" without reservations or exceptions? And what difference is there, in the final analysis, between Christians, whom Nietzsche denounces when they preach resignation in the expectation of better days to come and who perceive suffering as a trial that an authentic believer must accept with joy and gratitude, and materialists, who invite us — admittedly from a totally different point of view — to do the same? Epictetus stated that never in his life had he encountered a genuine Stoic sage, someone who loves the world in all circumstances, even the most atrocious ones imaginable; who consistently abstains from both regret and hope. Must we really see this failure as folly, a passing weakness, a lack of wisdom, or is it not instead a sign that theory vacillates, that *amor fati* is not only impossible but can at times become obscene?

Finally, how are we to understand the assertion that the will to find a meaning in life is merely an illusion, an insidious figure of a nihilism that claims to judge life *from the outside*? Here, too, the argument seems foolproof: we cannot judge the whole of existence (for the good and simple reason that there is nothing outside of it) unless we reintroduce, more or less surreptitiously, a supernatural, a transcendence, in short, a "beyond." Very well. But, for one thing, are we really certain that there exist no other ways of thinking of transcendence than the religious or metaphysical modes? Has not phenomenology — Husserl's in particular — taught us the contrary? For another thing: if immanence is the prime motif of our lives, if we must accept all that is as it is, in all its tragic dimension of radical senselessness, how are we to avoid — even ignoring the "hangman's argument"—the accusation of complicity or, worse, of collaboration with what Marx might have called "the universe of merchandise"? How can we not see in Nietzsche's apology of the "will to power" a way of legitimizing the existing relations of force? It might be said—and rightly—that we have to avoid committing the usual misreading of that will to power: it is not some bestial desire for power, and Nietzsche has no intention of taking the side of the "powerful." The will to power must be understood as a will that desires itself; that seeks its own intensification and active increase and flees its weakening in the various aspects of the reactive forces. Perhaps. But, under such conditions, is not that "will to will"—precisely—the supreme philosophical legitimation and the most fully realized figure of the "world of technology," of a universe in which the infinite increase of power is, in effect, deprived, perhaps for the first time in the history of humanity, of all finality and all meaning? Is that such good news? Is it possible that the desire to have done with the question of meaning is simply one way of adhering fully to the nonmeaning of the real, finally shattered and stripped of ends, that the globalized capitalist economy promises us? Can it be that the broken subject that Nietzsche hopes for already exists, more for the worse than for the better; that it is nothing but the individual delivered over to the unconscious, dispossessed of himself, deprived of free will, of all responsibility, and of all influence over the course of history—the minuscule and atomized being that the modern individual has become, drowned in the powers of a universe that is everywhere beyond his grasp? Must we further deconstruct the will to mastery in the age of a globalization whose surest effect is to deprive us of all mastery over our destiny?

Whatever we may think of such questions, they should not lead us to underestimate the crucial, historic importance of Nietzsche's response to the question of the good life. For the first time, that question was inscribed within a thought in the manner of the classical transcendences. Thus it opened the era of the great materialisms, of thought about the radical immanence of being in the world in which we are now immersed. As such, it was to have a long and fertile posterity. It expresses or presents themes regarding upheavals that were to give rise to other visions of the world and to as yet unheard-of representations of the successful life. Two of these in particular followed Nietzsche's lead directly, at times even explicitly. The first was an aspiration to rupture and to marginality, a rejection of repetitive traditions and of banal and boring "provincial" lives, and a search for intensity and adventure, as expressed in the ideal of the bohemian life. The second was a will to fulfill, *for oneself,* in private life, the program of total disengagement from oppressive illusions; a desire to achieve "perfect health" by freeing oneself from the idols of a superego that prevents us from enjoying and acting and from the anxieties and feelings of guilt that are the symptoms of such prevention. In this new light, both of these approaches merit a brief analysis.

CHAPTER 6

After Nietzsche

~ ~ ~ ~ ~

Four Versions of Life after the Death of God:
Daily Life, the Bohemian Life, the Life of Enterprise,
or Life Freed from Alienation

When philosophical speculation had finally come back down to earth, un-burdened by the transcendences of yesteryear and the old metaphysical "superegos," the first effect of a "wisdom of this world" seems to have resided in an emancipation or, to put it better, a hitherto unimaginable multiplica-tion of the possibilities inherent in human life. Welcome to earth: less reli-gion, less *religare*—did that not means fewer constraining ties, fewer tradi-tions, fewer communities within which the destiny of individuals seemed determined from all eternity? Did that not also mean increased freedom from the legacies that constrict and pre-form human existence, more diver-sity in existential choices, more individualism and less communitarianism—to use terms that may be overworked but are still pertinent in this context? A new demand for authenticity began to emerge; a demand to be "oneself" at last; a search for a full development of the individual personality no longer restricted by classic moral categories such as honesty and sincerity. Act or relax, command or obey: the new categorical imperative of eternal recurrence states, at the very least, be yourself! Stop spending your life trying to live up to principles that centuries of cosmological, religious, or humanistic nihilism have fallaciously presented as external to you and superior to you! It is hardly by chance, in this sense, that the subtitle of *Ecce Homo* opens a path destined to a fine future in contemporary societies when it declaims programmatically, *Wie man wird, was man ist* ("How one becomes what one is"). Be yourself!—stop taking "alienating" criteria, foreign to you, as your models. Human existence no longer has to conform to transcendent values that claimed to guide it only in order to limit it more surely. Its center of gravity shifts to the internal life of an "I" that, although "shattered" and open to the infinite unconscious of its most tumultuous vital forces, nonetheless constitutes the alpha and omega of the new destiny of humankind.

In this regard, the "Nietzschean moment" is situated at the crossroads of two major tendencies in lay societies, the underlying thrust of which it both accompanies and powerfully expresses. Although these two tendencies are in apparent contradiction, they are in fact closely interconnected and display an impressive coherence.

The first arose well before Nietzsche, even though he followed in the path it had traced. Launched with the Renaissance, this tendency blossomed in the seventeenth century and reached its height in the eighteenth. It was the movement—often analyzed but ever problematic—of *secularization, or the disenchantment of the world.* As it turned out, this process, during which there was a slow but sure erosion of idols "superior" to humanity, was—and this is almost a tautology—a *humanizing of the world.* While denouncing the ideals of modern humanism (equality, the rights of man, progress, the republic, etc.), Nietzsche nonetheless contributed to deepening the principal motif of those ideals: the *emancipation* of the human being as such—no longer a member of an all-embracing cosmic totality, nor a creature of God, nor even an isolated fragment of an overriding political project or a revolutionary cause—who simply wants to be himself. As the faces of transcendence dimmed, the face of humankind came to be seen more and more clearly, with our humblest traits, precisely the ones never considered eminent by the traditions. The corporeal, the sensible, the unconscious, the chaos of impulses—in short, the part of ourselves that from time immemorial referred back to aspects judged to be inferior, to the "animality in us"—came to be, not rehabilitated, but simply valued as never before. In this connection, Nietzschean genealogy paradoxically prolongs and continues the grand movement of "humanism" (understood here in the broadest sense as a pendant to secularization) far more than opposing it. Moreover, on this route to deconstruction, humans are never "too human"; to the contrary, their emancipation must be accomplished up to and including its most trivial, most quotidian, not to say most common manifestations.

In contrast, the secularization of the world, in which Nietzsche took such an active role, implies a totally different attitude toward the banality, even the boredom, that also emanates from "the quotidian." Given that God is dead, given that traditions are no longer invested *a priori* with indisputable legitimacy but instead are disputed as a matter of principle, given that no saving cause now justifies the painful and repetitive nature of existence, nothing compels us to accept life as an obligatory passage, even as a salutary trial. If there is no more "beyond," no more "after," no other life in which we can "catch up," it is here and now that we will have to accede to "true life." Hence (and this seems to contradict the first movement) the will to emancipate oneself from the "herd," scorn for ordinary life, soon even the cult of "marginality" and "solitude"—if possible in select company, as in a model that appears with late romanticism and blossoms in the age of Nietzsche, that of the "bohemian life" or the "artist's life," as opposed to that of the "philistines." When innovation, genius, originality, and a break with the past become the watchwords of human existence, how can one accept, in the new life, what was so vigorously denounced in the old one? A continual return of the "works and days" that made up the essence not only of tradition but also of daily life—even "modern" daily life—becomes unacceptable, indeed unbearable, to anyone who claims to move "among ice and high mountains."

On the one hand we have bourgeois existence and daily life, calm but boring. On the other, the artist's life, the bohemian life, adventurous but marginal. How has it come about that we swing between the contrary temptations of these two possible versions of modern life? What links them together, beyond their manifest oppositions, if their duality appears paradoxically before a common backdrop of the rejection of transcendence and of the traditions inherent in the humanization and secularization of the world? The question deserves attention, especially because it suggests life possibilities that are still with us today. If for a moment we follow the thread of the history of art, as the imagery of the artist's life that underlies the contrast between "bohemians" and "philistines" invites us to do, this existential contradiction will find rich and luminous clarification.

1. The Humanization of Art, or Praise for "Daily Life": The Case of Dutch Painting

One definition of art has run through the entire history of philosophy since Plato. It states that a great work of art is first and foremost an incarnation of a "great idea" in material form. It is the "presentation" or the staging of great principles in a reality that seems, *a priori,* to resist the mind: the sculptor's marble, wood, or bronze; the canvas and colors of the painter; sound vibrations for the composer. In every case the artist, unlike the philosopher or the scholar, is someone who has the genius to express ideas, not through concepts or abstract formulas, but by shaping a sensible *material* immediately *perceptible* to all. Art is a language, yes, but its language is not that of words. It is that of *materials.* That is what makes it *moving,* what enables it to be literally *touching* as it connects with the sense organs that are its natural receptacles.

Still, beyond the extraordinary permanence of this definition, common to all ages and all genres,[1] art possesses a history. The problem is that ideas change as art transfigures them. The historicity of art is in fact an expression of this variation of the principles that artists have sought to make sensible by inventing new languages as becomes necessary when the content to be expressed changes. So it is hardly by chance if part of the history of art closely parallels the history of conceptions of the good life: Greek art sought to translate (for example, in the serene faces of statues or the proportions of their bodies) the cosmic harmony and the perfection of the Great All, of which every particular work, like a microcosm, was but one of many possible representations. The Middle Ages celebrated the splendor of the attributes of the divine; in turn, humanization and secularization brought radical changes in perspective.[2] From that moment on, what is portrayed and presented in a work of art is completely human, as the lay viewpoint demands, and transcendent, cosmic, or divine principles external to humanity become a thing of the past.

The most striking illustration of this change is perhaps Dutch painting of the seventeenth century. Enthusiastic admirers of the Dutch school, beginning with Hegel in his lectures on painting, were quick to note that praise of a human life that was "quite simply human"—life at its most quotidian, most banal, even most "bourgeois"—was one effect of the secularization of Western European society. Perhaps for the first time in the history of humanity, works of art are called upon to show everyday scenes, the humblest and most ordinary moments of the daily lives of people who were themselves anonymous. Admittedly, certain medieval works had shown scenes of daily life. For example, there are illustrations of the work cycle through the year, season by season, of the seven capital sins, the five senses, the four elements, and so forth. But as Tzvetan Todorov notes in his discussion of the new approach to the world of culture:

One feels immediately that this old representation of daily life is subjected to a superior objective: to draw up an exhaustive and systematic repertory of life's situations; to illustrate a preexistent order. Or a picture with a religious or edifying subject matter will show a particular saint occupied in an utterly common sort of manual labor. In a certain period, sacred subjects that permitted maximal participation in the profane world were even preferred: the tribulations of the prodigal son, Christ at the house of Mary and Martha, motherhood. But here too we see that if this activity was elevated to the dignity that its appearance in an image presupposes, it is because it is the attribute of a famous person.[3]

One can clearly see that the persons represented in the works of Pieter de Hooch, Gerard Ter Borch, Judith Leyster, Pieter Jannens Elinga, Gabriel Metsu, Jan Steen, Gerrit Douw, and even Jan Vermeer are no longer necessarily drawn from Greek mythology or sacred history. Nor are they "great men"—heroes of famous battles, illustrious figures, kings, princes, nobles, or wealthy men—but, rather, simple human beings, shown in the most obviously profane moments of daily life: a dairymaid preparing a dish of food; a woman reading a book, having kicked off her shoes; another, peeling an apple while children play with a little dog; men drinking together in a tavern in gallant company; a wife scolding a drunken husband; peasants at supper, around a modest wooden table; a young girl at her dressing table in the morning; an old woman ill in bed. In short: nothing grandiose, but life in its least adventurous, commonest, and most *repetitive* mode. As Todorov shows, counter to all the past traditions of transcendent art, these artists were interested in praising daily life as it is. This sort of painting

> is thus not content to renounce history; it makes a choice, and even a very restrictive choice, within the many actions that form the fabric of human life. It rejects the representation of everything beyond the bounds of the ordinary that remains inaccessible to common mortals: there is no place here for heroes or saints. . . . Beauty is not beyond or above commonplace things; it is at their very heart, and one look suffices to extract it and reveal it to everyone. The Dutch painters were, for a time, inspired by a grace—in no way divine, in no way mystical—that enabled them to dispel the curse that weighed on matter; to rejoice in the very existence of things, to intertwine the ideal and the real, and therefore to find the meaning of life in life itself.[4]

Hegel had already made the same point: this praise of simple human beings went deep, being inseparable in the Holland of that time from the
Protestant Reformation and its struggle to free the bourgeoisie from the
weight of religious tutelage, even to make Christianity itself, in Marcel
Gauchet's apt formula, "*a religion for departing from religion.*" It was, in fact,
this early secularization of the world, Hegel tells us, that caused the "movement away from the Catholic Church, with its representations of piety, to
joy in the world as such, to natural objects and the details of their appearance, to domestic life, in its decency, cheerfulness, and its quiet seclusion."
Moreover, "if we look at the Dutch masters with these eyes, we will no
longer suppose that they should have avoided such subjects and portrayed
only Greek gods, myths, and fables, the Madonna, the Crucifixion, martyrs, Popes, saints male and female." Henceforth what was to be "rendered"
was, finally, "the vision of what man is as man, what the human spirit and
character is, what man and *this* man is."[5]

An art that is finally human and nothing but human nonetheless poses
a crucial question: To what extent can this humanity be reduced to the
quotidian? The paradox is striking: it is because we have emerged from the
world of cosmic and divine transcendence, because we have left the universe of traditions inherited from outside, that this reduction seems inevitable. But does not the quotidian, by its very repetitiveness, reestablish
almost a "new tradition" of gestures, tasks, and obligations repeated daily?
What have we gained by liberating people from the old transcendences if
they are immediately burdened with immanence? The entire challenge of
Dutch painting was, precisely, to show that this banality itself can have a
certain charm. There is a problem, however:

> "Daily life," as we all know, is not necessarily joyful. Very often, it is
> stifling: a repetition of acts that have become mechanical, a sinking
> down into imposed cares, an exhaustion of our strength in the sim-
> ple aim of maintaining existence, our own and that of those who are
> close to us. It is for that reason that we are so tempted by dreams, es-
> cape, heroic or mystical ecstasy—solutions that all turn out to be
> factitious, however. What is needed is not to abandon daily life (to
> contempt, to others), but to transform it from the inside, so that it is
> reborn illuminated with meaning and beauty. . . . That is when daily
> life would cease being opposed to works of art, to works of the
> mind, to become, in its entirety, as beautiful and rich in meaning as
> a work of art."[6]

This is an ambitious program, and there is no doubt that it traces one of the possible versions of the good life *after the death of God.*

Still, as Todorov rightly recognizes, it is impossible for anyone caught in the repetitive, mired in the anecdotal, not to dream of escape, of alterity, of adventures in distant places, of more enchanted, airier lives. Impossible, that is, unless such a person can be content with a life without savor or color, like the Swiss writer Henri-Frédéric Amiel, the author of a private journal 16,000 pages long devoted to the insignificance of the quotidian, which Pascal Bruckner, in his *L'euphorie perpétuelle,* summarizes, with neither remorse nor regret, in these terms:

> A sanctuary of paper dedicated to a new divinity, the infinitesimal. . . . Humors, anecdotes, migraines, digestive troubles, respiratory difficulties, all those little nothings end up constituting a history. A fiercely dedicated explorer of the inward, devoted to unraveling his impressions and "to the defects of microscopic analysis," he literally invents a new domain: the promotion of the trifle as an epic of the modern psyche, of the accidental as a means of access to the essential. . . . If the hero is someone who lives in urgency, simply transiting the parentheses between two exploits, Amiel knows nothing but the dead times along extended shores of emptiness.[7]

Not everyone is Vermeer, and when the only horizon of our lives becomes the merely quotidian, the vicissitudes of the weather might seem, against a background of vacuity, to be considerable events, and our inner life tends to be reduced to our gastric difficulties. Pascal Bruckner remarks, in this context: "The hell of our contemporaries is called platitude; the paradise that they seek, plenitude. There are those who have lived and those who have lasted."[8] This is perhaps a severe judgment, but no one could, in good faith, be totally insensitive to it. The least one can say is that it is a perfect expression of the post-Nietzschean need to evaluate life without moving away from life, to separate the successful existence from alternatives that are mediocre, lesser, or failed, without referring to transcendent principles but simply by contrasting platitude to plenitude, vacuity to intensity.

This provides a further measure of the degree to which the humanization of the world bears within it both praise of the quotidian and its absolute opposite: the will to escape from daily life at all cost; to be done with oppressive traditions, even when they are henceforth secularized or outright irreligious; the demand for innovation, originality, a tabula rasa, a rupture with everyday life—in short, a preference for a "bohemian" and avant-garde life as against the philistine life that increasingly affirms its legitimacy in modern culture.

It may be useful to retrace the origins of this tension, this alternative that is still quite broadly offered, if only in general terms. The two versions of a modern life that is terrestrial and immanent to itself—praise of the quotidian and its opposite, the bohemian life—are in fact two possible faces of an existence that accompanies the slow dying of the divine. Despite its more grandiose outward appearance, the second of these is also the child of a secularization of society that, in the history of art and of culture, led creative artists to think like *geniuses,* totally focused on innovation and originality and, by that token, dedicated to making a break with all forms of tradition from the past or admiration of the past. One decisive step in this direction was the revolution launched by theories of genius that appeared in the eighteenth century and were fully developed with romanticism. That revolution was a necessary preliminary to the emergence of the contrast between daily life and the bohemian life. Here, very briefly, is why.

In the civilizations of the past, works of art fulfilled a sacred function.[9] In ancient Greece, as I have already suggested, their mission was to reflect a cosmic order external to humankind. They were, in the etymological sense of the term, a "microcosm," a small world supposed to represent, on a small scale, the harmonious properties of the cosmos. From this they drew their grandeur and their capacity to *impose themselves* on individuals, who received them as a gift from something outside themselves. In this context, a work of art had "objectivity": rather than expressing the subjective *inspiration* of the architect or the sculptor, it expressed the cosmic or divine order as seized by the artist, acting as a modest intermediary. We perceive this so well that we hardly need to know the identity of the artist of an ancient statue or bas-relief. Nor would we think of seeking the name of an artist behind the bronze cats that we can admire in the Egyptian wings of our museums: what is essential is that these are sacred animals, transfigured as such within the space of art. The statue embodies a transcendent symbol, and that is undoubtedly how it was perceived by contemporary viewers. For all traditional societies, then, what was essential in art, and more generally in culture in the broader sense, was not originality, and even less innovation, but instead the transmission of a patrimony in a translation of symbolic values that were *religious* in the root sense of the word—that is, capable of binding together the individuals of a given community. As contemporary ethnologists have noted in a similar perspective, not only do traditional societies assign no value to innovation, but they forbid it in the firmest, most explicit manner. To innovate, to challenge tradition, is to risk one's life. This point is made, for example, by Pierre Clastres in his analysis of Amerindian native cultures.[10] Among the Guayaki band, the chief was not, as in Western societies, someone who got himself elected by promising reforms, improvements, hence innovations that necessarily introduce a break with custom, but, quite to the contrary, someone who promised *to make no changes,* to devote all his energies to maintaining the established order just as it is—that is, just as it has been transmitted by the Ancestors, who, back through the generations, are themselves connected to the tutelary divinities of tribal origins. This is why old age is respected in such societies. It is also why fashion is totally ignored in them.[11] For centuries the Roman toga, the Japanese kimono, and the Indian sari remained unchanged, but in the domain of art as well, works necessarily reflect repetition and the maintaining of shared cultural symbols.

Needless to say, our attitude toward works of art has changed. In certain regards the situation has been reversed, to the point that we may know the name of a creative artist, and even be familiar with certain aspects of his or her life, while knowing nothing about that artist's "production." This is particularly true in the sectors of art that are less affected by the market, as is the case with much serious music today. In Bach's day the burghers of Leipzig listened to his works, even with pleasure, without knowing that they were composed by Bach. Today we are probably familiar with the names of contemporary composers but—let us confess—cannot always name any of their works, let alone recognize one when we hear it. Nietzsche's prediction has become a general rule in lay societies: henceforth the truth of a work of art resides in the artist, not in nature or divinity. The work is no longer the reflection of a suprahuman, transcendent world; it is the highest expression of the personality of the artist, who may be better known than his or her creations. Even when the work seeks to express a reality not directly linked with the reality of the "I"—as is the case with abstract art—a demand for originality takes priority, replacing ancient art's satisfaction with imitation. Now artists must invent, not just discover. There were, to be sure, "authors" in premodern civilizations, but they were probably not perceived as "geniuses," in the sense of creators *ex nihilo,* artists capable of finding within themselves all the sources and resources of their inspiration. The ancient artist was more of an intercessor between individuals and the cosmos, between men and the gods, than he was himself a demiurge. So we can understand how the demand for radical innovation and originality is directly connected with the modern conception of the author as genius, as an inventor who must break with the past. If praise of daily life, simple human life, is without any doubt an effect of the secularization of society, so also is its contrary, the cult of the bohemian life as a means of rupture, hence of innovation. This is why the cult of marginality deserves mention as a new figure of a purely human destiny within the lay space consecrated by the Nietzschean moment.

2. "True Life Is Elsewhere": Bohemians versus Philistines

It is always difficult to date the appearance of a new concept. Nonetheless, it seems that the notion of "bohemian" first appeared, at least in its metaphorical sense, in *La dernière Aldini,* a late-romantic novel by George Sand. At that time, the term no longer referred to the Romanies, or Gypsies, who were thought to come from Bohemia (the region around Prague), but rather to young artists who chose to live in precarious circumstances. In France of the 1830s, these "bohemians" gathered in small, closed groups like the "Petit Cénacle" (named in honor of Victor Hugo) that included Auguste Marquet, Gérard de Nerval, and Théophile Gautier in their student days. One thing at least is certain: it was Henri Murger who popularized the theme with his *Scènes de la vie de Bohème.*[12] The novel appeared in installments in March 1845 in a Parisian gazette, *Le Corsaire.* It was then adapted for the stage, where it met with considerable success, and in 1896 the stage version was immortalized by Puccini's famous opera. We still listen to Puccini's music, but Murger's work has largely fallen into oblivion. This is a pity, because, aside from Rodolphe and Mimi's ill-fated love, it offers a splendid description of the artist's life in Paris, at the time "the capital of the nineteenth century," in Walter Benjamin's words. In the novel we see a group of penniless young people who live in attics, wear outlandish clothes, haunt the Paris cafés, drink absinthe, passionately adopt noble causes, fall in love frequently, scandalize the bourgeois, organize savory practical jokes, and even create innovative works. Above all, we gain a concrete idea of what that new mode of life could have meant in the eyes of its first practitioners. Murger was one of them, and his description of his fellow disciples is at times so accurate that it earned him quarrels with his old friends, who were themselves shocked by this merciless public depiction. This is how Murger defines *la Bohème* in the preface to his novel:

> Today, as of old, every man who enters on an artistic career, without any other means of livelihood other than his art itself, will be forced

to walk in the paths of Bohemia. The greater number of our contemporaries who display the noblest blazonry of art have been Bohemians, and amidst their calm and prosperous glory they often recall, perhaps with regret, the time when, climbing the verdant slope
of youth, they had no other fortune in the sunshine of their twenty
years than courage, which is the virtue of the young, and hope,
which is the wealth of the poor. For the uneasy reader, for the timo-
rous citizen, for all those for whom an *i* can never be too plainly dot-
ted in a definition, we repeat as an axiom: "Bohemia is a stage of
artistic life; it is the preface to the Academy, the Hôtel Dieu, or the
Morgue." We will add that Bohemia only exists and is only possible
in Paris.[13]

This says it all, or nearly all. If "life in the provinces" is the target of scorn
(and it is worth remarking that the expression *la vie provinciale* seems so
shocking to the French today that it has almost disappeared), and if it
elicited horror among the bohemians, it is because it was the perfect incarnation of the quotidian; it represented the repetitive and unadventurous
life of philistines who would never take the risk to attempt to rise above the
common lot or perish. Because Murger was interested in conferring incontestable legitimacy to a new movement, the bohemian life is not tied to one
point in time. It belongs to all ages. For him, it is an existential attitude, a
life choice, a possibility that is always open and that reaches back into the
night of time. He obviously was underestimating his own age: bohemia is
modern, even typically modern, and really cannot be compared to anything
that came before it. Murger seeks a precedent among the Greeks, however,
evoking the emblematic figure of Socrates, the tutelary authority of the
Cynics, another group that lived on love and cold water, seemingly in contempt of bourgeois conventions. This is fair game, but the truth is that
Greek transgressions are not our own; the Greeks lived in a world in which
the bourgeoisie did not exist, and they operated in the name of a life in
harmony with a cosmic nature, the very notion of which we have lost.
Once again, we need to guard against retrospective illusions.

The truth is that if the burden of daily existence terrifies young people
in search of adventure, it is in the perspective of a radical secularization of
society. There are three crucial reasons for this.

First, if the ultimate aim of an artist's life is henceforth connected with
his capacities for innovation and originality—a cultivation of eccentric
clothing is the external sign—then repetition, which furnishes the basis
for tradition, *but also for daily life,* must necessarily be detestable. A century

later the formula *métro, boulot, dodo* (subway, job, beddy-bye) stigmatized repetitiveness for the very same reasons. So hatred for bourgeois life, already present among the romantics, became increasingly radicalized in avant-garde movements toward the end of the nineteenth century and throughout the twentieth century. As is known, the expression "avant-garde," originally a military term, first appeared in the figurative sense, referring to the world of artists, in Saint-Simon.[14] If we can believe his *Opinions littéraires, philosophiques et industrielles,* it was artists, "men of imagination," who would henceforth, "marching forcefully," stand at the vanguard of history and "proclaim the future of the human species; they will remove the age of gold from the past in order to enrich future generations." At a later date but in the same spirit, the "Incohérents" have been seen as the earliest aesthetic avant-garde group worthy of the name.[15] This movement, which was much talked about in the years between 1882 and 1889 (when it petered out and the group disbanded), took up the legacy of bohemia. The Incohérants consisted of a number of smaller groups, habitués of the Parisian cabarets who labeled themselves "Hydropathes," "Hirsutes," "Zutistes," or "Jemenfoutistes," and the movement's principal activity was the organization of exhibitions relying on humor and primarily designed to "shock the bourgeois" and to mark a symbolic difference between the bohemian life and the philistine life. Signs of recognition played a role of capital importance, as seen in a manifesto stating the most typical traits of an ideology that was at once elitist and reliant on schoolboy humor but that, first and foremost, rejected all the distinguishing marks of daily life: "The Incoherent is young, and he does indeed need suppleness of members and mind to give himself over to perpetual dislocations, physical and moral. . . . As a consequence, the Incoherent has neither rheumatism nor migraines; he is high-strung and robust. He belongs to all the professions connected with art: a typographer can be an Incoherent, a roofer never. . . . The Incoherent goes into retirement when he marries or is afflicted with rheumatism."

In a more serious vein, it was during the early years of the twentieth century that artists themselves contributed greatly to portraying the avant-garde as a locus of rupture with ordinary life. An essay by Wassily Kandinsky, in French translation as *Du spirituel dans l'art et dans la peinture en particulier* (1912), constitutes one of the most remarkable examples of this enthusiasm. In describing this new and innovative movement, Kandinsky uses a metaphor that merits attention because it contains all the elements that would soon become sacred as the ideal type of the artist's life: "A great triangle divided into unequal parts, the smallest and sharpest at the top, provides a fairly good schematic figure of the life of the mind. The whole triangle, its motion barely perceptible, slowly advances and rises, and the part closest to the summit will 'tomorrow' reach the place where the point was 'today.' In other words, what 'today' seems incomprehensible drivel for the base of the triangle and has meaning only for the peak will tomorrow seem charged with emotion and new meaning to the part closest to the top."[16]

We can conclude from this metaphor that the solitude of the genius, who is that singular point formed by the tip of the triangle, is only provisional. Bohemia, Murger tells us, only lasts so long; it is only a "stage" in life that corresponds to youth, to beginnings. Moreover, precisely because of the triangular structure of the artistic life, at least when that life plays out at the summit, it is lived by an infinitely small elite or else is downright solitary. This is why avant-garde movements are naturally small: "At the very top of the triangle, there is but one man, alone. His vision is equaled by his infinite sadness." His mission is to advance "the recalcitrant chariot" of the masses situated at the base of the triangle. On one hand we have "the superior men" brave enough to question tradition; on the other, the ordinary beings who remain mired in conformity. Among the latter, Kandinsky adds, "no one has ever managed to resolve the slightest difficulty. It is others, superior to them, who have always made the chariot of humanity advance." The metaphor of the avant-garde returns here to the military accents of its origin: superior men, artists or savants of genius, "forge ahead, mindless of all prudence, and fall in the conquest of the citadel of new knowledge, just like soldiers who, having made a sacrifice of their person, perish in the desperate assault of a fortress that refuses to capitulate." The genius stands alone, for the summit of the triangle is a point. He is the object of derision, he is "called mad."

This solitude, however, is the surest sign of a break with the ordinary world, with common life, as Schönberg confessed to Kandinsky in a letter dated 24 January 1911: "For the moment, my works are debarred from winning the favor of the masses. They will reach individuals all the more easily. These individuals of great value are the only ones who count for me." This theme, which comes directly from Nietzsche, seemed to Schönberg so essential that in 1937 it became the central theme of an essay entitled "How One Becomes Lonely." Here elitism and the question of a public (or, rather, the lack of a public) centers on the notion of individuality: the artist's solitude is the most reliable indication of his singularity and the surest sign of his individualization in comparison with common mortals dully absorbed by their daily tasks.

If the imperatives of creativity impose a break with the quotidian—and this separation, another commonplace in the biography of "geniuses," is almost always described as difficult for those close to the genius—a second reason joins with the first to make the bohemian life a typically modern necessity. It states that now, after the disappearance of transcendence, what threatens our lives is platitude, understood in the literal sense as the absence of all relief, all height, all relation to the "grandiose." The theme merits reflection. It runs throughout contemporary culture and at time inspires diagnostics imprinted with pessimism. Is there—can there be—such a thing as a "modern grandeur"? Is that not self-contradictory? Isn't grandeur inextricably connected to the representation of a universe external to and superior to humans and, for that very reason, *imposing*? How can what is merely immanence within humanity possess the sacred character without which everything is but amusement and vanity—or, at least, familiar proximity? When still a theology student, Hegel wondered what "the religion of a free people" might be like. This led him to reflect on the conditions that might permit humanity finally to *recognize itself* in a common culture, freed of all dogmatism and of the opaque transcendence exuded by "authoritative arguments" founded on the representation of a revealed truth. According to Hegel, the Christian religion needed to be emancipated from its "positivity," from all that still remained *foreign to the human spirit in it.* But was this not tantamount to wanting to do away with religion itself and to transform it into a simple, *transparent* culture, wholly produced by humans and for humans, rather than given to them by the divinity? If the source of all works is human and therefore (from a traditional viewpoint and, without seeking a facile play on words, "too human"), is not lay culture also fated to be on a human scale as well? But after the eclipse of the sacred, how can humans draw from within themselves, without reference to any radical externality, what it takes to reconstitute grandeur? Were not "great men," be they politicians or artists, above all the embodiment of sublime entities such as Cosmos, Divinity, Science, Homeland, Revolution, and the like? If I no longer represent anything outside of myself; if I am, to parody Jean-Paul Sartre's formula, as worthy a being as any other, but those others are also worthy, how can I still aspire—whatever my talent—to reconstitute grandeur? Nietzsche responded to this question by distinguishing, within life itself, between weakened, "nihilist" forms of existence and other forms capable of attaining intensity and the grand style. Whatever we may think of his "solution," in his eyes it implied a radical break with the ordinary forms of bourgeois life—for which reason Guillaume Apollinaire was probably right to see him as the founding father of the avant-gardes.[17]

A final theme, also typically modern, helps to legitimate this separation. It resides in the simple fact that after the death of God, humans have only one life available to them. There is no longer a "beyond," no longer an "elsewhere," in our secularized age, which means that every moment wasted is irretrievably lost. As Pascal Bruckner has rightly noted, "Now nothing saves us from the prosaism that once constituted that humble part of existence and could be amended by prayers, faith, and rites. If we need to free ourselves now, it is from the quotidian that exasperates us, and we are less apt to contrast sin and grace than the ordinary and the exceptional."[18]

In spite of hypocrisy and sham, reality is stubborn: bohemia can scorn this world's goods; but because, in the final analysis, this is the only world we know, power and wealth demand their due. Lack of humility and wisdom? Contradiction with respect to the purity of bohemia's early ideals? Certainly. "Success," in the most trivial sense of the term, continues to be one of the possible horizons of modern life, and it is an ideal that reiterated denials from the virtuous (or from virtue within us) will never manage to hide. Nietzsche himself sought success throughout his life: he was crushed when he was forced to publish at his own expense, and wild with joy when one of his works elicited even a small response or when a "man much in view" came to encourage him and draw him out of his terrible solitude.[19] This was doubtless a sign, as Murger had already noted, that the artistic life is not, or ought not be, other than a transition, a movement toward public recognition, and that the desire for recognition pays homage—perhaps involuntarily, but nonetheless certainly—to the bourgeois life.

3. Artists and Entrepreneurs: Capitalism, the World of Technology, and the Will to Power

The pattern seems set: according to the mythology so efficiently passed on by Murger, the authentic bohemians, the "pure" ones, cared little for fortune. Adepts of art for arts's sake, they threw themselves into living "on the outskirts of life," dying, "for the most part, decimated by that disease to which science does not dare give its real name, want." These clichés are intended to describe a deliberate choice, an explicit rejection, of what we would today call a "consumer society." According to Murger, many of these artists could "escape from this fatal *dénouement* which suddenly terminates their life at an age when ordinary life is only beginning. It would suffice for that for them to make a few concessions to the stern laws of necessity; for them to know how to duplicate their being, to have within themselves two natures, the poet, ever dreaming on the lofty summits where the choir of inspired voices are warbling, and the man, worker-out of his life, able to knead his daily bread."[20] But the bohemian was not one to compromise, and even less to compromise with his conscience. He knew no duplicity, which is why those who devote their entire being to the artist's life "die young, leaving sometimes behind them a work which the world admires later on and which it would no doubt have applauded sooner if it had not remained invisible." This is why Murger, who basically is not deceived by this imagery, proposes a distinction between two variants of bohemia, the "unknown" or "ignored" bohemia and the "real" or "official" bohemia, as he calls them. The first (and unfortunately the commonest) "is not a path, it is a dead end." Its principal failure is to confuse what is only a provisional means with an ultimate aim. This is a tragic mistake, for bohemia is not an objective in itself and should correspond to the very beginning of the artist's life. Like the avant-gardists later, Murger was persuaded that real genius is not fated to remain unknown forever: "All truly powerful minds have their word to say, and, indeed, utter it sooner or later. . . . Genius is the sun, everyone sees it. Talent is the diamond that may for a long time remain hidden in obscurity, but which is always perceived by some one. It is, therefore, wrong to be moved to pity over the lamentations and stock phrases of that class of intruders and inutilities entered upon an artistic career in spite of art itself, and who go to make up in Bohemia a class in which laziness, debauchery, and parasitism form the foundation of manners." So much for "unknown Bohemianism."

This judgment, which Murger's old friends greeted with animosity, was accompanied by a veritable sacralization of "official Bohemia," the "real Bohemia" that Murger declares is the sole object of his book, and that he defines in terms that leave little doubt as to his own ambitions:

> This Bohemia, like the others, bristles with perils, two abysses flank it on either side—poverty and doubt. But between these two gulfs there is at least a road leading to a goal which the Bohemians can see with their eyes, pending the time when they shall touch it with their hand. It is official Bohemia so-called because those who form

part of it have publicly proved their existence, have signalized their presence in the world elsewhere than in a census list, have, to employ one of their own expressions, "their name in the bill," who are known in the literary and artistic market, and whose products, bearing their stamp, are current there, at modest rates it is true.[21]

Clearly, the modest rates held true only at first. There could hardly be a better statement that art, too, is part of the market economy; that it is not totally disinterested—far from it!—and that recognition, notoriety, and even money are not excluded from its ulterior motives, or even from its thoughts in general. Unknown at first, bohemia must work ceaselessly to become official, and, for bohemians whose "mind is kept ever on the alert by their ambition" and who know how to overcome all the obstacles that separate them from success, "to arrive at their goal, which is a settled one, all roads serve."

From their closely related but much more sophisticated viewpoint regarding the avant-garde, Kandinsky and Schönberg are equally persuaded that, for an authentic genius, "success" stands inevitably at the horizon of a transitory marginality. To be sure, in order to innovate, the artist must break with tradition, with the result that "each epoch creates an art that is its own and that will never be reborn." Hence the imitation of out-of-date forms inherited from the culture of the past is "for monkeys" whose "mimicry is denuded of all meaning."[22] The avant-garde is linked to the idea of revolution: its mission is to "bravely shake the established order," understood as a never-ending task. Artists' originality or individuality thus condemns them to a certain form of purgatory. But despite this pessimism, associated with the triangular structure of a spiritual life that, as we have seen, imposes solitude on artists, an unshakable belief in progress permits optimism to be resuscitated: "In spite of the blindness [of the masses], the spiritual triangle in reality continues to advance." Better, it "climbs slowly, with an irresistible force," with the result that one fine day the base of the triangle will reach the point now occupied by the summit. The elite can rest assured: its solitude is only provisional, and sooner or later it will be understood by a "base" that it serves as scout and guide: "The pictorial and musical dissonance of today is but the consonance of tomorrow,"[23] Kandinsky asserts.[24]

This does not mean that the ends of art lie entirely in the conquest of notoriety and wealth—to say so would be an error parallel to the unknown bohemianism's confusion between ends and means. Nonetheless, it is as if ambitious artists who wanted to escape from the stagnation and platitude of daily life and take their place among the "elite" were faced with a choice between two *concurrent* possibilities of existence, two ways to dominate the scene. On one hand was bohemia, provided it had become of the "official" variety and did not spend too much time lurking in unhealthy attics; on the other was *the life of enterprise.* In spite of the obvious (indeed, too obvious) gap between the two in bohemian mythology, these two forms of life share a radical and definitive departure from the daily life that Dutch painting had transfigured into art. They share a cult of elitism and innovation. As Karl Marx declared: "The bourgeoisie cannot exist without constantly revolutionising the instruments of production. . . . All fixed, fast frozen relations, with their train of ancient and venerable prejudices and opinions, are swept away, all new-formed ones become antiquated before they can ossify."[25] As a result, capitalism, which bohemia usually regarded as "reactionary," is in fact revolutionary, like bohemia and in spite of itself. For capitalism, too—as Marx stresses—a break with tradition and an imperative demand for innovation is its daily occupation, which means that a liberal society, more than any other form of social organization known to date, is diametrically opposed to traditional societies totally oriented toward respect of ancestors and the maintenance of custom.

Although obviously in different ways from those of enterprise, marginality thus appears as but one means—one strategy, one might say—for obtaining a rank equal to, if not superior to, that of the powerful of this world.[26] The bohemian is of course fully aware of this: as Murger writes: "Art, the rival of God, strides on, the equal of kings. Charles V stoops to pick up Titian's brush, and Francis I dances attendance at the printing office of Etienne Dolet," while Clément Marot, "the familiar of the antechamber of the Louvre," becomes, "even before she was a monarch's mistress, the favorite of that fair Diana whose smile lit up three reigns."[27]

Thus with the secularization of the world there are not two but three models for life: daily life and, opposed to it but in competition with each other, the life of the bohemians and that of captains of industry, both of whom can, each in their own way, claim the glorious title of Destroyer of Traditions.

So Heidegger's hypothesis—that Nietzsche's doctrine of the will to power is the true "superstructure" of the world of technology, the spontaneous philosophy of capitalism—is far from absurd. To be persuaded of that, paradoxical as the notion might seem to a "leftist Nietzschean," all it takes is to understand the term "will to power" correctly, as Gilles Deleuze invites us to do: not as a flat and bestial will to "have power," but rather as a "will to will," as an aspiration to an "endless" (both infinite and without specific aims) intensification of one's own force. The capitalist can, of course, desire and seek power on a personal basis. But if we consider the overall system, the "mode of production," or the social structure rather than the individual, these seem indeed to furnish a perfect incarnation of the will to power, understood as a will to will. As mentioned in the prologue to the present volume, Heidegger contended that if we want to take a wholly technological view of the world, we have to take one step beyond the Enlightenment in the will to dominate the universe that appeared as early as Descartes. For the will to take itself as its object, it must cease having external ends. This, Heidegger tells us, is just what happens with the "revolutionary" primacy of Nietzsche's "will to power," the metaphysical underpinnings of the technology in which the entire planet is immersed today. In Nietzsche, in fact, authentic will, out-and-out will, ceases to be will *for something* and becomes will in itself, a force that aims at the increase of the vital force, will that seeks its own vivification as will. This is the way, and the only way, that it attains the perfection of its concept: in desiring itself, it becomes mastery for mastery's sake, brute force for brute force, domination for domination, movement for movement. Nothing resists it because it has ceased believing itself subjected to external ends, as it was in the era of transcendence, and still was in the progress-oriented ideal of the Enlightenment.

It is this exigence without end, hence infinitely mobilizing, that threatens the contemporary individual. The *bobo*, the daily occupation or job, at once bourgeois and bohemian but mired in the quotidian, is compelled by a new quest for *happiness in lucidity* to replace philosophical preoccupations (now reputedly out of date) with the more concrete help, *better adapted to situation*, of depth psychology. The many things that Freud owed to Nietzsche have often been noted — in particular his discovery of the unconscious. Like Nietzsche, but in a different mode, Freud registers and pursues the deconstruction of metaphysical and religious illusions under all their forms. Again like Nietzsche, he is suspicious of abstract or excessively rational thought, and he works to set back in motion (in circulation, to use an appropriate idiom) the affective energies, blocked by alienating idols, so that the individual can fully "enjoy and act." Above all, and also like Nietzsche, Freud invites individuals, if not to "make a success of their lives" — the formula is immediately suspect because too normative — at least to think of their lives more clear-sightedly, avoiding the fatal and pathogenic

error of seeking to measure it by the standard of a transcendence now undeniably neurotic.

4. The Successful Life as Liberation from Alienation:
The Philosophical Message of Psychoanalysis,
or In Praise of Lucidity

Daily life or the bohemian life? The life of an artist or of a captain of industry? At base, does it matter? Is not what is essential, in a truly lay perspective, finally to be oneself, to feel right in one's skin and one's head? And
isn't a modicum of clear-sightedness the trump card in this game? Should
not one clearly state all that these life models, although secularized in principle, secretly owe to the imaginary of immortality? Whether one hopes for
personal survival through children or to remain in history by virtue of one's
works, does not the phantasm of surmounting death—to some degree at
least—continue to haunt the modern schemata of success? Freud, taking
the opposite view, thought himself without illusions. On the topic of reflection that remains slanted, even if unconsciously, toward metaphysics, he
is admirably clear, as demonstrated in a well-known passage from a letter
to Wilhelm Fleiss: "When we begin ask ourselves questions about the
meaning of life and death, we are sick, for none of that exists objectively."
Assigning a purpose to human existence implies judging it; it means
adopting a normative and necessarily repressive point of view with respect
to it. Though the style differs, Freud's statement could have been written
by Nietzsche.[28] It contains an irrevocable condemnation of the metaphysical line of speculation that, since the Greeks, held that to philosophize is to
learn how to die.[29] As for religion, Freud, a resolute post-Nietzschean, does
not mince words: for him (and the phrase has become famous), religion is
quite simply the "obsessional neurosis of humanity."[30] If Freud always admitted to taking "intense pleasure" in reading Nietzsche, it was precisely
because Nietzsche seemed to him to announce "in a prophetic manner" his
own deconstruction of metaphysical and theological illusions. But of
course Freud intended to go further into the question and move from the
stage of "lightning intuitions" (where Nietzsche had remained) to that of
scientific analysis of the way phantasms are produced.

Nietzsche's critique of religion, although radical, still resembles an "explanation" between equals. His stressing how crucial it is for a thinker worthy of the name to have "good enemies"; his determination to preserve "the
Church within us"; his desire to rival the Gospels, to the point of imitating

their style; and his refusal to break all ties with the eternal—all these attitudes reflect a certain form of *respect* even within a marked lack of respect.
There is none of this in Freud, who brings the cold gaze of the clinician to
his treatment of religion. Freud's most consistent thesis in this connection
is well known: the great monotheistic dogmas are no more than purely
imaginary realizations of childhood's earliest aspirations—not to die, not
to be exposed to solitude, not to be abandoned by one's parents, to be loved
no matter what we do. In short, they are "not the residue of experience or
the final result of reflection," but rather "illusions, fulfillments of the oldest,
strongest and the most insistent wishes of mankind; the secret of their
strength is the strength of these wishes. . . . The terrifying effect of infantile helplessness aroused the need for protection—protection through
love—which the father relieved, and that the discovery that this helplessness would continue through the whole of life made it necessary to cling to
the existence of a father, but this time a more powerful one. Thus the
benevolent rule of divine providence allays our anxiety in face of life's dangers."[31] This is how we have collectively invented the great monotheistic
deliriums.

This theme is a familiar one, and common enough today so that we
need not linger over it. What is important is to understand why, according
to Freud, we should strive not to remain within that delirium if we want to
make a success of our lives. Not that religion lacks certain advantages: it
can, as has just been suggested, calm infantile anxieties. Above all, by presenting individuals with a ready-to-use neurotic structure, religion can
spare them the trouble of fabricating their own "personal neurosis."[32] This
benefit—admittedly a small one—comes at a high cost, however. The lack
of lucidity that it involves concerning the real nature of the human condition can, quite simply, prevent us from being truly happy, to the extent that
religion warps our efforts to adapt to reality. Freud insists (and once more
his formulations echo Nietzsche) that the method of religion "consists in
decrying the value of life and promulgating a view of the real world that is
distorted like a delusion, and both of these imply a preliminary intimidat-
ing influence upon intelligence."[33] Thus religion forces us to both "psychic
infantilism" and "collective delirium." This means that it is bound to fail:
"Its doctrines bear the imprint of the times in which they arose, the ignorant times of the childhood of humanity. Its consolations deserve no trust.
Experience teaches us that the world is no nursery."[34]

Freud states that for anyone who wants to make a success of his life
and be happy—in any sense of the word, but at least in some real man-

ner—there are many ways to do so, not one alone, as religion would have us believe.[35] The first and perhaps the principal teaching of psychoanalysis regarding the way to lead one's life is that it is better to have the courage to face necessity as it is. Hence Freud stresses that the "reality principle" is not the opposite of the "pleasure principle," but rather "a simple modification" of the latter. The reality principle, indeed, is the surest and most useful prolongation of the pleasure principle, as Bruno Bettelheim has delightfully shown in his commentary on the three little pigs.[36]

We all know the outline of the story: the smallest pig builds his house out of straw and in the shortest possible time. His only care, in conformity with the pleasure principle, is to spend the least time at a boring task—building a house—so as to go out to play as soon as he can and to eat in the beautiful fields around the house. The second pig spends more time and energy in protecting himself against life's dangers, symbolized by the wolf: his house is built of sticks and is more resistant than that of the first. Only the third pig takes reality seriously. His house, carefully built out of brick, will resist the assaults of the ferocious wolf. But to bring this about, he will have to have made an effort—unlike his two little brothers—to *postpone satisfaction of his immediate desires,* for the moment sacrificing pleasure to the reality principle. He will be rewarded for it: not only does he escape the sad fate reserved for the two other pigs, but when the wolf falls down the chimney into the soup pot, it is the wolf—against all expectation—who will be eaten. Bettelheim shows convincingly that in the English version of the tale, as soon as we understand that the three little pigs are really one, we see that they are the same figure at three different stages. Not only are the two first pigs presented as "smaller" than the third, but when the third pig eats the wolf, he is also swallowing his two "brothers," recuperating them and integrating them into himself. This reveals the moral of the tale: we have to know how to outgrow childhood, to get past the dangerous pleasure principle, because it is in being lucid—in taking into account reality as it is, not trying to escape it—that we can master reality and, by that very token, derive satisfactions that, although not immediate or easy, are all the more real and durable. In other words, rather than fleeing from the difficulties of life into the phantasms of metaphysics or religion, we will profit immensely from perceiving the human condition as it is, without embellishment and with no evasion on our part. This, psychoanalysis tells us, is the first requisite of a life finally anchored in reality. Not that we can always avoid illness: in certain cases it even seems a necessary "solution." A surgeon who realizes the unexpected extent of a problem that he underestimated at the moment of diagnosis may decide not to operate; similarly, Freud himself recognizes that recourse to analytic therapy is not indicated at all times or for all patients. The fact remains, however—as the analogy with surgery suggests—that mental illness is a last resort and lucidity an ideal, perhaps impossible to realize fully but always to be sought. This leads to a question that we must put to psychoanalysis if we want to know in what measure it can offer a response to the question of the good life: What does it have to tell us about the human condition? What, precisely, is our *real* situation? If, as in the case of the three little pigs, it turns out to be preferable to seek conformity with reality, we need to know what that reality is like before we attempt the adventure.

Freud gives a masterly response to that question in chapter 22 of his *Introduction to Pyschoanalysis*. The chapter, which Freud writes in a style of unequaled clarity, concerns the history of the libido and, more generally, the destiny of our psychic life as a whole. I shall limit my remarks to a brief review of its principal theme, then draw a few crucial conclusions that touch on the question central to the present work.

Like Nietzsche, Freud considers that living reality, human reality included, is based on instincts, impulses, and desires that he groups under the general term of "libido." From infancy to adulthood, the libido possesses a history; it evolves through three major stages: the "oral stage," in which the infant's desires, which are still mostly auto-erotic and narcissistic, are for the most part realized in activities related to sucking; the "anal stage," which coincides roughly with the child's learning control over bodily functions; then, after a transition period called "latency," the appearance at adolescence of adult sexuality, when all the primary impulses are regrouped under the primacy of the genital. At that point the libido clearly turns toward external objects. One might say, using Jean Piaget's term, that the libido undergoes "decentering," henceforth expressing itself in the search for a partner for sex and love. Traces of the earlier stages of the evolution of the libido nonetheless play a certain role, if only a partial and timid one, in the mature sexual act, where their importance varies with individuals. The kiss, for example, which recalls the first stage of our affective life, always occupies an important place in adult sexuality, and the anal libido, although for the most part the object of a particularly powerful taboo, nonetheless continues to play a certain role in adult erotic life.

This evolution is inherent in the human species as a whole, which means that for Freud it pertains, in essence, to our purely biological dimension: we are all equal, or nearly so. This is our common lot. Still, here and there, according to individuals and by virtue of the training they receive, this history will show slightly different orientations that will in turn dictate our individual destinies. The course of the libido in no way resembles a tranquil river, and many accidents can occur along the way. Two of these accidents, which Freud calls "fixation" and "regression," play a decisive role in our lives. Fixation may be defined as a quantity of affect that remains "stuck" at an earlier stage in the development of the libido. Instead of the libido's evolving as a whole from one stage to another, a part of it remains fixated at, for example, the oral stage, probably because of strong pleasure experienced in infancy. It is normal, after all, that one should want to remain where one has been happy, and the libido, from this point of view, is no exception to the rule. As for regression, in one sense it is directly connected to the importance of fixations: when we reach maturity—which means the primacy of the genital—our impulses encounter many obstacles on their way to realization. This is a daily experience, and we do our best, with varied success, to deal with the problem, either by overcoming the obstacles; by renouncing, at least for the time being, the objects that they keep us from reaching; or by getting around the obstacles, choosing secondary objects that resemble the original ones as closely as possible ("sublimation"). But if those obstacles (or experiences of "deprivation") seem truly insurmountable and we find it impossible to get around them—in short, if the situation remains desperately "blocked"—then our unfortunate libido has little choice: it will have to regress, to return to old satisfactions, even though these are by definition infantile or archaic, thus to some extent pathological. This explains the dual connection between regression and fixations: the greater the quantity of affect fixed in the libido's past, the more "tempting" it will be to return to that past in cases of insurmountable privation in the present. Inversely, the greater the quantity of affect, the more the libido, which can be compared here to a tumultuous stream of water, is weakened by being "held back" in its attempt to surmount privations; hence will incline to regression.

To elucidate his point, Freud proposes a metaphor that is highly interesting because it reveals his entire vision of the human condition. He compares the evolution of our libido to that of a people who, constrained to abandon its first habitat, crosses an entire country to find a new place to settle Along the way, some, out of lassitude, fatigue, or, quite to the contrary, because they find a place that appeals to them, will choose to stay behind and settle before the group as a whole has reached its final destination. It is also clear, however, that the more the families who decide to stop along the way, the weaker will be the group that continues its journey and the less able to overcome obstacles (hostile natives, for example). This means that if the group as a whole encounters a particularly difficult obstacle, it will tend to turn back and—in the absence of a better choice—rejoin those who settled along the way. It will do so all the more willingly when this choice alone offers a perhaps not negligible chance for survival. We can suppose that those who stopped did so because the place they found was agreeable and offered a maximum of possibilities of adaptation. As Freud says, stressing the connection between fixation (the premature stop) and regression (a return to previous fixations): "If you think of a migrating people who have left large numbers at the stopping-places on their way, you will see that the foremost will naturally fall back upon these positions when they are defeated or when they meet with an enemy too strong for them. And again, the more of their number they leave behind in their progress, the sooner will they be in danger of defeat."[37]

To translate: if regression marks entry into illness (and in a moment we shall see why), fixations are not a good thing. The more numerous the fixations, the greater the chance that a regression will take place in the course of our life. This can occur in two, equally pernicious, forms. First, regression can occur without being "repressed"—that is, without being actively sent to the unconscious under the impulse of the grand censor designated as the "superego." In this case, one has a "perversion"—that is, a satisfaction of the libido that no longer takes place in the sex act properly speaking but that, to the contrary, is diverted to archaic objects or phases of its development. More often, however, the regression, for obvious reasons, will be "forbidden"—censored by the superego—and driven into the unconscious. Indeed, ordinary morality—whatever one might think of it—generally disapproves of infantile libidinal satisfactions. One cannot easily imagine, for example, a normal adult who would blithely regress to the anal stage and play with his feces without the least shame, like a small child. His regressive impulses would be subject to a prohibition, and, as in the case of sublimation, he would have to find a satisfaction that bore only an analogical relation (preferably, not too visible) with the object of his repression so as to avoid awakening the vigilance of the superego. Neurotic symptoms arise as "sublimations of regression" according to a process that can be schematized, as in the accompanying diagram.

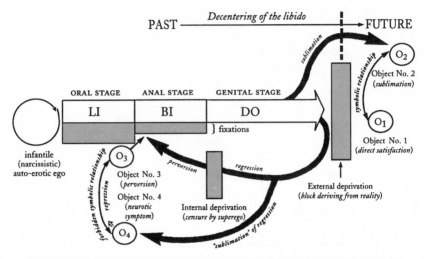

HUMAN PSYCHOSEXUAL DEVELOPMENT ACCORDING TO FREUD

Four (and only four) types of satisfaction are available to the mature libido. The first is direct satisfaction, which fortunately does occur. The libido finds an object that does not elude it (we fall in love), and all in all, things go fairly well. The second type is more problematic: an obstacle or a privation obstructs the libido, which is prevented from enjoying direct satisfaction of one of its desires, even a highly cherished desire. For example: a dedicated hunter paralyzed in an automobile accident has to give up an activity he passionately enjoys. But he can *sublimate* that passion: he can collect guns, trophies, stuffed or model animals, books about hunting, and so forth. We see here one of the basic traits of sublimation, a trait that we shall encounter again in symptoms of neurosis: the second, substitute object must bear an important symbolic relation to the first object of desire in order for sublimation to fulfill its function as a substitute satisfaction. A third possibility occurs when the situation is more serious and the deprivations apply to both direct and sublimated satisfactions. The case is not rare, notably because not everyone is capable of sublimation to the same degree (culture assists sublimation, but culture, as we know, is unequally distributed). In this case, regression seems the only possible solution and, as has been remarked, it is more likely to be chosen when there are strong fixations in the past of the libido. It is toward those fixations, of course, that regression takes place (as with the migrants who turn back to rejoin the group they have lost along the route). Still, this third "solution" (barely a solution, but a last resort) in turn follows one of two possible paths: regression can be "direct," not repressed (hence attached to object no. 3 in the diagram), and thus necessarily takes the form of a perversion (that is, a libidinal, but not a genital, satisfaction). Or else, if the superego of the person in question is particularly strong, the regression has every chance of being prohibited, hence repressed, which will constrain it to turn aside (object no. 4 in the diagram) to what is at that point necessarily a paradoxical object, not to say an "insane" one. As in the case of sublimation and for the same reasons, this object must resemble the first object of the regression (no. 3) as closely as possible, but at the same time—so as not to upset the superego—it must avoid too close a resemblance to the object that was just prohibited! Hence the appearance of the neurotic symptom, which alone responds to this dual requirement and can be roughly defined as an "unconscious sublimation of the regression."

It should also be noted that, quite obviously, all who share in the human condition participate in these four satisfactions, although in varying proportions. We all—fortunately—have experienced direct satisfactions, but also some sublimated satisfactions, a few perversions, and a neurotic symptom or two. Among neurotic symptoms I might cite the nearly universal case of phobias or, for those few people who have no phobias, obsessions. Who has never in his or her life felt an irrepressible but unjustified repulsion, whether in a certain situation (claustrophobia, fear of underwater weeds, fear of depths, etc.) or toward an animal (insect, mouse, snake, even when it is known to be totally inoffensive)? Who has never doublechecked to make sure the door is locked, the lights are out, and the gas has been turned off? Who has never made a mental wager with him- or herself; has never worried about stepping on cracks in the sidewalk; has never walked around a ladder, touched wood, or given in to those thousand and one little superstitions to which we pay no attention as long as the defense mechanisms that they replace function without noticeable difficulty? Yet these are obviously minor neurotic symptoms, perfectly explained by psychoanalysis, as in our diagram.

Another observation, this time in the form of a question: Given these conditions, how can we distinguish between the normal and the pathological? We know the usual response of psychoanalysis: it is a question not of quality but of quantity, of degree. The difference between "madness" and sanity is not absolute, and the dividing line between the two universes—this is the least one can say—is far from clear. Perhaps. We could point to two qualitative criteria, however, that alone give full meaning to the quantitative aspect. We could say, first, that health (and perfect sanity) lies more in the future than in the past. The more an individual's path is sown with fixations and regressions, the more it is mired in the past and the less "successful" it is (whatever fear of the "normative" might lead us to say). I might add, once again closely following Nietzsche, that what exhausts us to the point of making us sick or preventing us from "enjoying and acting," is *internal* conflict, anxieties caused by inner censure and the desires that it prohibits. It is in this sense—and Freud constantly returns to the topic—that only *internal privations, the ones engendered by the superego and its moral prohibitions,* are truly pathogenic and generate symptoms. As Bruno Bettelheim has rightly shown, human beings can bear nearly all external privations without becoming insane: even in German concentration camps, people managed to survive without losing their minds. Internal privations are unbearable, however, because they set up—even by definition—psychic conflicts that, like the reactive forces described by Nietzsche, cause both anxiety and exhaustion.

The psychoanalytical interpretation of the famous folktale of the three wishes is pertinent here. A genie promises a poor peasant couple living on the edge of starvation that he will make their first three wishes come true. The woman, who smells cooking nearby, reacts without thinking and wishes for her favorite dish, sauerkraut and sausages, which immediately appear on the table. The husband, furious to see one wish wasted so stupidly, when he could have asked for all the gold in the world, punishes his wife by crying: "May the sausages stick to your ugly nose!" No sooner said than done. As is so often the case in these tales, the husband and the wife represent different symbolic aspects of one ividual. In this case, the wife symbolizes the id-dominated personality, the immediate desires of the pleasure principle. The husband of course reflects the superego, moral censure and punishment. The couple is the whole person, the famous "I" or ego who is charged with doing its best to regulate conflicts between those two capricious fractions. It has only one wish to make, which is unfortunately the third and last: that the sausages become unstuck from the woman's nose and return to the plate. The moral of the tale? Simply that psychic conflicts are *exhausting* (Nietzsche would say, "reactive"); they block our vital forces and keep them from being deployed in the world without inhibition or mutilation. The couple starts off with three wishes to be granted miraculously; but ends up roughly as before, not exactly with nothing, but with only a plate of sausages and sauerkraut that must have had a bitter aftertaste. The couple has lost its chance, if not its life.

Does this mean that psychoanalysis, like Nietzschean genealogy, invites us to choose the grand style, total health? That might perhaps be a natural tendency, and I suppose that in their heart of hearts many psychoanalysts, in spite of their suspicion of the idea of a normative model, might prefer clear-sightedness to the unconscious, the future to the past, harmony (even relative harmony) to conflict, and fluidity to blocks—in short, the more or less normal to the avowedly pathological. After all, if transference has any meaning, if psychoanalysis is above all a practice rather than a theory, it is in order to bring back into circulation energies that have been "stifled" by psychic conflict and to liberate the vital forces from the snares that hold them prisoner. As far as I know, however, psychoanalysis offers no ultimate answer. Regarding the question of why liberation from alienation is preferable to alienation, it is not even certain that it can respond otherwise than in terms of *function,* of pleasure and distress. After all, if a seriously deranged person is happier with his symptoms than without them, it is hard to see what justifies depriving him of them. As Freud recognized, psychoanalysis is basically just a *technique.* Its philosophical pretensions are deliberately null. This is, what is more, its grandeur, but it may also be, depending on one's point of view, its weakness. Radically lucid and disenchanted, psychoanalysis leaves it up to each individual to find his or her own way and destiny. Psychoanalysis sees all modes of life as of equal worth, provided that they are best suited to the person living them. Indifferent to ends, refusing at any cost to be normative, thus never offering anything but means, the psychoanalytic approach once again rejoins Nietzsche's thought and confers on the world of technology a visage that is no longer philosophical but therapeutic. Is this supreme wisdom, or is it a forced surrender to the world of merchandise?

To give an honest evaluation of the implications of that question, we need to return, without *a priori* considerations and if only to encourage comparison and reflection, to the alternatives that psychoanalysis claims to have gone beyond—that is, to the alternatives that ancient philosophy offered from its beginnings, and to its conviction that the value of life can only be measured by a standard of transcendence going beyond "instrumental reason," thanks to an "objective reason" that fixes objectives and provides superior goals for the guidance of humanity. In my opinion, there is no reason to deny that Nietzsche and Freud, as the common phrase goes, "were right," or that they were the first in the history of thought to have had the final word on a human existence at last fully disenchanted—which is also to say, to put the matter positively, liberated, as never before, from past illusions. In many ways, and whatever latter-day revolutionaries might say, our democratic societies are in great part in the image of their thought: whatever dysfunctions they may contain, whatever impression of injustice or emptiness they may at times project, no one can seriously deny that in them we are freer today than at any other time or place. This freedom, of course, includes the right to express all possible criticism of those same societies—criticism that they alone are programmed to tolerate. Religious nations filled with "superior" meanings and values may still exist, as well as "communities" that rise above the "individualism" that we are so quick to stigmatize in words. But let us admit it: those societies repel us, and for nothing in the world would we want to return—for us this would be a real regression—to the past or to outmoded figures of the theologico-political. Yet there is no reason to stay put, in my opinion, nothing to suggest that freedom of this kind is sufficient in itself, or that we can or must be satisfied with a disenchanted clear-sightedness. Nothing stops us—to say it all—from thinking that other forms of spirituality might exist, other representations of the meaning of life compatible with the lucidity that we cannot and must not deny. At base this would be the program of a "non-metaphysical humanism"; of the philosophy that I have called a "humanism of the man-god." Far from espousing any sort of "return to," I am suggesting that perhaps we need to think, at long last, beyond the disenchantment of the world, without rejecting what it contains that is inevitable and even salutary, but also without desperately seeking to conform to it. In order to do this, it is helpful—if only as a preparatory exercise—to return to this history at its origins, when it still promised us transcendence and meaning. Beyond a merely historical interest (which is not negligible), our task is to grasp the significance of such promises—not naïvely to yield to them, but rather to measure how, and above all why, they still have something to tell us. We shall discover, I believe, a surprising and profound thought according to which the exigencies of meaning and salvation are not incompatible with the secularization of the world. We may also find that the idea of a lay spirituality or, if you will, a wisdom of the Moderns, is not necessarily acquired at the cost of diminished rigor or lucidity.

PART III

The Wisdom of the Ancients: Life in Harmony with the Cosmic Order

CHAPTER 7

Greek Wisdom, or The First Image
of a Lay Spirituality

~ ~ ~ ~ ~

The Secularization of Salvation

A Preliminary Question

Why should we be interested in the wisdom of the Ancients if it no longer exists? That question might seem superfluous, if not preposterous. Isn't it obvious that, because philosophy was born in antiquity, we should retrace our own traditions to know who we are? Doesn't a modicum of respect for the historical landmarks of European civilization command us to defend classical studies, without which we would be cut off from our deepest roots? And even beyond historical or cultural justifications, is it not in Greece that the first inklings of contemporary thought emerged, so that when we practice the archaeology of knowledge, we become aware of something deep within ourselves?

It may well be so. Still, I cannot help thinking that such legitimations of the Ancients fall a bit short or, to put it better, are too narcissistic to be utterly convincing. It is always in relation to ourselves, because they are supposed to hint at or lay the groundwork for our modern modes of thought, that we must *still* read the Greeks. I dislike the idea that we should discover or rediscover profound and difficult works merely for the pleasure of finding ourselves in them in a nascent state. Yet this is why many readers—and highly prestigious ones—proclaim their love of Greece. Marx hails Democritus as the ancestor of his materialism, and Heidegger reads in the pre-Socratics the first outlines of a thought recalling Being. More recently, some have seen the advent of direct democracy and self-government in the century of Pericles, glints of Lacanian psychoanalysis in the Sophists, American pragmatism in Plato and Aristotle, or the dawn of scientific thought in the physicians of Ionia. As if the Ancients were admirable only by virtue of their proximity to us! At that rate, why not spare ourselves the detour? Why not go directly to current thinkers for what we are supposed to find, in an immature and less elaborate form, among the Ancients?

I shall propose a different reading of them, one that emphasizes what they *are*—strangely distant from us—rather than what we would like them to be, a notion that relies on a line of descent that is all too often purely imaginary.[1] Not that distance in itself is any better guarantee of our interest than proximity. The wisdom of the Ancients offers us the two basic conditions of all fruitful dialogue: kinship with, if not complicity in, the nature of philosophical interrogations that still shapes our thought, and a sometimes radical alterity in the responses and the visions of the world that underlie those interrogations. Like ethnologists attempting to understand the usages and customs of a "primitive society," we are fascinated by the Other, and its strangeness sends us back to ourselves. Let me be clear: Although the thought of the Ancients founded a philosophical tradition that is in many ways still our own, it operated in a world now lost. Finding an entry into that world provides a double benefit. We discover an intellectual universe that possesses the charm of sunken cathedrals, but we also have a chance to understand ourselves better by comparison with others. If we want to become conscious of ourselves, we need to find a way to see ourselves from the outside. Tocqueville would never have taught us so much about the birth of democratic societies if he had not viewed that world with the detached gaze of an aristocrat. Similarly, in many ways and despite the undeniable permanence of their questioning, the Greeks remain *our* most radical "outside," the one that provides the broadest and deepest perspective on our modern humanism. It is this mixture of connection and detachment that, in my opinion, gives the Ancients their savor.

First, the connections, because the Ancients formulated their questions about "living well," which form the heart of their thought,[2] in ways that explicitly break with traditional religious attitudes. Beginning in classical antiquity, philosophy was to rival religion on one crucial point. Like religion, philosophy situated the good life in relation to the issues of death and salvation. Also like religion, it responded to those issues by referring to a radical transcendence (that of cosmic order). But, unlike all religious discourse, philosophy endeavored, right from the start, to "secularize" doctrines of salvation. Even in classical Greece, it attempted to place man in a position to save himself, by his own means rather than by the grace of a *personal* deity. This created a space for reflection that has remained the province of philosophy up to our own day.

Next, the detachment, because the responses of classical philosophy to the question of an objective transcendence of an ordered universe endowed with meaning are simply not our own.[3] For basic reasons (to which I shall return), the representation of a "world order," of an organized, purposeful cosmos, was destroyed by modern physics — the physics of Galileo, Descartes, and Newton — and in particular by the emergence of the notions of infinite and neutral space and time. As late as the seventeenth century, that scientific revolution was cause for anxiety. People worried that it would lead ineluctably to the collapse of the old world. Pascal's libertine, frightened by the silence of the new infinite spaces, offers further evidence: once the universe was endowed with infinite dimensions, it no longer was a house that one could live in cozily. To find one's place in the universe now required the use of arbitrary coordinates, the choice of an "abscissa" and an "ordinate" forming the x and y axes. The infinitely small points that we became in a universe stripped of meaning were no longer capable of finding any kind of "natural place" in that universe. But this distance between the Ancients and ourselves, which might seem to prejudice the interest we owe them, acts in a contrary manner, I think, guaranteeing their relevance. In order to understand what there is, it may help to measure the distance that separates us from what there no longer is.

Philosophy as the Secularization of Religion

One of the most profound theses ever put forth regarding modern philosophy holds that it was first and foremost a massive attempt to secularize (or "rationalize") the Christian religion.[4] Hegel analyzed this question on several occasions, in particular in his lectures on the history of philosophy and on aesthetics, in which he developed the notion in the context of an enlightening comparison of art, religion, and philosophy as three great moments in the life of the mind. To summarize his thesis: the essence of art aims at embodying certain representations of the absolute within a sensible material. The sculptor, for example, makes divinity perceptible in the form of statues of marble, clay, or stone; the painter uses color and drawing—*perceptible* elements—to render grand scenes of mythology, of the Gospels, or some other sacred text. Art pleases because it speaks to the heart, to the emotions, and to sensibility, which is of course its special charm. The downside is that art necessarily remains limited in its spiritual aims because it rests—one might say from the outset—on an unresolvable contradiction: its object is ideal—in the final analysis, it is divinity itself, or at least spirit if it is "human" art—but the form in which it is expressed is always inadequate to the task because it is material. Thus art must be surpassed by religion, which has the same objectives as art—to express the divine, the absolute spirit—but has recourse to the more appropriate forms of myth, symbols, and parables like the ones Jesus used to explain his evangelical message. In other words, religious means of expression are already more spiritual, more adequate to their object, than those of the artist, even an artist of genius. Myth is not reason, however. It still derives in some fashion from the heart and the sensibility, which means that, like works of art, it touches even those whose knowledge is scant or who lack erudite culture. Only rationality, Hegel tells us, is truly capable of expressing the absolute, of being in full sympathy with its object and in perfect harmony with it. In the long run, then, art and religion must give way to philosophy, which surpasses them but shares their basic goal of attaining and thinking the divine.

To some extent Nietzsche and Heidegger confirm this understanding of philosophy as "in competition" with religion, with which it shares an object and a goal, but not its form or means of expression. Hence the reproach that both men address to classical metaphysics, which they considered merely a "disguised religion," an "onto-theology" secularized by the demands of a human reason claiming to replace faith. Of course, both men criticized and attempted to reach beyond that conception of philosophy, and both claimed to have broken with the illusions of metaphysics, shattering them "with a hammer" or "deconstructing" them. It is by no means certain that, in doing so, they did not retain a more secret continuity with metaphysics, which consisted simply in *pursuing* the business of secularizing religion in order to bring to fruition the disenchanted quest for an "intense" or "authentic" good life.

Whatever the accuracy of these criticisms, they agree in their diagnosis of what had preceded them. For thousands of years, philosophy had done little but pursue religious ends by other means—those of reason rather than faith; of argumentation rather than initiatory rites; of the use of public space rather than a secret community; of the universal rather than the particular; and so forth. Moreover, if this thesis strikes me as so important—if it alone (in my opinion) truly elucidates the meaning of philosophical activity from the Greeks to our own day—it is because it enables us to understand how and why philosophy, albeit in a manner different from and even opposed to that of religion, has retained a relation to wisdom, even to salvation, as its ultimate question. We need to guard against certain current tendencies to push philosophy toward specialization in order to endow it with a legitimacy akin to that of the sciences. A philosophy can never be partial, limited to the thought processes of law, science, politics, morality, language, and other areas, without losing its essence and very soon finding itself overwhelmed and overtaken by the hard sciences or the human sciences, which would soon regard it as out of date or useless. Thus my answer to the ritual question "What is philosophy?" would be a simple one: It is an attempt to take on religious questions in a nonreligious or, as the case may be, an antireligious mode.

Even admitting that this thesis applies to a portion of *modern* philosophy (essentially, German idealism), some might object that it could not possibly be extended to *all* of philosophy.[5] It is hard to see what sense there would be in claiming that Greek philosophy was a secularization of the Christian religion. As the reader may have guessed, that is not what interests me. What I think necessary is to show how all the great examples of philosophical thought were indelibly marked by a very special relationship with the *religion of their times;* to indicate how that relationship defined them as great lines of thought and how it enables us to comprehend the questions they *inherited,* albeit reinterpreting those questions in new ways.

Philosophy has always declared itself in *rupture* with the religious attitude in its approach to and treatment of the questions it considers; it nonetheless conserves a less visible but just as crucial *continuity* with religion—crucial in the sense that it is from religion that philosophy takes up lines of inquiry that *become its own only after they have been forged in the religious sphere.* It is that continuity, beyond rupture, that enables us to understand how philosophy deals with the question of the good life in terms of *salvation,* thus in relation to finitude and death, all the while abandoning the illusory status of the religious responses. Thus philosophy can claim to speak to all human beings rather than to believers alone, and can attempt to move beyond particular discourse and toward a dimension of universality that, from the start, placed it in opposition to all forms of religious communitarianism.

Leading classicists have taught us to acknowledge that both this rupture and this continuity are attested in Greece from the time of the rise of philosophy. To understand how and why the Greek philosophers answered the question of the successful life and in what sense they linked it to the question of salvation in the face of finitude and death, but without falling back on religious discourse, we must begin with their attempts to move beyond that question, yet keep it alive.

Greek Philosophy as a Secularization of Greek Religion

Jean-Pierre Vernant, taking inspiration from the works of Francis Macdonald Cornford on the transition from religion to philosophy in Greece, has discussed the secularization of religion in Greece with great acuity. Vernant has shown how the birth of philosophy in antiquity was not the result of any "miracle," as had often been said, but rather can be explained by what might be called the "secularization" or "laicization" of the religious universe in which the Greeks lived. This point deserves attention, for the process that inaugurated the "disenchantment of the world" is two-sided: on the one hand, the earliest philosophers *took over* a part of the religious heritage, in particular the themes preserved in the great poetic narratives about the birth of the gods and the origins of the world; on the other hand, that very heritage was "translated" into a new form of thinking—rational thinking—which gave it a new meaning and a new status. For the most part, Vernant tells us, ancient philosophy "transposes into a secularized form and on the plane of a more abstract thought the system of representation developed by religion. The cosmologies of the philosophers took over and continued the cosmogonic myths. . . . This was no vague analogy. Cornford shows that the structure of the philosophy of Anaximander and the theogony of an inspired poet like Hesiod correspond even in detail."[6]

Without analyzing these analogies in depth (for they are extremely complex, as might be imagined), we can gain some notion of the revolutionary changes that philosophic thought introduced in passing from the realm of the sacred to that of the profane by looking at just one example: philosophy's attempt to "extract" or "abstract" the Greek divinities from the four "material" elements that make up the universe. It is fair to say that in the philosophers' eyes there was a transfer from Zeus to ether (fire), from Hades to air, from Poseidon to the sea, and from Gaia to the earth. Some centuries later we find echoes of this "lay" revolution in Cicero, when he interprets the gods of the Greek myths in terms of physics. Consider, for example, the case of Saturn:

An ancient belief prevailed throughout Greece that Caelus was mutilated by his son Saturn, and Saturn himself thrown into bondage by his son Jove: now these immoral fables enshrined a decidedly clever scientific theory. Their meaning was that the highest element of celestial ether or fire, which by itself generates all things, is devoid of that bodily part which requires union with another for the work of procreation. By Saturn again they denoted that being who maintains the course and revolution of seasons and periods of time, the deity actually so designated in Greek, for Saturn's Greek name is *Kronos*, which is the same as *chronos*, a space of time. The Latin designation "Saturn" on the other hand is due to the fact that he is "saturated" or "satiated with years" (*anni*); the fable is that he was in the habit of devouring his sons—meaning that Time devours the ages and gorges himself insatiably with the years that are past.[7]

Let us leave aside the philological value of this reading of the great Greek theogonies. What is important is that it elucidates the mechanism of secularization at this early stage: it is less a matter of breaking with religion than of rearranging its contents; less a question of creating a tabula rasa than of turning the great themes around and seeing them in a new light. From the very beginning, that duality—rupture and continuity—marked, *and indelibly marked,* the ambiguous relations between philosophy and its only serious rival, religion. Contrary to an opinion endlessly reiterated as if it were supported by blindingly clear evidence, philosophy engages in competition with theology, not science. The various sorts of science and philosophy are complementary in that they represent two distinct faces of the same and equally rational thought. We have difficulty imagining an Aristotle who knew nothing of the biology of his time, or a Kant unaware of Newton, let alone their being "bothered" by the presence of science. Quite to the contrary, such thinkers ceaselessly drew nourishment from it. Both Cornford's and Vernant's remarks invite us to accept the view that—from the beginning and perhaps for ever, given that the connection is so essential[8]—religion "preforms" the fundamental metaphysical questions that philosophy inherits, rearranges, puts in new terms, turns around, or even deconstructs. One can choose to emphasize one moment or another of this relation, one can stress the continuities or the betrayals, but it is impossible, even if we feel more at home with philosophy, to eliminate religion.

This thesis is by no means restricted to the realm of Greek thought: its scope is so wide that we can see confirmation of it throughout the history of philosophy, and it holds true even in thinkers regarded as the least religious. Spinoza and Nietzsche, for example, each in his own way and while declaring a radical break with constituted religions, continued to take an interest in the problematics of salvation and eternity. It is not just by chance that Spinoza claims that his ethics goes beyond purely formal moralities and leads us toward "beatitude." According to him, there is no good life that has not been freed of the fear of death. He seems to say that a successful life and a successful death are one and the same: we cannot live well unless we have vanquished all fear, and the way to attain that goal is to work on our lives, to render them so wise and so untouched by folly that we succeed in dying "as little as possible." In short, in order to live well one must be ready to die well, with no fears and no regrets, and in order to die well one must have lived in such a way that only an infinitely small and inessential part of the self disappears. Nor should we be surprised that the texts in which Nietzsche presents his doctrine of eternal recurrence are so often cast in the form of a parable, a form typical of the great New Testament texts. The point is to describe a criterion of existence that permits us to distinguish between what is *absolutely* worth experiencing and what hardly deserves to last.

From Religion to Philosophy: Three Breaks in Continuity

What the classicists teach us about antiquity is that the secularization of religion, which conserved but also moved beyond religion (preserving the problematics of salvation and finitude but abandoning strictly religious responses to these questions), had already been put in place, clearly and firmly, at the dawn of philosophy. Regarding that early period, some specialists have shown a greater interest in what linked philosophy to the religions that preceded and informed it, while others have concentrated on what distanced philosophy from those religions and on what might be called its lay or rationalist moment. Cornford is sensitive to the connections between the two problematics; Vernant, without denying the religious paternity of philosophy, tends to accentuate what sets them apart. To be sure, Vernant tells us that the first "philosophers did not invent a system for explaining the world; they found it ready-made. . . . But today, when, thanks to Cornford, the filiation is recognized, the problem necessarily takes a new form. It is no longer just a question of finding the ancient in philosophy, but of disengaging from it what is truly new: what causes philosophy to cease being myth and to become philosophy."[9] This near revolution in continuity operated on at least three levels. We shall trace them briefly, following Vernant, before considering their consequences for the ways in which philosophical thought had to rephrase and, in part, recast a question that preceded it, overtook it in scope, and in a sense guided it, by virtue of philosophy's religious origin. It was the question of the connections between the problematic of salvation and that of finitude and death within the definition of a new understanding of "living well."

The first mutation is as easy to grasp as it was fundamental in its effects. In philosophy, questions replaced religious responses, and investigations regarding the origin of the world and the ends of man replaced the great narratives that explained destiny *in terms of lineages.* In myths of the origin of the world, says Vernant, "the explanation of becoming relied on the mythic image of sexual union. To understand was to find the father and the mother, to draw up a family tree." In many ways this is true of all the great religions in which the problematic of lineage is central, as in the Bible. Among the earliest philosophers, to the contrary, as soon as the material elements (air, fire, earth, water) had replaced the gods, genealogies no longer functioned as explanations. Thought had to become both interrogative and explicative; not only did it have to pose questions—which implies the famous "astonishment" that philosophers ever since Plato have declared consubstantial with philosophy—but it also had to make those questions explicit, formulate them clearly, and begin to respond to them by means of reason. As Vernant puts it, "Cosmology, by that token, did not only modify its language. It changed its content. Instead of recounting successive births, it defined the first principles that constitute being. No longer a historical narration, it was transformed into a system that exposes the deep structure of reality."[10] This also means that at its birth philosophy was still indistinguishable from scientific activity, with which it was inextricably mixed. It was religion that philosophy opposed, not the scientific spirit; it was in reaction to religion that philosophy was constituted, even though it also borrowed the principal interrogations of religion, but in a new mode, *diverting them.*

In this move from the gods to the elements, however, a second mutation took place: the very content of the world changed and the supernatural disappeared. Among the first philosophers, the ones who are, in fact, called physicists, "positivity suddenly invaded the totality of being, including man and the gods. Nothing was real that was not nature. And nature, cut off from its mythical background, itself became a problem, the object of rational discussion."[11] This was a first "disenchantment of the world," since henceforth it is "the force of the *phusis*, in its permanence and in its diversity, that takes the place of the ancient gods; by the power of life and the principle of order that it contains, the *phusis* itself assumes all the characteristics of the divine." Vernant's observation goes to the heart of the matter: we see again the duality, not to say the ambivalence, of the process of secularization. By emphasizing the moment of rupture, we underline the retreat of the divine, the birth of naturalism and rationalism, in short, the appearance of scientific and positive thought. On the other hand, by restoring continuity, we can show how, in the mental universe of the Greeks, nature remained a fundamentally *animated* being, organized and harmonious, in short, *divine*, because, as Vernant rightly points out, it inherits all (or almost all) the characteristics formerly those of the gods. This also explains the fact—an important one, as we shall see, for understanding how the Greeks, the Stoics in particular, responded to the question of the good life—that nature bore immediate values and meaning for the Ancients, whereas for us Moderns, nature in itself is merely raw material, having no ethical or aesthetic values other than those we choose to lend it. Because the cosmic order is no longer directed by divinity but has become what one might call divinity itself, it establishes by its own power and within itself the ends that humans have every interest in making their own if they want to find their place in the cosmos and begin to live well. It is, paradoxically, because it is secularized that the cosmic order becomes a "cosmologico-ethical" order "reposing not on the power of a sovereign god . . . but on a law of justice (*dikē*) *inscribed in nature*, a rule of allotment (*nomos*) implying for everyone the elements that constitute the world in an egalitarian order, in such a way that no one can dominate others and prevail over them." In this sense, it is no exaggeration to say that the order of the world includes not only the "cosmologico-ethical" and the inscription of moral ends, but also the "cosmologico-political." A certain line of thought on cosmic equality, which found its place in the city by way of Greek democracy, is not unconnected to the process of secularization by which nature is removed from "royal power" and itself becomes the bearer of *laws of allotment*, which is to say, law itself.

Finally, the same duality of rupture and continuity that we find in philosophy's relations to the religious and that marks the secularization by which philosophy becomes possible occurs in the figure of the philosopher. Like the priest, or the poet who relates the history of the gods to men, the sage is someone who maintains a privileged connection with transcendent entities: like them, he possesses the power to see the invisible and to enable others to see it;[12] he accedes to the contemplation of the celestial harmony, penetrates the world of ideas beyond the cave, perceives the unity of all things behind their apparent diversity, and so forth. Here, too, one can emphasize either connections or change. Taking the second choice, we can say with Vernant that the early philosopher, in spite of everything that links him to the poet and the priest, is "no longer a *shaman*," because his role, precisely, is not to live on what is secret, not to nourish himself with a mystery that he maintains at all costs, but rather to share his knowledge, to form a school and to teach, which implies submitting what he knows to rational and public discussion. As Vernant writes, "Divulgation of a religious secret, extending a reserved privilege to an open group, making public previously prohibited knowledge—these are the characteristics of the turning point that permitted the figure of the philosopher to become disengaged from the person of the magus." In this regard, the philosophical schools that flourished in fourth-century B.C. Greece were in their essence distinct from the religious sects that, even when they grew in size and increased in number, nonetheless remained closed, esoteric groups focused on revealed verities not to be shared with noninitiates: "To the contrary, philosophy, in its progress, broke out of the confraternity setting in which it had arisen. Its message was no longer limited to a group, to a sect. Through the spoken and written word, the philosopher addressed the entire city, all cities. He delivered his revelations in full public exposure. In bringing mystery into the public square, to the 'agora,' he made it the object of public and contradictory debate." In short, the true philosopher was already a "media specialist." He was not yet subject to the prohibition that an avant-garde ideology was to impose on him twenty-four centuries later, when a new sectarianism and elitism declared that a genius, someone ahead of his time, can by definition have only a tiny, select public, won over in advance to his cause.

But it is just as easy to focus on the early philosopher's close resemblance to the magi who preceded him as on the distance between them. Like the magus, the philosopher was presumed to be a sage—that is, to possess privileged access to the transcendent, to an invisible realm of cosmic harmony that underlies a better organization of life, both within the city and in the individual. Hence the philosopher's exceptional prestige, at least in ancient Greece.

Here also we see how the quest for salvation continues to serve as an Ariadne's thread for reflection in this shift from the religious to the philosophical. Understanding the nature of that persistence correctly should lead us to raise questions about analogies that must also persist in the responses themselves, even after the changes introduced by secularization. If we have moved from the earliest forms of the "theologico-ethical" to the emergence of the cosmologico-ethical, the cosmic order on which the new orientation is based must possess qualities that help us to fit into that order, and must provide the same services as the old beliefs. How does philosophy's revelation of the harmony of the world permit me to respond to the question of salvation? How can it lead me, taking into account my radical finitude, to rid myself, if not of death itself because that is impossible, at least of the fear of death, for myself or my loved ones, which in some fashion prevents me from "living well"?

The Desire for Eternity, or the First Secularization of the Problematic of Salvation

As Hannah Arendt has remarked, traditional Greek culture offered two main ways of responding to the challenges presented to humans by the unavoidable fact of mortality, two ways of conquering death, or at least our fear of death.

The first, totally natural way resides in procreation. By ensuring progeny, one could hope to join the eternal cycle of nature and take one's place in the universe of things that cannot die. The problem is, of course, that this means of access to eternity is available only to the human species: although the species is potentially immortal, the individual is born, matures, and dies, so that when human beings aim at perpetuity through procreation, they not only fail to accomplish this goal but also fail to rise above the condition of the other animal species.

The second way is more elaborate: it consists in accomplishing heroic and glorious actions capable of providing subject matter for a narrative, given that the *written record* of a life has the virtue of partially defeating transience. Indeed, for the Greek historians, beginning with Herodotus himself, the task of historiography was to rescue certain men, by relating their exceptional actions, from the oblivion threatening everything that does not belong to the realm of nature. Natural phenomena are cyclical, repeating indefinitely as day follows night, winter follows autumn, and good weather follows a storm. Their very repetition guarantees that they will not be forgotten: the natural world, in this sense, attains immortality without difficulty, whereas "all things that owe their existence to men, such as works, deeds, and words, are perishable, infected, as it were, by the mortal-

GREEK WISDOM ~ 147

ity of their authors." It was that dominance of the ephemeral that had to be fought against, at least in part, in a combat made possible by the quest for glory. According to Arendt, this was the tacit thesis of ancient historiography when, in reporting "heroic" deeds, it attempted to uproot them from the realm of the perishable and place them in the realm of nature: "If mortals succeeded in endowing their works, their deeds, and words with some permanence and in arresting their perishability, then these things would, to a degree at least, enter and be at home in the world of everlastingness, and the mortals themselves would find their place in the cosmos, where everything is immortal except men."[13]

With the birth of philosophy a third way to meet the challenge of immortality makes its entry onto the scene. Epictetus considered fear of death the ultimate motivation for an interest in philosophical wisdom, and he was surely expressing a conviction shared by all the great cosmologists. Thanks to philosophical wisdom, existential anxiety could at last reach beyond the false consolations of procreation and glory to find not one but two responses.

The first response makes no claim to change the course of things. It resides rather in a process of operating within the self, aiming less at vanquishing death than at dominating the fears aroused by death. It is not a matter of revolt, or of yielding to some consoling illusion of promised immortality, but rather of striving, with open eyes, to accept the inevitable. To paraphrase a famous Stoic formula, one cannot change the order of the world (which includes the necessity of death), but one can modify one's own expectations and desires. One way to accomplish this aim is to distinguish (as the Stoics constantly urge) between what depends on us and what does not depend on us and therefore should not frighten us. The mechanisms of this procedure for combating existential anxiety are far more profound than they might seem at first glance. I shall return to the topic. For the moment, let me simply observe that this invitation to wisdom does not challenge the reality of death, but rather attacks the pusillanimous way in which we perceive death. In this sense, Stoicism sets itself at a distance from the great religions that hold out hope for the soul's immortality.

A second response focuses more on the underlying problem. Unlike the first, it brings philosophy singularly closer to the religious attitude. According to the Stoics, the sage may attain a certain human form of eternity, if not immortality, thanks to a proper exercise of thought. Death is not the absolute end of all things, but rather a transformation, a "passage" from one state to another within a universe endowed with a *global* perfection and with a degree of *stability*, even of divinity. It is a fact that we will die, just as it is a fact that ears of wheat will one day be harvested. But does that mean, Epictetus asks, that we must veil our faces and abstain, as if out of superstition, from formulating such thoughts because they might somehow be "ill-omened"? Not at all, he replies, for "it signifies the destruction of the ears, but not of the universe." His comments deserve a moment's consideration: "Say that also for leaves to fall is ill-omened, and for the fresh fig to turn into a dried fig, and a cluster of grapes to turn into raisins. For all these things are changes of a preliminary state into something else; it is not a case of destruction, but a certain ordered dispensation and management. This is what going abroad means, a slight change; this is the meaning of death, a greater change of that which now is, not into what is not, but into what is not *now*. — Shall I, then, be no more? — No, you will not be, but something else will be, something different from that of which the universe now has need."[14] As Marcus Aurelius put it in one of his Meditations, "You exist but as a part of the Whole. You will disappear into the Whole which created you, or rather you will be taken up into the creative Reason when the change comes."[15]

To comment briefly: in this passage, unlike the first response, the disciple is not invited to change his desires rather than try to change the order of the world, to no longer desire eternity and to accept death without surrounding it with fears that are not only useless but harmful. Instead, the disciple is invited to understand that once the human being arrives at a certain level of theoretical wisdom, he will see that death does not really exist; that it is merely a passage from one state to another, not an annihilation but a different mode of being. As members of a divine and stable cosmos, we too can participate in that stability and that divinity. Provided that we understand it, we will also perceive the extent to which our fear of death is unjustified, not only subjectively but also, in a quasi-pantheistic sense, objectively.

This, Epictetus tells us, is the aim of *all philosophical activity*. It is what should permit every individual to make a success of his existence and to attain a good and happy life, because philosophy teaches not only how to live but how to die "like a god,"[16] in other words like a being who attains serenity by perceiving his privileged connection with all other beings within cosmic harmony, aware that although in one sense he is mortal, in another sense he never dies completely. This is why, Cicero tells us, tradition has sometimes attempted to "confer the deification of renown and gratitude" on such illustrious men as Hercules or Aesculapius. Because their souls "survived and enjoyed eternal life," these figures "were duly deemed divine, as being both supremely good and immortal."[17] Here Cicero is speaking *as if there were degrees in death; as if one died more or less, according to whether one was more or less wise and "aware."* From this point of view, the good life, the "successful" life, is the life that, despite Epictetus's disillusioned avowal of his own finitude, retains the closest possible connection with eternity—in this case, with the cosmic divinity to which the sage accedes by contemplation, by *theōria.* In assigning this supreme mission to philosophy, Epictetus is simply associating himself with a long tradition that goes back at least to Plato's *Timaeus,* by way of Aristotle, and that continued in odd ways even into modern philosophy among thinkers closest to the Ancients, primarily Spinoza, who is often wrongly presented as the least religious of them all.

Let us first turn to Plato and the famous passage from the *Timaeus* that speaks of the sublime powers of the superior part of man, the intellect (*nous*):

We declare that God has given to each of us, as his daemon [genius; guardian angel], that kind of soul which is housed in the top of our body and which raises us—seeing that we are not an earthly but a heavenly plant—up from earth towards our kindred in the heaven. And herein we speak most truly; for it is by suspending our head and root from that region whence the substance of our soul first came that the Divine Power keeps upright our whole body. Whoso, then, indulges in lusts or in contentions and devotes himself overmuch thereto must of necessity be filled with opinions that are wholly mortal, and altogether, so far as it is possible to become mortal, fall not short of this in even a small degree, inasmuch as he has made great his mortal part. But he who has seriously devoted himself to learning and to true thoughts, and has exercised these qualities above all his others, must necessarily and inevitably think thoughts that are immortal and divine, if so be that he lays hold on truth, and in so far as it is possible for human nature to partake of immortality, he must fall short thereof in no degree.[18]

Plato immediately adds that such a man "must be supremely blessed." Thus in order to make a success of one's life and to render it both good and happy, we must remain faithful to the divine portion of ourselves, which is the intellect. It is by means of our intellect that we attach ourselves, as if by our "roots," to the superior and divine universe of celestial harmony: "We ought to try to escape from earth to the dwelling of the gods as quickly as we can; and to escape is to become like God, so far as this is possible; and to become like God is to become righteous and holy and wise."[19]

Provided that it not remain mere discourse but be truly put into practice, philosophy should therefore enable us to make a success of our lives—*that is, "in so far as it is possible" to escape the mortal condition.* The two convictions that animate these great Platonic texts cannot fail to strike the modern reader. One conviction is that there are degrees of finitude: one might almost say that one dies "more or less" according to the degree of elevation in wisdom that one attains (or descent into folly that one suffers). This explains the extraordinary importance of philosophy and of its vocation for *salvation*—the word is not too strong. It is philosophy alone that can save us, at least in part, from the most absurd death there is: the death that we have constructed for ourselves, in a sense by our own acts, when we pursue objectives that distance us from a *reconciliation with the divine cosmos.* But just as astonishing is the symmetry of the phrase "in so far as it is possible" applied to both mortality and immortality: someone who chooses the wrong road, that of the lower, less celestial portions of the soul tending to the passions and to ambition, must prepare himself to die entirely or at least "in so far as it is possible"—that is, not completely. Similarly, someone who chooses the other road prepares himself for eternity "in so far as it is possible"—that is, without attaining it perfectly. Here we have further confirmation of the idea that there are degrees in death and that, as a part of the divine cosmos, the human being can neither die totally nor wholly achieve eternity. It is between the two that he has room to maneuver, and here is where he can fail or succeed. In a hierarchized and harmonious universe, each being has a place, miserable though it might be, and cannot totally leave that place, even by death. The fact remains—and this is the ultimate task of all human existence worthy of the name—that a being can rise within that hierarchy to the point that death, at the very limit and like an infinitesimal quantity, becomes almost nothing.

The corollary—and this is probably the ultimate meaning of this reflection on human finitude—is that there also exist *degrees in life.* Just as I die more or less, according to whether I am more or less wise (or "celestial"), so my life before the "greater change" evoked by Epictetus will be more or less intense, more or less alive, more or less worth living. Once again, philosophy comes to our rescue: it saves us not only from death but also from a failed life, not only from annihilation pure and simple (which is impossible in the absolute) but also from the impoverishment or shrinking of life itself.

Aristotle expresses a similar thought in in one of the most frequently commented passages of his *Nicomachean Ethics*, where he too defines the good life, the "theoretical or contemplative" life, as the only way to "perfect happiness" and as a means for escaping, at least in part, the condition of mere mortals. It might be said, he states, that "such a life as this will be higher than the human level: not in virtue of his humanity will a man achieve it, but in virtue of something within him that is divine. . . . If then the intellect is something divine in comparison with man, so is the life of the intellect divine in comparison with human life. Nor ought we to obey those who enjoin that a man should have man's thoughts and a mortal the thoughts of mortality, but we ought so far as possible to achieve immortality and do all that man may to live in accordance with the highest thing in him."[20]

As Pierre Aubenque neatly points out in his commentary on this text, which so evidently follows that of Plato and precedes Epictetus, we cannot accuse Aristotle of the sins of pride or exaggeration. Undeniably, such an accusation should have a broader aim, "for it is not only Aristotle's project but that of all philosophy to enter into rivalry with the gods for the possession of wisdom."[21] We find confirmation, so to speak *a fortiori*, of this view of philosophy as the great rival of theology when it reappears in the atheism of Spinoza. To be sure, philosophic "soteriology" aims less at being consoling than the theological version; it is less promising but more lucid, less enchanted but more solid, less symbolic but more rigorous. And each "less" is inverted as soon as one perceives that the apparent modesty of this statement is the surest sign of its efficacy.

Admittedly, Spinoza's doctrine does not promise the immortality of a soul separated from its mortal body. It actually does better by assuring us that already, here and now, we "feel" and "experience" that we are "eternal." Moreover, like Epictetus, Plato, and Aristotle before him, Spinoza is not concerned, as has often been wrongly suggested, to vanquish only the fear of death; rather, "in so as far as it is possible," he is seeking a way to surmount death itself. Spinoza's formulas equal what we have just read from the *Timaeus*, where Plato asserts that thanks to philosophy it is possible to die "in so far as it is possible." Like Plato, and for reasons that are less distant from his than might be thought *a priori*, Spinoza is persuaded that the wise man dies less than the fool, and the child more than the mature man because he has not had either the occasion or the time to raise himself to a true intelligence of what he is. This is why, as Gilles Deleuze emphasizes in his commentary on these passage from the *Ethics*, "what one calls a happy life is to do all that one can, and this is something that Spinoza says formally, precisely in order to conjure away premature deaths . . . in order to arrange things so that death, when it arrives, *finally concerns only the smallest part of myself.*" This implies not only conquering one's fears, which is already a fine thing, but dying the least possible, which, it must be admitted, is even better. This is what we are promised by a soteriology that can, at a stretch, be called "atheist" and "materialist," but that brings us back, at the very least, to the heart of the religious problematic.

To return to the Greeks, we can now measure to what extent the rupture with religion also signifies continuity with it: first by returning to questions about salvation, but also in the conviction that if nature takes the place of the gods, it nonetheless remains in some fashion divine and, in the root sense, "animated." We are still far from the modern concept of a universe without soul or meaning, raw material delivered over to human domination and exploitation. Not only is the cosmos organized and hierarchized; not only does it offer the image of a harmonious organization to be contemplated; it is also endowed with meaning. Thus, we may safely say, to borrow a term from of Hans Jonas, that moral ends are "domiciled" in the cosmos: it is by observing the cosmos and comprehending it by means of reason—even more, it is by imitating it—that human beings improve their chances of raising themselves toward authentic wisdom in the aim of escaping, "in so as far as it is possible," from the fear of death and even, in part, from death itself. We must explore that conviction further to gain a better understanding of how this Greek universe provides a foundation for an alternative to religions in its response to the question of the good life.

CHAPTER 8

The "Cosmologico-Ethical"

~ ~ ~ ~ ~

Power and the Charms of Moralities
Inscribed in the Cosmos

It is time to say something more about the neologism "cosmologico-ethical," which I have used to qualify the grand philosophical tradition of the Greeks from Plato's *Timaeus* and Aristotle's *Ethics* to the founding fathers of the Stoic school. This tradition was to exert a decisive influence over all of Christian Europe until the end of the Middle Ages. The term "cosmologico-ethical" may be incomprehensible for anyone who adheres to the viewpoint of the Moderns: beginning with the Galilean revolution and the appearance of the positive sciences we have thought it evident that nature as such cannot have any normative value. We can of course admire nature's beauty, its perfection, its richness, its power, perhaps even (although metaphorically) its "intelligence," but we are totally incapable of perceiving it as bearing moral values. There are two basic, intimately interconnected reasons for this.

The first is that we Moderns, the heirs of Galileo and Newton, no longer perceive the world as an organized, "animated" being: the notion of the "soul of the world," so frequent in ancient philosophy, has disappeared from our physics texts, and we take it for granted that, outside the logical systems of obscurantism or magical thought, it is absurd to imagine that the universe might not be radically neutral with regard to our ethical principles.

Moral ends belong to another sphere, that of the "should be" and not that of being, to the ideal more than to the real. These ends are now expressed in terms of imperatives and demands, in contrast to the simple factual givens of the natural realm. To put it differently, the natural sciences describe what is; they cannot, as *natural* sciences, indicate what we ought to do. I can observe the fact that big fish eat little fish without drawing the conclusion that, on the moral plane, the human world should follow the same rule. Furthermore, although egotism and the instinct of self-preservation seem manifestly to guide natural creatures, that does not mean that I should take them as a model. To the contrary, on an ethical level I may even consider it an elementary rule to struggle against those aspects of nature both within myself and outside of myself. Whatever admiration nature may arouse in us on other levels, it is not an infallible guide for conduct. Just as it would seem silly, like a superstition from a bygone age, to call a particular virus or microbe "wicked," it is equally senseless to consider the tree that gives us apples or the stream that slakes our thirst *morally* good—whatever benefit we may draw from them. Yet, to take an extreme case, even though biology teaches us that tobacco is surely harmful to our health, its consumption is still situated "beyond good and evil." That such an activity has been proved to endanger health does not in itself imply any ethical value: the question of deciding whether I prefer a short life but a good one to a long and boring existence, whether a certain number of dangerous activities are part of the short but merry life, whether I care to take the risk, and so on, cannot depend uniquely upon observation of natural events.

One might even say that our moral universe, today largely dominated by a philosophy of the rights of man, is almost entirely constructed on a rejection of what is brutal and blind in nature. Laws such as natural selection by the survival of the fittest and the elimination of the weak, for example, constitute a foil more than a model. More often than not, we assume that imitating that law would be contrary to all the values of mutual aid, charity, solidarity, and respect of others that, at one time or another, have formed the basis of our value systems, however they may differ or even contradict one another. It has thus become clear to us that nature, in the best of cases, is morally *indifferent;* that it corresponds to the sphere of fact and not to that of law. Perhaps certain visions of the world—Nazism, for example—have at times attempted to set up nature as an ideal for human behaviors, but such visions have hardly succeeded in becoming universal on the ethical level, to put it mildly.

Nonetheless, we need to be clear from the start and must eliminate a misunderstanding that might arise from these remarks on differences between the Ancients and the Moderns. Although the Greeks invite us to imitate nature and to draw our ethical values from it, they had absolutely no intention of speaking in favor of brute force, egotism, or a natural selection aimed at the weak. In order to comprehend their conception of the "cosmologico-ethical"—a morality rooted in the cosmos—we must recall that their representation of nature was in many ways totally different from our own. We tend to see natural reality more as a vast field of forces embodied (or not) in organized beings; it offers a spectacle of a permanent confrontation, of a war of all against all, rather than a well-regulated arrangement in which harmony, cooperation, and solidarity occupy an essential place.[1] Hence, the dictum that one must "imitate nature" can have totally different, if not contrary, meanings according to context. For the Ancients, not only was nature characterized primarily by a harmonious order rather than by a perpetual, mortal struggle for survival (although they were not unaware of that aspect of reality); nature was also, in itself and by itself, the bearer of the highest moral values. Ethical ends could therefore seem "domiciled" in it. Not only could people find a guide for conduct in the cosmic order; but it was their obligation to decipher in the cosmos— given sufficient practice in contemplation—the ultimate ends and the meaning of mortal life. This "conception of the world" is what I have in mind when using the term "cosmologico-ethical."

As Rémi Brague has written in a fine work on the "wisdom of the world": "For our ancestors . . . man could, in fact should borrow the criterion of his action from nature. Nature was then the source of morality. As a consequence one could turn physics into a propaedeutic to ethics."[2] The Stoics, who were perhaps the first to articulate systematically the various parts of philosophy, made a point of doing just that, as attested by an aphorism of Chrysippus, the second director of the Stoic school: "There is no other means, or more appropriate means, to reach a definition of good and bad things, of virtue, and happiness, than by starting from common nature and from the government of the world."[3] It is as if the cosmos were an open book in which we must learn to decipher the ends of man—which certainly does not imply that man can do without reflection or give up using his reason, because it is reason that enables him comprehend nature's signs. The fact remains, however, that for the Stoics the ends of morality are *objectively*, and not merely subjectively, inscribed in the very being of the world, with the result that the path to a comprehension of what is proper to man and to man's supreme ends on this earth—or, if you like, an adequate perception of the meaning of his life—is through the cosmos. In this tradition of Platonic origin, anthropology and the cosmos are inseparable, as Brague shows in a passage in his book that perfectly focuses on the difference between the Ancients and the Moderns in this context—the difference between the universe of the cosmologico-ethical or the "wisdoms of the world," on the one hand, and the universe of humanism and the "rights of man," on the other:

> It is indeed nature, and not physical science alone, that determines man's humanity; nature as an object of study, not the study of nature as the activity of a subject. The ethical value of physics does not come from the human process of learning, but from nature itself. . . . The world, and above all that which is most cosmic in the world— the sky—provided ancient and medieval man with brilliant evidence that good is not only a possibility, but a triumphant reality. Cosmology has an ethical dimension. In turn, the task of transporting such good into the here below where we live enriches ethics with a cosmological dimension. It is through the mediation of the world that man becomes what he must be, consequently, what he is. Wisdom thus defined is indeed a "wisdom of the world."[4]

It would be hard to express this point any better, and Brague is right to insist that the determination of the ends of man belongs, in this grand tradition of the Greek cosmologies, *to nature itself.* Seneca, among many other heirs of these earliest philosophical visions of the world, clearly perceived this: "I follow the guidance of Nature—a doctrine upon which all Stoics are agreed. Not to stray far from Nature and to mould ourselves according to her law and pattern—this is true wisdom."[5] Cicero states: "Man himself however came into existence for the purpose of contemplating and imitating the world; he is by no means perfect, but he is 'a small fragment of that which is perfect.' . . . Again, man's nature is not perfect, yet virtue may be realized in man, how much more readily then in the world! Therefore the world possesses virtue. Therefore it is wise, and consequently divine."[6] Clearly, it is not the way we look at it that constitutes the ultimate foundation of ethical values, but being itself, the cosmos as such, because it is "divine." That does not mean, of course, that human beings are relieved of the tasks of study and learning. If they were, what would be the good of philosophizing? What would be the good of granting value to *theōria,* the contemplation of that very divine, or of recommending that the schools teach physics and logic as a preliminary to ethics? The use of reason obviously remains indispensable. Reason is nonetheless fragile, difficult, and at times uncertain, for it does not give way before nature as it would before a revelation delivering ready-made verities, self-contained and self-referential truths that are handed to us and require no effort of thought.

Reason itself, however, as the Stoics constantly remind us, is not an entity external to the cosmos: it is instead its most intimate and most divine structure. Men participate in reason but are not its proprietors; they do not own it as if it were a simple tool, a neutral instrument capable of being applied in a wholly subjective manner to an external universe unconnected with it. In short, we are still at the opposite end of the scale from what the Moderns would later call "technique" (using a word of Greek origin)— that is, an "instrumental reason" characterized both by radical indifference to the ends that it might be called upon to pursue and by its no less radical externality in relation to the real, which it seeks to transform, to manipulate, and to explicate rather than to contemplate. Here the order of the world and reason form two facets of one entity, as Socrates suggests in a famous passage in the *Republic:*

> A man who has his understanding truly turned toward the things that *are* has no leisure to look down toward the affairs of human beings and to be filled with envy and ill will as a result of fighting with them. But, rather, because he sees and contemplates things that are set in a regular arrangement and are always in the same condition— things that neither do injustice to one another nor suffer it at one another's hands, but remain all in order according to reason—he imitates them and, as much as possible, makes himself like them. Or do you suppose there is any way of keeping someone from imitating that which he admires and therefore keeps company with?[7]

For Plato the answer is obviously no, and it is quite clear from this passage that the great cosmologies of the ancient world were deeply persuaded, not only of the beauty of the world, but also of its goodness.

These characteristics of the Greek cosmos make it possible (a possibility that we have in great part lost) for humans to use them to create a representation of the good life. We need a firm understanding of them if we are to grasp their consequences for an ultimate comprehension of the relationship between ethics and the cosmology on which that representation depends, albeit in a complex, nonmechanical fashion.

In the first place, this cosmos is *a world radically "transcendent" in relation to humans.* This notion calls for clarification, as it can lend itself to confusion. In contrast to monotheistic religions, the notion of transcendence here does not refer to the representation of a being situated in a beyond totally foreign to the real universe. It is, rather, a "transcendence within immanence": the cosmic order and the harmony of the universe exist solely as embodied in that universe; they are not, strictly speaking, abstract ideal objects or beings. Nonetheless, from the human viewpoint they constitute external and superior principles, if Chrysippus is correct when he states that "the heavenly bodies and all those things that display a never-ending regularity cannot be created by man."[8] Thus we are dealing with transcendence not in relation to natural reality but in relation to the individuals who make up humanity and participate in natural reality only as infinitely small parts of an organism as imposing as it is admirable.

That order, organized as a living, harmonious, and good being, is divine. Here Cicero defends the Stoic tradition against Epicurean criticism of the great cosmologies, a criticism that he thinks so foreign to the ancient world that he almost doubts whether Epicurus is really Greek:

> Let Epicurus jest at this notion as he will—and he is a person who jokes with difficulty, and has but the slightest smack of his native Attic wit,—let him protest his inability to conceive of god as a round and rotating body. Nevertheless he will never dislodge me from one belief which even he himself accepts: he holds that gods exist, on the ground that there must necessarily be some mode of being of outstanding and supreme excellence; now clearly nothing can be more excellent than the world. Nor can it be doubted that a living being endowed with sensation, reason and intelligence must excel a being devoid of those attributes; hence it follows that the world is a living being and possesses sensation, intelligence and reason; and this argument leads to the conclusion that the world is god.[9]

This is exactly what today's physics prohibits us from thinking and, consequently, what keeps us from basing ethics in a cosmos that we can no longer find.

No matter. For the Greeks, with the notable exception of the Epicureans and perhaps the Sophists, that divinization of the world that makes it, in the etymological sense, the privileged object of *theōria,* provides a foundation for unequaled qualities of harmony,[10] and for attributes worthy of imitation by a human wisdom, in the sense indicated in a remarkable passage from the *Meditations* of Marcus Aurelius. He states: "One should continually think of the universe as one living being, with one substance and one soul—how all it contains falls under its one unitary perception. . . . What happens next is always intimately related to what went before. It is not a question of merely adding up disparate things connected by inevitable succession, but events are logically interdependent. Just as the realities are established in tune with one another, so, in the world of sense, phenomena do not occur merely in succession, but they display an amazing affinity with one another."[11]

We see here that the universe, as Jacques Brunschwig stresses, obeys the mechanical order of the efficient causes that link historical events, but also, like a living being, is governed by an internal systematic order:

> The cosmic picture is clothed in biological and vitalist colors: the differences between natural beings are of degree rather than of nature, and the world itself is imagined, according to the ancient analogy of the microcosm and the macrocosm, as possessing the properties that its most perfected parts posses: life, to begin with, but also the sensitivity characteristic of an animal and the rationality characteristic of man. It would not be contrary to the spirit of the Stoa to say that man is "at home" in this great warm cocoon that resembles him, where everything that is not man is made for him, where evil is but an illusion, a detail, or an inevitable ransom for the good. Still, we must add that man himself, a rational but mortal animal, does not achieve fulfillment except by acknowledging the whole of which he is a part, a great, perfect, rational being—that is, God. Fate is a form of providence, at the last stage of initiation into the mysteries (the image is from Chrysippus) physics turns out to be a theology.[12]

So the world that is harmonious and organized like a living being is also just and good. Marcus Aurelius declares with a serenity that derives from certitude, "'Everything which happens, is right.' Examine this saying carefully and you will find it so. I do not mean right merely in the sense that it fits the pattern of events, but in the sense of just, as if someone were giving each his due."[13] The sentiment that evil exists in nature is thus an error connected to prejudice. The error occurs because we judge the value of the whole by relying only on the observation of an extremely small part of the universe, the part in which we live, the "sublunary" world. But we are looking through the wrong side of the magnifying glass, and the disorders we sometimes see in the universe are infinitely small in comparison with the beauty and the perfection of the whole. According to Aristotle, those who think the world is imperfect "deserve censure in that they have maintained about the whole material universe what they have observed in the case of a mere minority of sensible things. For it is only the realm of sense around us which continues subject to destruction and generation, but this is a practically negligible part of the whole; so that it would have been fairer for them to acquit the former on the ground of the latter than to condemn the latter on account of the former."[14] One cannot judge the whole by considering infinitesimal parts. Where we have acquired the conviction that nature is morally neutral, or even too violent to furnish any ethical model, the Ancients were animated by the conviction that "the evil that reigns here on earth is basically only an exception. The rule that it confirms is manifest in the regularity and majestic order of celestial movements. It is owing to that order that the world deserves its Greek name of *Kosmos,* which rightly means 'order,' good arrangement, arranged and harmoniously articulated totality, etc. Here below it is possible that everything is falling apart; above, 'all is order there, and beauty.'"[15] We shall return to the implications of this ancient pantheism when we take a closer look at Stoic wisdom and its final response to the question of the good life. Two thoughts need to be stated now, however: first, for the Greeks, reason must not be thought of as merely a human faculty, subjective, instrumental, and external to the real, but rather as an objective and common order in which both we and the world itself participate in equal measure;[16] second, we must take the real itself as an ethical model.

It is because the cosmos is endowed with the qualities we have just seen that it turns out to be *an intrinsically moral world, and it is in that affirmation, of course, that the idea of a cosmologico-ethical finally takes on its full meaning.* In his *De finibus bonorum et malorum* (On good and evil ends), Cicero explains with exemplary clarity why, in the Stoic vision of the world, physics—that is, the study of the cosmos—possesses a dimension that is immediately or intrinsically ethical:

> He who is to live in accordance with nature must base his principles upon the system and government of the entire world. Nor again can anyone judge truly of things good and evil, save by a knowledge of the whole plan of nature and also of the life of the gods, and of the answer to the question of whether the nature of man is or is not in harmony with that of the universe. And no one without Natural

Philosophy can discern the value (and their value is very great) of the ancient maxims and precepts of the Wise Men, such as to "obey occasion," "follow God," "know thyself" and "moderation in all things" Also this science alone can impart a conception of the power of nature in fostering justice and maintaining friendship and the rest of the affections.[17]

Not only do the maxims that Cicero cites give a faithful translation of the mental universe of Stoicism and more generally of the great Greek cosmologies, but this passage also shows how far Cicero is from modern thought. It is inadequate merely to suggest that the study of nature might be "useful" to moral life or that we might find salutary correction by drawing certain teachings from nature; rather, Cicero asserts that man's ends, the objectives that he should propose for himself on the ethical plane, *are lodged at the very heart of the real,* domiciled in a nature that Cicero, as we have seen, views as conscious and wise—"all things are under the sway of nature and are carried on by her in the most excellent manner"—and that he calls "the sustaining and governing principle of the world."[18] That is to say, contrary to what moralists of the modern age were to teach,[19] values are situated in being and not in the should-be; they are rooted in facts and not hanging from an ideal of "law."[20] Although it seems exotic to us, this vision of the cosmologico-ethical is easy to understand when it is associated with the organic metaphor that dominates the representation of the cosmos: if the order of the world resembles a living organism, it is clear that within it every being possesses a function of its own, a particular intended purpose. How could one not think it preferable, under those conditions, that such purposes be realized, and realized well, rather than remaining virtual? It is on this model that the idea of a finality immanent in the real can acquire a coherent meaning. It is also by following this road that one can imagine an almost "objective" response to the question of the good life. The wisdom of the world that prevailed in Europe during the long period from antiquity to the end of the Middle Ages can no longer be our own, if only because of evolutions in modern science.[21] The fact remains, however, that it still exerts a strong appeal, to which we cannot be indifferent. It still speaks to us, provided that we take the trouble to analyze its innermost mechanisms.

It has often been said of the grand moral visions rooted in Greek cosmology that they were, first and foremost, eudaemonistic: that their ultimate ideal was exclusively happiness on this earth. We cannot rule out the possibility that the ethical convictions founded on the idea of a harmonious cosmos may have defeated all forms of anxiety, that they may have succeeded in vanquishing the existential fears that prevent humans from living in serenity, and that the Greek sage may have been the happiest of men. If nature is good and if it is divine, whatever fate it reserves for us fully merits the name of providence, and, like Christians or Muslims who humbly put their fate into the hands of God and learn to accept that fate with joy, the Stoic must be able to assert tranquilly, with Epictetus: "Always I wish rather the thing which takes place. For I regard God's will as better than my will."[22] God is probably not a real person here, as he is in monotheistic representations, but rather just another name for nature. The fact remains that one can trust this cosmic nature as if it were a god; we can, so to speak, let ourselves be carried along by it as by a gentle and welcoming wave. Even when fate seems contrary to our desires, we must be able to accept it without ceding to unhappiness, because "the rational animal, man, possesses faculties that enable him to consider all these things, both that he is a part of them, and what kind of part of them he is, and that it is well for the parts to yield to the whole." We shall return in the next chapter to the deeper philosophical themes of this "wisdom of providence." It is already clear, however, that in the age of the Greeks and still today, the idea of providence offers its disciples a dual benefit: on the one hand, confidence, like faith, is destined to chase away anxiety; on the other hand, cosmology provides the basis for an attitude that is in radical rupture with a common consciousness immersed in daily life.

Epictitus's *Discourses* leave no doubt regarding the first of these benefits: the good life is a life without hopes or fears, a life reconciled to what is. But how could this reconciliation come about if not guided by the conviction that the world is divine, harmonious, and good? From "your own mind" you must cast out "grief, fear, desire, envy, joy at others' ills; cast out greed, effeminacy, incontinency. These things you cannot cast out in any other way than by looking to God alone, being specially devoted to Him only, and consecrated to His commands. But if you wish anything else, with lamentation and groaning you will follow that which is stronger than you are, ever seeking outside yourself for peace, and never able to be at peace. For you seek peace where it is not, and neglect to seek it where it is."[23] Once again, this injunction must be read in a "cosmic" or pantheistic sense rather than a religious one: God is simply equivalent to the cosmos, another name for universal reason, a visage of the fate that we must accept and even wish for with all our soul, although as victims of the illusions of the common consciousness, we always think we must stand up to God in our attempts to bend him to our desires: the philosopher "should put his own will into harmony with what happens, so that neither anything that happens happens against our will, nor anything that fails to happen fails to happen when we wish it to happen. The result of this for those who have so ordered the work of philosophy is that in desire they are not disappointed, and in aversion they do not fall into what they would avoid; that each person passes his life to himself, free from pain, fear, and perturbation."

It goes without saying that such injunctions seem *a priori* absurd to common mortals, who can see little in them other than a particularly inane form of "quietism." Wisdom passes for folly in the eyes of the greatest number because it rests on a vision of the world, a cosmology, that can be thoroughly understood only through an extraordinary exercise of theoretical thinking. But is that not precisely what distinguishes philosophy from ordinary discourse, and is it not by such means that it acquires a unique fascination? As Pierre Hadot states: "This is a complete reversal of the usual way of looking at things. We move from a 'human' vision of reality, in which our value judgments depend on social conventions and on our passions, to a 'natural' or 'physical' vision of things, which restitutes each event within the perspective of nature and universal Reason."[24]

Once again we see here to what extent philosophy is, from the start, the paradoxical heir of religions: not only does it invite us to a veritable *conversion*, a thought experience after which nothing will be as it was before, everything will be different from ordinary life, but it does so in the name of a principle that is clearly not human—the cosmic principle that, as we have seen, although immanent in the world, embodies a radical transcendence in relation to humans. In order to understand how ancient philosophy responds to the question of the good life, we will need to investigate this principle further. On this path we can find no better guides than the Stoic philosophers. Without a doubt, in fact, in Greek antiquity it was they who accorded the most importance to that question.[25]

CHAPTER 9

An Ideal-Type of Ancient Wisdom

~ ~ ~ ~ ~

The Case of Stoicism

In conformity with the custom of designating philosophical schools by the names of the places in which they became established, the word "Stoicism" derives from the Greek, *stoa,* or portico: the founding father of the doctrine, Zeno of Citium (ca. 334–262), taught in Athens under arcades "covered with paintings" (*stoa poikilē*). His lessons, which were free and public, received considerable acclaim, to the point that at his death his disciples continued his teaching. The first of Zeno's successors was Cleanthes of Assus (ca. 331–230); and the second, Chrysippus of Soles (ca. 280–208). These three great names together form what is usually called "Old Stoicism." Aside from one brief poem, a "Hymn to Zeus" by Cleanthes, practically nothing has been preserved of the many works of the early Stoics. We know that they wrote important works on the three major divisions of their philosophy—logic, physics, and ethics—but because these works are lost, we know their thought only indirectly, with many lacunae and probably many distortions—through much later authors (Cicero, for example), many of them hostile to Stoic thought (Plutarch, for example); or through the authors of manuals or collections of the opinions, aphorisms, or maxims of the ancient philosophers (by Diogenes Laertius, for example), whose statements must be interpreted with caution.

The second, or "Middle," period of the Stoic school, mainly in the second century B.C., is even less well known than the first: Diogenes of Babylon, Antipater of Tarsus, Penaetius of Rhodes, and Posidonius of Apamea are its principal representatives.

The great works of the third wave, that of imperial or "Late Stoicism," are, in contrast, much more accessible. They come to us, not from philosophers who headed the school and lived at Athens, but from a member of the Roman imperial court, Seneca (ca. 8 B.C.–A.D. 65), who was also the tutor and minister of Nero; from Musonius Rufus (A.D. 25–80), who taught Stoicism at Rome was persecuted by Nero; from Epictetus (ca. 50–130), a freed slave whose oral teaching was faithfully transmitted by disciples, notably by Arrian (Flavius Arrianus), the author of the famous *Discourses of Epictetus* and the *Manual* (*Encheiridion*, or *Handbook*);[1] and finally from the emperor Marcus Aurelius himself (121–180).

The relative scarcity of the works that have come down to us in their original state contrasts singularly with the extraordinary importance and permanence of Stoicism throughout history, from its birth in fourth-century Greece down to the modern age. Montaigne, Descartes, and Pascal were imbued with it; it prompted discussion by Kant, Hegel, and Nietzsche. How are we to explain this? Quite certainly by the power of a cosmological message that permits both the great and the humble of this world (that is, both Marcus Aurelius and Epictetus) to offer a concrete response to the question of the good life. Their teaching begins with a distinction that, somewhat oddly, can seem both simple and contestable. We shall see that it is more profound than it first appears. Here is where we need to begin if we want to see how the ideal of wisdom was derived from it and how that ideal managed to attain a power of conviction sufficiently impressive to last through the ages.

Distinguishing between What Depends on Us and What Does Not

The fundamental, omnipresent, tenet of the Stoic doctrine is presented by Epictetus in these terms in his *Manual:* "Some things are under our control, while others are not under our control. Under our control are conception, choice, desire, aversion, and, in a word, everything that is our own doing; not under our control are our body, our property, reputation, office, and, in a word, everything that is not our own doing."[2] Included in the latter category, according to Epictetus, are sickness and health, wealth and poverty, pleasure and pain, beauty and ugliness, fame and obscurity, and, of course, life and death. Pierre Hadot offers the following commentary on this text:

Everything in our life escapes us. The result of this is that people are unhappy because they passionately seek to acquire things which they cannot obtain and flee evils which are inevitable. There is one thing, and only one, which does depend on us and which nothing can tear away from us: the will to do good and to act in conformity with reason. There is thus a radical opposition between what depends on us and can therefore be either good or bad, since it is the object of our decision, and what depends not on us but on external causes and fate and which is therefore indifferent. The will to do good is an unbreachable fortress which everyone can construct within themselves.[3]

One can hardly imagine a better summary of Stoic thought. In spite of its apparent simplicity, however, this passage raises three formidable problems that will have to be resolved before we can comprehend the full breadth of the Stoic response to the question of the good life.

On attentive examination of the list that the Stoics themselves usually give of the things that do not depend on us, we notice first that they seem somewhat odd to today's reader. We can certainly agree that some things in our lives escape our control, beginning with the most important of these—the inevitable facts that we will all grow older and die, that an accident or an illness can take away our health or our mind, that tragedy can befall our loved ones without our being able to do anything about it, among others. But just how does that prove that everything that happens is totally beyond our control? Is there no middle term between all and nothing? Take wealth, for instance, which is often mentioned by the Stoics as the best example of what does not depend on us: can it not, at least in part, be the result of our efforts, our talents, or our enterprise? And what about prudence, which will permit me to avoid certain accidents or certain illnesses and to conserve my life and my health longer? Is exercising prudence not in part my responsibility? In other words: what are the suppositions underlying the conviction that everything that goes on in the world radically escapes our control, and how is it that only the internality of the self—the "inner citadel" in Hadot's terms—falls within our competence?[4]

Next, Hadot's text supposes (although it does not state explicitly) a definition of virtue that may also seem more than a bit odd. Yet it, too, seems "close to us." Virtue resides in action that is free and "in conformity with reason." Indeed, why not? But we can understand this in two quite contrary ways. In a modern, Kantian sense, to act in conformity with reason is, more often than not, to undertake to *struggle against nature within oneself and against the course of the world outside of oneself.* For example, one acts "reasonably" in opposing the irrational in injustices, inequalities, threats to the rights of man, exploitation, and the like. It is obviously not in this sense that Stoic virtue should be understood, because its starting point is the principle that any influence on the course of the world is denied us. That being the case, in what does this totally internal virtue consist? What exactly does it change if it in no way modifies events themselves? And is it not a pretty sorry liberty and a chilly sort of ethics that would guide us in making a virtue of necessity? "The willing soul Fate leads," Seneca tells us, "but the unwilling [it] drags along."[5] Is this the only room for maneuvering that Stoicism leaves us?

Finally, this message also implies that all of our unhappiness stems from the fact that we have not distinguished well enough between what does and does not depend on us. Here again, at first glance this seems comprehensible and coherent: we are unhappy because we tend to strive for objectives that are totally out of our reach or flee from ills that are out of our control. All very well. But does this mean that all we have to do to be happy is to be virtuous and accept the course of the world as it is? If that is the case, we would have to accept the equation "virtue = reason = happiness." Fair enough. But are we really sure that it is sufficient to be virtuous and to act rationally to attain happiness? Does not reality give us endless examples of the opposite: of virtuous but unhappy individuals, and of evil ones unjustly rewarded by social success, money, honors, society's recognition, and—why not?—the love of those around them?

These questions may help to clarify the three essential themes that function as the three pillars of Stoic thought: first, the precise foundations of the "cosmological" determinism that provides basic justification for this famous distinction, but also the conviction that everything that happens in this world is beyond our control—except for the perception (which may be a vague feeling or the product of reflection) that we have of those events, which can introduce fundamental changes in the meaning that we give to life. Next, and as if in compensation, the status of the freedom that seems to reign only at the heart of the "inner citadel." Finally, the definition of virtue that results from this and the connections it maintains with the ideal of a blessed life.

1. A Resolutely Deterministic Cosmology. It is within Stoic physics, within cosmology, that we should seek the answer to our first question. This segment of philosophy will give us a better understanding of a first and basic equation in Stoicism that declares that there is perfect equivalence between the three terms "God," "nature," and "reason." *Deus sive natura sive ratio* we might say, parodying Spinoza: there exists an order of the world, a cosmological system that is perfectly *determined, rational, and divine.* The *logos*— in other words, the rational—is the essence of this ordering, which means that reason is at once objective (it is the most intimate structure of the world insofar as the world is harmonious), subjective (it is the mode of thought specific to us as humans), and divine (it is the reconciliation or the very identity of these two orders).[6] As Cicero states, commenting on Stoic thought: "The world possesses wisdom, and . . . the element which holds all things in its embrace is pre-eminently and perfectly rational, and therefore the world is god, and all the forces of the world are held together by the divine nature."[7] Of course, this perfect rationality of the universe also implies that nothing occurs in it without reason. Every event necessarily has a cause, and Chrysippus, for example, cannot find words harsh enough against "men [the Epicureans] who constrain nature with no cause."[8] The Stoics keep insisting, against Epicurus and his disciples, that "there is no movement without a cause." They add, "If this is so, everything happens . . . by fate." Pierre Hadot comments on this formula: "The slightest event implies the entire series of causes, the linkage of all previous events, and finally the whole universe. Whether people like it or not, then, things thus necessarily happen the way they happen. Universal Reason cannot act otherwise, precisely because it is perfectly rational."[9] Following this line of thought, Chrysippus uses rhetorical devices prefiguring the famous anecdote of Buridan's ass to present a forceful defense of the idea that events we take to be without cause (because they are undetermined) are actually engendered by an implacable mechanism that has simply escaped our attention. Plutarch brings up the case of "dice and scales and many of the things that cannot fall or incline now one way and now another without the occurrence of some cause, that is of some variation either entirely in the things themselves or in their environment, it being [Chrysippus's] contention that the uncaused is altogether non-existent and so is the spontaneous and that in these movements which some people imagine and call adventitious obscure causes insinuate themselves and without our notice direct our impulse in one way or the other."[10] As was the case later with Spinoza, belief in the indetermination of the world is simply one of the many facets of our ignorance of the causes that utterly determine the least event that takes place in the world.

This is why, in the final analysis, all that is *in the world*—that is, the totality of everything that is, outside of *our reflective thought inasmuch as it is immaterial*,[11] belongs to the list of the things that do not depend on us: health does not, any more than life; suffering does not, any more than death; even honors, wealth, love, and friendship do not depend on us. Everything is determined, through and through, in the course of things, if one can believe this anticipation of Spinoza, and it is why we need to learn not to desire the impossible, not to want to flee ills or seek goods that in no way depend on our will. That intellectual error will surely lead to moral misery.

This leads to our second question: What can we say, under these conditions, about virtue, which, we are told, depends on our freedom? Should we not eventually, again like Spinoza, reduce freedom to a simple "intelligence of necessity"? Virtue seems excluded by this determinism, and yet ethics requires it: What would be the use of philosophizing and why should one preach wisdom if nothing, absolutely nothing—not even the fact of grasping the distinction between things that do and do not depend on us, which is supposed to raise us up to wisdom—requires us to exercise liberty? We humans must have some choice available to us, if only the choice between virtue—even a totally internal virtue—and its opposite in order for ethics to be meaningful. And yet physics seems to make that impossible. How to resolve this contradiction?

2. On the Nature of Liberty: What, Precisely, Depends on Us and Why Is It Important to Be Aware of It? As is obvious, Stoic liberty is not that of the Moderns. It is not free will, the power to choose between possible things as if we could look down on the world from some great height; nor does it reside in some sort of faculty for transforming the world. We have just seen that the world is totally determined and that everything in it in no way depends on us. If everything happens according to an order that is, while harmonious and good, completely beyond the reach of our will, then we should, Epictetus tells us, learn to live with "this ordaining" in mind, and should "go to receive instruction, not in order to change the construction of things,—for this is neither vouchsafed us nor is it better that it should be,—but in order that, things about us being as they are and as their nature is, we may, for our own part, keep our wills in harmony with what happens."[12]

Unhappily for them, most people choose the attitude of rebellion, carried away by a senseless passion the minute reality opposes their subjective desires. But this is pure illusion: we can always imagine that by refusing to accept fate we are choosing to oppose the entire cosmos, but—aside from the fact that this supposed "choice" has already from all eternity been part of our fate—the only result, as Marcus Aurelius teaches his disciple, is that the poor fool who attempts such a rebellion ends up as a pitiful member torn away from its body: "If you ever saw a severed hand or foot, or a severed head lying somewhere apart from the rest of the body—that is what a man makes himself like, as far as he can, when he refuses to accept his lot and sets himself apart, or performs an unsocial act. Suppose you have torn yourself away from the unity of nature of which you had been born a part, and from which you have cut yourself off."[13] The metaphor is pertinent: it skillfully presents the cosmos as an organized body, and anyone who detaches himself from it is like a member or an organ that, once separated from the body, has no consciousness and no life. A fairly similar attitude—in a quite different but still analogous perspective—can be found in certain currents of Christian fundamentalism: to complain of one's fate on undergoing a reversal of fortune, losing a loved one, contracting a serious illness, and so forth, borders on blasphemy, because if everything happens in this world according to the will of God, the true believer must not only reject rebellion but submit himself to providence *with a joy that goes far beyond all resignation.*

To state the matter clearly: for the Stoics, the "choice" of someone who rebels—to the extent that this is an authentic choice, of course—is at once irrational, illusory, unfortunate, and, by that very fact, immoral. These four points merit a brief comment. The choice is *irrational* because it results from an error of judgment concerning the rationality of the world and the nature of what does and does not depend on us; it is *illusory* because this rejection changes nothing in the order of the world, which, to parody Seneca, pulls us or pushes us whether we like it or not. If man is like a dog attached to a cart, he will trot along quietly behind the cart, accepting his fate; but if he refuses to accept it, nothing will change fundamentally, except that he will be dragged along willy-nilly. To further refine the argument: given that his supposed choice is an integral part of fate (a fact he is unaware of), it is not even the expression of an authentic liberty. The choice is *unfortunate* because the result of his rebellion is inevitable: cut off from the cosmos, human beings are destined for unhappiness. Confusing what depends on him with what does not, he ceaselessly pursues goals that will always escape him in the end. Thus he loses all the happiness of a true reconciliation with his natural, reasonable habitat. Finally, it is *immoral* because—as we now can understand—virtue resides in that very reconciliation or (and this amounts to the same) in a life in conformity with divine, cosmic, and universal reason.

Before discussing this point, however, we need to draw the proper conclusions regarding the true nature of human liberty. Authentic liberty is obviously not a liberty that one directs against the world, as if from the outside, in order to change it in the name of an indignation born of rebellion; rather, it consists in comprehending, accepting, and loving the world. Here again the Stoics foreshadow Spinoza's response to the question: liberty, in fact, is nothing more than the intelligence of necessity. It is not free will, but liberation; not an intangible given inherent in the human species, but the ultimate result of a process by means of which we can progressively liberate ourselves from "reformist" or "revolutionary" illusions by understanding exactly what depends on us and what does not. Is this notion self-contradictory, as Plutarch believed?[14] Possibly. But the Stoics themselves, in any event, thought it perfectly logical to affirm that human reason, far from standing opposed to liberty because it would reveal the causes of events, is its supreme auxiliary; that reason is actually liberty itself because it constitutes the royal road to universal Reason, to the cosmic and divine order; and that a correct understanding of this order must enable us to conquer all fear, including the fear of death, and to attain the blissful life.

What difference does this make, some might ask, if the course of the world remains unchanged? All the difference, the Stoics respond. As Pierre Hadot suggests, what changes is *the meaning one gives it.* "The form of reason proper to human beings is not universal Reason—the substantial, formative reason which is immediately immanent within things. Instead, it is a discursive reason, which has the power, in judgments and in the discourses it enunciates about reality, to give meaning to the events which Fate imposes upon it and the actions it produces. Human passions, as well as morality, are also situated within this universe of meaning."[15]

Everything plays out, in fact, not in deeds that transforms the world, but in thought that gives meaning to the real or, more precisely, to the relations that we maintain with the real. This is the ultimate meaning of Seneca's anecdote; it is what makes the difference between someone who is led by fate and someone who is dragged along by it. The former understands and serenely accepts what happens to him. Having "let go," he bathes in the serenity of letting things take their course—and here Stoicism resembles certain aspects of Buddhism. It is hardly surprising to find something similar in the metaphor of the archer or the spear thrower in Cicero's commentary on the Stoics: if he is wise, he will do his best to aim straight; hitting the mark can be wished for, but it is not to be sought for its own sake. This is because success in that objective never depends completely on him: a sudden breeze, an earthquake, a defective bow or arrow can keep him from hitting it. What *is* in his power is to do his best, to carry on with order and calm, according to nature, and if he has done this well he will be satisfied and happy. Whether he strikes the mark or not will change nothing in his well-being, for the meaning of his action was not to change the world but to put himself in accord with it. It is also this access to meaning that permits us to deliver ourselves of passions and to attain "ataraxia," peace of soul, and a life that is ultimately successful. If we become impassioned, if we are carried away by our emotions, if we hope or fear, it is because we have not understood the true distinction between what depends on us and what does not. Doing so not only guarantees unhappiness but also promises the absence of virtue, which means the absence of reason and, in the last analysis, the absence of excellence and wisdom

3. The Equation "Intelligence = Virtue = Liberty = Happiness." The equivalence of intelligence, virtue, liberty, and happiness is the culmination of Stoic thought. It merits commentary because today we may find it quite surprising: for us Moderns, the four individual terms not only do not imply each other but, for the most part, are radically opposed to each other. Reality offers us daily examples of happy fools, unhappy virtuous persons, the wicked unjustly rewarded, as well as examples—rarer, to be sure—of worthy persons who sacrifice their happiness to the demands of liberty. At first view, that is. But in the Stoic perspective, this is just the froth on the surface of things. According to what we have seen in the preceding pages, we can connect the four terms of the equation without much difficulty. Reason reveals the harmony of the cosmos and helps us to perceive that fate is out of our hands. At this point, virtue consists in reconciling ourselves with that perfect world, in wanting and loving what is, rather than in ceding to the torment of unsatisfied desires. This is how we attain true liberty, which is emancipation, mastery of the self, hence happiness, given that from that point on nothing can deceive us or frighten us.

As might be imagined, thanks to the doctrinal rigor of its formulation, this "wisdom of the world" has been the target of criticism throughout history. By reviewing these critiques, we may see how, despite some basic objections,

Stoicism was able to deliver a message of life whose principal themes—beyond the limits specific to a particular epoch—are astonishingly pertinent for us today.

Plutarch, in "On Stoic Self-Contradictions," was among the first to point out a difficulty that seems to have affected Stoic thought from the outset. It is less evident but more troublesome than it might seem at first sight, and it involves an opposition between external determinism and internal liberty. We can certainly understand what led the Stoics to posit the two terms: without the hypothesis of a fate just as implacable in its whole as it is minute in its detailed workings, reality would immediately be a source of anxiety again. If I do not have an entire and absolute conviction that the course of the world escapes my control in every way, and if, as a consequence, I introduce even the slightest idea that by my free action I might be able to bend or modify that course, then I lose all possibility of adhering to it with the serenity and the quietude recommended by Stoicism. In order to accept fate, I must be absolutely certain that it is truly a destiny—that is, a series of events occurring by means of a mechanism regulated completely outside of my personal will. But unless I also accept a minimum of liberty—be it uniquely in the sphere of pure internality inherent to my consciousness—how can I even distinguish between a disciple who *tries* to live well and one who understands none of the philosopher's enlightened advice? What is the source, if not of free choice, at least of the difference between someone who performs his philosophical exercises with the aim of rightly accepting the real in order to live in conformity with nature and someone else who gives himself over to the most foolish passions? We need only reflect for a moment to understand that even in Stoicism the idea of free will cannot be totally eradicated, because the ideas of effort and virtue and the notion of spiritual exercise suppose it, so to speak, *a priori*. Furthermore, why should the philosopher waste his time transmitting his doctrine to students if he does not think that a comprehension of the truth could permit them to make *the choice* of a good, intelligent, and virtuous life rather than an unreasonable and unhappy one? But, under these conditions, what place shall we accord to that liberty, which seems so totally opposed to the idea of destiny? Plutarch stresses this point, and not without reason: "If it is not because of destiny that men get fancies and suffer injuries; obviously it is not because of destiny either that they perform right actions or are sensible or have steadfast conceptions or are benefited; and there is nothing left of the doctrine that destiny is cause of all things."[16]

Plutarch remarks that Stoic doctrine, which is in part ultradeterminist but in part attached, in spite of all, to a form of what we would have to call free will, leaves us deep in ambiguity: "So then, shall we say that we do not have control over acts of assent or over virtues or vices or right action or wrong-doing; or shall we say that destiny is deficient and Determination is indeterminate and the motions and stations of Zeus are frustrate?" It has to be one way or the other: either "destiny is a cause sufficient of itself" and, if so, "abolishes the sphere of our control and volition," or else we admit liberty, without which there would be no distinction between vices and virtues, in which case destiny, for its part, "loses the character of being unimpedible and fully effective."[17]

Plutarch's criticism has often been repeated—by Kant, of course, but also, paradoxically, and in a fairly similar form, by Nietzsche. In *Beyond Good and Evil* Nietzsche reproaches the Stoics for being totally inconsistent in their presentation of life "according to nature," as a "moral obligation," an imperative, or an "ideal," whereas it is simply a fact. If nature is indeed all, if cosmological determinism is omnipresent and omnipotent, *how could we even live otherwise than in accord with it?* What, then, is the source of the absurd hypothesis of a liberty that might work against the destinies of the cosmos? "And supposing your imperative, 'live according to nature,' meant at bottom as much as 'live according to life'—how could you *not* do that? Why make a principle of what you yourselves are and must be?"[18] Indeed, if nature is all-powerful, it is hard to see what kind of human behavior could not be in conformity with it in the final analysis! The next step, as Plutarch rightly perceived, was to assume that the very idea of nonconformity with nature supposes a "minimal free will." The criticism is fair and, what is more, could be addressed to all schools of thought that reject free will, beginning with Spinoza, and to Nietzsche himself, in whom it is just as hard to see how it would be possible *not to live* according to nature or to life, and even less how such a hypothesis—even admitting that it makes any sense—could in some fashion be imputed to human liberty.

But that does not matter; what we do know is that when the Stoics equated the intelligence that reveals the destiny of the world with the liberty that accepts it, both parts of the equation prompted numerous and very serious criticisms. Moreover, it is not even certain that the major Stoics themselves found the connection totally convincing. One might wonder whether the frustration they associated with the figure of the sage was not originally connected with that difficulty. The Stoics conceded that perhaps no one in the history of humanity has ever been able to welcome with real, unfeigned joy the news of having contracted a fatal and painful illness or the news of the death of a loved one. Epictetus seems to recognize this dilemma when, in a famous passage of the *Discourses*, he contrasts the authentic sage to those who simply adhere to the abstract principles of doctrine: "You can show me thousands who recite the petty arguments of the Stoics," he complains, but they are not truly Stoics. "As for a Stoic, show me one if you can! . . . Show me a man who though sick is happy, though in danger is happy, though dying is happy, though condemned to exile is happy, though in disrepute is happy. Show him! By the gods, I would fain see a Stoic! But you cannot show me a man completely so fashioned; then show me at least one who is becoming so fashioned, one who has begun to tend in that direction; do me this favour; do not begrudge an old man the sight of that spectacle which to this very day I have never seen."[19]

This statement might well have discouraged a number of vocations, even in those days. And today, *a fortiori*, we may wonder why we should still interest ourselves in a thought that frankly declares itself beyond the reach of simple human beings. And yet, as we shall see, even for those who do not share the expectations of Stoicism, and even over the centuries that separate us from the great cosmologies of antiquity, at least two messages of a rare profundity remain, two guiding ideas of lasting significance that deserve meditation even today.

A Wisdom of the Present Moment:
Beyond Nostalgia and Hope, It Is Here and Now
That We Must Attain the Good Life

The first of these messages is rooted in a conviction still timely today: it states that the two ills that weigh on human existence, the two things that block it and prevent it from attaining successful forms of life, are nostalgia and hope, attachment to the past and worry about the future. Time after time, these attitudes make us miss the present moment and keep us from living fully. Where nostalgia is concerned, Stoicism anticipates one of the deepest findings of psychoanalysis: someone who remains a prisoner of his past will always be incapable of "enjoying and acting." Today, we all know that nostalgia for a lost paradise, notably for the joys and sufferings of childhood, burdens our lives all the more strongly because we misunderstand it. As for hope, Stoic thought echoes one of the subtlest themes in Eastern forms of wisdom, Tibetan Buddhism in particular: contrary to the commonplace that one cannot "live without hope," hope is the greatest misfortune that exists. By its very essence it falls into the category of things lacking, unresolved tension. We live constantly in the dimension of the project, subjected to ends set in a more or less distant future, and we think—supreme illusion!—that our happiness depends on the full realization of the objectives (modest or grandiose) that we have set for ourselves. Buying a bigger apartment, a more beautiful house, a faster car, or a more high-powered boat; climbing the career ladder; getting access to power; enhancing our physical appearance; finishing a piece of work; winning salvation; accomplishing any sort of enterprise: in each case we yield to the mirage of delayed happiness, a paradise still to be constructed, on earth or in the great beyond, and we forget that there is no reality other than the one we are living here and now, in which this strange race to keep ahead guarantees our failure. Moreover, we almost always face the painful experience of indifference, if not disappointment, once we have conquered our objective: possession of the goods we so ardently coveted does not make us much better or happier than we were before. All this striving does little to modify life's difficulties or the tragic aspect of the human condition. As Seneca puts it, "While we are postponing, life speeds by."[20]

This is why, as a Buddhist proverb suggests, the most important moment of our life is the one that we are living right now, and the people who count the most are the ones who are facing us. The rest of life simply does not exist: the past is no more, and the future has no reality. Past and future are temporal dimensions, fictive entities that we "burden" ourselves with—just like the "beasts of burden" that Nietzsche mocked, which lose the "innocence of becoming"—only to justify our inability to love the present as it is. Lost happiness, felicity to come, but also a fleeting present, although it is the only temporal sphere of real existence, are all packed off to nothingness. This is perhaps the simple, profound, and principal conviction underlying the sophisticated but contestable theoretical edifice of Stoic wisdom. Marcus Aurelius expresses this thought perhaps better than anyone else. He begins book XII of his *Meditations* thus: "All those things, which you pray you may secure after a time, you can possess right now if you do not grudge them to yourself, that is, if you cease to think of the past, leave the future to Providence, and only redirect the present on the path to piety and justice: to piety, that you may regard your lot with affection, for nature brought it to you and you to it; to justice, that you may, freely and without prevarication, speak the truth and do what is in accord with the law and the worth of things."[21]

For a proper understanding of this passage, we should recall that in Stoicism, theology and cosmology are inextricably mixed: the "piety" to which

Marcus Aurelius calls us as an aid for lessening the burdens of the future and the past is none other than love of the world as it is and as it goes. This love exists in the certainty that the "share" assigned to us by nature, here and now, is (all things being equal) just and good: we must think it and must proclaim it loud and clear if we want to live, at the very least, without vain fears and superfluous nostalgia. "Let not the picture which imagination draws of your whole life disturb you, let not your mind concern itself with all the kinds of troubles which are likely to have happened in the past or are likely to happen in the future, but for each event as it happens ask yourself: what is there in this task which is a burden I cannot endure? . . . Then remind yourself that it is not the future or the past which weighs upon you, but always the present." We must therefore learn to shake off the burdens so strangely anchored in the two figures of nothingness. Marcus Aurelius insists that the present is what matters, "and that this present burden is lightened if you consider it in isolation and rebuke your mind if it cannot stand merely against this."[22] The scope of the life that we have to deal with in the realm of reality is small indeed. And Seneca, in his *Letters to Lucilius,* says: "These two things must be cut away: fear of the future, and the memory of past sufferings. The latter no longer concern me, and the future does not concern me yet."[23] One might add that it is not just "old woes" that spoil the present life of someone who sins by lack of wisdom but also, and paradoxically, the memory of happy days gone by, now irremediably lost. In Edgar Allen Poe's poem "The Raven," the bird that serves as the incarnation of hell on earth and in heaven says only one word, "Nevermore," and it may be the irremediable loss of time, a first death in the very heart of life appearing in the form of what may be our happiest memories, that pulls us back and prevents us from attaining serenity.

This attitude toward time, which the Stoics derived from their cosmology and the philosophical representations connected with it, has clearly lost little of its force and its interest, even for those who do not subscribe to the major doctrinal options of Stoicism. It is an attitude than can be extended in two directions, one practical and the other spiritual, which have no direct and necessary connection with any dogmatic stance.

On the practical level, the Stoic schools (like all the Greek philosophical schools) made use of a certain number of "spiritual exercises" designed to enable disciples to move on, as far as is possible, from a simple knowledge of principles to actually putting them into practice; from a philosophy that is still only love of wisdom to wisdom itself, which has value only in action. One of these exercises consisted, as in Buddhism, in using the processes of thought to rid oneself of various "attachments"—to things and to persons but also, more especially, to passions rooted in the past or the future. Pierre Hadot provides a magnificent description of the meaning of such wisdom exercises in the Stoic schools in general and in Marcus Aurelius in particular. It consists in "separating oneself" from everything that is not truly the self but is "attached" to the self accidentally and weighs on our life like a heavy burden. The student must strive to use thought to detach from himself everything "that others do or say, and what he himself has done or said in the past. He encourages himself also to separate from his 'I' everything in the future which might worry him (by this he means his body, and even the soul which animates his body), including events which stem from the mutual linkage of universal causes—in other words, destiny—and things which have become attached to him because he has attached himself to them. He promises himself that if he separates himself from the past and the future, and lives within the present, he will attain a life of peace and serenity."[24]

We can see here how Stoicism pleads—again like Buddhism—in favor of attaining a subjectivity finally stripped of all hypertrophy of the "I" and cultivating an attitude, not of indifference, but of "nonattachment" regarding earthly possessions. As Epictetus suggests, in a text that the Tibetan masters might not have quarreled with:

> The highest and principal discipline, and one that stands at the very gates of the subject, is this: Whenever you grow attached to something, do not act as though it were one of those things that cannot be taken away, but as though it were something like a jar or a crystal goblet, so that when it breaks you will remember what it was like, and not be troubled. So too in life; if you kiss your child, your brother, your friend, never allow your fancy free rein, nor your exuberant spirits to go as far as they like, but hold them back, stop them. . . . Do you too remind yourself that the object of your love is mortal; it is not one of your own possessions; it has been given you for the present, not inseparably nor for ever. . . . What harm is there if you whisper to yourself, at the very moment you are kissing your child, and say, "To-morrow you will die"?[25]

Attachments make us forget the reality of "impermanence," the fact that nothing is stable in this world and that if we fail to understand that we are preparing ourselves for the worst sort of suffering—the suffering brought on by nostalgia and hope. Reason, which guides us and invites us to live in accordance with cosmic nature, must thus be purified of the sediment that weighs it down and falsifies it the minute it loses its way in these unreal dimensions of temporality. Once this truth has been grasped by the mind, however, it is still far from being put into practice. That is why Marcus Aurelius invites his disciple to embody it: "If, I say, you separate from your directing mind what is linked to it by passion, what is beyond us in time, and what is past, you will make yourself, like the sphere of Empedocles, 'rounded and rejoicing in its solitude.' Practice to live only the present which you are now living, and you will be able to live through to the time of your death in imperturbability and kindliness, and at peace with the divinity that is within you."[26]

This brings us back to death, and to the victories over death that philosophy, once it has become wisdom, can enable us to attain. Thus the most concrete exercises are close to the highest spirituality. If we strive to live in the present, to cast off the remorse, regrets, and anxieties that are crystallized by the past and the future, it is so that we can enjoy every instant of life as it deserves, in full awareness that, for the mortals that we are, the present moment my be our last. As Pierre Hadot notes, Stoic serenity paradoxically conveys a sense of urgency: anyone who puts off life while waiting for better days, who delays his happiness until one objective or another is realized, surrenders to folly, for "death can arrive at any moment." Marcus Aurelius declares: "Each of life's actions must be performed as if it were the last"; hence, "when we view things from the perspective of death, it is impossible to let a single one of life's instants pass by lightly."[27] The spiritual stakes in the practical exercise by which the subject rids himself of his burdensome attachments to the past and the future are clear. One must conquer the fears connected with finitude by use of a conviction that is intimate, almost carnal, rather than intellectual and that states that there is no basic difference between eternity and the present, provided that the present is not overshadowed by the past and the future. The sage is thus permitted to live "like a god" in the eternity of an instant relative to no other, in an absolute happiness that no anxiety can spoil.

From the Wisdom of the "I" to the Wisdom of the World:
A Western Version of Buddhism

The seeming paradox of those exercises that focus on the self as it lives in the here and now but are in no way egocentric, either in Stoicism or in Buddhism, is easily dissipated. The opposite is true: by reconciling us with the world as it is, with the lived present that temporal ecstasies frequently cause us to miss, those exercises invite us to enlarge thought to the dimensions of the cosmos. It is from the point of view of the entire universe, and from that point of view alone, that we can understand why, destiny being what it is (that is, globally just and good), we must accept it without remorse or regrets, without rebellion or hope. The "I" that "attaches" either to itself or to some possession, and then, because of that attachment, fears for its future and defends its past, is not the authentic "I." To the contrary, it is the weightless "I" that merges into the Great All. At that point it finally fully grasps that, despite appearances, "everything that happens, happens justly." We must learn to fear and hope a bit less in order to love a bit more: "As for the Stoic sage, as soon as he discovers that indifferent things depend not on his will but upon the will of universal Nature, they take on infinite interest for him. He accepts them with love, but he accepts them with *equal* love; he finds them beautiful, but all of them inspire him with the same admiration. He says 'Yes!' to the entire universe and to each of its parts and to events, even if specific parts and events seem painful or repugnant."[28]

Just as in Christian theology the true believer, given that the ways of the Lord are inscrutable, must believe that the course of providence is always good, even when at first sight it seems distressing, so too the Stoic sage must rise above his limited self to comprehend that although the world can seem imperfect in detail, it is in reality harmonious and good as a whole. Parallel to theodicy, which relieves God of the suspicion of having acted badly, there is a "cosmodicy," which also aims at absolving the cosmos. Marcus Aurelius describes one of the finest properties of the human soul and one of the most useful exercises for a concrete realization of an authentic wisdom in this way: "The rational soul travels through the whole universe and the void which surrounds it, and observes its form; it stretches into infinity of time and grasps and understands the periodic rebirth of the Whole; it observes that those who come after us will see nothing new, nothing different from what our predecessors saw."[29] Time does not enter into the picture, given that it must be reduced to the one dimension of the present.

Just as "nonattachment" to earthly possessions, by revealing the authentic nature of an "I" freed of the burdens of past and future time, had already liberated humans from the anxieties of death, so now, by opening up the cosmic dimension to us, by elevating us toward the totality of being, we will be able to end our struggle against mortal fears. There are two reasons for this. First, we need a change of scale regarding the universe as a whole: with it, we can measure our smallness better and, hence, see the relative insignificance of the "little deaths" that are our lot and that change nothing, absolutely nothing, in the harmony and perfection of the All. But also, it is by situating ourselves on that level that we can prepare ourselves to welcome with serenity the events that common mortals usually regard as catastrophes. Again as in Buddhism, one might say that for Stoicism the temporal dimension of the struggle against the anxiety of death is expressed in the future anterior—or, to put it more simply, the sage is the person who, far from blocking meditation on the brevity of life, will say to himself: "When destiny has struck, I will have prepared myself for it." When catastrophe (or at least what men usually consider such: death, sickness, poverty, etc.) *has already taken place;* I will be able to confront it thanks to the capacity to live in the present that was granted to me—the capacity to love the world as it is, no matter what happens. Then, if something happens that would be called undesirable, "immediately the thought that it was not unexpected will be the first thing to lighten the burden. . . . You will say, and again, 'I knew that I was mortal,' 'I knew that I was likely to leave my home,' 'I knew that I was liable to banishment,' 'I knew that I might be sent off to prison.' And in the next place, if you reflect with yourself and look for the quarter from which the happening comes, immediately you will be reminded of the principle: 'It comes from the quarter of the things that are outside the sphere of the moral purpose, that are not my own.'"[30] Such things are sent to us by nature in a just and good manner, provided that one view them, not through the wrong end of the magnifying glass, but adopting the viewpoint of general harmony.

Once again, Stoicism seems closer to Buddhism than to Christianity. Like Buddhism, it makes the divine a reality immanent in the world, an entity that merges with the cosmic harmony. Again like Buddhism, it seeks no consolation in the beyond. Finally, like Buddhism, it invites us not to flee meditation on death and suffering. This ethic raises many objections, but it also sketches out an early form of spirituality without God—a lay spirituality—that finds multiple echoes in the preoccupations of contemporary humanity.[31]

This "wisdom of the world" was also, and simultaneously, a wisdom of men: the Stoics were perhaps the first—even before the Christians—to elevate their thoughts to an idea of a unified, fraternal humanity; to consider, on the moral and political planes, that we are all members of one and the same universal community. They were thus the founding fathers of what is still called "cosmopolitanism," understood here in its etymological sense as placing everyone in one and the same cosmos. As Marcus Aurelius puts it, "If we have intelligence in common, so we have reason which makes us reasoning beings, and that practical reason which orders what we must or must not do; then the law too is common to us and, if so, we are citizens; if so, we share a common government; if so, the universe is, as it were, a city—for what other common government could one say is shared by all mankind?"[32]

Why does this wisdom of the Ancients, which at times speaks to us so directly, seem to us to belong irremediably to the past? Why does it seem to us so difficult—and, at times so dispiriting—to adhere to its thought, even when we find certain notions attractive? Perhaps it is because the vision of the world and the cosmology in which it took root simply are no more. That vision lasted only from postclassical antiquity to the end of the Middle Ages, when it gradually gave way to a totally different representation of the universe. The Christian world, which at its beginnings was rooted in the philosophical universe of the Greeks, eventually shook free of it, at least in large part. It was that world that embraced, perhaps to a greater degree than any other, the desire to represent human destiny in a more credible way so as to eradicate humanity's primitive fears in the face of finitude and death.

PART IV

The Here & Now
Enchanted by the Beyond

The way of the good and blessed life is to be found
entirely in the true religion.

St. Augustine, "Of True Religion"

CHAPTER 10

Death Finally Conquered
by Immortality

~ ~ ~ ~ ~

Philosophy Replaced by Religion

Greek philosophy had the genius to develop powerful doctrines of salvation without God, thus offering us the first model of a "lay spirituality" in the West. How did religion manage to take back control and reverse the process of secularization that began with the rise of philosophy in Greece? By what intellectual contrivance did Christianity, soon to be followed by the two other great monotheistic religions, show that it was capable of turning Greek philosophy to its profit, at the same time proposing a new doctrine of salvation that went on to dominate Western thought for more than fifteen centuries? How did that unprecedented competition take place, and why did philosophy lose? These questions are all the more pertinent because the content of the Christian religion—the first religion to establish a connection with Athens—seems quite simple in comparison to the extreme sophistication that Greek thought had already achieved. The situation can be summarized in a few lines, as one Christian philosopher, Etienne Gilson, attempts to do with false naïveté:

> A man was born in marvelous circumstances: his name was Jesus; he taught that he was the Messiah announced by the prophets of Israel,

the Son of God, and he proved it by his miracles. This Jesus promised the coming of the kingdom of God for all those who would
prepare for it by observing his commandments: love for the Father,
who is in heaven; mutual love among men, now brothers in Jesus
Christ and children of that Father; penitence for sins, renunciation
of the world and of everything that is of the world, out of love of the
Father above all things. The same Jesus died on the cross to redeem
men: his resurrection proved his divinity, and he will come again, at
the end of time, to judge the living and the dead and to reign with
the elect in his kingdom. There is not a word of philosophy in all of
this.[1]

Indeed. Yet it was "pagan" thought—that is, Greek thought—that the
Christian religion took as its standard for measurement; it was pagan
thought that Christianity invested and placed in its own service before Judaism and Islam followed its footsteps on this difficult path along which
philosophy, losing its old status of an apprenticeship in life and wisdom,
was gradually relegated to the status of a modest auxiliary to theology.
When Christianity put the idea of an incarnation of the divine *logos* into a
human being, Jesus Christ, it founded not only a new conception of providence but also a new promise of salvation—a promise that guaranteed
that, through love of God and love of all created beings "in" God, we can
accede to a *personal* immortality and vanquish all the fears aroused by finitude. The history of this long change began with the writings of John, and
it played out essentially during the first centuries of our era.

John, Paul, and Justin: The Divine Logos
versus the Cosmic Logos, or The Birth of a New Doctrine
of Salvation Breaking with the Greek Philosophers

The opening lines of the prologue to the Gospel According to John are
universally familiar within the Christian world and outside of it: "In the
beginning was the Word [*logos*], the Word was in God's presence, and the
Word was God. He was present to God in the beginning. Through him all
things came into being, and apart from him nothing came to be. . . . The
Word became flesh and made his dwelling among us, and we have seen his
glory: the glory of an only Son coming from the Father, filled with endur-
ing love."[2]

I am not certain, however, that except for priests and scholars, Christians today know, even approximately, what is implied in the notion of the "Word," or that they know why John the Evangelist's explicit borrowing from Stoic philosophy seemed iconoclastic to the principal heirs of that tradition. The question would be of only historical or philological interest if it did not symbolize, in a nutshell, the conflict that later opposed a nascent Christian philosophy to Greek philosophy under the Roman Empire of the second to the fifth centuries. A bitter and often mortal struggle took place—Christian martyrdom is no myth—to win a monopoly of the legitimate doctrine of salvation. We must attempt to define what was at stake in that struggle if we want to understand the extraordinary novelty of Christian thought and the deep-seated reasons for its universal hold, almost without exception, over the population of Europe until the seventeenth century. It offered a new definition of the good life, replacing the wisdom of antiquity. The reasons for its success are interesting, and in many ways they remain pertinent for millions of people today.

Let us, too, begin at the beginning: What is there in John's statements on the incarnation of the divine Word in the flesh of Christ that a Greek philosopher would find so shocking? In what way did the new definition of the *logos* found both another doctrine of salvation and a novel conception of the blessed life? In spite of the unsoundable depth of the metaphysical and historical aspects of the problem, the answer can be put quite simply. John invested the term *logos*, which he borrowed from the Stoic philosophers, with a meaning that they deemed truly senseless. No longer did it designate the harmonious and rational structure of the world, the divine organization of the cosmos as a whole; it now referred to a particular human being, Jesus Christ. To put it even more simply: the *logos*, once impersonal, had become personal, and despite the word's apparent continuity, the new definition changed everything in the Greeks' view of the world, life, and salvation. This new representation of the Word produced three revolutions in thought, which concerned *theōria, praxis,* and soteriology. As it happens, Plato's heirs found all three of these new definitions strictly inadmissible.

First, the very nature of *theōria* was turned upside-down: it was no longer, as in the entire philosophical tradition since the Greeks, by *reason* alone that all men must strive to arrive at a proper comprehension of the cosmic universal rationality (*logos*) reflected in the organization of the world. Now it was by faith, by putting trust (*fides*) in the message of another person, that the *logos* was to be received. It no longer had to be fought for and won. Even if the old imperative remained in part valid, it was now less important to *think for oneself* than it was to *give one's trust to an Other,* accept the news that he brings, and believe in the promises that he makes to us. In other words, philosophical pride had to give way to religious humility. Faith, one might object, does not abolish reason, and we shall see that when philosophy became Christian, reason did not disappear. But the least one can say is that religion dominated philosophy; henceforth it was up to revelation to guide thought in its striving toward intelligibility, whether such efforts were directed to deciphering Scripture or to understanding the world itself.

Extremely significant, in this regard, are the opening lines of the First Epistle of John, which return to the theme of the prologue of his Gospel but present it as a direct witness, a narration that is *credible,* deserving of faith and trust: "This is what we proclaim to you: what was from the beginning, what we have heard, what we have seen with our eyes, what we have looked upon and our hands have touched—we speak of the word [*logos*] of life. (This life became visible; we have seen and bear witness to it, and we proclaim to you the eternal life that was present to the Father and became visible to us.) What we have seen and heard we proclaim in turn to you so that you may share life with us. This fellowship of course is with the Father and with his Son, Jesus Christ." Gilson, faithful in this to Augustine,[3] provides a cogent summary of the meaning of John's cooption of the Greek heritage:

> Beginning with the concrete person of Jesus, the object of Christian faith, John turns to the philosophers and tells them that Jesus is what they call the *logos,* that the *logos* was made flesh and lived among us, so that—and this is what was intolerably scandalous for minds in quest of a purely speculative explanation of the world—we have seen it (John 1:14) To say that it is Christ who is the *logos* was not a philosophical assertion but a religious one. As Aymé Puech has so rightly put it: "As with all Christianity's borrowings from Hellenism, what was at stake, beginning with this one, which is to our knowledge the first, was the taking over of a notion that would later serve for the philosophical interpretation of faith rather than as a constituent part of that faith."[4]

The statement is accurate: it applies not only to the early church fathers but also, at a later date, to Thomas Aquinas (even though references to Greek philosophy changed between the one and the other, shifting, one might say, from Plato to Aristotle). In other words, and if I may use a bellicose metaphor (justified, however, by the violence of the polemics), the Christian religion—beginning with John's Gospel—strove to colonize, even to subjugate, Greek philosophy. Or, to change the metaphor, it attempted to make philosophy the "handmaid" of theology, as Peter Damian called it, launching a term that proved successful all the way to Aquinas, by whose time theology had been consecrated as the only true doctrine of salvation.

Just as the Greek *logos* was no longer cosmic but was personalized by its incarnation in Jesus Christ, so the notion of providence changed totally. The Stoics invited us to put all our "trust" in destiny. This was still a rational conviction, dictated by a wholly intellectual comprehension of perfect determinism and of the *logos* that rules the course of the world. It was in the name of that speculative knowledge that the Stoics urged us to change our desires rather than attempt to alter the order of reality. Even when they spoke of "providence" or of the "goodness of God," such formulas were by no means to be understood in a personal sense. God, in the pantheistic perspective, was, first and foremost, the divine, not a real person; God was the perfect and harmonious structure of the world considered as a Whole. But when the *logos* was made flesh and was incarnate, before our eyes, in a real person, Jesus Christ, it lost its former meaning of an ineluctable and blind destiny. Exactly contrary to the way the Stoics saw things, providence henceforth became one with the benevolent and conscious attention that a (divine) person bears to other (human) persons. Once again, everything becomes a question of trust, of faith in the probity and veracity of a given word.

Justin Martyr was probably the first Christian philosopher to start out as a Platonist but later to do battle with the errors of the Greek philosophers. In his *Dialogue with Trypho* he says of the disciples of Aristotle and Plato: "They try to convince us that God takes care of the universe with its genera and species, but not of me and you and of each individual, for otherwise there would be no need of our praying to him night and day."[5] The converse is also true: the Christian God, *because in him and by him the logos is a person and no longer the impersonal structure of the world,* is occupied with everyone, in general and as individuals, as Augustine stresses in his essay on true religion. Writing in much the same spirit as Justin, that is, speaking explicitly against the Greek tradition, he states: "Divine providence not only looks after individuals as it were privately, but also after the whole human race publicly. How it deals with individuals God knows, who does it, and they also know, with whom he deals. But how he deals with the human race God had willed to be handed down through history and prophecy."[6] John's new interpretation of the Stoic *logos* places it in direct opposition to the idea of a course of the world determined anonymously and to which reason alone commands us to adhere. Providence now operates within the element of consciousness, person to person.

The promise of salvation was transformed just as radically. Among the Greeks, and in particular among the Stoics, fear of death was finally surmounted when the sage understood that he himself was a part, perhaps infinitesimal but nonetheless real, of the eternal cosmic order. It was as such, and by his adherence to the universal *logos,* that he came to think of death as a simple *passage* from one state to another rather than as a radical and definitive disappearance. Eternal salvation, however, like providence and for the same reasons, remained *impersonal.* It is not as individuals but as unconscious fragments of a perfection that itself has no consciousness that we could think of ourselves as eternal. The personalization of the *logos* changed all the givens of the problem: if the promises made to me by Christ, the incarnate Word that trustworthy witnesses have been able to see with their own eyes, are true, and if divine providence takes me in charge as a person, humble as I am, then my immortality will also be *personal.* It is of course in this perspective that the Gospels narrate the three resurrections performed by Jesus (beside his own): those of the son of the widow from Nain, of Jairus's daughter, and of Lazarus. But what merits our attention in the context of our pursuit of the victory of Christianity over Greek philosophy is the ironic incredulity that greets Paul when he mentions the resurrection of the dead before an Athenian public: "Epicurean and Stoic philosophers disputed with him, some of them asking, 'What is this magpie trying to say to us?' Others commented, 'He sounds like a promoter of foreign gods,' because he was heard to speak of 'Jesus' and 'the resurrection.'"[7] This is hardly surprising, given the message that Paul was transmitting, nor is it surprising that it was Jesus and his resurrection that attracted the philosophers' most pointed attacks, for Paul was preaching that *it was death itself, and not only our fear of it, that was finally vanquished. Immortality is no longer the anonymous, cosmic immortality of Stoicism, but the individual, conscious immortality of the resurrection of souls accompanied by their "glorious" bodies.*

The dimension of "love in God" gives ultimate meaning to the revolution that Christianity brought to Greek thought. It is that love that lies at the heart of the new doctrine of a salvation that proves, in the end, "stronger than death." I shall return to the topic shortly. What has already been said, however, should explain the extraordinary hostility—within Judaism, but above all within the Greco-Roman world—that greeted John's appropriation of the highly prestigious philosophic concept of the *logos*, but also the no less extraordinary success of Christian soteriology. Paul outlines the terms of this polemic thus:

> Has not God turned the wisdom of this world into folly? Since, in God's wisdom, the world did not come to know him through "wisdom," it pleased God to save those who believe through the absurdity of the preaching of the gospel. Yes, Jews demand "signs" and Greeks look for "wisdom," but we preach Christ crucified—a stumbling block to Jews, and an absurdity to Gentiles; but to those who are called, Jews and Greeks alike, Christ the power of God and the wisdom of God. For God's folly is wiser than men, and his weakness more powerful than men.[8]

This text, which the fathers of the church and the theologians commented on incessantly in their attempt to come to some sort of understanding with Greek philosophy,[9] lays the groundwork for the program put into effect by the first Christian authors, Justin in particular. In many ways, Augustine carried through this same program in certain passages of the *Confessions* (and, even more, in the *City of God*), where he argues the superiority of Christianity over Hellenism.

The profound meaning of Paul's message has been brilliantly summarized (from a Christian viewpoint) by Etienne Gilson. We shall let him speak for himself:

> As he puts it in the First Epistle to the Corinthians, the new revelation was set up as a rock of offence between Judaism and Hellenism. The Jews sought salvation by way of a literal observance of a Law and by obedience to the commands of a God Who made His power manifest in miracles of glory; the Greeks sought a salvation to be achieved by way of the rectitude of the will and the certitude afforded by the natural light of reason. What had Christianity to offer either? Salvation by faith in Christ crucified, that is to say a scandal to the Jews who asked for a sign of power and were offered the infamy of an humiliated God: a folly to the Greeks who sought after the intelligible and were offered the absurdity of a God-man, dead on a cross and risen again from the dead to save us.[10]

In both cases, though from differing perspectives, it was the *humility* of the Christian doctrine of salvation that raised problems—for the Jews because the divine Word, even admitting that it could become incarnate, could not be ridiculed and put to death by mere humans. Weakness was not, so to speak, the Word's forte. The true God could not be other than a power of salvation that operated by incontestable signs: he is the One who, when his people were enslaved in Egypt, delivered them after raining plagues on the pharaoh and his people. How could God be incarnate in the weakness of an unhappy man who allows himself to be martyred? The Christian doctrine of salvation raised problems for the Greeks because all of their philosophy, which was based on reason—that is, on the divine in us inasmuch as it is able to join with the divine outside of us (the eternal cosmic harmony)—taught that it is possible to save oneself by oneself alone, without the aid of an Other, of whom it is absurd, incidentally, to believe that he could be the sole repository of the divinity of the *logos*. To the strength of the Jews, Christ opposes the weakness of his martyrdom, and to the proud reason of the Greeks he opposes the humility of the faith that he calls forth within us as the sole, sufficient response to his given word.

When the representatives of Greek wisdom were challenged in this manner, they did not remain silent. As one might imagine, their principal criticisms were aimed at this question of the incarnation of the *logos* in a human being, even if he be the Christ. Augustine recalls this confrontation in the *City of God:* the Platonists, he tells us, would have liked the opening lines of the Gospel According to John to be "inscribed in letters of gold and set up in the most prominent place in every church." Not only did those lines suit them, but they also gave evidence, for the Platonists, that the best in Christianity had been taken over from Plato. "But God, the great teacher, became of no account in the eyes of the proud simply because 'the Word became flesh, and dwelt among us.'"[11] That Jesus alone could be the incarnation of the truth of the divine *logos* seemed absurd to them. The anecdote that Augustine relates is quite real, and the polemic between Platonists and Christians prompted Ambrose, the bishop of Milan, who had baptized Augustine, to put out a pamphlet. So we see the extent to which the question of the incarnation of the *logos* was an apple of discord between Platonists and Christians. Though disputable, the reasons that Augustine offers in explanation for the philosophers' reticence are more profound than they may seem: according to him, it was out of pride that the heirs to the great Greek thinkers rejected the incarnation of the Word in the figure of Jesus, and that was why they rejected the teachings of religion, even though the underlying tenets of their philosophy might have brought them close to it on more than one point. That said, however, it is not impossible that Augustine touches on the crucial point: as regards religion, the philosophical doctrines of salvation have a touch of arrogance about them. They are aimed at permitting us to save ourselves by our own efforts, without the aid of any Other. As the Neoplatonist Porphyry later stated in the early pages of his *On the Life of Plotinus* (and Plotinus was Augustine's target in the passages just discussed): "Try to bring back the god in you to the divine in the All!"[12] That was where salvation, which implied entry into communication with the eternal world, was situated, and the philosophers saw no need to receive grace from a God. Reason alone sufficed.

The sufficiency of reason was precisely what the earliest Christian authors contested. Their arguments are all the more interesting because they had originally been disciples of the Greek schools. Their accounts of their conversion offer us a further opportunity to evaluate the reasons that in their view justified their decision to leave philosophy and enter into religion. In this regard, no testimony is more meaningful than that of Justin: he was the first and one of the very few writers of his age whose works have been in large part preserved, and he explains, in a lively manner, how and for what reasons a second-century philosopher and follower of Platonism could quit that vision of the world on discovering Christianity. Moreover, in his account of his own conversion Justin presents himself as "testing out," one after the other, Stoicism, Aristotelianism, and Pythagorism; he then became an ardent Platonist, and finally came around to confessing the name of Jesus Christ. His comparison of lay doctrines of salvation and the Christian faith is paradigmatic, and it exerted a decisive influence in the history of Christian theology.

Let us briefly recall who Justin was and in what context he operated. Classified among the Greek "apologists," he was the principal representative of that movement in the second century. The pagan persecutions of Christians, and also the hostility of the Jews toward them, had induced the early Christian theologians to write apologies—that is, pleas addressed to the Roman emperors with the aim of defending their community against the rumors about their cult that were circulating. Public opinion accused them, among other absurdities, of worshiping a god with the head of an ass, of conducting cannibalistic rites, of ritual murder, and of giving themselves over to all manner of debauchery, none of which bore any relation to Christianity. Justin's own apologies were aimed at testifying to what Christian practice really was. The first, which dates from A.D. 150, was sent to the emperor Antoninus; the second, to Marcus Aurelius. What makes them irreplaceable as documents is that they offer a description unique at that period, and probably equally unique in its accuracy, of the way in which the early Christian communities celebrated Mass and performed baptisms. To evaluate the authenticity of his evidence, it may be helpful to recall that Justin lived less than a century after the death of Christ and that he had met people who had actually known Peter and Paul. After his conversion to Christianity around the year 130, Justin founded a highly successful Christian school in Rome. In 160 he wrote his *Dialogue with Trypho,* Trypho being a rabbi (possibly the rabbi Tarphon), whom he had met at Ephesus. Completing the program sketched out by Paul, Justin explains his reasons for rejecting both Greek philosophy and Judaism. Roman law stated that Christians were not to be molested unless they had been denounced by someone "credible." It was a philosopher of the school of the Cynics, one Crescens, who played that sinister role: a determined adversary of Justin's and a man jealous of the fame of Justin's teaching, Crescens had Justin condemned, along with six of his disciples. All seven were beheaded in 165, under the reign (and this seems highly symbolic) of Marcus Aurelius, the most eminent Stoic philosopher of the imperial era. The record of Justin's trial has been preserved and is, even today, the only authentic document describing the martyrdom of a Christian thinker in second-century Rome.

In his *Dialogue with Trypho,* Justin attacks both the Greeks and the Jews. It may be convenient to return to the three major categories that have lent structure to our entire inquiry, *theōria, praxis,* and *soteriology.* I shall try to present, in simplified form, the decisive ruptures between Christianity and Greek philosophy in these three domains that define the good life.

Theōria first. Like most of the great Christian theologians who came after him—or at least until Aristotle was rediscovered in the thirteenth century under the influence of Arabic and Jewish philosophy—Justin considered Platonism the highest true knowledge achievable without the aid of revelation, by reason alone. His admiration for Plato was to remain, if not intact, at least considerable, up to and even after his conversion. On the purely theoretical level, however, two major ruptures occurred, which gradually led to many others. First, of course, was the question of the nature of the *logos.* Like John, Justin believed in the incarnation of the Word, the doctrine responsible for diverting the course of pagan philosophy: "Not only among the Greeks through Socrates were these things revealed by reason [logos], but also among the Barbarians were they revealed by logos personally, when He had taken shape, and become man, and was called Jesus Christ."[13] This passage is crucial because it shows that for the early

Christian philosophers of Greek culture (and probably for John himself), pagan and Christian doctrines of salvation spoke of "the same Word." Hence the message of revelation was perceived as being in explicit dialogue with Greek thought, so that it seemed more a prolongation of Greek thought than its refutation. For that reason, Christian theology, far from simply rejecting pagan philosophy, appropriated its essence on the speculative level of *theōria*, putting it to its own service.

The second rupture derived from the first. If henceforth faith replaced reason in its relation to the incarnate Word, that did not mean that reason had been annihilated; Justin himself continued throughout his life to wear the mantle of the philosopher. Instead, it meant that revelation assumed the role of guiding rational thought, and theology that of appropriating philosophy and providing it with the objects that it should help us to understand. These objects are essentially two: one is Holy Scripture, the message of which, in spite of all, had to be *thought*, which supposes a certain use of reason; the other is nature, because, as God's creation, it bears witness to the splendor of the divine. It is in this sense, for example, that Paul declares in the Epistle to the Romans (1:20): "Since the creation of the world, invisible realities, God's eternal power and divinity, have become visible, recognized [by the intelligence] through the things he has made." Thus the study of nature should long ago have led those Greeks who called themselves sages to the content of revelation, if only their "senseless hearts" had not been "darkened." Thus from the start we can see emerging in Christianity—in contrast to Greek thought—the figure of philosophy as handmaid to theology and reason, operating in the service of a revelation that guides it but does not annul it.

Where *praxis*, or simple morality, is concerned, Justin tells us that Christianity is just as opposed to all of Greek philosophy of Platonic inspiration, even though it takes over and continues what is true in that philosophy. What Justin disapproves of in pagan philosophy is essentially that providence, as we have seen, is viewed as an ineluctable and cyclical destiny. Not only does free will seem to have no place in the Greek vision of the world, but in a more general sense and even among the Platonists themselves, the conviction that all things are fated to relive their destinies, unchanged and infinitely repeated, renders the very idea of morality totally nonfunctional: "Such reasoning . . . imparts a certain immunity and freedom of speech to those who hold these opinions, permitting them to say and do whatever they please, without any fear of punishment or hope of a reward from God.

How could it be otherwise, when they claim that things will always be as they are now, and that you and I shall live in the next life just as we are now, neither better nor worse?" Beneath the apparent naïveté of Justin's statements, a new continent emerges in his opposition to Greece—that of free will and of a historicity conceived for the first time detached from a cyclical idea of eternal repetition. It is because man is free, because he chooses his life and is responsible for his acts, that history must be thought of, not as a natural cycle, but as the sphere in which that liberty can be manifested as an *advance* or a *decline*, a rise or a fall. Contrary to the teachings of Porphyry, Justin insists that "man does not see God because of his affinity with him, nor because he possesses an intellect, but because he is temperate and just."[14]

In terms of *soteriology*, this new vision of the world implies another decisive rupture. Henceforth it is by the human being's free action and by the grace of God that salvation is won. Undoubtedly, as with the Greeks, salvation still (and more than ever) involved finitude and death. But beyond this surface continuity, a gap had opened up between the Greek and Christian worlds: no longer could the soul be called immortal as a soul and of its own doing, as if neither human liberty nor God's will had any input in the affair. To declare, as Plato did, that the soul is immortal no matter what choices it makes "would certainly be a benefit to sinners," says Justin. If the soul, because it has been virtuous, because it has, so to speak, taken the "first step," can reach immortality, it does so by the grace of God and not by its own powers, since it is God who has given it life and who can take back that life or prolong it for all eternity, "for, whatever exists or shall exist after God has a nature subject to corruption, and therefore capable of complete annihilation." Sages like Plato and Pythagoras, therefore, deserve our derision, and, as Paul invites us to do, their false wisdom should be annihilated and the "prudence of the prudent" should be laid low. Justin continues: "The soul partakes of life because God wishes it to live. It will no longer partake of life whenever God doesn't wish it to live. For the power to live is not an attribute of the soul as it is of God."[15] For someone who at least possesses faith, the Christian message thus seems infinitely more "promising" in terms of salvation than that of the Greek sages: immortality is no longer impersonal; rather, providence promises to save every one of us (if we are worthy of it) as a singular individual and, what is more, to do so from a point of departure where no one is guaranteed immortality *a priori*. As with Pascal's wager at a later date, the game was well worth the candle.

We will find a similar line of thought in a more elaborate but basically analogous form in Augustine's writings against the Platonic philosophers—in other words, against himself before his conversion, when he was still supporting their doctrines.

Augustine: The Grandeur et Misère of Platonism, or How the Humility of Religion Triumphed over Philosophic Pride

Like Justin, Augustine places Plato and the Neoplatonists at the top of the list of those who sought truth by their own powers alone. This fact deserves deserves emphasis, as it highlights the residual differences between Augustine and Plato. According to Augustine's essay "Of True Religion," Plato was the philosopher who had the genius to discover almost all of the Christian message by reason alone, without benefit of Christian revelation. What, in fact, did Plato want when he spoke to his disciples? According to Augustine, he simply wanted to persuade them of certain truths that are found intact in Christianity:

> You have persuaded me that truth is seen not with the bodily eyes but by the pure mind, and that any soul that cleaves to truth is thereby made happy and perfect. Nothing hinders the perception of truth more than a life devoted to lusts, and the false images of sensible things. . . . "Therefore the mind has to be healed so that it may behold the immutable form of things which remain ever the same, preserving the beauty unchanged and unchangeable, knowing no spatial distance or temporal variation, abiding, absolutely one and the same." . . . "Other things are born, die, are dissolved or broken up. But so far as they do exist they have existence from the external God, being created by his truth. To the rational and intellectual soul is given to enjoy the contemplation of his eternity, and by that contemplation it is armed and equipped so that it may obtain eternal life."[16]

We see here the extent to which Augustine, in his polemics against the Platonists, was aware that the points that Platonism and Christianity shared were far more numerous than were their differences and antagonisms. The same thought can be found in only a slightly different form in the *Confessions*.[17] There Augustine states plainly that nothing is closer to Christianity than Platonic philosophy. Of course, essential differences remain, and the former is clearly superior to the latter: Christianity alone could succeed in convincing ordinary people of truths that in philosophy were still reserved to an elite. Here Augustine appears as the first author to state a theme later popularized by Nietzsche: Christianity was a Platonism for the people, and Christ's talent—though to have such a talent he had to be the incarnation, in himself and by himself, of the divine Word—consisted in rendering the highest ideas comprehensible and sharing them through other means than those of an elitist reason.[18]

This leads Augustine to the conviction that Plato and all his great disciples would have converted to Christianity without the least hesitation if they had had the benefit of revelation: "This, however, I will say with complete confidence in spite of all who love so obstinately the books of the philosophers. In Christian times there can be no doubt at all as to which religion is to be received and held fast, and as to where is the way that leads to truth and beatitude. Suppose Plato were alive and would not spurn a question I would put to him; or rather suppose one of his own disciples, who lived at the same time as he did, had addressed him." Both Plato and his disciples, Augustine continues, would certainly have seen the way in which Christ succeeded in communicating their own convictions to the people infinitely better than they themselves could do, and would have paid honor to the wisdom of God and recognized its source: "So if these men could live their lives again today, they would see by whose authority measures are best taken for man's salvation, and, with the change of a few words and sentiments, they would become Christians, as many Platonists of recent times have done."[19] Unfortunately, Plato's philosophic heirs rejected what might justifiably appear to be the crowning of Platonic doctrine. Why? Simply out of pride, *superbia*.

Augustine's reference to pride is essential to an understanding of the quarrel that separated the Christians from the Platonists. On this point, the philosophic project as such stood sharply opposed to the presumed humility of the religious attitude.[20] Contrary to paganism, conversion to Christianity entailed a double humility: both an "objective" humility, because Christianity accepts the human incarnation—too human in the eyes of both the Greeks and the Jews—of the divine *logos;* and also a subjective humility, because it demands of us that we believe in the word of an Other rather than in the virtue of our reason alone, and that we accept him as our savior. The new problematic of the good life depends entirely on this humility.

A highly significant passage of the *Confessions* enumerates the truths found in Plato's works. Here again, Augustine's sole aim is to emphasize what is tragically absent in Plato and to insist that Christ alone brings to humanity "immense mercy on your part [as] the way of humility was demonstrated to us when your Word was made flesh and dwelt among men and women." Augustine admits that he has read fine things in Plato, but he nonetheless insists that "God, the Word, is *the true Light, which illumines every human person who comes into this world; and that he was in this world, a world made by him, but the world did not know him. But that He came to his own home, and his own people did not receive him; but to those who did receive him he gave power to become children of God: to those, that is, who believe in his name*—none of this did I read there." Why this absence? Quite simply because the philosophers, "grossly swollen with pride" by the high opinion they have of their knowledge, do not listen to Christ when he says: "Learn of me, for I am gentle and humble of heart, and you shall find rest for your souls."[21] The question of the incarnation is directly connected to the representation of a new doctrine of salvation, and the *City of God* stresses, once again, that such a doctrine is infinitely more functional than that of the Greeks. Porphyry

> refused to recognize that the Lord Christ is the "principle," and that by his incarnation we are purified. The fact is that he despised Christ as he appeared in flesh, in that very flesh which he assumed in order to effect the sacrifice of our purification. It was of course his pride which blinded Porphyry to this great mystery, that pride which our true and gracious Mediator has overthrown by his humility, in showing himself to mortals in the condition of mortality. It was because they were free from that mortal condition that the false and malignant "mediators"' vaunted their superiority, and deluded unhappy men by false promises of assistance, as immortals coming to the aid of mortals.[22]

In this magnificent and remarkably precise text, Augustine connects the two fundamental themes in the name of which the Platonists reject Christianity and Christians are converted to it: philosophic pride implies a rejection of the incarnation of the *logos* in a person judged—no matter the circumstances—unworthy of it, but it is also a rejection that deprives philosophy of all access to true soteriology. The impersonal and anonymous immortality of the Greeks is shoddy stuff compared to the immortality that Christ, who by his incarnation is exposed to finitude and ill fate just like us, promises to us individually.

This speaks to the humility of Jesus, who, although divine, willingly lowers himself to the level of a mortal, but also to the humility of the Christian who puts his trust in Jesus's words and recognizes that reason alone is powerless to grant us authentic salvation. Thus the Platonic philosophers, "even if they know God, . . . do not honor him as God or give him thanks; their thinking has been frittered away into futility and their foolish hearts are benighted, for in claiming to be wise they have become stupid."[23] This irrevocable judgment, which of course alludes to Paul's Epistle to the Romans (1:21–22), traces once more the line of demarcation that the early Christian authors, and all Christian theology after them, drew between philosophical pride and religious humility. Another example appears in the *City of God* in a passage directly addressed to Porphyry, the Neoplatonist who published a number of books against Christianity: "If you were a genuine and faithful lover, you would have recognized 'Christ, the Power of God and the Wisdom of God,' instead of shying away from his saving humility, inflated with the swollen pride of useless learning." This is the same Christ, Augustine adds, returning once more to the Pauline legacy, who is scorned by the Greeks and the Jews "on account of the body which he received from a woman, and because of the shame of the cross."[24] And yet

> the grace of God could not be commended in a way more likely to evoke a grateful response, than the way in which the only Son of God, while remaining unchangeably in his own proper being, clothed himself in humanity and gave to men the spirit of his love by the mediation of a man, so that by this love men might come to him who formerly was so far away from them, far from mortals in his immortality, from the changeable in his changelessness, from the wicked in his righteousness, from the wretched in his blessedness. And because he has implanted in our nature the desire for blessedness and immortality he has now taken on himself mortality, while continuing in his blessedness, so that he might confer on us what our hearts desire; and by his sufferings he has taught us to make light of what we dread.[25]

In this decisive passage the connection is once again affirmed between the personal incarnation of the *logos* and the new doctrine of salvation in the face of human mortality. Only Christ, because he has taken human form and understands us as we are, because he has shared our sufferings and our anxieties, can enable us to vanquish our fears.

Nonetheless, still speaking against Porphyry and his disciples, Augustine adds, "But humility was the necessary condition for submission to this truth; and it is no easy task to persuade the proud necks of you philosophers to accept this yoke. For what is there incredible—especially for you who hold certain opinions which should encourage you to believe—what is there incredible in the assertion that God has assumed a human soul and body?" We know the answer to that question, and so did Augustine: if the Greeks hold the incarnation of the *logos* in a *person* to be an absurdity, it is because they prefer to see the *logos* operating in the entire cosmos, a notion that leads to positing the existence of a "soul of this visible world," and of a rationality immanent in "this visible world . . . this vast corporeal mass." Augustine continues: "For you allege, on the authority of Plato, that this world is a living being, and a being of utter blessedness." Why should what is true of bodies in this world, the planets, for example—that they are the incarnation of the divine *logos*—not also be true of the Christ who is infinitely superior to them in all ways? "And yet," Augustine continues, "you refuse to recognize the incarnation of the unchanging Son of God, which brings us salvation so that we can arrive at those realities in which we believe, and which we can in some small measure comprehend." Why should this be? The answer is, as always, out of pride: "The only reason, I repeat, is that Christ is humble, and you are proud."[26] Pride here is undoubtedly the pride of reason, but also, and perhaps primarily, it is the cosmological vision of salvation, which could never be satisfied with being reduced to one person alone. It was the sin of reason against faith, but also, and perhaps even more, of intelligence against love.

At the Heart of the Christian Doctrine of Salvation: Why Only Christian Love (agapē) Is Stronger Than Death

It is obvious that love is the principal saving virtue in Christianity. Everyone knows how Jesus responds to the Pharisee lawyer who tests him with the question, "Teacher, which commandment of the law is the greatest?" Jesus replies: "'You shall love the Lord your God with your whole heart, with your whole soul, and with all your mind.' This is the greatest and first commandment. The second is like it: 'You shall love your neighbor as yourself'" (Matthew 22:34–39). Jesus was of course aware that he was couching his response within the phraseology of his interlocutor's tradition. In appearance at least, all he does is to repeat two passages from Scripture that no one in the group he was addressing could reject: the first is from Deuteronomy (6:5): "You shall love the Lord, your God, with all your heart, and with all your soul, and with all your strength"; the other from Leviticus (19:18): "Take no revenge and cherish no grudge against your fellow countrymen. You shall love your neighbor as yourself." The idea that Judaism had ignored the "law of love" to the profit of the "law of fear" alone is false. Nonetheless, the Christian vocabulary was enriched by a new term to signify the most authentic sort of love: *agapē*—from the Greek verb *agapan*, which simply means "to cherish" or "to love" and is usually translated as "charity." It is the term that Jesus uses, according to John 13:35, when he declares: "This is how all will know you for my disciples: your love for one another." It is this love that is stronger than death when Jesus raises Lazarus from the dead. It underlies the belief that Jesus demands of his faithful when he promises them: "I am the resurrection and the life: whoever believes in me, though he should die, will come to life; and whoever is alive and believes in me will never die" (John 11:25).

The specific sense of *agapē*, in relation to forms of love known under other terms by the Greeks (notably *eros* and *philia*) has been scrutinized and commented innumerable times. We shall not return to the question here.[27] It seems to me more important, in the context of an analysis of the ruptures effected by the Christian doctrine of salvation in the great Greek wisdom traditions, to investigate how Christianity, with its new conception of a love stronger than death, hence a saving love, revolutionized the old soteriologies. In a nutshell: salvation, a problem among the Stoics, became a solution in Christianity. It is love that led us astray and made us unhappy by making us excessively attached to the good things of this world; now it is love that saves us and enables us to enter into the blessed life. Things are, of course, more complex than this succinct statement makes it seem, for Christian love cannot be confused with the passion that leads to a pathological attachment to terrestrial beings. Still, given that love comes from the "heart" and leaves room for tenderness, it does not exclude certain forms of attachment to individual beings, something that Stoicism, for its part, rejects with all its might. So we need to define our terms more precisely: as we shall see, it will be worthwhile. In the final analysis, the entire meaning of Christian soteriology stands or falls on such definitions and, along with it, all the allure that the new definition of the good life might exert among converts to Christianity who had dwelt among the ancient philosophies for a time.

The point is crucial. Stoicism—and here it is close to Buddhism— held the fear of death to be the worst impediment to the blessed life. As it happens, that anxiety is not unconnected to love. To put it very simply:

there is an apparently insurmountable contradiction between love, which leads almost ineluctably to attachment, and death, which is separation. If the law of this world is that of finitude and change, to become attached to things or beings is to sin by lack of wisdom. Not that one should sink into indifference, which neither the Stoic sage nor the Buddhist monk would recommend; compassion, good will, and solicitude toward others, even toward all forms of life, must remain the highest ethical rule for our behavior. But passion is, to say the least, not well viewed by the sage, and even family ties must be relaxed when they become too much of an "attachment." It is in this context, as we have seen, that Epictetus offers a disciple some advice that may seem strange to modern ears, but that, for him, summarizes the entire wisdom of the world:

> If in this way you long for your son, or your friend, at a time when he is not given to you, rest assured that you are hankering for a fig in winter-time. For as winter-time is to a fig, so is every state of affairs, which arises out of the universe, in relation to the things which are destroyed in accordance with that state of affairs. Furthermore, at the very moment when you are taking delight in something, call to mind the opposite impressions. What harm is there if you whisper to yourself, at the very moment you are kissing your child, and say, "To-morrow you will die"? So likewise to your friend, "To-morrow you will go abroad, or I shall, and we shall never see each other again"?[28]

If one must practice thinking ceaselessly about death, separation, and the *impermanence* of all things, it is not out of a taste for the morbid, but rather out of an interest in happiness: if separation is the law of this world, we should anticipate it and prepare ourselves for it so that, when the day comes, we will not be taken aback and filled with sadness. True liberty and the most authentic sort of joy depend upon this preparation.

Thus the Buddhist monk, like the Greek sage, has every interest in living in relative solitude as much as possible: "You will make every attempt, in virtue of your spiritual practice, to detach yourself from the objects of attachment,"[29] an ideal that is very difficult to attain in ordinary social and family life. "Among human beings, the life of laypeople is beset with all sorts of troubles and problems. And they are more involved with worldly activities that are not very conducive to the practice of the Dharma. Life as a monk or nun is said to be far more conducive to the practice of the Dharma, to put an end to this cycle of existence."[30] This is because the monastic life exposes us to infinitely fewer temptations of attachment than any other. It is precisely from these temptations that we must free ourselves if we want to overcome the fear of death, for "the ideal way for a person to die is having given away everything, internally and externally, so that there is as little as possible yearning, grasping, and attachment for the mind at that essential moment to latch onto. So before we die we should try to free ourselves of attachment to all our possessions, friends, and loved ones,"[31] an operation that cannot be carried out at the final moment but demands an entire previous life of wisdom.

Christian love, it might be argued, is not all that far from this Hellenic or Eastern wisdom. In many ways it does seem to exclude any notion of attachment to the creatures of this world. As André Comte-Sponville has stressed in a debate in which he and I took opposing views on this point: "Charity [*agapé*] culminates in love of one's neighbor. But, precisely, one is not *attached* to one's neighbor! A neighbor is by definition anybody. Hence charity is precisely, in Pascal's phrase, a love *without attachment.* Besides, what characterizes it and is the special mark of the Gospel is not the love that we bear our children or our friends, to whom we are attached, but the love that we should bear even for our enemies! What greater detachment? In short, love without attachment is not only a Buddhist notion; it is also a Christian virtue, which is called charity: to love without wanting to possess or to keep."[32] I agree, up to a point. André Comte-Sponville is correct, and, in fact, one could hardly find a better guide than Pascal, who confirms his point, as if in advance, in a fragment that Voltaire (wrongly, from a Christian viewpoint) judged to be unreasonable: "If there is a God, we must love Him only, and not the creatures of a day. . . . And this is the conclusion of the wise: 'There is a God, let us therefore not take delight in the creatures.' Therefore all that incites us to attach ourselves to the creatures is bad; since it prevents us from serving God if we know Him, or from seeking Him if we know Him not. Now we are full of lust. Therefore we are full of evil; therefore we ought to hate ourselves and all that excited us to attach ourselves to any other object than God only."[33] But who could move us "to attach ourselves to any other object than God only" if not our loved ones—not our neighbor, but those whom we love in a *singular,* individual, personal manner, like beings apart from all others? Jesus says as much, and in an even more radical manner: "Do not suppose that my mission on earth is to spread peace. My mission is to spread, not peace, but division. I have come to set a man at odds with his father, a daughter with her mother, a daughter-in-law with her mother-in-law: in short, to make a man's enemies those of his own household. Whoever loves father or mother, son or daughter, more than me is not worthy of me" (Matthew 10:34–37). This statement seems to contradict the first commandment, given that its terms are more suitable to the demonic than to the saintly: separation, enmity, hatred. This is of course not the case, and Jesus's meaning is clear enough: human love, love that is purely human, excludes God, and as such is to be hated. The passage at least seems to bring striking confirmation to the idea that authentic Christian love is not a love of attachment and even less a passion, and that, as such, it is not as distant as I have seemed to suggest from the recommendations of the Stoics and the Buddhists. Moreover, between Jesus's words and Pascal's thought, we have the entire works of Augustine to confirm the point, if need be, as evidenced by this passage (among many others) from *De vera religione:* "No one can perfectly love that *to* which we are called unless he hate that *from* which we are called." This is why "man is not to be loved by man even as brothers after the flesh are loved, or sons, or wives, or kinsfolk, or relatives, or fellow citizens. For such love is temporal. . . . Let no one think that is inhuman. It is more inhuman to love a man because he is your son and not because he is a man, that is, not to love that in him which belongs to God, but to love that which belongs to yourself."[34] In short, love of one's neighbor not only is not love of those close to you but is the very opposite. Augustine's reasoned conclusion leaves no doubt on this point. Since "no man can serve two masters" (Matthew 6:24), "if we are ablaze with love for eternity we shall hate temporal relationships. . . . Human nature is to be loved whether it be perfect or in process of becoming perfect, but without any condition of carnal relationship."[35]

If we take the trouble to pursue the question, however, to dig below the surface and to reflect a bit more on the exact nature of the Christian condemnation of love that is attachment, it soon seems quite different from that of Buddhism and Stoicism. Here, too, Pascal sets us on the right track. In fragment 471 of his *Pensées* he clearly explains why it is unworthy to let someone else become attached to oneself (and, consequently, why it is absurd to permit oneself to give in to a love that is an attachment for another). In order to comprehend the passage, we need to read it as a whole:

> It is unjust that men should attach themselves to me, even though they do it with pleasure and voluntarily. I should deceive those in whom I had created this desire; for I am not the end of any, and I have not the wherewithal to satisfy them. Am I not about to die? And thus the object of their attachment will die. Therefore, as I would be blamable in causing a falsehood to be believed, though I

should employ gentle persuasion, though it should be believed with pleasure, and though it should give me pleasure; even so I am blamable in making myself loved, and if I attract persons to attach themselves to me, I ought to warn those who are ready to consent to a lie, that they ought not to believe it, whatever advantage comes to me from it; and likewise that they ought not to attach themselves to me; for they ought to spend their life and their care in pleasing God, or in seeking Him.[36]

Once again the argument seems to parallel that of the ancient wisdom traditions: for Pascal, too, it is because the object of attachment is mortal that all complaisance toward it is unworthy or absurd. As Paul states in his Epistle to the Galatians (6:7–8): "A man will reap only what he sows. If he sows in the field of the flesh, he will reap a harvest of corruption; but, if his seed-ground is the spirit, he will reap everlasting life." Or, as Augustine says regarding those who attach themselves to mortal creatures out of love: "You are seeking a happy life in the realm of death, and it will not be found there. How could life be happy, where there is no life at all?"[37] But the contrary lurks between the lines of his argument: if the object of my attachment were not mortal, how would it be wrong or unreasonable? If my love were directed at eternity in the other, why should I not attach myself? This is something that Augustine, before Pascal but already in the same line of thinking, willingly concedes: "Do not, then, let us serve the creature rather than the Creator, or become vain in our thoughts. That is the rule of perfect religion. If we cleave to the eternal Creator we must necessarily be somehow affected by eternity."[38] In other words, when love is directed toward God, the *attachment* that it implies becomes legitimate. By the same logic, however, if it is directed toward creatures *insofar as they are divine*—and the reverse of man's *misère* is his *grandeur*—does not love once again become licit, and even desirable? This is the entire theme of the love "in" God that, contrary to the universal compassion of the Stoics and the Buddhists, in no way prevents consideration of the singular qualities of each individual.

Two or Three Loves? Love "in" God as a Reconciliation of the Love of God and the Love of Human Beings

We must not be fooled by the simplistic alternative that Augustine's words suggest. They are often quoted and commented on in a reductionist sense implying that there are only two loves: love of God to the point of self-contempt, and love of self to the point of contempt for God. It is obvious, in fact, that this dichotomy does not exhaust either the meaning of *agapē* or Augustine's authentic thought: how could a Christian unreservedly recommend self-contempt while also encouraging us to love our neighbor "as ourselves"? In a Christian perspective the self can only be hated to the extent that it tends to exclusivity in love. One must thus conclude that there are not two but three possible forms of love. First, of course, there is the love of God, which cannot be surpassed. Second, there is self-love, which, when it excludes the love of God, approaches self-centredness and urges us to love others only out of egotism, for our own purposes. To return to Pascal's categories, the first sort is related to conversion, the second to "amusement": it is the love of attachment in its most condemnable and even senseless form. On this point, as we have seen, Christianity joins Stoicism and Buddhism: it is supremely unreasonable to become attached to mortal creatures, given that separation is ineluctable and brings unhappiness. It follows—and Pascal was right on this point—that it is just as unworthy to permit others to become attached to us in an exclusive or possessive manner as it is to let ourselves become attached to them in that manner. A case in point is the legitimate fear that visits all parents at one moment or another, when they fear their own death more for its effect on others than for themselves. We are well aware (more or less consciously) that our children's attachment to us constitutes a major risk for them: what will become of them if we disappear? And will that eventuality not become a reality, one day or another, given that we are mortal? There is a third form of love, however, that reconciles the first two and thus surpasses the ancient wisdom traditions and their rejection of individual attachments: it is the love "in God" that includes all creatures inasmuch as they too, thanks to salvation, can attain immortality.

Augustine gives a remarkable description of this third form of love in the *Confessions* where he speaks of the loss of a "friend most tenderly loved." With genuine psychological insight, Augustine evokes the pangs of a bereavement that he suffered before his conversion, when he still knew nothing of the Christian doctrine of salvation: "The more I loved him, the more I hated death, which had taken him from me; I hated it as a hideous enemy, and feared it, and pictured it as ready to devour all human beings, since it had been able to make away with him. Yes, this was my state of mind: I remember it." Augustine dwells at length on the contradiction between love and death in that state of mind: "I was miserable, and miserable too is everyone whose mind is chained by friendship with mortal things, and is torn apart by their loss, and then becomes aware of the misery that it was in even before it lost them." At this stage in his life, hence in a still pre-Christian perspective, Augustine of course echoes Stoic thought and, more generally, all the wisdom traditions hostile to attachment to mortal beings: "How had that sorrow been able so easily to pierce my inmost being, if not because I had poured out my soul into the sand by loving a man doomed to death as though he were never to die?" This was the unhappiness to which all human loves are destined when they are too human and fail to seek in the other anything but the "signs of his goodwill" that make us feel worthwhile, reassure us, and satisfy our egos: "From this springs our grief if someone dies, from this come the darkness of sorrow and the heart drenched with tears because sweetness has turned to bitterness, so that the dying lose their life, life becomes no better than death for those who live on." This is the same indignity that Pascal speaks of when the person who allows himself to love as if he were immortal knows very well that he is just a mortal among others. One must know how to resist attachments when they are exclusive, because everything wastes away in this world, and everything is subject to decline and to death. Where mortal creatures are concerned, Augustine writes:

> Let my soul use these things to praise you,
> O God, creator of them all,
> but let it not be glued fast to them by sensual love,
> for they are going whither they were always destined to go,
> toward extinction;
> and they rend my soul with death-dealing desires,
> for it too longs to be, and loves to rest in what it loves.
> But in them it finds no place to rest,
> because they do not stand firm;
> they are transient, and who can follow them with the senses of the
>   body?[39]

It would be difficult to express this thought better, and it seems to me that the Stoic sage and the Buddhist might subscribe to Augustine's thoughts.

But who has said that humans are mortal? Not to become too attached to the transitory makes good sense. But why should this nonattachment also apply to what is not transitory? And does not the whole originality of the Christian message reside in the announcement of the good news of the resurrection, not only of souls, but also of individual bodies, of persons as persons? Where the Buddhist sage considers the individual as nothing but

an illusion, a temporary aggregation destined for dissolution and impermanence, and where the Stoic sees the self as fated to be fused into the totality of the cosmos, *Christianity promises the immortality of the individual person when saved by the grace of God.* Moreover, it is precisely by love, not only
love of God, or of one's neighbor, but equally love of one's family and
closest friends, that salvation is won! Here we see *how love, formerly a problem, becomes a solution: provided that it is not exclusively love of God, but directed to individual creatures, that is, to persons, it is nonetheless love in God.*
This is, of course, what Augustine is getting at when he addresses the
Lord: "Blessed is he who loves you, and loves his friend in you and his
enemy for your sake. He alone loses no one dear to him, to whom all are
dear in the One who is never lost. And who is this but our God? . . . No
one loses you unless he tries to get rid of you, and if he does try to do that,
where can he go, whither does he flee?"[40] We might add, pursuing this
thought, that no one loses the individual beings he loves unless he ceases to
love them in God.

Just as Pascal does not exclude concupiscent love, if it is directed to God
himself rather than to creatures as such,[41] so Augustine does not exclude
love that is attachment when its object is the divine—God himself, of
course, but also creatures in God inasmuch as they also escape finitude to
enter into the sphere of eternity. "If kinship with other souls appeals to you,
let them be loved in God, because they too are changeable and gain stability only when fixed in him; otherwise they would go their way and be
lost. . . . Stand with him and you will stand firm, rest in him and you will
find peace."[42] Nothing is more striking, in this regard, than the serenity
with which Augustine speaks of his own losses, this time after his conversion to Christianity. The first of these was the death of his mother, to
whom he was very close: "By this means something boyish in myself,
which was sliding toward tears, was also restrained by the man's voice in
my heart, and it too grew quiet. We judged it unfitting to mark this death
by plaintive protests and laments, since these are customarily employed to
mourn the misery of the dying, or death as complete extinction. But she
neither died in misery nor died altogether. The evidence of her virtues and
her sincere faith gave us good reason to hold this as certain." Similarly, Augustine speaks of the "happy death of two friends, men who were very dear
to him" and who had, to his happiness, been converted themselves, which
meant that they could in turn benefit from "the resurrection of the just." As
always, Augustine finds the right word, for in the final analysis it is the resurrection that is the basis of this third form of love, which is love in God.

It is thus in and by the resurrection that the Christian concept of the good life finds its high point.

Christ, by causing "the death of our death" and "rendering immortal this mortal flesh," is the only one who promises us that our life of love will not end with terrestrial death. From the subterranean Sheol of the Hebrews, the sojourn of the dead after their earthly life, to the reincarnation of souls presented by Plato's *Republic* in the story of Er, the idea of an immortality of beings was clearly present in many forms in a number of philosophies and religions before Christianity. Christian resurrection, however, offers the special characteristic of closely associating three themes fundamental to the Christian doctrine of the blessed life: that of the personal immortality of the soul; that of the resurrection of the body (I am thinking of the singularity of beloved faces, for example); and that of salvation by love, even highly individual love, provided that it be love in God. It is as such that resurrection constitutes the nucleus of the entire Christian doctrine of salvation. Without it—and it is significant that the Acts of the Apostles call it the "good news"—the whole message of Christ collapses, as the First Epistle to the Corinthians (15:13–14) unambiguously declares: "If there is no resurrection of the dead, Christ himself has not been raised. And if Christ has not been raised, our preaching is void of content and your faith is empty too." The resurrection is, so to speak, the alpha and omega of Christian soteriology, given that it occurs not only at the end of this earthly life, but just as much at its beginning, as witnessed by the liturgy of baptism, considered as a first death (symbolized by immersion) and a first resurrection to the authentic life, that of the community of beings destined for eternity and, as such, worthy of a love that can, without fear of loss, be individual.

It must be stressed that it is not only the soul that is resuscitated but also the composite of soul and body, the individual person as such. When Jesus reappears before his disciples, he invites them to touch him in order to remove all their doubts; then, as proof of his "materiality," he asks for food, which he eats before their eyes: "If the Spirit of him who raised Jesus from the dead dwells in you, then he who raised Christ from the dead will bring your mortal bodies to life also, through his Spirit dwelling in you" (Epistle of Paul to the Romans, 8:11). No matter that such a thing is difficult, if not impossible, to imagine (With what body will we be reborn? At what age? What is the meaning of a "spiritual" or "glorious" body?); no matter that this is quite surely part of the unsoundable mysteries of a revelation that, on this point, far surpasses our reason. The teachings of Christian doctrine permit no doubt: "'The flesh is the hinge of salvation.' We believe in God who is creator of the flesh; we believe in the Word made flesh in order to redeem the flesh; we believe in the resurrection of the flesh, the fulfillment of both the creation and the redemption of the flesh. . . . 'We believe in the true resurrection of this flesh that we now possess.'"[43] The question of the incarnation of the divine *logos* in a human being, Jesus Christ, and the difficulties that it raised for both the Jews and the Greek philosophers, were in no way theoretical: what was at stake was nothing less than the ultimate tenet of any doctrine of salvation, or (which amounts to the same thing) of any version of the good life, which is how to surmount finitude and death.

In this regard the Christian response, at least for those who believe in it, is surely the most "functional" of them all: if love and even attachment are not excluded, provided that they are directed to the divine as such—and, as we have seen, this is explicitly stated by both Pascal and Augustine—and if individual beings (not only one's neighbor but one's loved ones as well) are an integral part of the divine inasmuch as they are saved by God and called to a resurrection that is also individual, then it appears that only Christian soteriology will permit us to surpass not only the fear of death but even death itself. Operating on an individual level rather than anonymously or abstractly, Christianity alone appears to offer humanity the good news of a victory, finally and truly won, of personal immortality over our mortal condition: "This, then, is the full satisfaction of souls, this the happy life, to recognize piously and completely the One through whom you are led into the truth, the manner in which you enjoy the truth, and the bond that connects you with the supreme measure."[44] Augustine's equation for the fulfillment of the blessed life, as we can see, is opposed in its very principle to that of philosophy. Admittedly, it returns to the three main axes of philosophy: *theōria*, which identifies the "supreme measure"; *praxis*, which attempts even in this life to adhere to that "supreme measure" as far as possible; and the doctrine of salvation, which teaches us at what cost we are saved from the finitude that is our lot. But underlying these common categories a difference (even a contrast) prevails. Religion, far from inciting us to save ourselves by our own efforts, recommends humility in salvation by an Other upon whom we are utterly dependent. Even more important, if what is essential in attaining eternal life and liberating ourselves here and now of all of our anxieties is, as Augustine states, to be "attached to the supreme measure," then philosophy has something diabolical about it since it invites us to doubt, therefore to stray, if only in thought, from the measure that links us to life eternal. Doubt, as any attentive reader of Genesis knows,[45] is the devil's work par excellence, the ultimate objective of one who, by the temptations he offers us, strives to separate us as far as possible from the Being who can alone save us from a death and a solitude as eternal as the life that we would have had, by the grace of salvation, if we had remained "in" him. The force of this message of humility striking down the pride of a too-human reason was to contribute strongly, over the centuries, to relegating philosophy to the subordinate rank of handmaid to theology. How, at the dawn of modern times, did philosophy manage to regain the upper hand? How did the lay thought that emerged out of Christianity confront the old questions about the good life? We must explore this question if we are to put our problematic situation as "Moderns" into proper perspective.

CHAPTER 11

The Renascence of Lay Philosophy
& the Humanization
of the Good Life

How did modern humanism (in all senses of the term) "emerge" from religion? What were the effects of that emergence on new definitions of the good life that are still forming on the horizon of our thoughts today? To comprehend this phenomenon, we first need to grasp what occurred in the history of thought when philosophy, replaced by theology, entered into servitude. It is only by taking that subjugation into account that we can understand the motives and the strategies that led philosophy to shake off its subordinate status and raise new questions about man's destination—questions that were new because they were inscribed within the intellectual perspective of the secularization inherent to a democratic space.

Among all the explanations that have been suggested for the "disenchantment of the world," two strike me as having been notably underestimated—at least from the viewpoint adopted in the present work. The first has to do with the changes that the rediscovery of Aristotelian rationalism in the thirteenth century introduced into the relations between theology and philosophy. The entire problematic of the relations between faith and reason took a new path in the Augustinian tradition that resulted in freeing philosophy from religion and giving it greater autonomy. The second explanation, which is perhaps better established, has to do with the scientific revolution of the sixteenth century, a turning point between the closed world of the Greeks and the infinite universe of the Moderns and a transition that spawned a new type of rationalism. But I shall treat this topic not from the point of view of the history of science but rather from an ethical perspective, taking the word "ethical" in a broad sense. The first task is to see just how the Greek wisdom traditions suffered from the repercussions of a scientific revolution hostile to their cosmological bases, but we also need to understand how Christianity experienced the same event as a veritable earthquake, thanks to its conversion to Aristotelianism under the influence of Thomas Aquinas.

These considerations might seem to be limited to the purely historical or the factual. Yet they are indispensable to providing a genuinely philosophical perspective to what Hannah Arendt has called the "condition of modern man"—that is, the situation of individuals when largely deprived of apparently incontrovertible notions inherited from cosmological or religious traditions. To put the matter differently, we must now turn to an archaeology of radical materialism if we hope to define the power inherent in that new human condition or to understand the impasses that it so clearly encounters today.

Augustine's Legacy: Philosophy as Handmaid of Religion, or How Reason Was Put to the Service of Revelation

If the roads to salvation are indicated by revelation, if it is faith that saves and reason that leads pagan thinkers astray on the paths of vanity and pride, what is the good of philosophizing? Is it not preferable, in the long run, to devote one's life to exercising the cardinal virtues of faith, hope, and charity rather than attempting to construct systems whose very sophistication is dubious, if not downright deadly? It was more or less in these terms that the question of the status of philosophy was posed as soon as religion was accepted as offering the sole authentic doctrine of salvation. Christian thinkers quickly brought a response to these questions, the essence of which is contained in the famous phrase that Peter Damian, a doctor of the Italian Church close to Pope Gregory VII, proposed to theological meditation in the eleventh century: philosophy is and must remain the "handmaid of theology" (*philosophia ancilla theologiae*).[1] Thomas Aquinas himself, even though he was the Christian thinker who most resembled a philosopher, repeated the expression on several occasions. "Sacred doctrine" should occupy the first and highest place among possible sciences open to the human mind, for "this doctrine is wisdom above all human wisdom, not merely in any one order, but absolutely. . . . In the order of all human life, the prudent man is called wise, because he orders his acts to a fitting end. . . . The knowledge proper to this science comes through revelation, and not through natural reason," which also means that "whatsoever is found in other sciences contrary to any truth of this science, must be condemned as false: *Destroying counsels and every height that exalteth itself against the knowledge of God* (II Corinthians 10:5)."[2] As is always the case in this context, we can sense the theme of pride, the *superbia* of a philosophical discipline that must be put back in its place, which was subordinate and instrumental.

That said, and although all Christian authors had long been in agreement on this point, the servile status reserved to philosophy can be understood in two quite different ways.

In an earlier interpretation inherited from Augustine, philosophy, while relegated to a secondary plane, continued to occupy the eminent position of a science that was expected to give, as far as possible, profound meaning to the content of revelation. It was in this perspective that the apostle Paul, in a much earlier age, invited us to use our reason both to reach a deep understanding of the meaning of the Gospels and to fully appreciate the natural beauties of creation. The task of philosophy as the use of human reason thus has two complementary aspects. As a theory of interpretation ("hermeneutics"), it permits us to pass from the figurative or symbolic meaning to the real meaning of Christ's words. Jesus speaks as if he were speaking to small children so that all can understand him, but he also speaks in parables, proverbs, metaphors, symbols—all forms of discourse that need deciphering, so they call for the same intellectual faculties that come into play in philosophy. But beyond reading the Gospels, we also need to take nature into consideration if we are to apprehend the divine perfection of the created world and to grasp the natural universe as a perfect order, a language of God that bears witness to his greatness and his infinite goodness toward us.

Philosophy is thus invaluable for pursuing both of these aims, provided that it remains within its designated role and is guided in all things by faith. Indeed, "faith is thought's assent to realities that it does not perceive. For us, reality thus constitutes a truth that is hidden and currently inaccessible to our thought. Yet the very certainty that we are denied knowledge, properly speaking, of that object does not completely discourage our reason. Faith, to the contrary, is like an appeal and a continual invitation to philosophy."[3] Philosophy, therefore, cannot possess other objects than those of revelation: it is, so to speak, merged with natural theology as its rational, hence subordinate, moment. It is in this spirit that the concept of philosophy as the handmaid of theology remained a constant in Christian doctrine from Augustine to Bonaventura in the thirteenth century. Most of the great theologians speak of moving from *faith to reason,* with faith always closely guiding reason in all its endeavors by setting themes and objectives for it to pursue. This is how the idea of a Christian philosophy acquires its full meaning and legitimacy.

Of course, a negative variant of this policy is also possible: it is always to be feared that pride might regain the upper hand, tempting philosophic reason to throw off the reins that revelation claimed to hold; that the slave might revolt, and human arrogance, instead of moving from faith to reason, might be tempted to take the opposite route from reason to faith, thus stripping faith of all the merit that religion accords it. What, in fact, would belief be worth if it were brought to bear solely on elements previously established by the unassisted power of the human mind? Would there still be a place for the contents of faith if these were the object of a demonstration that leads to firm and certain knowledge? Clearly not, for if I "know" that something exists, I no longer need to "believe" it. This is why Damian himself, and soon the papacy with him, tended toward a much more restrictive interpretation of the role of philosophy in its relation to theology, seeing it more as a dangerous slave than a trustworthy and valuable servant.[4] It was urgent that matters be taken in hand, which is why the church, speaking through Pope Gregory IX, condemned the liberties taken by the Paris "artists,"[5] who all too often claimed the right to discuss theological questions in light of the philosophy of Aristotle rather than with the guidance of the church fathers. As we shall soon see, not even the rationalism of Thomas Aquinas himself escaped this criticism.

Before we analyze this new stage in the relations between religion and philosophy—a stage largely dependent on the rediscovery of Aristotle on the part of twelfth-century Arab and Jewish writers and the impetus it gave to the independence of philosophy from theology—we need to mention one crucial consequence of the new, instrumental status of philosophy. Whether it is viewed positively or pejoratively; whether it is taken to be the valued servant or the restive slave of theology, what the Greeks saw as the ultimate ends of philosophy were turned upside down. For Greeks of all schools of thought, philosophy was above all an apprenticeship in wisdom;

a mode of life rather than a discourse. Pierre Hadot has written with particular acuity on this aspect of philosophy.[6] Modern philosophy (with the exception of its greatest exponents) has too often accepted as ineluctable a sort of historical or academic commentary in which it is at times difficult, if not impossible, to discern any message for real life. More often than not, the lives of today's philosophers have little connection to their thought; they do not even see such a connection as an enviable ideal. The person is one thing; that person's work is another; and anyone who attempts to merge the two or even relate the one to the other invites the sharpest sort of criticism. Even when they study antiquity, our historians of ideas declaim their conviction that philosophy cannot and should not be related to notions of wisdom or of the good or successful life.[7]

This revolution in the way philosophers of classical antiquity are regarded seems mysterious in other ways as well, given that it appears so contrary not only to the etymology but also to the spirit of a discipline that is in no way destined *a priori* for either specialization or technical jargon. The history of Christian theology provides the key to the problem.[8] If the doctrine of salvation is to be sought no longer in philosophy but in religion; if philosophy itself is reduced to an instrument that may be more or less useful or dangerous but is always subordinate because it is cut off from the supreme objectives of salvation, then philosophy is fated to become mere scholastics, a conceptual analysis no longer in the service of an initiation to the blessed life but, as the name indicates, a discipline in the service of scholarly teaching and reserved to academia. Philosophy, even after its emancipation in the modern period, was never to fully recover from its demotion to an inferior status when Christianity won out over the Greek soteriologies. With rare exceptions—Montaigne, for example, or, in part, Kant and Nietzsche—philosophy never got back to those "wisdom exercises" that were intended for everyone, not just specialists, for which it was prized in antiquity. How can we explain this situation today and draw a lesson from it?

Paradoxically, it was precisely from within Christianity that philosophy was to draw the nucleus of its future emancipation from religion. But it owed its liberation to the two other great monotheisms, which—well before Christian doctrine—had rediscovered Aristotelianism, the supreme tradition of Greek rationalism, while Christian thought remained with Augustinian Platonism. Aristotelianism constrained the three great religions (Islam and Judaism mainly in the twelfth century; Christianity in the thirteenth century) to find new terms in which to pose the question, deci-

sive for the good life, of the relations between faith and reason and between revelation and "natural light": in short, the relations between religion
and philosophy.

The Truths of Reason and Revealed Truths: Toward a "Double Truth"

In Andalusia, where it left a legacy that still enlightens humanity, and soon
in the rest of Europe, the rediscovery of Aristotle obliged the three
monotheistic religions to enter into a dialogue that remains unique in history, past or present.[9] The pioneers were Averroës for Islam and, in the
same century, Maimonides for Judaism,[10] but Albertus Magnus, and then
his leading pupil, Thomas Aquinas, soon added their reflections on the relations between philosophy and religion. It was in great part thanks to
these men that Christian doctrine was to "convert" (if we may use that
term) to Artistotelianism. In order to evaluate the consequences of this dialogue for the new relationship that was arising between faith and reason
and, hence, for its relevance to our principal question (whether the good
life was to be guided by religion or philosophy), we need to keep two things
in mind.

For all four of these theologians, Aristotle was obviously not Moses,
Mohammed, or Christ. But it is hardly an exaggeration to say that he came
as close to being on their level as was possible for a human being—or, to
put it better, his status was somewhat analogous to theirs, notably that of
Jesus. In his own way, Aristotle, like Jesus, was an "incarnate *logos*," a "word
made flesh," a terrestrial incarnation, if not of the divinity, at least of reason. Admittedly, Augustine had held Plato and the Neoplatonists to represent the height of natural enlightenment, but he also subjected them to
many criticisms. Not only Averroës and Maimonides but also Albertus
Magnus and Thomas Aquinas regarded Aristotle as unsurpassed; they believed he embodied the perfect and absolute truth in philosophy, a genre
that was admittedly thought to be inferior to religion, but that was nonetheless essential. Averroës, the true founding father of religious Aristotelianism, had no doubt that "the doctrine of Aristotle is the sovereign
truth. No one can have knowledge that equals or even approaches his. It is
he who is given to us by God to learn all that can be known." In his commentary on the *Physics* of Aristotle, Averroës describes this unequaled intellectual discovery: "We address endless praise to God, who distinguished
that man for perfection and who placed him alone at the highest degree of
human superiority, which no man in any century had attained; it was to

him that God was alluding when he said: 'this superiority, God accords to whomever he wishes.'"[11] Maimonides is scarcely less generous in his praise; in a letter to Samuel ibn Tibbon he recommends reading Aristotle with the commentaries of Averroës, but also suggests not bothering with the other ancient philosophers. According to Maimonides, it is unnecessary to read Plato, whom he considers needlessly obscure, and he tells his friend not to occupy himself with the books written by Aristotle's predecessors because Aristotle's intellect is "the supreme degree of the human intellect."[12] As for Thomas Aquinas, he simply calls Aristotle "the philosopher," as if it were taken for granted that there was no other, either before or after him, and describes Averroës as "the commentator" of Aristotle.

For the Christian West, the shift from a philosophical model based on Platonism (the Augustinian model) to an Aristotelian model posed a problem, and it would be a mistake to underestimate the importance of this problem for the future of an autonomous secular thought. If Aristotle—as Averroës, Maimonides, and Thomas Aquinas asserted—was indeed the incarnation of philosophy on earth, if he was reason at its highest degree, how can we explain that, at least at first sight, there are a number of major differences between the content of his philosophy and the content of revelation, be it Christian, Jewish, or Muslim revelation? Between the lines we can read here the entire relationship between faith and reason and the need to recast it. How can these relations be reconciled in the apparently numerous instances in which they seem to differ noticeably? What role does each play in the religious experience? On at least three essential points, there is a danger of their leading to radically opposed conclusions.

It is clear, first of all, that in an Aristotelian perspective, since God is defined as "thought of thought," he has no other imaginable object than himself. He can in no way interest himself in individual beings, in creatures, which means that the entire notion of a personal and benevolent providence—the *particular* providence *attentive to each one of us* that was, as we have seen, so important to Justin Martyr and Augustine—is fundamentally cast into doubt.

Next, if the world is eternal, as Aristotle continually asserts as one of his most constant and most certain theses, is it not rather difficult to maintain revelation's thesis that the universe was created? Ultimately, the first few chapters of Genesis, and with them the creation of the world, of man, and of all other creatures, become highly problematic.

Finally, if man is an indissociable composite of matter (his body) and form (his soul), it is hard to see how the soul, in detaching itself from the body at the moment of death, could continue to exist as an entity. At most one can imagine the immortality of a universal intelligence common to the species, but the immortality of particular beings becomes more than problematic—with the result that we would have nothing to hope (or to fear) from life after death. Does this not challenge the very nub of the Christian doctrine of salvation, along with any thought of a resurrection implying the idea of a personal life after death? On a still deeper level, is not the link between that doctrine and the moral perspective broken when fate seems to regain its rights over liberty and individual responsibility?

It is understandable that Augustine's heirs within the official church did not look favorably on the Aristotelianization of Christianity. Most of the apparent contradictions between Aristotelian philosophy and Christian revelation could be resolved—which was just what Thomas Aquinas did—and when contradictions remained, one could always appeal to the existence of unfathomable mysteries and the superiority of revelation. The fact remains, as Etienne Gilson rightly notes, that in the eyes of Augustine's heirs, "a wide gap appeared between so-called natural revelation and true Revelation. To discover Aristotle was to discover, first, that human reason does not spontaneously direct its path toward Revelation."[13] This is well put, and the temptation soon arose simply to prohibit the teaching of Aristotelianism. Gregory IX, in a decree dated 1 April 1272, forbade the Paris "artists" to engage in any philosophical debate that treated both philosophy and faith. On 10 December 1270, Etienne Tempier, bishop of Paris, had already condemned thirteen philosophical propositions of Aristotelian inspiration; and in 1277, at the request of Pope John XXI, that condemnation was extended to 219 theses, including the most controversial ones: "The world is eternal; the soul, which is the form of man as man, perishes at the same time as his body; God does not know individuals; God knows nothing other than himself; and so forth."[14] The heresy was Aristotelian inspiration itself, but along with it all philosophy—once it had been identified with Aristotelianism by Averroës and his successors, including Albertus Magnus and Thomas Aquinas—became increasingly suspect. What was needed was to counter the supposed "truths of reason" with a firm reminder that revelation alone must win out in any case of conflict, and that it alone must dictate the authentic truth should reconciliation prove impossible.

This is how the doctrine of the "double truth" entered the scene. In spite of the difficulties that surround it, it can be summarized thus: if reason, identified with Aristotelianism, leads us to think about certain things that openly contradict the content of revelation—a providence that once again becomes blind and general, an impersonal immortality of the soul, the eternity of an uncreated world—must we not then admit that the two types of truths (those known by reason and those discovered by revelation) are in clear contradiction to each other?

The matter deserves a moment's attention, because it involves philosophy's independence of theology, thus the origins of the secularization of thought in the modern era.[15] If philosophy, in its purely autonomous and rational exercise, should ever rise to encompass truths that are no longer those of revelation, it follows that the latter, and with it all of theology, would no longer enjoy an evident monopoly of the legitimate definition of the good life. This opens the way to new doctrines of salvation and shows just how problematic the rediscovery of Aristotle could seem for the Christian religion and, more generally, for all three major monotheistic religions. But it also shows how that same rediscovery began to open up new horizons for them.

In a paradox that itself merits reflection, one might say that it was Thomas Aquinas who made the doctrine of the double truth possible at precisely the same time that he was striving with all his might to condemn it.[16] In his polemic with Averroës and his disciples—more precisely, in his controversy with a Belgian theologian, Siger de Brabant, who had been "converted" to Aristotelianism under the indirect influence of Averroës— Thomas suggests the possibility of the absurd heresy of admitting the hypothesis of a "double truth" in face of the new conflicts between reason and revelation. Thomas's quarrel focused on what was known as "monopsychism"—that is, the unity of the intellect—given that a certain comprehension of Aristotle could, as has been suggested, lead to the notion that there is no individual soul after the soul's separation from the body, which in turn would challenge the notion of personal immortality. This led Siger to the hypothesis that philosophy might defend the idea of a unique and universal intellect, whereas revelation invites us, to the contrary, to think in terms of a personal soul and personal thought. It would also explain Thomas's horror at a reading of his master, Aristotle, that threatened to introduce an insurmountable contradiction between philosophy and revelation, thus legitimate the notion of a "double truth" according to which, as Thomas states, "through reason I conclude necessarily that intellect is numerically one, but I firmly hold the opposite by faith"—an aberrant hypothesis that would lead, by the paths of simple reason, to thinking that "faith consists of propositions, some of whose opposites are necessary truths," which would thus oblige the believer to make a choice as impossible as it is tragic.[17]

The substance of this quarrel is not important here: what is essential, however, is to perceive how the quarrel threatened to dissociate philosophy from religion. As the best analysts have noted, in reality no one had defended the doctrine of a double truth—at least not before Thomas had invented the idea to place his adversary in difficulty by confronting him with its evident absurdity. Siger de Brabant did not defend the notion: as a theologian and a faithful believer, he had not the slightest hesitation to accord revelation primacy over reason in the case of an eventual conflict. When all was said and done, only one truth remained in the field, the truth of authentic faith and religion. Nor did Averroës defend a double truth, although in the same situation he would certainly have opted for the truths of reason. Nor, of course, did Thomas himself do so: having chosen the middle road of a perfect reconciliation of the two truths, he did his utmost to demonstrate that the idea of a unique intellect common to all humanity but excluding the individual thought of each single human being did not in the least correspond to Aristotle's true thought and was the simple result of an erroneous interpretation of his works.

The fact remains, however, that the worm was in the apple. Many classical theologians, the heirs of Augustine's Platonism, saw reason-Aristotle as a threat to revelation. In their eyes, philosophy as philosophy, imported from Andalusia by the philosophical versions of Islam and Judaism propounded by Averroës and Maimonides, was once more a menace to religion. Even the arguments of Thomas himself, although they were critical of Averroism (or at least of the heresies in large part wrongly attributed to Averroës), and although they brought reason down to the established limits of its accord with revelation, were worrying for those who saw them as potentially emancipating the "handmaid" from its theological tutelage. Moreover, the danger initiated by the Cordova philosophers soon became a reality. Thomism itself, despite its declared distance from Averroism, real or supposed, was not spared condemnation. After 1277, when Etienne Tempier, bishop of Paris, denounced the errors of the Paris arts faculty, Thomism was also attacked by Robert Kilwardby, archbishop of Canterbury, and again in 1284 by Kilwardby's successor, John Peckham. The condemnations were not revoked until 1325, when Thomas was canonized by Pope John XXII. Thomistic Aristotelianism, which today appears as the most traditional base of official church doctrine, was considered a modernist thought, if not a revolutionary one, in its own day.

In the meantime, however, philosophy had begun to regain its autonomy in relation to theology. Under the effect of Thomistic thought, it had freed itself from religious tutelage and shaken off the role of servant that theology had assigned to it. This process played such a major role in the birth of secular thought in the modern period that before we evaluate its impact on a renewed humanist problematic of the good life, we must retrace the basic stages of its development.

The Great Monotheisms and the Rediscovery of Aristotle: The Birth of Religious Rationalism, or The First Emancipation of Philosophy from Religion

If space allowed, we could recount here the many processes that made possible the rediscovery of Aristotle, evoking the various lines of descent and tracing the history of translations. More important here, however, is to identify the new ideas Aristotle might offer to religious thinkers. Such innovation included not only a doctrine of logical reasoning and an impressive theory of demonstration, which Aristotle's religious disciples could reinvest in proofs of the existence of God, but also, and perhaps even more useful, an incomparable grasp of concrete empirical existence. Where Platonism invited its disciples to move rapidly from the sensible world to the intelligible world, Aristotle proposed to accord that sensible world all the importance it merited. For the empirical sciences today, Aristotelian physics, astronomy, and biology have lost credibility. But in the early Middle Ages they manifested the practical value of observing events, of closely associating those events to the elaboration of a theory, and of offering a sufficiently positive and harmonious image of this world to make it the worthy creation of a divine artisan.

In the twelfth century, then, with Averroës and Maimonides, a new rationalistic attitude began to challenge the prerogatives of revealed theology. Beginning in the thirteenth century, the relations between faith and reason were expressed—for Christians themselves, Albertus Magnus and Thomas Aquinas in the lead—in terms unfamiliar in the already long Augustinian tradition: How should the relations between reason and revelation, between philosophy and theology, be envisaged in this new context, the quasi divinization of Aristotle?

Averroës clearly stated his position in several treatises, notably in a major work whose complete title outlines his program: "The Book of the Decisive Discourse in Which One Establishes the Connection That Exists

Between Revelation and Philosophy."[18] A philosopher and a Muslim, Averroës states in the very first lines of his treatise the objective of a reflection that is addressed not only to the cultivated public but also to those who hold political power. He aims "to investigate, from the perspective of Law-based reflection, whether reflection upon philosophy and the sciences of logic is permitted, prohibited, or commanded—and this as a recommendation or as an obligation—by the Law."[19] In spite of Averroës' somewhat esoteric style, the subject, as we can see, was and still is timely, and Averroës' response to his own question—Yes, philosophy (by which he means Aristotle's rationalistic and pagan thought) is obligatory—may still seem incredibly audacious in many parts of the world today. So it was thus a "decisive" book or, rather, a "decisional" work, given that it was intended to settle the question in the form of a "legal" opinion or, in Muslim religious terms, a "fatwa." And even if the object of the treatise was not primarily to reconcile faith and reason, as Alain de Libéra recalls in his excellent introduction to the 1996 edition of the *Discours décisif,* but rather to justify the philosophical interpretation of the Koran, it goes without saying that the two questions go hand in hand. Averroës' argumentation is extremely subtle. I will limit my remarks here to summarizing three strands that touch directly on the status of philosophy in its relation to religion—in this case, Islam.

The first strand consists in demonstrating, by the use of reason alone and the letter of the Koran, that philosophy is indispensable: "If the activity of philosophy is nothing more than reflection upon existing things and consideration of them insofar as they are an indication of the Artisan—I mean insofar as they are artifacts, for existing things indicate the Artisan only through cognizance of the art in them, and the more complete cognizance of the art in them is, the more complete is cognizance of the Artisan—and if the Law has recommended and urged consideration of existing things, then it is evident that what this name indicates is either obligatory or recommended by the Law." Averroës cites the many passages in the Koran that invite believers to "think what is" in light of an increasingly deep comprehension of the creator from the starting point of a consideration of created beings. His conclusion is inevitable from the viewpoint of revelation (here, the Law): philosophy is obligatory for all those who have the means (in particular, the intellectual means), and, since the "Book of God" so states, " the Law calls for consideration of existing things by means of the intellect."[20]

This leads to the second question, which is just as crucial and arises from what today we might call "multiculturalism" or even the "clash of civilizations." Philosophy—by which Averroës means Aristotelianism—comes from the Greeks. Not only is it a rational and profane discourse, but its very origin situates it wholly within the pagan world. How can Islam make use of it, and why should comprehension of the Koran have any need of a framework for reading that derives from a vision of the world totally different from the one from which the Koran emerged? Averroës' response is couched in a logic that we know well today: *mutatis mutandis,* we have already seen it at work among the early church fathers with regard to Plato. Although philosophy is obligatory, it is never anything but an instrument of religion. Whatever its importance, it is still secondary to the verities of revelation. Averroës displays admirable skill here: in order to persuade his readers to accept philosophy as obligatory, he presents it in the least disturbing guise possible. That it comes from the pagan world is no longer an obstacle as soon as its instrumental status is acknowledged: "For when a valid sacrifice is performed by means of a tool, no consideration is given, with respect to the validity of the sacrifice, as to whether the tool belongs to someone who shares in our religion or not, so long as it fulfills the conditions for validity." As for intellectual syllogistic reasoning, "If someone other than us has already investigated it, it is evidently obligatory for us to rely on what the one who has preceded us says about what we are pursuing." Next, "since it has been determined that the Law makes reflection upon intellectual syllogistic reasons and its kinds obligatory . . . it is evident that if someone prior to us has not set out to investigate intellectual syllogistic reasoning and its kinds, it is obligatory for us to begin to investigate it and for the one who comes after to rely upon the one who preceded." He concludes: "Since this is so, if we find that our predecessors in former nations have reflected upon existing things and considered them according to what is required by the conditions of demonstration, it is perhaps obligatory for us to reflect upon what they say about that and upon what they establish in their books. Thus, we will accept, rejoice in, and thank them for whatever agrees with the truth; and we will alert to, warn against, and excuse them for whatever does not agree with the truth."[21] We see here, incidentally, that, as always, the choice of reason—whatever certain varieties of contemporary thought may say—is also a decision to opt for a more open spirit, not to say for universalism.

Although philosophy is an instrument in the service of religion, its teaching must never contradict that of revelation. But for Averroës—and on this point he seems to foreshadow Thomas Aquinas more closely than is usually admitted—such a thing is inconceivable, because if the Koran reveals the truth to us when it invites us to reflect on the created world by using our own means, it also guarantees that the ways of demonstration, if used with care and rigor, cannot contradict those of revelation: "Since this Law is true and calls to the reflection leading to cognizance of the truth, we, the Muslim community, know firmly that demonstrative reflection does not lead to differing with what is set down in the Law. For truth does not oppose truth; rather, it agrees with and bears witness to it."[22] So we see that Averroës explicitly rejects the fateful hypothesis of a double truth.

In spite of the outward trappings of a humility appropriate to faith that appears to keep philosophy within proper limits, philosophy nonetheless plays a quite considerable role. In many passages in his *Decisive Treatise*, Averroës seems close to thinking (like Lessing and Hegel several centuries later) that recourse to revelation is useful to the people for pedagogical purposes, but is almost useless for an authentic philosophy that can attain the same result, if not a higher one, by reason alone. This may explain his aversion to theologians as an intermediary class between true philosophers, who by themselves are capable of achieving a just comprehension of the divine, and the ignorant masses, for whom pious images suffice. Between the truths of reason and those of revelation, theologians merely confuse things and lead both others and themselves astray. Maimonides was not far from sharing this iconoclastic conception, and for similar reasons. For him as for Averroës, the philosopher has no need of miracles in order to believe, but miracles are extremely useful for an ignorant populace incapable of raising itself to a proper comprehension of the existence of God by thought alone.

Still, it is within Christianity that the Aristotelianization of theology, in what has been called the "Albertine-Thomist revolution," was to carry the debate into the public space that the University of Paris had become in the thirteenth century. Ruptures with the Platonic and Augustinian tradition were many. They have been analyzed so often that we need not dwell on them here: the soul, henceforth seen as inseparable from the body, has little illumination. Deeply rooted in the experience of an empirical world from which it cannot escape, the intelligence discovers a nature that had lost almost all substance in a Christianity of Platonic heritage. Proofs of the existence of God also had to start off from experience and proceed by following the utterly rational paths of causal reasoning. As for the question of personal immortality, which posed no particular problem in a Platonic-Christian perspective, it tended to become more difficult in the Aristotelian view, where it was difficult to imagine the soul outside of the body. It would be useless to belabor these multiple discrepancies. We need merely recall, aside from the difficulties they might raise for theologians of the Augustinian tradition, that they gave Christianity a hitherto unheard-of rational power. They offered Christianity the possibility of becoming reconciled with intelligence of the real universe, of the sensible, empirical world that Platonism invited its disciples to flee in favor of the intelligible world. But this new rationalism also forced Christianity to cast the question of the relations between faith and reason in new terms.

On the one hand, it was quite clear to both Albertus Magnus and Thomas Aquinas (who followed his mentor word for word on this point) that knowledge and belief were mutually contradictory: I cannot believe what I know because I know it; nor can I know what I believe because I believe it. Faith and knowledge are mutually exclusive because faith requires the inexplicable in order to flourish, and knowledge tends toward certainty. Thomas, despite his rationalism, considered it self-evident that some mystery should subsist in revelation and that certain elements of faith—the trinity, the incarnation, redemption, resurrection of the body, and all the sacraments associated with these fundamental elements of theology—could never have been known by reason alone. He concludes that faith not only cannot be abandoned to make way for knowledge alone, but that faith retains all the merit that Christ himself attached to it: happy are those who believe without having seen, through trust in the divine word rather than because of some demonstration. To ask continually for proofs is to enter into the devil's logic and into the logic of doubt, as seen in Satan's vain attempts to tempt Jesus. Here Thomas is so firm in both his thought and his statements that he leaves no ambiguity and permits no doubt of his sincerity (as has sometimes been suggested of Averroës). Thomas declares: "There is a twofold mode of truth in what we profess about God. Some truths about God exceed all the ability of the human reason. Such is the truth that God is triune. But there are some truths which the natural reason also is able to reach. Such are that God exists, that He is one, and the like. In fact, such truths about God have been proved demonstratively by the philosophers, guided by the light of the natural reason. . . . There are, consequently, some intelligible truths about God that are open to the human reason; but there are others that absolutely surpass its power."[23] This is why Thomas, perhaps rebutting Averroës, could write and undoubtedly believe as he was writing it, that "no philosopher before the coming of Christ, try as he might, could know as much about God or as much as is necessary for eternal life than any little old woman knew after the coming of Christ."[24]

We should note, however, that even at the heart of the domain that seems reserved to revelation and faith (which he analyzes in book IV of his *Summa contra Gentiles*), Thomas continues to consider reason highly useful for the interpretation of Scripture. Philosophy may well act as a servant to theology, but it does so in the best and highest sense. Without philosophy, the words of revelation might remain mere "noise," sound without meaning.[25] There is much more to it, however: a considerable portion of theology is open to simple reason (as analyzed in books I though III of the *Summa contra Gentiles*) and even, as demonstrated by Aristotle, without the aid of revelation. Moreover, it is even rational (as later, with Hegel) that there should be something irrational about revelation,[26] so that the Thomist doctrine of truth culminates in the conviction that a perfect synthesis of reason and revelation is not only possible but necessary. In order to be authentic, this sort of synthesis can never be forced, either on one side or on the other. Traces of this philosophical attitude can still be found in a recent encyclical of Pope John Paul II, *Fides et ratio*. Following a line of thought laid down by Thomas Aquinas, the encyclical reasserts the need to avoid constraint in the free exercise of a thought that, when authentic and rigorous, will not long diverge from revealed truths.[27]

Thus the truths of revelation (the trinity, for example), by which "sacred doctrine" is raised infinitely higher than pagan philosophy, in no way contradict the truths of reason; conversely, the truths of reason complement those of revelation. It is not by chance that Thomas cites Paul in this context, repeating the apostle's exhortation to make use of one's intelligence, which, even in a pagan universe, would have sufficed to lead men to God, even though revealed truths are superior to the ones that philosophy discovers on its own. For "although the truth of the Christian faith . . . surpasses the capacity of the reason, nevertheless that truth that the human reason is naturally endowed to know cannot be opposed to the truth of the Christian faith." Put the other way around, "it is impossible that the truth of faith should oppose those principles that the human reason knows naturally."[28]

The fact remains that the margin for maneuvering that Thomas accords the new powers of a reason given full rein opens up an autonomy previously unheard of in Christian tradition. So great is that independence that its full extent cannot be determined *a priori*, nor is it certain that it can be contained. To be persuaded of this we need only remember the terms that Thomas uses when he attributes to reason alone the ability to put an end to humanity's existential anxieties: Speaking of "how even the brilliant minds" of the ancient philosophers "suffered from the narrowness of their viewpoint," he contends that we shall be freed of such narrow attitudes "if we grant in accord with the foregoing proofs that man can reach true felicity after this life, when man's soul is existing, immortally; in which state the soul will understand in the way that separate substances understand."[29] Thomas is speaking here as a rationalist, and it is indeed to *philosophical demonstration* that he entrusts the task of persuading us that the fears connected with finitude can be surmounted in the light of an ultimately successful life. The powers of reason alone, as Thomas conceives of them, are considerable: not only does reason, with no help from revelation, permit us to demonstrate the existence of God; it also defines an important part of God's essence and proves the world's dependence on God, the immortality of the soul, the conditions of the soul's beatitude after death, and more.[30] To be sure, many mysteries remain, and revelation, like the faith that accompanies it, continues to be more than legitimate. Still, Peter Damian's fears are no longer unfounded, and the statement that philosophy must remain the handmaid of theology continued to be too open to inversion to prevent the danger from being perceived by the heirs to the Augustinian tradition. It was only a step from there to thinking, as Averroës sometimes suggests in barely disguised fashion and as Lessing and Hegel later state openly, that religious revelation is not indispensable to attaining truth; that it is little more than a crutch, an aid to reason useful for the education of the human species but superfluous for the philosopher. That step may have been gigantic in the eyes of a believer like Thomas, but for a lay thinker it was an easy one to take.

There is another explanation for the almost ineluctable beginning of the process of the secularization of thought. The Thomist position, although modern in one sense, is not at all modern in another. In order to produce a "revolution" in relation to the Platonic and Augustinian tradition that preceded it, the Thomist position was considered—with respect not to its past but to its future—much too closely linked to the Aristotelian cosmology not to be strongly influenced by the birth of modern science. After considering the internal aspects that explain, at least in part, the shift of rational thought away from theology toward autonomy, we need to examine external aspects. When the ancient cosmologies collapsed under the blows of modern science, it was not only the great Greek ethical traditions that were called in question, but also theology of Aristotelian inspiration.

The Second Emancipation: From the Closed World to the Infinite Universe, or The Birth of Modern Science and the Disenchantment of the World

In less than a century and a half—say, from the publication of Copernicus's *De revolutionibus orbium coelestium* (1543) to that of Galileo's theses regarding the earth's relation to the sun (1632), Descartes' *Principia philosophiae* (1644), and Newton's *Principia mathematica* (1687)—a scientific revolution unprecedented in the history of humanity took place. The new era that was born is one in which we are in many ways still living. It is not just humans, as is sometimes said, who have "lost their place in the world"; rather, the world itself—or at least the world that had formed the closed and harmonious framework of man's existence since antiquity—has simply disintegrated. The "wisdom of the Ancients" may continue to speak to us beyond the "catastrophe" that struck it in the move from the closed world to the infinite universe. If that ancient wisdom still retains multiple and valuable meanings for us today, we must at least recognize that the "scientific" foundations that it claimed as a base have collapsed. The physics of Plato, Aristotle, and the Stoics is no longer our physics, and because the old physics underlay a number of ethical as well as religious considerations, the question was raised—and is still raised today [31]—of how far ancient philosophy as a whole was affected by the ruin of its cosmological bases.[32] We need to reach beyond the Greek universe, however, to evaluate the effects of that revolution on religions that were too dependent on the Greek heritage, in particular after the advent of Thomism, not to be affected, at least in part, by the rise of modern science.

A thorough and detailed analysis of the reasons behind the rupture that put an end to the reign of a centuries-old cosmology that founded an ethics and even a spirituality is beyond the scope of the present work. This task has been largely accomplished by others, and their works are available for consultation.[33] The underlying causes of the change from the closed world to the infinite universe are extremely complex and diverse. They of course include technological advances, in particular new astronomical instruments such as the telescope that permitted observations that would have been inconceivable in the ancient image of the world. To cite two examples among many, neither the discovery of novas nor the disappearance of certain stars would have harmonized with the dogma of celestial immutability. Other technological innovations that have been cited are the rise (or the revival) of perspective in the plastic arts and considerable improvements in marine cartography, which, combined with innovations in astronomy, prompted revision of the principles of Aristotelian cosmology. Another topic that some scholars have pursued is the rise of modern individualism, which, combined with certain economic and commercial trends, also led to ruptures with the "holism" of the Ancients. Without entering into a discussion of these multiple causes, we need to look briefly at three decisive aspects of these changes that will help to comprehend how (if not why) we have come to situate ourselves in a universe diametrically opposed to the ancient cosmologies.

1. **From the Inhabited Cosmos to the Disenchanted Universe.** Alexandre Koyré tells us that the scientific revolution of the sixteenth and seventeenth centuries brought forth nothing less than the destruction of the cosmos,

> the disappearance, from philosophically and scientifically valid concepts, of the conception of the world as a finite, closed, and hierarchically ordered whole (a whole in which the hierarchy of value determined the hierarchy and structure of being, rising from the dark, heavy and imperfect earth to the higher and higher perfection of the stars and heavenly spheres), and its replacement by an indefinite and even infinite universe which is bound together by the identity of its fundamental components and laws, and in which all these components are placed on the same level of being.[34]

The controversy has been forgotten, but at the time many people found the emergence of this new vision of the world deeply disturbing. In 1611, after he had become aware of the principles involved in the "Copernican revolution," John Donne wrote:

> . . . New philosophy calls all in doubt,
> The Element of fire is quite put out;
> The Sun is lost, and th'earth, and no mans wit
> Can well direct him where to looke for it.
> . . . .
> 'Tis all in peeces, all cohaerence gone;
> All just supply, and all Relation.[35]

Pascal's libertine expresses a similar anxiety when he contemplates the eternal silence of newly infinite space. The world is no longer a cocoon or a house: it is no longer habitable. As a simple reservoir of objects formed out of raw, inanimate, and unorganized matter, nature no longer has any particular meaning and contains nothing inherently worthy of respect. Nature is no longer a model that serves as a standard and a guide for the life of men. So one can make use of it at will, instrumentalize it in order to become its "master and possessor." The idea that the good life might reside in an agreement with nature disintegrated, with the result that the inner heart of the old representations, the deepest sense that those representations gave to human existence, suddenly collapsed with the emergence of the "new philosophy" that bothered John Donne, which is of course none other than modern science. If the world is no longer harmonious and closed, if high and low, right and left, no longer indicate the "natural places" or niches in which beings are called to lodge as a function of their most essential nature and their ends, then the world offers no particular orientation for human life. Disoriented, humans are left to find new guidelines within themselves.

If an image of this state of affairs were needed, the best indication of its absurdity would lie in the invention of the "Cartesian coordinates," which are, in many ways, its perfect symbol. Whereas in the closed world each locus had, by definition, a unique and absolute place in relation to the All, once space becomes infinite, and the universe, no longer comparable to a living organism, becomes a mere reservoir of raw materials, to situate a point in this new infinity requires tracing an arbitrary framework, the vertical and horizontal coordinates of the abscissa and the ordinate. All precise specifications of place, which formerly were absolute, become relative to these new references, and, in both the strict and the figurative senses, all localities are henceforth equal. The universe can no longer be the spatial embodiment of the hierarchy of values mentioned by Koyré. Space becomes radically neutral on the moral plane, with the result that the "new philosophy" signals the end of the "cosmologico-ethical" and, along with it, the ancient wisdoms, inasmuch as they were rooted in it. Although those wisdoms have left many messages of undeniable actuality and interest, we are forced to understand and accept the fact that their philosophical foundations have been undermined by the modern scientific revolution.[36]

2. **From the Harmonious and Good Cosmos to the Indifferent or Malevolent Universe.** The Stoics' confidence in fate and their constant appeal to an acceptance of destiny was justified, as we have seen, by the intimate conviction that providence was good, the cosmos was just, and the role to which we were assigned within it, like that of the organs or the members of a living being, was necessarily fitting. To comprehend the world and to love it were one and the same. No doubt certain natural beings could—then as

now—at first seem harmful or repugnant. Still, the Stoics invited us, as does the genuine sage, to take the trouble to understand them at a deeper level and to see that they, too, are admirably made according to their own kind. We should look closely at "the wrinkles of a lion's brow, . . . the foam flowing from a boar's mouth, and . . . many other things. Looked at in themselves they are far from attractive, but because they accompany natural phenomena they further adorn them and attract us. As a result, the man of feeling and deeper understanding of the phenomena in Nature as a whole will find almost all these incidentals pleasantly contrived. . . . He will see a kind of fulfillment and freshness in the old, whether man or woman: he will be able to look upon the loveliness of his own slave boys with eyes free from lust."[37] Stoicism culminated in a "cosmodicy." A little intelligence distances us from the cosmos; much brings us back to it, and the sage, in contrast to the ignorant man, understands that what can seem bad from a partisan viewpoint can turn out to be good when viewed from the perspective of the whole: the "misfortunes" that seem to rain down on human life from time to time can be justified from a more all-embracing point of view, for example because later they turn out to be the condition for a higher good.

The modern revolution gradually put an end to that sort of reasoning, at least on the scientific level, if not on those of metaphysics or theology. Once it is no longer animate, organized, and endowed with purpose, the world becomes indifferent. There is no reason to think that natural events are the result of any sort of providence. Henceforth they occur by chance or by necessity, thanks to blind, radically meaningless mechanisms. After the fall of the great ancient cosmologies, says Goethe,

> For nature
> Is unfeeling:
> The sun's light shines
> On the wicked and the good.[38]

Furthermore, if the world were seen as a neutral space in which the movements of bodies were governed uniquely by relations of pure force analyzed by "shock theories," taking the world as a model would be ultimately contrary to all the moral representations, Christian or even ancient, that invite us to solidarity and charity. Given that the way nature is conceived has changed radically, retaining the imperative to imitate it would promote the law of the strongest to an ethical principle, with the result that acting morally would no longer be following the teaching of nature, but rather opposing nature in all its aspects, both outside ourselves, in combating its maleficent effects on human existence (for example, in natural catastrophes), and within ourselves, where nature now appears in the form of the rule of special interests and ineluctable tendencies to egocentrism, if not plain egotism. If all morality is in some fashion altruistic, biased toward care for others, it can no longer be founded in nature, but rather in God or in humanity, inasmuch as neither now appears totally integrated into nature; to the contrary, both appear as beings in contrast to nature. The human being is henceforth perceived as the only living creature that can and must struggle against nature in order to transform it and impose human law on it. This leads to the radical rupture, induced by the collapse of the great cosmologies, that marks the emergence of new relations between nature and virtue.

3. From Virtue as Imitation of a Divine Nature to Virtue as a Struggle against a Maleficent Nature.

Without returning here to the philosophical foundations of this reversal,[39] we can summarize them thus: for the Ancients, at least for those involved in the great cosmological tradition inaugurated by Plato's *Timaeus*, virtue, understood as excellence in its genre, is not opposed to nature. It appears instead as a successful actualization of the natural dispositions of a being, as a passage, in Aristotle's terms, "from power to act." Among the Moderns it tended to be the exact opposite, a struggle for liberty against the natural in us. Dominated by blind powers, the natural universe, from the moral point of view that we are taking here (aesthetics might see things differently), is a universe governed by the law of the strongest and by a principle of generalized egotism. One of the dominant convictions of the modern world is that civility, peace, altruism, solidarity, and democracy itself are not natural, inborn qualities, givens that only require development in the child. To the contrary, they are laborious and fragile conquests that demand effort from human beings, self-directed effort in particular. These qualities are so far from being natural that they are imposed on humans in the uncomfortable forms of duty and imperatives. Not all currents of modern thought concur in this attitude, and certain of them—romanticism, for example—attempted to rehabilitate the idea of a harmonious nature. But we need only contemplate our Western juridical systems to measure the degree to which they display a deep-rooted conviction that the moral world is constructed against an egotistic and rebellious nature rather than in accord with nature. Even the economic liberals who tried to find a "natural" articulation between egotistical individual interests and the general interest came to share the sentiment, at least on the level of personal morality, that we need to use our free will to control the self-centeredness inherent to our nature if we want to respect the interests and the liberty of others. This is also why "labor," a notion not highly valued in the ancient world, took on a new and positive significance in the modern universe.

In the aristocratic vision of an organized nature in which every being must find its rightful place according to its own nature and within an inviolable hierarchy, labor is an activity that is servile in the strict sense of the word—reserved for slaves or, as Plato says, for the inferior class. The aristocrat is, by definition, someone who does not work. As Nietzsche puts it, the aristocrat commands, imposes, decrees with authority. He makes war and participates in the arts and in sports. Above all, he contemplates, in the sense of Greek *theōria:* he grasps the natural and cosmic order in the midst of which his place is, by nature, that of the best. Where this representation of the world prevails, labor bears no value. But when the meaning of virtue changes, when it is no longer defined as the actualization of a wellborn nature, but rather as a struggle of liberty against the natural in us, labor changes in meaning as well as status and acquires a value previously unknown. Among the Moderns, the person who does no work runs the risk of being not only a poor man but a poor sort of man, given that work is identified with one of the essential manifestations of what is proper to man, of liberty as a faculty for transforming the world and, in so doing, transforming and educating himself. The primacy of *theōria* has given way to that of *praxis.* Virtue is no longer expressed in words or ideas, but by undertakings and acts aimed at modifying reality and changing ourselves. Unlike the ancient cosmos, the order that humanity is henceforth called upon to construct and put in place no longer preexists humankind; it no longer possesses the transcendence of anteriority. Now humanity must not only invent order but engender it. We have entered into the reign of humanism, where values are no longer in the domain of being. They belong not in nature but in the sphere of the must-be, of the hoped-for ideal. Values are not part of a reality that is *a priori* harmonious and good, given to men in advance and ready to welcome them with benevolence.

Christianity's Attitude in Face of the Scientific and Anti-Aristotelian Revolution

The relationship between Christianity and the Greek cosmology is ambiguous. Christianity set itself apart from the old cosmology (notably with Justin Martyr and Augustine), then reinvested in it (with Thomas Aquinas), so that the shock of the scientific revolution shook it but without damaging its fundamental principles.

Drawing from the Old Testament, Christianity explicitly introduced into the heart of the problematic of salvation, in contrast to Greek "cosmologism," the idea of a dual transcendence of both God and humankind over the world. It is that new aspiration to salvation that the Epistle of Paul to the Romans (12:2) expresses in the imperative language of exhortation and the "must be," which breaks with the classical prescription of accord with the cosmos: "Do not conform yourselves to this age, but be transformed by the renewal of your mind, so that you may judge what is God's will, what is good, pleasing and perfect." There could hardly be a clearer illustration of the distance between Christianity and the Greek universe. Not only is the world no longer a model, and agreement with it no longer an ultimate human aim, but to the extent that humans have the possibility, the liberty, to separate themselves from the world, they can raise themselves above the world in order to fulfill what God requires of them. Salvation may still reside in an accord, but that accord is now established between two beings, man and God, both of whom transcend the cosmos. In his studies of medieval philosophy, Etienne Gilson has shown a profound understanding of the links between modern philosophies of liberty and Christianity, but he has also shown that the philosophies of necessity, beginning with Stoicism, had inherited their cosmological principles from Greek religion:

> Christianity is addressed to man, to comfort him in his wretchedness, by showing him what its cause is and offering him the remedy for it. It is a doctrine of salvation, and that is why it is a religion. Philosophy is a knowledge that is addressed to the intelligence and tells it what things are; religion is addressed to man and speaks to him of his fate, so that he will either submit to it, as in Greek religion, or shape his own, as in the Christian religion. Further, this is why, influenced by Greek religion, the Greek philosophies are philosophies of necessity, while the philosophies influenced by the Christian religion are philosophies of liberty.[40]

Gilson might be reproached for a habit adopted early on by the church fathers—that of considering philosophy, from the start, more as an intellectual discourse than a mode of life, thus reserving the problematic of salvation to religion alone, whereas salvation was already an integral part of Greek ethics, although in a nonreligious form. Nonetheless, there are arguments for the connection that Gilson establishes between philosophy and religion, and the idea that Christianity reopened the question of free will in a new way and in a break with the world is a fertile one. It is even quite clear that it is this new representation of human liberty that came to constitute, within Christianity, a major theological problem with a promising future: that of the conditions under which our free will accords with the ideas of a divine providence and a divine grace. Beginning with Augustine's polemics with Pelagius and his disciples, that problem haunted Christian tradition. But whatever the solutions to it might be, the problem certainly originated in a doctrine of salvation aimed at reconciling the dual transcendence of man and God in relation to the world.

Christianity, therefore, gives high priority to knowledge of oneself as a free being. This was already true of Platonism, of course, as witnessed by the famous Socratic injunction to "know yourself." But for Plato, as in the entire tradition of the great cosmologies, self-knowledge is achieved through knowledge of the world: to know oneself is first to situate oneself within the cosmos, to know one's natural place — that is, one's place in the universe as a part of its most intimate nature. The city described in the *Republic* is a just city when all occupy their rightful places: the philosophers at the top, the warriors at the center, the workers and craftsmen at the bottom. The same is true of the body: the mind belongs in the head, courage in the heart, and desire in the belly, each in its proper place. To know ourselves well is to occupy the right place, to know the role assigned to us in the cosmic order by reason of our function. Augustine disagrees, however. Even Thomas Aquinas tells us that Augustine has "followed the Platonists as far as Catholic doctrine would permit"; knowledge of the world, for Augustine, even in its most celestial regions, no longer brings anything to knowledge of the self: "People go to admire lofty mountains, and huge breakers at sea, and crashing waterfalls, and vast stretches of ocean, and the dance of the stars, but they leave themselves behind out of sight."[41] For henceforth there are "two heavens," one corporeal, one celestial, and the second of these, which man does not possess as long as he remains in this world but to which he must aspire, is infinitely superior to the first. Augustine borrows from the Psalms a sublime image of a "heaven's heaven"; it expresses, perhaps better than any other formula, the distance that has been established between Christianity and profane philosophy. Each one of Augustine's terms deserves close attention:

> But where, Lord is that *heaven's heaven* of which we hear in the psalm: *Heaven's heaven is for the Lord; but he has assigned the earth to humankind*? Where is that heaven we cannot see, in comparison

with which all we can see is but earth? This whole material world has been endowed with beauty of form even in its furthest parts, the lowest of which is our earth (though not uniformly throughout, for the material world is not the same or wholly present everywhere); yet compared with *heaven's heaven* the heaven that overarches our earth is itself no better than earth. And not without good reason are those two vast realities—our earth and our sky—to be regarded as mere lowly earth beside that unimaginable heaven which is for the Lord, not for humankind.[42]

This is the "heavenly Jerusalem," the sojourn of the saints, which is not for men but is a place to which all men can aspire. Infinitely higher than the stars, which the philosopher's gaze had not exceeded, it relativizes the Greek cosmos and, so to speak, crushes all terrestrial hierarchies, which seem flat in contrast to its superiority.

One is reminded of Pascal: "All bodies, the firmament, the stars, the earth and its kingdoms, are not equal to the lowest mind; for mind knows all these and itself; and these bodies nothing." And here is another of Pascal's thoughts, one so familiar that we sometimes forget that it signals the end of Greek tragedy as a setting for a universe that always claims its rights against hubris and human rebellion: "Man is but a reed, the most feeble thing in nature; but he is a thinking reed. The entire universe need not arm itself to crush him. A vapour, a drop of water suffices to kill him. But, if the universe were to crush him, man would still be more noble than that which killed him, because he knows that he dies and the advantage which the universe has over him; the universe knows nothing of this."[43]

So the Greek world has come to an end. Yet how can we forget all that Augustine owed to Plato, and Thomas Aquinas to Aristotle? The dual transcendence of God and man, the idea of a universe created and subordinate to both, is probably foreign to the Greeks. But both transcendences proved able to resist the catastrophe represented by the rise of modern science and to persist after the "end of the world." The role of Greek thought was no less decisive for the fathers and doctors of the church, so that the collapse of the Greek cosmology could not have left them indifferent. Gilson, who wholly subscribes to the Christian view of profane philosophy, once again helps us to a better evaluation of what Christianity stood to lose in the affair and also what it managed to gain, while the Greek ethical systems largely disintegrated: "Plato had gotten as close to the idea of creation as he could without attaining it, and yet the Platonic universe, along with man contained in it, are only barely real images of what alone merits the title of being. Although Aristotle had turned away from that same idea of creation, the eternal world that he described still enjoyed a substantial reality and, one might say, an ontological density worthy of the work of a creator. In order to make Aristotle's world into a creature and to make Plato's God a true creator, both of these needed to be surpassed."[44] In other words, with his theory of ideas, Plato has almost imagined the creation, but the real world, which he compares to the images of the cave, has insufficient reality to be worthy of being the work of a divine creator. Aristotle, on the other hand, opposed the idea of a God who created heaven and earth within time. Instead, his description presents a picture of the world so varied and so profound that it is worthy of being the work of a supreme being. Thanks to Augustine, Christianity was able to take from Plato all that it considered good before molding Platonic logic, by virtue of the revelation of Christ, into a doctrine of creation. With the help of Thomas Aquinas, Christianity took what was good in Aristotle, notably his description of the cosmos, but went counter to him in making the cosmos (following the teaching of Plato revisited by Augustine) into an authentic creature, which Aristotle would never have done. Here, in brief, is the connection of both continuity and rupture between true religion and true philosophy: a creator God inherited from an improved version of Plato, a cosmic universe borrowed from Aristotle but transformed, contrary to Aristotle, into a creature of God.

This is how things stand: on the one hand, Christianity—in particular after Thomas Aquinas's gigantic effort to reinterpret Greek cosmology in a Christian perspective and to integrate into Christian theology the best of what pagan philosophy had to offer—could not remain indifferent in face of the "end of the world" that was introduced by the modern scientific revolution. It is clear that if Paul's pronouncement regarding the analogy between the creature and his creation was to retain any meaning—and how could it not?—the destruction of the order inherent in the sphere of creatures risked affecting the creator as well, albeit indirectly as if by ricochet. The transition from an ordered, harmonious, and good universe to an infinite and chaotic one, henceforth presented with total certainty as a vast field of meaningless forces, could not operate painlessly. The ecclesiastical authorities were long consumed by the urge to emit condemnations and papal interdicts against the scientific discoveries that, from Galileo to Darwin, they deemed most threatening to Christian requirements for a creation worthy of its creator. On the other hand, if we compare the situation of Christianity to that of the Greek ethical systems founded on the cosmos, Christianity faced a lesser evil: after all, the modern scientific revolution affected only the order of terrestrial creatures, and the infinitely higher "heaven's heaven" could remain in many ways intact. If we follow Thomas Aquinas himself—at least concerning principles, if not their Aristotelian application *stricto sensu*—we might even hope that by giving free reign to man's natural reason, it would in the end attain, albeit in a non-Aristotelian mode—the truths of revelation. When all is said and done, the church lived through and, indeed, managed to surmount a bad phase in its history, as witnessed by its current positions on the relations between faith and reason, or God and science.

To skip a century or two, the current attitude of the church finds perfect expression in the recent encyclical of Pope John Paul II, *Fides et ratio* (Faith and Reason). At the risk of surprising all those, even among the faithful, who still think that belief begins where the powers of understanding stop, and that belief is rooted more in the heart than in the mind, the pope delivered an apology of reason tinged with Thomism freed from an overly cumbersome Aristotelian orthodoxy. In this brief but profound text, the pope forcefully rehabilitates the philosophical and scientific uses of rationalism. He clearly states the principal theme of the encyclical: there is not, nor should there be, any opposition between the truth that "God reveals to us in Christ Jesus" and "the truths which are derived from philosophy"; thus there is no opposition between revelation and reason or between faith and thought. Quite to the contrary, they display an indispensable complementarity.[45]

Today, in a period strongly marked by the rise of mystical and sentimental spiritualities—as demonstrated by the worldwide success of works supposedly inspired by Eastern wisdom—the pope's message offers food for thought. Of course, we need to define what he means by "rationalism" and to understand how it fits into a well-attested theological tradition still connected to the spirit, if not to the letter, of the works of Thomas Aquinas, and critical of the instrumental reason and "positivist approach" that at times characterizes "scientific investigation."[46] Many of the findings of modern science (from the theory of the big bang to that of evolution) are accepted by the church today, even explicitly. Reference to a Thomist tradition that has neither neglected experimental observation of reality nor scorned the operation of reason continues to animate the church's message: by comprehending nature and its laws and by practicing science, the grandeur of the Creator will be all the more clearly perceptible. In many regards, nature—even nature reviewed and corrected by the natural sciences—continues to be seen as a marvel of beauty and organization, the creation of which one might be tempted to attribute to a supreme being. The church today can thus, without hypocrisy, make use of this tradition, well attested in its own history, in order to invite believers to be reconciled, if need be, with science and philosophy and to follow Pasteur's maxim that a little science takes us away from God, while a lot of science brings us back to him.

The fact remains that the break with Aristotelian physics has been completed. It is impossible to maintain intact Aristotle's theories of space, place, motion, and causality. Not only has reason become independent of revelation, but modern science has dealt a decisive and perhaps fatal blow to the Aristotelian-Thomist heritage: its form and principles may continue to be perceived as valid, but its doctrinal content has had to be abandoned on many points, at least on the scientific level. There is no doubt that the new autonomy of rational thought made a powerful contribution to the emergence of new visions of the world, which, although still religious in form, have largely become emancipated from the dimensions of traditional theology. Modern utopias or "religions of earthly salvation" are relevant here. They merit our attention because they form a kind of link or channel between religions, on the one hand, and the materialist thought that culminated in the philosophy of Nietzsche, on the other.

The Secularization of Religion and the Birth of Secular Thought: From Revealed Religions to the Religions of Earthly Salvation

The notion of religion can be understood in at least three different ways.

For believers, it designates a doctrine of salvation, a reflection on what can save us from the vicissitudes inherent to our status as humble mortals. What religions promise to those who accept their dogmas is eternal salvation and victory over the fears and the suffering engendered by the prospect of death's inevitability. Like all the great philosophies (which they resemble), religions attempt to give meaning to human existence, but they do so by reference to a radical alterity, that of the divine. Untouched by philosophical pride, religions are less interested in permitting us to save ourselves by the sheer force of our own thought than they are in persuading us to accept with humility being saved *by an Other*. It is at this point that they break with the discourse of reason.

For nonbelievers, that break seems contestable, even illusory. Thus another perspective on the religious has become widespread in Europe since the eighteenth century: far from being the supreme verity of human life, faith has come to be seen as the height of illusion. According to a familiar witticism of Voltaire's, "If God created us in his own image, we have more than reciprocated." What, in fact, do we want? To be loved, not to be alone, not to be separated from those whom we love, to find them again after death, and, if possible, not "really" to die. That is what religion promises us, and, according to its critics, the content of that hope is simply too beautiful to be true. Hence a long series of "deconstructions" of belief that denounce its phantasms as "superstition" (Diderot), "alienation" (Feuerbach), "the opium of the people" (Marx), "nihilism" (Nietzsche), "humanity's obsessional neurosis" (Freud), and so forth.

A third option is possible, however. It does not choose to side with either the believers or the nonbelievers, but is content to describe the effect of the religious on the social and political organization of historical societies. Whether faith is legitimate or not matters little here: the point is that human organizations founded on religion—what the ethnologists call "traditional societies"—present a full range of contrasts to secular societies. Secular societies (the societies in which we live today in Europe) appear to have "emerged" in some fashion out of religion-based societies, and this long and painful birth, completed only in the twentieth century, leaves so many traces that if we fail to take into account the entire, complex process, we cannot possibly understand the ideologies and passions of the world in which we live or its intellectual, moral, artistic, and political life. This, roughly speaking, is the conviction that Marcel Gauchet invites us to share and to meditate in *The Disenchantment of the World*.[47] The simplest way to understand Gauchet's viewpoint is to accept it for the moment, if only as a hypothesis, and to try to see, point by point, what is distinctive in our modern societies and in religious societies and how they differ. Not that the religious has disappeared from our secular universe: far from it. Almost 70 percent of the population of France today is still Christian. But belief—whatever its intensity—now has the status of an individual opinion; belief no longer structures the public space and is no longer the official source of either the law or political power. Today it is not even the foundation of morality or the arts or, *a fortiori*, the scientific representations that we forge, little by little, of the physical world. This revolution, which follows millennia of religious civilization, has had profound effects.

In order to evaluate the impact of that revolution, we should first pinpoint the characteristics of traditional religious societies—the very traits that democracy was to challenge one by one, sometimes for the better, sometimes for the worse. I shall follow Gauchet's analysis, but discuss only four of these traits, limiting my remarks to the most salient.

Religion—and believers themselves cannot totally reject this description—is first and foremost heteronomy, a term that refers, etymologically, to the fact that the law is given to us other than by ourselves, by an Other *external to humanity and superior to humanity.* This is in fact a primary characteristic of traditional societies: human beings do not fashion the law themselves, as we claim to do in our modern parliaments. Among the indigenous peoples for which Pierre Clastres provides an ethnological description, customs appear to have been given to men from the outside and are experienced as an inheritance going back to an immemorial past—that of the ancestors, who merge, as one generation succeeds the other, with the gods at the time of origins. The second major characteristic of these societies follows from the first: the dimensions of the future, of innovation, and of reform, not to mention revolution, are not valued. Indeed, they are sometimes fiercely prohibited: among certain indigenous peoples, the chief, unlike today's politicians, is not someone who promises to improve society or to transform it in the name of an ideal, but rather someone who swears to guarantee the continuance of custom. Where we Moderns fix our eyes on the future, the chief's eyes are fixed on the past; it is in the name of the past that the social connection perpetuates itself as best it can, given that respect for traditions creates a conservative temporality that is difficult to maintain today. A third characteristic of traditional societies follows naturally from the second: where we assert (at least in principle) that all people are equal, traditional societies reproduce the hierarchical principle of the dependence of inferiors on their superiors. Just as humans are dependent on the gods, the young are dependent on their elders, women on men, slaves on members of the community, and so forth. Religious societies are basically caste societies even before they are class societies. The difference might seem minor from the viewpoint of our modern demand for genuine equality, but it is decisive, because the principle involved states that hierarchical difference is inscribed in the very nature of beings. Inequalities may persist in our democracies, but the least one can say is that they are not perceived as inviolable. After the symbolic date of 4 August 1789, when privilege was abolished in French society, social mobility, although still difficult and limited, was at least not prohibited in principle. With time, it became valued. Since people in religious societies—and this is the fourth trait that characterizes the traditional society—are linked under the tutelage of a law that they experience as radically transcendent and inscribed within a fabric of hierarchical relations presumed to accord with nature, they possess a strong feeling of belonging to a *community*. To put it perhaps better: the individual, in the sense in which we understand the term—that is to say, someone presumed free to live, at least in private, as he or she chooses and to hold opinions and beliefs of his or her own choosing—does not exist in the traditional society. Human beings have a real existence only as members of a totality that surrounds them and surpasses them in every way. This means that traditional societies are "holistic" societies.

The birth of the modern world—and a convenient milestone is the French Revolution—occurred in rupture with the old visions of the world. It was a move to counter religious heteronomy by aspiring to make one's own laws—an aspiration that became an event with the creation of the French National Assembly in 1789 (the source of norms was no longer divine but human, and human beings, with their reason and their will, finally claimed autonomy). It was a move to counter the respect of a sacralized past, replacing it with the hope of a better future that would gradually lead to valuing the young, henceforth supposed to embody the march of progress, over the old; to denying the natural basis of inequalities and affirming equal rights for all; to declaring an end to the superiority of the whole over individuals (in communitarianism, or holism); and to insisting on the preeminence of the individual over the collective. From now on, disorder is preferable to injustice! Let there be no misunderstanding, however: heteronomy and autonomy should be understood here as purely descriptive categories pertaining to the values experienced by the individuals in the two sorts of society. The terms have no claim to truth in themselves. To be perfectly clear: there is no proof that the law of traditional societies really comes from the outside (quite to the contrary, humans obviously create laws). Similarly, there is no reason to think that modern individuals are truly autonomous (alienation besieges or threatens them at every turn).

Of all these upheavals, which are interconnected, the second is perhaps the most visible. It is the tipping of the balance from past to future that enables us to understand how our societies, as they emerged from the world of the ancien régime and of tradition, were to move from revealed religions to the secular religions that became modern utopias: fascist nationalism, on the one hand, as a paradoxical temptation to transform a return to the past into a future under the banner of a "national revolution"; communism, on the other hand, which claims to reestablish a lost community in a better future. In both cases, the form of the religious persists, in the sense that politics is likened to a doctrine of salvation: by claiming a monopoly of the authentic definition of the successful life ("all is politics"), and by giving an ultimate meaning to human life, it aims at saving humanity from the perils that threaten it. By that token and like any religion worthy of the name, the reactionary or progressive utopia posits values superior to individual life, values in the name of which it will infallibly demand its tribute of human sacrifice. Moreover, because the future is as mysterious as the past, militant action inevitably supposes a measure of hope and even of faith. What we are experiencing today, Gauchet tells us, is the end of this process of disenchantment: our religious beliefs have finally ceased to be political, now that they have been relegated to the private sphere. But, on the other hand, political belief has broken with religion.

Do our democracies no longer have transcendent principles or internal enemies? Is the radical immanence announced by Nietzsche to be the sole rule of our existence? I think not, and that is why we have not exhausted our questions regarding the good life. To the contrary, what we need to do—at least those of us who are not believers—is to think about those questions not only outside the framework of traditional religions but also outside the confines of a materialism that I do not hold to be the unique and ultimate horizon of modern humanism.

PART V

A Humanism of the Man-God: The Good Life as a Life in Harmony with the Human Condition

CHAPTER 12

Materialism, Religion, & Humanism

We have now returned to our point of departure: the primacy of a "terrestrial" thought, a vision of the world that strives to rid itself of the "illusions" of transcendence. If we exclude the "returns to" and the many restorations that the contemporary world seems so fond of, at least three paths seem promising. First, we can follow Spinoza or Nietzsche and investigate materialism further, pursuing its "deconstructionist" logic to the limit; second, we can go the opposite way and attempt to refit the religious, seeking to accommodate its conditions with democratic ideology and the demands of that ideology for individual autonomy; third, we can try to rethink the relations between modern humanism and novel figures of transcendence. I would like to suggest briefly and from a lay perspective why only the third path seems to offer ways for surmounting the current "disenchantment of the world."

1. Radicalizing Materialism: A Paradoxically Metaphysical Spirituality

Materialism has presented different faces through history, but it has retained two essential traits: the conviction that human beings are not free to choose their own destinies but are totally determined by forces beyond their control; and a resolute rejection of the classic figures of transcendence, beginning, to be sure, with that of the divine. To put it even more simply: for a consistent materialist, we do not *have* a body and a history that we can survey and guide as we see fit; we *are* that body and that history: we are the end product of two implacable determinisms, and nothing more.

After its setback on the philosophical and political levels by the defeat of communism, materialism found new impetus by shifting to the domains of science and nature. This shift is reflected in the renewed discussion, during the past thirty years, about our relations with the nature that surrounds us, notably with animals, our closest kin. Although I have no intention of presenting an exhaustive treatment of this difficult dossier, its philosophic implications are easy to draw.

Major advances have led biologists to rethink the difference between human nature and animal nature, beginning with the now well-known fact that human beings and chimpanzees share 98 percent of their genes. This is a lot, too much in any event for the question of our resemblances and our differences not to be explored on the basis of new criteria, no longer according to *a priori* principles, but taking into account the concrete acquisitions of contemporary genetics. What is more, the theory of evolution has been enriched and further confirmed by research in recent decades that has thrust the relationship between humans and other primates into sharp relief. If we go back, generation after generation, into the genealogy of our ancestors, we will have to admit, like it or not, that quite soon (a few hundred thousand years is but a blink in the history of the universe!) we encounter beings with simian faces and hairy bodies who would hardly be presentable in a Paris *salon*. If we go back even further, more than seven million years, we can have no doubt: we are looking at "monkeys." In global terms, Darwin was right. This makes it obligatory—even within the Roman Catholic Church—to abandon the old creationist idea according to which the various living species came out of the hands of the creator ready-made, once and for all, in their unique forms. With the exception of a few fundamentalist sects, everyone has accepted the obvious: the species, the human species first among them, have *evolved* over time, thus they derive from one another.

This also leads to profound questions currently being raised in a spate of works about the consequences of the theory of evolution for the very definition of humanity: if the human being was originally an animal, if our species has in some manner "emerged from" the great apes, how can the human be called anything but a beast among others, a "third chimpanzee," according to the provocative phrase of the American biologist Jared Diamond;[1] a creature only slightly more evolved than the pygmy chimpanzee (the bonobo) or the common chimpanzee? In other words, what are the truly *distinctive* signs that mark the difference between humans and our humbler brethren, now that the nonmaterialist or supernatural characteristics with which certain religious and philosophical traditions endowed us seem to have been rendered singularly fragile? This first question, which revives one of the oldest debates of classic metaphysics, but with a new foundation, is joined by a second and no less bewildering question. Just how did this evolution take place? What were its stages or principal moments? Also, and perhaps especially, is this history of the birth of the human in the animal the result of pure contingency, or does it obey a certain logic (as some Christians, notably Teilhard de Chardin, continue to think) or even a finality hidden in a principle of "anthropogenesis"?

On the animal side, research has made continual progress, especially concerning the notion of "animal culture." Where are we to set the line of demarcation between man and beast? In language, morality, art, funerary rites (signs of which have been observed in elephants and great apes), or in the manufacture of tools and the use of clothing? Why not in the use of drugs or the practice of assassination, torture, and war? We cannot enter into detail here: what is essential is to grasp what guides this sort of investigation. If humans were once animals, if they are (or were originally) completely "natural" beings, continuity dictates that we should be able to find early indications of all human behaviors in other animals. Hence the attempt to trace the origins of language or the manufacture of tools in animals, but also the beginnings of morality, art, even metaphysics or any other characteristic generally held to be absolutely and specifically human. What animates the scientific spirit here is a desire to establish continuities that it views as too long denied by ancient "spiritualisms."

If this was a comprehensible and legitimate project at the start, is it still convincing in its realization? We are far from certain. Zoologists' investigations are no doubt fascinating in that they clearly show how animals that had been thought "beasts" (Descartes considered them mere machines) in reality possess a highly developed intelligence and strong emotions. This is confirmed by a number of observable behaviors that are finally receiving the attention they deserve. Still, in a general manner, we have the feeling that the human being cannot be reduced to an animal as easily as our biologists might like. There are two significant indications of discontinuity. The first is in the sphere of ethics: even as our materialists argue in favor of a perfect continuity between beast and man on the theoretical level, they behave in their laboratories as if there were a radical break between them on the moral level. Dissecting mice or rabbits and even monkeys, cats, or dogs is hardly a problem for them, but no one would think for one minute of substituting small children. One might object that this attitude is a persistence of old prejudices on their part, and that practice simply lags behind theory. But it is doubtful that such an objection would win the argument over our inner convictions; surely we should think about such convictions rather than simply denying them, so as to understand the grain of truth they might contain. Be that as it may, there is a striking contrast between what science sees as continuity and ethics sees as rupture. The reason may lie in the fact that we are all more or less aware that the human being is the sole creature engendered by nature that is capable of detaching itself from reality in order to evaluate it; to stand at a distance from reality. Humans can thus be, in certain regards, "antinatural" and can construct laws or works that control nature rather than extend it. In short, humans are the only living beings capable of resisting nature, the only form of life able to revolt against life itself and, hence, to gain access to the sphere of morality, culture, and politics.

The second indication of discontinuity is that the hypothesis of humankind's free detachment is indissolubly linked to our entry into historicity, which seems to remain the true criterion of what is inherent to us. By emancipating ourselves from the immutable rules of nature, both on the individual level (by education) and on the collective level (by culture and political action), and being no longer mired in the reality of the natural, we are enabled to enter into a history to which animals have no access, since they are fixed within rules that have remained inviolate for millennia. This ability also enables us to enter into a common world thanks to the specifically human faculty of narration. Animals are often said to lack nothing but speech. This comment sins by lack of reflection: even if animals had speech, they might easily have nothing to say to us, whereas a person who has accidentally lost the capacity for speech will still retain the dimension of the human condition that enables him or her to form a narrative and communicate it to others. Why? Simply because totally natural beings, those who lack the liberty that permits them to escape—if only for an instant—the natural, hence ahistorical, laws that guide their existence (except, perhaps, on the scale of thousands, if not millions of years), those who have no access to historicity, will have no tales to tell. They would find it impossible to enter the sphere of "common sense" and forge a world of culture and the mind through communication with others. We can discuss endlessly the question of whether or not the finch possesses a culture because it sings slightly differently in different localities, whether the chimpanzee is "cultured" because it breaks open nuts with the aid of a stone in certain parts of Africa and not in others, or whether the elephant has a natural disposition to metaphysics because it reacts to the death of another elephant. That is all well and good. We would have to have lost all sense of the meaning of words if we use them so loosely. The truth is that the animal not only lacks a world, as Heidegger said, but above all, lacks history. What might a talking lion tell us? Do we need proof? The much talked-of language of the great apes—Kanzi, for example—gives us an approximate idea of what animal discourse might be like. Unfortunately, Kanzi's mastery of language never gets beyond the performance stage: he comprehends the orders given to him and in turn emits demands, but his communications never rise to the level of narration. Contrast this with human children, who, from the age of two or three, are so delighted with their discovery of the world that they soon feels a pressing need to share their feelings and experiences with those around them.

The possibilities inherent in narrative are much more fundamental than a capacity for language itself, though the two are often and obtusely confused. Narration involves the very existence of a world that is shared because it is exclusive to humankind. In that world, moreover, language, art, education, religion, love, and hate need not be equated with their animal analogues, as contemporary tendencies to scientism suggest. Education is not apprenticeship, culture is not behavior, brutality is not wickedness, attachment is not love, egotistical discomfort is not sacrifice. What we notice here, through the ordinary confusions of contemporary biological discourse, is that the notion of a common world, signified by the possibility of narration, is missing.

But enough of the terms of this debate. We need to focus on its underlying logic. I would like to show how the strength of materialism, and also its weakness, resides in the fact that it always operates within a double paradox.

The first paradox will not surprise readers familiar with the philosophical tradition. Contrary to what might be imagined *a priori,* materialism culminates in an ethic, an invitation to wisdom, even—and the word is not too strong—a spirituality that comes close to mysticism. Far from sinking

into immoralism, its criticism of traditional moralities signals an approach
to the good life and points the way to a soteriology that, in order to define
itself in the absence of a god, claims more legitimacy than religions or idealist philosophies. It takes over the doctrine of salvation (following Spinoza) and adds to it a demand for lucidity that, in its eyes, no other doctrine
has been able to assume. We have to admit that, taken on its best level, materialistic spirituality offers an authentic and powerful vision of the happy
life. It may not, however, be as tenable as one might suppose from its desire
to don the prestige customarily conferred by the exact sciences.

The second paradox is that while materialist wisdom claims to effect a
radical break with established religions and the classic systems of metaphysics in the name of the same demand for lucidity that urges it to deconstruct "idols," it never manages to reach fulfillment without falling back
into the rut of metaphysics from which it set itself an absolute duty to escape.

Let us summarize briefly.

Any reader of Spinoza or even, as we have seen, of Nietzsche must
admit that materialism has blossomed within the confines of an ethic, a
"lay spirituality," that offers human beings a definition of the good life and
a doctrine of salvation emancipated from the trappings of both metaphysics and religion. In the realm of contemporary philosophy, André
Comte-Sponville has shown how that third type of wisdom (neither religious nor idealist) culminated in a critique of hope and, as a corollary, in an
appeal for reconciliation with the world as it is. In his eyes, "to hope a bit
less; to love a bit more" is the key to the successful life, for hope, contrary to
what the Christian religion has vainly attempted to make us understand
(and after it, the political utopias), far from enabling us to live better,
makes us fall short of what is essential in life, which must be grasped here
and now. In this light (and on this point Western materialism coincides
with a long tradition in Eastern thought), hope is more a misfortune than
a helpful virtue if, as Comte-Sponville claims, "to hope is to desire without
enjoyment, without knowledge, and without power." Without enjoyment,
because it is clear, even by definition, that we do not possess the objects of
our hope: to hope to be wealthy, to be young, to be in good health, and so
forth, implies that this is not (or not yet) the case, so we are in a situation
of absence—lack of what we would like to be or to have. To hope is also to
desire without knowledge, however. If we knew when and how the objects
of our hope were going to be granted to us, we would probably be content
to *wait* for them, and, if words have any meaning, expectation and hope are

quite different. Finally, to hope is to desire without power, for—again, obviously—if we had the capacity or the power to realize our wishes, we could do so without detouring through hope.

Frustration, ignorance, powerlessness: these are the major characteristics of hope. This is where materialism's critique of hope rejoins a spirituality that, on two essential points, draws on both the ancient wisdom traditions and, paradoxically, on a certain reading of Christianity itself. From the ancient wisdom traditions materialism borrows the notion of *carpe diem*, the conviction that the only life worth living is in the here and now, in reconciliation with the present. For both materialism and those ancient traditions, the two ills that cloud our existence are nostalgia for a past that no longer exists and the expectation of a future that has not yet arrived. In the name of these two voids we absurdly miss out on life as it is, on the only reality that has value because it alone is real—the life of the moment that we must finally learn to love for what it is. Like Spinoza, materialism accepts Christianity's message of love. After all, charity (that is, love) is one of the three theological virtues of Christian doctrine, along with faith and hope. But in the Kingdom, when we are finally admitted into God's presence, it is understood that, as Paul insisted, charity alone will remain. Faith will have no reason for being, because we will know God, and his presence alone will make faith unnecessary; hope will disappear for the same reasons, given that all hope will be fulfilled. That leaves love. Materialism states that we must act as if the Kingdom had already come, as if it were already of this world, or, to put the point better, as if the Kingdom were the world itself, the reality that we must love as it is, as the Stoics and Spinoza insist, here and now, or else we do not truly love it. *Amor fati* is the last word in materialist spirituality.

This invitation to love should not leave us unmoved. It even has—I am persuaded of this—its share of truth, which corresponds to those moments of "grace" that we have all experienced in which, in a stroke of good fortune, the world does not seem to us hostile, sick, or ugly, but rather benevolent and harmonious. Such a moment can arrive during a walk along a riverbank, on viewing a landscape whose natural beauty enchants us, or even within the human world, when a conversation, a festive occasion, or a chance meeting fills us with sudden pleasure—all situations that I am borrowing from Rousseau. The precise occasion does not matter: each of us possesses a memory of one of these blessed moments of lightness in which we feel that reality is not something to be transformed, to be bettered laboriously by effort and hard work, but something to be savored immediately, with no thought of the past or the future, in contemplation and enjoyment rather than in struggle and the hope of better days.

In this sense, materialism is indeed a philosophy of happiness, and, when all goes well, who would not willingly cede to its charms? A fair-weather philosophy, in other words. But there's the rub: when a storm breaks, is that philosophy one we can still adhere to? Just when it might be of some help to us, it gives way under our feet, as the greatest philosophers, from Epictetus to Spinoza, were constrained to admit. The genuine sage is not of this world, and, unfortunately, the "third type of wisdom" remains inaccessible to us. To put it bluntly: when faced with an imminent catastrophe—a sick child, the possible victory of fascism, an urgent political or military decision, or something of the kind—I know of no materialist sage, no Spinozan, who does not immediately become an ordinary Kantian weighing the possibilities, suddenly persuaded that the course of events might in some fashion *depend upon his free choices*. I grant that we must be prepared for ill fortune and anticipate it, as has been said before, in the mode of the future anterior tense ("when it happens, I will at least have prepared for it"). But that we must love the real in all circumstances seems to me simply impossible, not to say absurd or even obscene. What meaning can the imperative of *amor fati* have in Auschwitz? And what are our rebellions or acts of resistance worth if they have been preordained, from all eternity, in the real, along with what they were opposing? I know this argument is trivial. Still, I have never seen a Spinozan, ancient or modern, who has found a way to respond to it.

That is not for lack of trying. But when materialism attempts to respond to that argument, it falls back—in a second paradox that reinforces the first one—into the most traditional sort of metaphysics. As with Stoicism, in fact, any philosophy of radical immanence and reconciliation with the real supposes the dogmatic conviction that free will is an illusion, if not the height of illusion, because only the real exists, to the exclusion of all the possibilities that our wild imagination represents to us as accessible to our choice. The inverse situation can enable us to grasp this necessity better: if I reintroduce multiple possibilities and admit the hypothesis of free will, and if I accept the notion that the course of the world depends—if only to an infinitesimal degree—on my free choice among those possibilities, then doubt, hesitation, even anxiety immediately reenter the picture, closely followed by the eventuality of guilt: Have I acted well? Have I made the right choice? And if serious consequences ensue, how can I escape my responsibility for them? By the same token, how can I avoid the tragedy of an existence with which I am henceforth unable to reconcile myself in perfect serenity? In short: How can we escape the utterly banal "moral point of view"?

This is why, in his commentary on book 1 of Spinoza's *Ethics*, André Comte-Sponville chooses (if I may be permitted the term) absolute determinism:

> Man is not an empire within an empire: he is but a part of nature whose order, or, to our eyes, disorder, he follows. Who would morally condemn an eclipse or an earthquake? And why must we condemn a murder or a war any more than that? Because men are responsible for them? Let us say that they are the cause of them, as others are in their turn, and so forth, *ad infinitum* (*Ethics* I, 28). There is nothing contingent in nature (*Ethics* I, 29), hence there is nothing free in the will (*Ethics* I, 32; II, 48). Men believe themselves free to will only because they are unaware of the causes of their volition. . . . The belief in free will is thus mere illusion, and that is why all morality (if we take morality as being that which authorizes the absolute blaming or praising of a human being) is also illusory.[2]

Or, as Spinoza himself says of the reasonable man, "Whatsoever he deems to be hurtful and evil, and whatsoever, accordingly, seems to him impious, horrible, unjust, and base, assumes that appearance owing to his own disordered, fragmentary, and confused view of the universe."[3] Conversely, if we could place ourselves at an adequate observation point — that is, what God's viewpoint on the world would be — it would seem to us that everything is necessary and determined and nothing appertains to man's free will. In that case, finally rid of the weight of a false responsibility and, with it, a futile culpability that is the archetype of all the "sad passions," we would accept the world as it is with joy.

This returns us to the possibility of a wisdom of love. But at what cost? Who guarantees us, in fact, that setting aside man's finite viewpoint and taking this mystical leap into the absolute does not in itself represent the worst of illusions, the classic illusion of all traditional metaphysics? "All these evils," Spinoza writes, "seem to have arisen from the fact that happiness or unhappiness is made wholly to depend on the quality of the object which we love. When a thing is not loved, no quarrels will arise concerning it — no sadness will be felt if it perishes — no envy if it is possessed by another — no fear, no hatred, in short no disturbance of the mind. All these arise from the love of what is perishable, such as the objects already men-

tioned. But love towards a thing eternal and infinite feeds the mind wholly
with joy, and is itself unmingled with any sadness, wherefore it is greatly to
be desired and sought for with all our strength."[4] This is an odd sort of materialism: even word for word, it is almost as if Pascal or Augustine were
speaking. Like them, Spinoza invites us to direct our love exclusively to the
eternal, risking disappointment if we fail to do so. He says that his only aim
is to return to the "spirit of Christ." And why not? It is not the objective
that seems contestable here, but the coherence of what Spinoza has to say.
One might object (and I am well aware of the objection) that Spinoza's
God is not quite the Christian God; that here God is not transcendent to
the world but inextricably mixed with it. The invitation to love, therefore,
bears on the real, the here and now, not on the beyond.

Be that as it may. But who will believe that it is purely by chance that
reality, for Spinoza, bears the name of God? It would be nice if every moment in life were like an instant of grace, but what would be the use of philosophizing, after all, if it only involved loving what is lovable? As was true
of Stoicism, however, in order to reach that goal one must leave finite consciousness—hence move out of materialism—and situate oneself at the
one viewpoint (God's) from which determinism, which justifies the *amor
fati* and turns every instant into an instant of grace, is conceivable. Absolute determinism is the condition of possibility of the *amor fati*. Without
it, reconciliation with the real and love of what is loses all meaning, for
when possibles take back their rights, then doubt, responsibility, and culpability also take back their own right to threaten serenity. The materialist attitude thus seems at once contradictory (by demanding fusion with God's
viewpoint, it turns inevitably to mysticism) and inoperative: in ordinary
life, materialists continue to be just as anguished as others, and they behave
as if they believed in free will just as much as in the illusion of the possibles.

This means that materialism, instead of a "deconstruction," an apogee
of the critical spirit, turns out to be a traditional onto-theology, a dogmatic
metaphysic that illegitimately surpasses the limits of experience and
human finitude in order to operate in a sphere in which no human being
can dwell. Genealogy turns against itself, and the suspicion arises that materialism may have been chosen less for the lucidity it is supposed to procure than for the peace it promises us by putting an end—as far as can be
done—to the questions that the very idea of multiple possibles suggests to
us.[5] Like no other philosophy, in fact, materialism claims to spare us the
tragic in life. I doubt that it succeeds in this aim, and I also doubt that it is
even desirable to do so: to be a thoroughgoing Spinozan, one would have

to be a god, or a stone flung from the same slingshot that gave him his motion, and, as the maxim states, *ultra posse nemo obligatur.*

Materialism thus brings us back to the religion from which it claims to free us. It displays the same passion for heteronomy, the same interest in ultimate foundations, the same focus on rooting human wisdom in a radical alterity that wisdom cannot attain or even imagine: the alterity of an eternal, absolute, and all-powerful reality.

2. Modernizing the Religious: Toward a More Humanist Theology

I have already suggested that according to one interpretation the religious organization of society might seem to be the element out of which a democratic modernity gradually emerged during the course of the nineteenth and twentieth centuries. As a first approximation, one might say that modern democracy prefers autonomy to heteronomy, innovation to tradition, and individualism to communitarianism. We need to clarify some of the terms used in this diagnosis. If it turned out to be correct, it would clearly, *a priori*, cause serious problems for the project of "modernizing" the religious and making it compatible with the demands of the secular universe, given that the latter is, so to speak by its very nature, hostile to the principal values that seem to nourish the religious.

First, what do we mean by heteronomy? The response may seem easy: it simply designates the fact that the great religions agree that humanity—its organization, its life, its salvation—depends on a principle radically external to and superior to itself. In temporal existence, that transcendence of the divine is manifested by a particular relation to the law, in the conviction that in its very principle, the law escapes the understanding of the individuals who receive it and are subject to it even in their daily lives. In this perspective, Marcel Gauchet has advanced the thesis that "the most religious" form of the religious can be found at the origins of history; that it can be found in what might be called its chemically pure state in "primitive societies" in which the underlying sources of social organization are the most external. But there is more: the religious does not simply imply heteronomy—the conviction that the law comes from elsewhere than from humanity itself—but also a *denial of autonomy*—that is, a refusal, on the part of human beings, to attribute to themselves social organization, history, and the making of laws. Through this denial of a human origin of the political, they place the founding principles of political connection elsewhere, in a radical transcendence and dependence.

In this light, we can also understand that the religious may seem to belong (and here again, almost by its essence) to the past, to a bygone time. This is not to suggest, in the manner of Auguste Comte, that the modern world, now that it has at last arrived at the age of science and democracy, has shed religious naïvetés; the point is rather to show that the modern world, by its nature, contains the *traditional* forms of political organization in which the law is envisioned as an immemorial and inviolable heritage. In the modern world, a politician presenting himself as a candidate for election with the sole program of doing his utmost not to change anything would obviously have little chance of being elected. The notion that the religious belongs to the past is not, in this regard, a superficial sort of belonging: because it participates in the notion of radical dependence on a suprahuman origin that precedes history itself, the religious idea is *structurally* linked to the sacralization of the concept of transmission.

Finally, whatever the precise etymology of the word "religion" may be, the various principles that transcend humanity have clearly had the effect of creating communities of belief in which the notion of the individual was secondary to those of heritage or tradition: in this perspective, the part is always inferior to the whole, the organ counts for less than the organism, the member less than the body and certainly less than the all-powerful creator of the whole within which creatures are as if soldered together within a hierarchy of beings that is intended to be inviolable. This explains, incidentally, the atrocity of wars of religion, which continue to bloody the world even today. Aimed at the adverse community as a community, they seldom draw any distinction between the individual and the nation, and even less between the person and the soldier, which means that they are always, although to various degrees, tempted to engage in extermination or genocide.

We should recognize (at least as a first step; I shall refine my discussion later) that the structure of traditional heteronomy constitutes, in many ways, one of the dominant traits of the religious, which for that very reason continues to be imposed under the outward appearance of an argument from authority. Rather than denying that fact, perhaps out of fear of seeming "dogmatic" and offending the democratic sensibility in which we are permanently immersed, the catechism of the Roman Catholic Church has the merit, not to mention the courage, to embrace it boldly: "What moves us to believe is not the fact that revealed truths appear as true and intelligible in the light of our natural reason: we believe 'because of the authority of

God himself who reveals them, who can neither deceive nor be deceived.' . . . Faith is *certain*. It is more certain than all human knowledge because it is founded on the very word of God who cannot lie. To be sure, revealed truths can seem obscure to human reason and experience, but 'the certainty that the divine light gives is greater than that which the light of natural reason gives.'"[6] It might be objected that the catechism is not a reference, that it belongs to a literary genre that does not indulge in nuance, and that philosophical discussion is hardly permitted to it. Perhaps, but Pascal, who was neither a bigot nor inclined to silliness, constantly says the same thing: if the "I" is hateful, it is because, while always claiming to have the upper hand, it makes humans forget what is essential, that "not in you yourselves will you find truth or good."[7] All truth and all justice come from God, not from human beings, whose principal virtue in this regard is humility.

A second, indirect authority is added to the first, which derives directly from the supreme being. It is that of the church, which—as the faithful are enjoined to agree—holds a monopoly on the legitimate interpretation of the content of revelation, including its moral aspects. The catechism states: "The Church's Magisterium exercises the authority it holds from Christ to the fullest extent when it defines dogmas, that is, when it proposes truths contained in divine Revelation or having a necessary connection with them in a form obliging the Christian people to an irrevocable adherence of faith."[8] (The latter provision of course refers to moral recommendations that do not appear in the Gospels but have been adapted by the church to today's world.) This could hardly be stated more clearly: the Magisterium does not deny personal liberty, or the role of consciousness in the "choice" of faith. But faith is never anything but a "response" in the face of a gift, a reaction secondary to a revelation that precedes it.

It is of course this relation to a "revealed authority"—which is interpreted in other ideologies to its utmost consequences—that democratic ideology spontaneously rejects. A conflict—sometimes open, sometimes disguised—was launched in the seventeenth century between revealed religions and the modern demand (in particular, as a result of Cartesianism) to subject all prejudices inherited from the past to doubt and to reject all arguments from authority. "To think for oneself" became the ultimate requirement, the fundamental, non-negotiable imperative that gradually led to a desire to submit even the truths most firmly rooted in tradition, starting with those of revelation, to critical examination.

Does this mean, as certain authors have made a show of believing,[9] that religion, totally devoted to heteronomy and to tradition, henceforth belongs to the ancient world, to the universe in which man has not yet, so to speak, gained access to himself, whereas the Moderns, infatuated with democratic autonomy, are finally free, aware, lucid, and autonomous? Obviously not. This sort of interpretation distorts—deliberately, no doubt—the analysis I have just evoked. By indulging in caricature for the needs of its cause, such an interpretation loses its own way and seeks to lead others astray where both heteronomy and autonomy are concerned. No one would dream of denying that faith, precisely because it claims to respond to an appeal, can be experienced by the believer as a "free choice" and an autonomous act—which in no way excludes the fact that it continues to refer to the idea of radical dependence, thus of an original heteronomy (here, a "theo-nomy": a founding of the law in God). The converse, of course, pertains among the Moderns: the Cartesian claim to "think for oneself," far from annulling all forms of heteronomy, simply emphasizes the existence of many determinisms—psychic, historical, and biological—that continue to weigh on individuals just as much as before, given that individuals have no control over their birth or their death, or even, in all probability, over much of the course of their lives. How are we to understand this double paradox of a radical heteronomy that does not exclude the autonomy of religious choice, on the one hand, and an ideal of autonomy that in no way puts an end to the multiform reality of heteronomy, on the other?

To tell the truth, it is easy to concede that religion *tends by itself* (and not through some malevolent injunction supposedly served on it from the outside) to declare that faith is an act of grace—that is, a gratuitous gift from a real being upon which we are radically dependent and to which we owe obedience. Heteronomy does not imply that faith has been *forcefully wrung out of us by arguments of authority imposed from the outside.* To the contrary, Christianity is above all the religion that leaves people free from its counsel, that recognizes a person's own conscience as a legitimate forum, and that attributes merit to faith only because it depends, at least in part, on free choice. This is why, moreover, Pope John Paul II, while recognizing the radical heteronomy of truth, nonetheless attempts to make it accord with freedom of conscience. According to the encyclical letter *The Splendor of Truth*, conscience and truth must be reconciled. As Vatican II had already declared, "God willed to leave man to his own counsel."[10] He did not take away man's liberty. Far from it. Just as God created man in his image, human beings fully accede to themselves by following the principles of divine truth in all their acts. The pope, using the language of theology, speaks of "participated theonomy." In short: moral law comes from God (theonomy), not from human beings, but that does not exclude human autonomy, since human beings, by participating in the divine in some fashion, accede to full liberty only by obeying the law that is prescribed for them: "Man's *genuine moral authority* in no way means the rejection but rather the acceptance of the moral law, of God's command. . . . If in fact a heteronomy of morality were to mean a denial of man's self-determination or the imposition of norms unrelated to his good, this would be in contradiction to the Revelation of the Covenant and of the redemptive Incarnation." Thus freedom of conscience does not exclude the radical heteronomy of the truth or absolute transcendence. Still, from his own point of view the pope is right: faith is a gift; there is a splendid revealed truth that originates in a supreme being, hence a truth that has a real foundation.

There is also no doubt that, conversely, democratic ideology tends to magnify the ideal of autonomy. But this is a fault that I have constantly denounced as deriving from *a logic of materialism rather than a logic of humanism*—that is, from a thought that, like contemporary sociobiology, professes the radical immanence of the values of the material reality of the human being. For the materialist, human beings do not discover values, they invent them; they are the creator and ultimate foundation of values—even if they are not aware of this fact and believe, in fetishist fashion, that what they have set up does not originate in themselves. The critique of fetishism is the key moment of the modern attitude of suspicion and of deconstruction, and this moment always results in a radical immanentism: values are relative to the human because the human produces them.

Unlike materialism, which may appear in this regard as an extreme radicalization of democratic ideology, authentic humanism seems always to have been based on the affirmation of an externality or a radical transcendence of values: I do not invent truth, justice, beauty, or love, I discover them, in myself, to be sure, but as something given to me from the outside, although I cannot identify the ultimate basis of that gift. A mystery of transcendence subsists, in fact—a mystery that materialism and theology cannot abide. They are both intent on having done with the intolerably loose, free-flying nature of transcendence and on tying it down, solidly and firmly, to an ultimate foundation—material in the first case, divine in the second, but in both cases certain and definitive. For an authentic humanist, on the other hand, the mystery of transcendence is totally rational (at least if one accepts the idea that it is rational that the irrational should exist). The reason is obvious: no causal explanation could ever lead to the discovery of an ultimate causality, a "first cause" that would be the "cause of it-self." For the same reason, all the positive sciences today assume that not one of them will ever come to completion, definitively closed within some sort of "absolute knowledge," but rather that scientific progress is bound-less, infinite, or indefinite, not only in fact but also by right. Thus, if words have any meaning, mystery will always persist in our knowledge of the world. But this is precisely what the two onto-theologies, the materialist and the religious, strive to do away with, each in its own way striving to identify the natural or spiritual basis of knowledge and of ethics, be it eco-nomics, God, genes, the libido, or some other explanatory principle.

The idea that transcendence might exist within the immanence of human consciousness, a kind of transcendence that is not a being or a basis but a horizon of meaning, has shocked certain Christian friends of mine, who have accused me of inconsistency. Some who, unlike my early critics, have realized that I was by no means equating modernity, autonomy, and immanence of values with the human being, but, to the contrary, that I was referring to a humanism that accepted the hypothesis of transcendence, even of mystery, therefore of the externality of such values in relation to the individual, have thought my attitude doubly contradictory. In the first place, they state, why reproach Christianity for its doctrine of heteronomy if you intend to transfer that doctrine immediately to humanism by ar-ranging a place for transcendence within it? But also, how are we to re-spond to the question of the origin of the values common to human beings unless we admit the idea of a real basis for them, in this case divine? Thus, in an interesting article that reflects genuine intellectual honesty, Damien Le Guay directs the following objection to me: "What, therefore, is the status of this externality accepted by Ferry? To speak of a 'morality external to nature and to history' is to speak of a morality that comes before human consciousness. As it happens, that anteriority is rejected, along with the theologico-ethical. At this point, thanks to a bit of theoretical hocus-pocus, there can be an externality compatible with man when it is human-ist and an externality incompatible [with man] when it is religious?"[11] Well yes, Damien Le Guay, you could hardly have said it better. There are, in fact, several conceptions of transcendence, and according to whether you define it as a real foundation, a supreme form of being, or, to the contrary, a simple horizon of meaning that cannot be explained in terms of ultimate foundation, you escape (or fail to escape) from the framework of a human-ism that attempts to be nonmetaphysical.

Faith—both that of Christians and that of materialists—begins beyond this, which is why their criticism of the humanism of the man-god is perfectly symmetrical. The Christian allows humanism its affirmation—unlike materialism—of a kind of transcendence, but deplores the fact that humanists fail to follow through in their pursuit of a logic that looked so promising. Why stop when the road seems so right? Why not found the transcendence of values in a God who will guarantee it and provide a satisfactory explanation for it? Materialists, on the other hand, praise humanists for not having done anything of the sort; they communicate with humanists, one might say, in atheism, but materialists too (again, but for the opposite reason) regret that the logic of humanist reasoning is not fully resolved and remains as if in suspense. If God does not exist, why not eliminate the absurd notion of transcendence? Why not have done with it, once and for all, by positing that all values are immanent to the materiality of the real? My response: if we did so, in each case we would fall back into the illusions of ultimate metaphysical foundations, into an onto-theology that, as we have seen, surpasses the limits of human finitude. There may be nothing illegitimate about faith, but it is and it must remain what it is: a wager, a postulate, a decision to believe that never engages anyone but oneself. Of course, nothing prevents our making such a wager: everyone is fully free to believe, with the materialist, that the real is eternal, that it excludes possibles along with free will; everyone is equally free to believe, with the Christian, that a God has given us the values to which we adhere. But this "leap outside of oneself" cannot engage others and, in the long run, no longer pertains to the realm of philosophy.

To conclude: what remains to be done is to clearly define the other perspective, the one that represents the humanism of the man-god, and to show what makes the horizons of meaning of our most intimate yet also our commonest experiences truly impervious to distortion.

3. The New Faces of Transcendence

From now on, do we have only one choice: between, on the one hand, the transcendences of yesteryear, which, even when reorganized and adjusted to the conditions of the democratic world, continue to contain their inevitable moment of "authority," and, on the other hand, the absolute immanence, the radical platitude of a secularized, democratic, and disenchanted universe totally dedicated to the materialist ideology? Because I could never persuade myself of this, I long ago decided to apply philosophical reflection to the possibility of a "nonmetaphysical" humanism that, standing apart from "restorations" and "returns to," would, on the contrary, follow the deconstructions of metaphysics, take their contributions into account, and begin to explore the possibility of a re-enchantment of the world. If I had to summarize that humanism and reduce it to its essence, as I have attempted to do for other positions discussed, I would say that it is based on an affirmation of the "divinization of the human"—on three postmetaphysical philosophical principles that concern the dual transcendence of liberty within human beings and values outside them, but that also launch a new interrogation pertaining to the question of happiness.

i. The Affirmation: The "Divinization of the Human." For over a century now, powerful thinkers, beginning with Nietzsche, through Freud, Marx, and Weber to Heidegger, have repeatedly announced the "death of God" and just as repeatedly analyzed the secularization of the world and the processes at work in the modern world that inexorably have led to the erosion and then the retreat of the paraphernalia of religion. The present work takes that perspective, at least in part, in that it describes how the various responses to the question of the good life became increasingly humanized until they culminated in a radical materialism. Yet, as I have already had occasion to demonstrate, a history of sacrifice—that is, of the motivations that induce human beings to risk their lives or even give them up for what they regard as *sacred*—suggests the opposite conclusion, even today: contrary to what should have been the logical consequences of a universe finally and genuinely disenchanted, we continue (whether or not we are materialists) to think that certain values might, in certain cases, lead us to risk death. The famous slogan of the German pacifists, *Lieber rot als tot* (better red than dead), has not, in the long run, persuaded all of our contemporaries, and it is clear that a number of them (who are not all "believers") are still persuaded that saving one's own life is not necessarily the supreme value. I am convinced that, if they had to, our fellow citizens would still be capable of taking up arms to defend their loved ones or even to resist oppression. At the very least, if they lacked the courage to carry out such acts themselves, they would not think them either unworthy or absurd. As it happens—and Nietzsche was right on this point—sacrifice, which refers to the sacred, always has a religious dimension, even for a convinced materialist. It implies an admission, albeit a surreptitious one, that there exist values that are *transcendent* because they are superior to material or biological life. The problem is, however, that the sacrificial entities of yesteryear have petered out. It is far from certain, at least in our Western democracies, that many individuals would be willing to sacrifice their lives for the glory of God, the homeland, or the proletarian revolution. On the other hand, their liberty and, perhaps even more, the lives of their loved ones might well seem to them, in extreme circumstances, worth fighting for. In other words, we have not replaced the old transcendences—God, the homeland, revolution—with a radical immanence or a renunciation either of the sacred or of sacrifice. Rather, we have replaced them with new forms of transcendence, "horizontal" rather than "vertical" forms—transcendences rooted in the human rather than in entities external to and superior to the human.

That is the way we must think if we wish to stop living (as materialists must resolve to live) in the untenable *denial* that consists in recognizing within our inner experience the existence of a "practical absolute" and of values that engage us absolutely, and, at the same time, in striving, on the theoretical plane, to defend a purely relativist morality that leads to reducing that same absolute to the status of a mere illusion to be dispelled.

ii. Three Postmetaphysical Philosophical Principles: The Excess of Liberty, Irreducible Values, Transcendence within Immanence. If determinism is itself no more than a metaphysical "choice" or even, as in Spinoza, a form of mysticism, of fusion with the viewpoint of God about whom nothing—short of a return to the old ontological argument—guarantees that he is one with the real or with nature, then we are forced to recognize that the hypothesis of free will also remains a possible philosophical choice. This was the choice of Descartes, Rousseau, and Kant, of course, but also of Husserl, Sartre, and even, under another name (*Ek-sistenz* or "transcendence"), the early Heidegger. Rousseau proposes to differentiate man from the animals by his genuinely "super-natural" ability not to follow instinct: whereas animals are totally ruled by nature, and even more surely guided by it than are humans, man ceaselessly reveals a strange and indefinable capacity for excess. In man, as Rousseau nicely puts it, "the will still speaks when nature is silent,"[12] whereas in the animal, we might add, nature constantly expresses itself both rigorously and imperatively. This view grants the human three characteristics that are seldom encountered in animals, whatever biologists might say: first, hatred, which becomes demonic when it leads people to cast aside all natural rationality and take on evil as a project; next, love, when people go beyond the utilitarian logic of possession and attachment and arrive at a simple enjoyment of the existence of others (what the Greeks called *philia*); and, finally, education or training, which cannot be confused, without descending to reductionism, with the learning process of an animal, given that it shifts us away from the natural within us rather than complementing it.

Transcendence is thus revealed to lie at the heart of the human being. But it also resides outside of humans. If materialism were right, if it were simply true, we would have to conclude that, from the moment materialism arose, encountering no obstacle and clashing with no prohibition, the values to which we constantly refer have possessed no transcendence and are nothing but the natural products of our desires. In other words, we would have to accept the clear conviction that relativism is the only "morality" with any value and agree that, as Spinoza claimed, "in no case do we strive for, wish for, long for, or desire anything, because we deem it to be good, but on the other hand we deem a thing to be good, because we strive for it, wish for it, long for it, or desire it."[13] Relative to our libido, values—whatever they may be—should appear to us as what they necessarily are in this perspective: entities immanent to our nature and nothing more. In my view, however, even the most banal aesthetic or moral experience immediately persuades us of the contrary: not only do certain values continue to seem independent of my will, like "givens from outside" of me, but also they seem to impose themselves upon me, even in the form of an imperative that can at times induce me to put my life in danger. The truth is that in the age of democratic individualism and the era of autonomy, values continue to seem superior to us and external to us, as they did in the time of religions, even when we reject the metaphysical framework that once permitted us to ground them on some sort of ultimate foundation. Not only does the slightest scientific truth resist my ego and impose itself on that ego as a given that it must admit in spite of its subjectivity, but even in the sphere of aesthetics, which is usually considered subjective, the experience of the transcendence of the beautiful continues to prevail. I do not invent the beauty of a suite by Bach or of a landscape. I am humbly content to discover them as if, despite the admittedly subjective sentiments that they arouse in me, they were not created by my subjectivity. *A fortiori* in the ethical realm, it often goes against my nature, against my penchants, against my normal inclinations to egotism or to communitarian particularisms that I have to admit the transcendence of the law or the primacy of justice. This explains the persistence, even at the heart of individualistic societies, of a republican ideal, of a reference to the universal, and to the *res publica,* when it is hard to imagine what meaning could still be attached to such notions if the sole and unique truth were situated in the innermost nature of each particular individual.

Rather than launching an inquiry, once again in the name of materialist immanence, into the denials imposed by dogmatic metaphysics, it will be more useful to consider the persistence of such a transcendence and to forge the new concepts that it requires. We can begin by distinguishing three general conceptions of transcendence. First, there is the transcendence that the Ancients mobilized in order to respond to the question of the good life in terms of cosmology. As we have seen, the harmonious order of the cosmos is both transcendent and immanent: it is transcendent in relation to human beings, who have neither created nor invented it but discover it as a given, external to and superior to them, yet immanent to the real because it is completely embodied in the world. The second is the transcendence of the God of the great monotheisms, as we have also seen. This transcendence is situated not only in relation to humanity but also in relation to the world, which is itself conceived entirely as a creature whose existence depends on a being outside itself. But a third form of transcendence, different from the first two, can also be imagined on the basis of transcendental philosophy (and on that of phenomenology, which is in many ways simply an extension of the latter). Like the transcendence of the Greeks, it is a "transcendence within immanence" in the sense that its embodiment is no longer found in the natural world, in the cosmos, but in the human world, within humanity, inasmuch as humanity cannot be reduced to the natural logic of animality alone, where, thanks to the liberty it enjoys, it constitutes what Wilhelm Dilthey called a "world view" (*Weltanschauung*). Unlike theological transcendence, phenomenological transcendence refers not to the idea of an ultimate foundation, but rather (using the vocabulary of Husserl once again) to the notion of horizon. When I open my eyes onto the world, objects are always presented against a background, and as I penetrate the universe that surrounds me, that background shifts constantly, as the horizon does for a sailor, never becoming fixed into one ultimate, unsurpassable setting. Thus, from one background to another, from horizon to horizon, I never manage to seize anything that I can take to be a final entity, a supreme being, or a first cause capable of guaranteeing the existence of the real that surrounds me. By its infinite mobility, the notion of horizon includes an element of mystery: the reality of the world, like that of the cube, whose six faces cannot all be seen at once, is never granted to me in perfect transparency or perfect mastery. To put it differently, if we insist on remaining within the viewpoint of human finitude, if we refuse to take the mystical leap to which materialism and theology both invite us, each in its particular fashion, we are forced to admit that human knowledge will never accede to omniscience and never coincide with the viewpoint of God or of nature, either by an "intellectual intuition" or a "third type of wisdom."

Thanks to this refusal of closure and this rejection of all forms of "absolute knowledge," this third type of transcendence appears as a "transcendence within immanence," uniquely capable of conferring a significance to the human experience that the humanism of the man-god attempts to describe and account for. It is "in me"—in my thought or in my sensibility—that values are revealed, outside of all reference to an argument from authority or to a heteronomy originating in a real substructure (God or nature). Yet I do not invent mathematical truths or the beauty of a work of art or ethical imperatives. To use an appropriate idiom, we "fall in love" rather than make a deliberate choice. The alterity or the transcendence of values is in this sense quite real: we can make a phenomenology of it, a description beginning with the irrepressible sentiment of a necessity, of the awareness that it is impossible to think or feel otherwise. I can do nothing about it: that $2 + 2 = 4$ is not a question of taste or subjective choice. Still, that truth, simple as it is, eludes all ultimate foundation. I can probably deduce it from certain initial axioms, those of classic arithmetic in this case, but beyond those axioms—which by definition are and will remain undemonstrated propositions—no real foundation is ever revealed to me. It is that openness that nonmetaphysical humanism intends to assume as its own, not out of impotence but because it must agree, for the sake of principle and even lucidity, to quit searching in genes or in divinity, in nature or in the supreme being, for the final explanation of our relation to common values, let alone universal ones. If it fails to do so, it relapses into the discourse of classical metaphysics. Nonmetaphysical humanism needs to think in other terms—terms deliberately more fragile, more human, but by that very token less illusory—about the question of the good life and, along with it, that of happiness.

CHAPTER 13

A New Approach to the Question of Happiness

Are you for or against happiness? The question seems absurd, but for more than two centuries modern philosophy has been tormented by it. A line of thinkers ranging from Kant to Nietzsche and Freud considered happiness a vague and naïve idea (if not an illusory one, given the tragic or contradictory nature of existence) but also believed that the demands of liberty and lucidity must at times take precedence to it—assuming that happiness can be defined with any degree of coherence. Each in his fashion, all these philosophers elaborated powerful "critiques" of the very notion of happiness. Another line of thought from Hobbes to Marx, including English utilitarianism, held, to the contrary, that material and moral well-being, in whatever sense one understands it, is the ultimate end of all human existence and nothing can or should be put ahead of it.

Without going into detail regarding these debates, we need to understand what led certain thinkers—and not the least of them—to criticize the idea of happiness and then to consider why modern utilitarianism, as against Greek philosophy, gave such a reductive version of the question that it could not help but elicit hostility. Beyond the apparently infinite number of possible definitions of happiness, two major "eudaemonistic" moral conceptions—two contrasting philosophies of the "sovereign good," one essentially ancient, the other typically modern—form the background of contemporary discussion.

We have already encountered the first of these philosophies, the one developed within the framework of the Greek cosmologies. It rests on two basic convictions, both of which were contested in the seventeenth century. The first states that there exists a "common good" connected to the cosmic harmony, completely independent of the will or the particular interests of each individual. Whether I like it or not, there is an "objective" order of the world, an organization that I myself have not invented and within which I can and must find my place: it is at that price, and only at that price, that I can bring together the conditions that will permit me to be happy. In this "holist" perspective, then, the All (the cosmos) precedes the parts (individuals) and predetermines the conditions in which individual access to the blessed life is possible. The second conviction is just as essential and flows directly from the first. It states that authentic happiness cannot be reduced to material and psychological well-being but must include the problematic of salvation. In order to be fully happy, one must have vanquished the fear of death, and the only way to do so, the only possible way of life, is the philosophical life, which means that the problematic of happiness goes far beyond the mere satisfaction of material desires and contains a soteriological dimension.

Modern utilitarianism takes a radically opposed position on these two characteristic aspects of the cosmologico-ethical. First, it completely reverses perspective, starting with the individual instead of the All, in its attempt to construct a new conception of happiness based on the individual. That conception reaches its apogee in the conviction that the blessed life resides quite simply in a satisfaction as complete and durable as possible of all individual "interests"—a generic term that covers all varieties of determinations, desires, needs, wishes, appetites, whims, and so forth. This does not mean that modern utilitarianism takes no account of the "common good." It modifies that notion, however, and in two ways. For one thing, the common good ceases to take precedence over particular interests and is presented as an attempt to bring them into accord, as far as possible, *a posteriori*. Consequently, it replaces the cosmological conception of the common good, perceived as an objectively harmonious order, by the individualistic idea of the "general interest," seen as the reconciliation, if not as the result, of particular interests (according to the model of liberal market theories). This leads to the second way in which modern theories of happiness have broken with ancient theory. If happiness is nothing but the satisfaction of particular interests (which, in certain cases, can also take into account the general interest), it tends to be reduced to a material and psychological well-being that excludes any metaphysical perspective. Not that utilitarianism never raises the question of the fear of death; it is simply one "interest" among others. So the fear of death belongs on a psychological level, in that it can trouble the psychic serenity of the individual, not on the soteriological level. The philosophical life ceases to constitute the human ideal. That ideal is now situated in commerce, even in the quest for wealth, rather than in wisdom as the Ancients defined it. From the common good of the Greeks we have shifted to the notion of the general interest, and from the idea of happiness to that of well-being.

This reductionist shift produced not only utilitarianism but also the first great philosophical criticisms of the idea of happiness. It is because happiness was reduced to this secondary materialistic and psychologizing image, to material and psychic well-being, that it elicited hostile reactions, notably on the part of Kant and Nietzsche.[1] Not that they contest the fact, which is banal, that happiness (admitting that the concept has an assignable meaning) in some fashion constitutes a horizon of human life. But they invite us, each in his own way, to situate it anew, as the Ancients had done, in a wider perspective and in a vision of the world that includes—as we have just seen in Nietzsche—the three fundamental moments of *theōria*, *praxis*, and soteriology.

It is in that same triple perspective that I would like to discuss the humanism of the man-god. Today, after the collapse of the cosmological models, the problematic of happiness can no longer be equated with that of the Ancients, but if we nonetheless refuse—as they invited us to do—to reduce that problematic to a mere logic of interests and well-being, how and on what basis can we possibly return to it? In order to answer that question, I must first suggest, as with all general philosophical perspectives, what the specific characteristics of *theōria*, *praxis*, and soteriology might be in our current age and in a humanist perspective.

Theōria: *The Age of Self-Reflection*

We can distinguish three ages of science. The first corresponds to the Greek *theōria*. As contemplation of the order of the world and comprehension of the structure of the cosmos, *theōria*, as we have seen, is not a science indifferent to values, nor is it, to use Max Weber's term, "axiologically neutral." Knowledge and values are intrinsically connected, in the sense that, in itself, the discovery of the intimate character of the universe implies an emphasis on certain practical aims for human existence.

The second age appears with the modern scientific revolution, which (contrary to the Greek world) witnessed the emergence of a kind of knowledge radically indifferent to the question of values: science describes *what is;* it does not speak of *what should be;* as science, it has no normative implications. In this view, which one might call "positivist" in the broad sense of the word, science is less interested in self-interrogation than in knowing the world as it is.

A third perspective challenges the second but also complements it. It is that of self-criticism or self-reflection, an attitude highly characteristic of our current age.

In his *Risk Society,* Ulrich Beck proposes a useful description of both the difference between the second and third ages of science and the connections between the two.[2] Without discussing Beck's analysis in detail, and without concurring with him in all of his conclusions, we can join him in accepting the idea that after the "first modernity," which arose in the eighteenth century, dominated the nineteenth century, and is drawing to a close today, our Western societies have entered into a second phase marked by an awareness of the risks engendered within them by the development and subsequent globalization of sciences and technologies. We need to understand both the frontal opposition between these "two modernities" and the secret links between them before we can grasp the radically new situation into which the more advanced portions of the West now find themselves. Let us pause for a moment at this diagnosis. It will repay the effort.

The first modernity, which was still "truncated" and "dogmatic," had four fundamental and intertwined traits.

The first of these was a conception of science that remained authoritarian and dogmatic. Sure of itself and domineering in its attitude toward its principal object, which was nature, science aspired, without the least doubt or self-criticism, to work hand in hand with emancipation and human happiness. It promised to free people from the religious obscurantism of centuries past and at the same time to provide them with the means to make themselves, in Descartes' famous phrase, into the "masters and possessors" of a universe that they could use and exploit at will in order to realize their material well-being.

The idea of progress, solidly anchored in this scientific optimism and defined in terms of liberty and happiness, was quite logically inserted into the framework of parliamentary democracy and the nation-state. Science and "national" democracies went hand in hand: Is it not taken for granted that the verities revealed by science, like the principles on which democracies are founded, are in essence destined to all, equally? Like the rights of man, scientific laws claim to be universal; at least in principle, they apply to all human beings regardless of race, class, or gender.

This means that the chief business of the new scientifico-democratic nation-states was the production and distribution of wealth. Their dynamic was equality, as Tocqueville stated, or, in Marxist terminology, the struggle against inequalities. In this difficult but resolute combat, confidence in the future was all-important, with the result that risks were mostly relegated to the status of second-tier concerns.

Finally, social and familial roles remained fixed, even naturalized. Distinctions of class and gender—to say nothing of ethnic differences—were perhaps rendered fragile in law and questionable in principle but continued to be perceived as inviolable *de facto*. People spoke of "Civilization," capitalized and in the singular, as if it were taken granted as being primarily European, white, and male.

On these four points the second modernity—*theōria* as we are beginning to live it today—is about to break with the first. It will do so, however, not by means of an external critique, nor on the basis of a radically new social and political model, but through a deeper pursuit of its own principles.

To turn to science first: a veritable revolution took place in its relations with nature at the end of the twentieth century. Today it is no longer nature that engenders the major risks for humankind, but scientific investigation; thus it is no longer nature that we have to tame, but rather science. For the first time in history, science furnishes the human species with the means for its own destruction. This is true not only of the risks created within modern societies by the industrial use of new technologies; there is also the possibility that others will use those technologies for political purposes. If terrorism worries the world today more than it did yesterday, it is not just because we have become aware that terrorists now have access, or soon will have, to chemical and even nuclear weapons. Control of the uses and effects of modern science is slipping out of our hands, and its unbridled power is worrisome.

This "process without a subject" in a globalized world of technology that no worldwide governance has yet managed to control makes the framework of the nation-state and, along with it, the traditional forms of parliamentary democracy seem strangely cramped. No republican miracle caused the clouds from Chernobyl to stop at the frontiers of France. For their part, the processes that govern economic growth and the financial markets no longer obey the dictates of the people's representatives, who now struggle to keep the promises they have made to the electorate. This of course enhances the residual success of those who attempt to persuade us, in the image of French neorepublicans, that we can turn back the clock and that the old alliance of science, nation, and progress is simply a matter of good citizenship and political will. We are so eager to believe them that we receive their nostalgic statements with considerable sympathy

In this evolution of the more developed countries, the distribution of wealth tends to take second place. Not that it disappears, of course, but it fades in comparison to the new necessities of *solidarity in the face of risks* that appear all the more threatening because, now globalized, they fall largely outside the competence of the nation-states and elude any real control by ordinary democratic procedures.

Finally, under the effects of universal self-criticism, the old social roles are being challenged. Destabilized, they no longer seem imprinted in nature, as exemplified by the multiple facets of the feminist movement.

This picture could, of course, be elaborated and discussed at length. It probably merits more detail and color. Its interest is considerable if we accept the notion that the "second modernity"—in spite of the objections just discussed—is merely an ineluctable extension of the "first modernity" under the species of *self-reflection*. If the traditional faces of republican science and democracy are more fragile today, it is not simply out of "irrationalism" or a lack of civic responsibility but—paradoxically—out of fidelity to the principles of the Enlightenment. This finds illustration in current environmentalist movements in countries that (unlike France) already have a long ecological tradition—Canada and the Scandinavian countries, for example. Debate over the principles involved in preventive measures and long-term development refers increasingly to scientific arguments as well as to an explicit democratic will. In attempting to distinguish between two modernities, we must learn not to confuse two quite different figures of antimodernism. The first appeared with romanticism and in reaction to the Enlightenment. Imbued with nostalgia for lost paradises, it denounced the artifices of the democratic universe; stressing the virtue of feelings and passions, it decried the desiccation of science. A large portion of the current environmental movement is probably still rooted in this view, but another segment of the same movement has emancipated itself from it, and when it challenges science and the democracy of the nation-state, it does so in the name of dedication to science and of a democratic ideal broadened to a global scale, but also with a certain introspection. In other words, the principal critiques of the modern world now draw on hypermodernism rather than on the spirit of reaction. If this analysis is correct, it has a decisive consequence: the demanding and corrosive spirit of *theōria* founded on self-reflection is not behind us but decidedly ahead of us; it is not an archaism or a survival of the old figures of resistance to progress but the most recent avatar of progress.

This explains the extraordinary rise, throughout the twentieth century, of the historical sciences. On the model of "critical theory," even of psychoanalysis, they promise us improved self-knowledge in the present by means of an increasing mastery of our past. They are rooted, more or less consciously, in the conviction that history, because it weighs on our lives even though we are unaware of it, is par excellence the location of the greatest heteronomy; and, by the same token, the democratic ideals of liberty, of thinking for oneself, and of autonomy cannot do without a detour through a knowledge of history, if only in order to liberate ourselves from history and approach the present with fewer prejudices. It is in this context that *theōria* has come to resemble a reflection on the self henceforth indispensable for any genuine emancipation. Although contemporary science is always linked to the idea of axiological neutrality, it reconnects (in a totally different mode, to be sure) with the ancient idea of the ethical vocation of *theōria*.

To a certain extent, and looking beyond the unbridgeable gap between our world and the Greek world, there is a similar continuity in the domain of *praxis*.

Praxis: *From the Natural Cosmos to the Human Cosmos*

Since the writing of the New Testament,[3] the notion of "the world" has taken on a dual, seemingly contradictory meaning. Beginning with the Gospel According to John, the Greek term *kosmos*, rather than designating only the natural universe in its harmony and order, also includes the men and women who people that universe. Retreat from the world, for example, does not refer to the (highly improbable) fact of leaving the earth on which we dwell, but rather to abstaining from human society or, as is said, from "worldly things."

Two different moral visions correspond to these two concepts of the natural world and the human world. The first is the one that dominated the ancient world: that ethics should, by and large, reside in behaviors that conform to cosmic nature. The second reached its height, after the rupture with classical antiquity, in the birth of modern law and modern morality. It is best known in Kant's notion of the "kingdom of ends." This is the conviction that humanity, if properly ruled by moral and juridical laws that are held in common (if not universally), can forge something like a "second nature" and constitute—but this time in the order of the intellect—the analogue of a "cosmos" (that is, a universe) that, although thoroughly human and even founded on human freedom and "manufactured" by human beings, nonetheless represents a harmonious and ordered whole. If we pursue the analogy, the successful moral life is thus defined formally in the same terms as it was among the Ancients, as a life in harmony with the cosmos, the only difference being that the term "cosmos" has changed meaning, now referring to a humanity capable of constructing an artificial universe. It is in this same context that we should understand Kant's categorical imperative, which invites us to live by applying moral maxims transformable into universal laws "of nature." The term "nature" has only an analogical meaning here: it designates the capacity, lent to us by this philosophy and, beyond it, by the whole of modern politics, to invent a moral universe by ourselves and for ourselves, a society pacified by the declaration of such "antinatural" laws as, for example, the law that my liberty stops where that of others begins. It is also in this sense, and recalling the ancient idea of the cosmos, that Kant opposes the "scholastic" concept of philosophy to his own "cosmic" concept. In the first view, philosophy implies little more than schooling, or apprenticeship in knowledge; and the philosopher is just one learned man among others. In the second, the philosopher is an authentic sage or even, Kant declares, a "legislator" capable of seizing the essential ends of human reason and transforming them into laws applicable to his own life. The first and most important of these, on the practical level, is respect for the general (or universal) interest and, by that token, a respect for the individuality of others.

There is more, however, and here formal ethics moves beyond its customary realm toward a soteriology. With this new humanistic (rather than naturalistic) concept of what might be called a supranatural cosmos, and with the novel definition of the good life that it implies, there gradually appeared a new representation of the successful life, beyond the moral ideal of the "kingdom of ends," hence beyond the invitation to a purely legal respect for other people. It was a demand for "the presence of others" and a "common world," as Hannah Arendt puts it, that would finally be in conformity with the principles of an "enlarged mentality" or an "enlarged way of thinking"—that is, of a certain way of understanding others. This notion, which Kant introduces almost incidentally in his *Critique of Judgment,* is crucial.[4] Only outlined in Kant, it needs to be elucidated if we want to grasp the reasons for its extraordinary subsequent success. In contrast to narrowness of mind, Kant suggests that an enlarged way of thinking, which he defines as "anticipated communication" with others, can serve not only as a means for understanding their thought but also, returning to ourselves, as if from outside, as a way to try to look at our own judgments and values as others would view them. The idea of an "enlarged mentality" was to find a posterity, not only in current theories of argumentation (for example, in Habermas or in the notion of a "veil of ignorance" as formulated by John Rawls), but far beyond academic philosophy in the essentially humanist and democratic conviction that we must be capable of setting up a distance from ourselves (the distance of the "critical spirit") in order to respect cultural differences and cultural identities unlike our own. Such a distance will, equally importantly, help us to understand ourselves and open up the possibility of regarding our own traditions objectively. This is what "self-reflection" demands. In order to become self-aware, we must in effect stand apart from ourselves, which, among other things, enables us to take into account viewpoints different from our own. Where the narrow mind remains mired in its own community of origin, to the point of believing that community to be the only one possible (or at least the only one that is good and legitimate), the enlarged or broadened mind, by seeing things from the viewpoint of others, can contemplate the world as an interested and benevolent spectator. Agreeing to decentralize its initial perspective and to tear itself away from the limited circle of egocentricity, it can penetrate customs and values foreign to its own and then, by returning to itself, can become aware of that egocentricity in a distanced, less dogmatic fashion, thus considerably enriching its own views.

In the speech that he gave on the occasion of receiving the Nobel prize in literature in December 2001, V. S. Naipaul, seemingly with no thought of the Kantian tradition, perfectly describes this experience of broadened thought and the benefits it can bring, not only to the writing of a book, but also, and more profoundly, to the conduct of a human life. Telling of his childhood on the small island of Trinidad, Naipaul evokes the limitations typical of all community life, bounded by particularisms, in terms that deserve to be repeated in full:

> We Indians, immigrants from India, . . . lived for the most part ritualised lives, and were not yet capable of self-assessment, which is where learning begins. . . . In Trinidad, where as new arrivals we were a disadvantaged community, that excluding idea was a kind of protection; it enabled us—for the time being, and only for the time being—to live in our own way and according to our own rules, to live in our own fading India. It made for an extraordinary self-centredness. We looked inwards; we lived out our days; the world outside existed in a kind of darkness; we inquired about nothing.[5]

Naipaul continues, explaining that once he had begun to write, the shadowy zones that surrounded the child—the island's natives, the New World, India, the Muslim universe, Africa, England—became favorite subjects that enabled him to set a certain distance between himself and the island of his birth and write about it. He then adds this, which is perhaps the essence of what he has to say:

> But when [writing the book] was over I felt I had done all that I could do with my island material. No matter how much I meditated on it, no further fiction would come. Accident, then, rescued me. I became a traveller. I travelled in the Caribbean region and understood much more about the colonial set-up of which I had been part. I went to India, my ancestral land, for a year; it was a journey that broke my life in two. The books that I wrote about these two journeys took me to new realms of emotion, gave me a world view I had never had, extended me technically.[6]

There is no denial here, nor any renunciation of the particularities of origin. Only the demarcation of distance, a broadening of view that enables him to grasp those particularities in another, more general, less immersed perspective and hence to transfigure them within the space of art so as to extract the truly singular moments, those moments that are both irreplaceable for him and meaningful for others. This is precisely how Naipaul's works have risen above folklore to attain the rank of "world literature."

On the deepest level, the literary ideal (but also the existential ideal) that Naipaul describes here signifies that we need to penetrate not only beyond egocentrism, but also beyond a purely formal or legal respect for differences in order to enter into a successful common life. We need others if we are to understand ourselves; we need their liberty and, if possible, their happiness, in order to fulfill our own lives. Here a consideration of morality points the way, of its own accord, to a higher problematic, one that takes into account elements susceptible of giving meaning or value to our existences *in a substantial manner,* and one that we will have to cultivate if we want to arrive, in some fashion, at "saving ourselves by our own efforts."

Soteriology, or Lay Spirituality: Singularity, Intensity, and Love

A humanist doctrine of salvation—understood here in a philosophical sense, not a religious one, as an invitation to conquer fears, to reconcile oneself with life, and to "save ourselves by ourselves"—should take into account several basic elements to undergird a "lay spirituality."

The first derives directly from the enlarged way of thinking that I have mentioned, and it resides in an invitation to "singularize" our experiences, not to say our lives. The great romantic tradition has bequeathed to us a definition of singularity that needs to be evaluated for our purposes. A first step is a very simple analysis of what characterizes all great works art: in any and all domains, a great work always reflects the *particularity* of the cultural context in which it originates. In brief, it is marked *historically and geographically* by the epoch and the "spirit of the people" from which it emerges. This is, precisely, its "folkloristic" aspect. One can see at a glance, even without special expertise, that a painting by Vermeer does not belong to the Asiatic or the Islamic world, and nor does it belong in the space of contemporary art; conversely, it is easy to see that it does have something to do with Northern Europe in the seventeenth century. Similarly, listening to just a few bars of music will tell us whether it comes from the East or the West, whether it is relatively old or recent, whether it is was created for a religious ceremony or for dancing, and so forth. But what is unique to great art (unlike folklore) is that it rises to the level of the universal, or, if that word seems too grand, *that it potentially addresses all of humanity.* It is what Goethe called "world literature" (*Weltliteratur*). The notion of "world" is in no way connected with uniformity here: worldwide access to a work of art is obtained not by scoffing at particularities of origin but, quite to the contrary, by respecting them, given that it is partly from those particularities that the work draws its nourishment. What happens is that the particularities, instead of remaining intact or being treated as sacred, which would restrict their meaning to their community of origin, are incorporated into a project that translates a great experience potentially common to humanity at large, a project that can speak to all human beings in all places and at all times.

If, as classic logic since Aristotle has declared, the terms "singularity" or "individuality" are defined as a particular quality that, while remaining particular, can nonetheless be reconciled, so to speak, with the universal, then we can ascertain the ways in which a great work of art offers us the most perfect model of that quality. It is because they are "singular" authors or composers, in this narrowly defined sense (that is, rooted in their culture of origin and their epoch, yet destined to speak to all men of all times by virtue of the universality of their message), that we still read Plato or Homer, Molière or Shakespeare, and still listen to the works of Bach or Rameau. The same is true of all great works and all great monuments. One can be French and Roman Catholic and still be profoundly moved by the temple of Angkor Wat, the great mosque of Kairouan, a book by Gabriel García Márquez, or a fine example of Chinese calligraphy. This conception of great works as "singularities"—as transfigurations of particularities that are local in origin but bear a relationship to the universality of the world— can also be applied to major scientific discoveries (one example would be algebra, which, as its name indicates, is Arabic in origin but is universal today), or to cultures taken as a global entity (as one might speak of "Greek art," "French classicism," or "German romanticism"). It is also in this sense that one might defend a nondogmatic, nontribal, nonnationalistic conception of cultural identities that, although (or, rather, because) they are particular, enrich the world to which they are addressed and of which they truly become a part as soon as they speak the language of the universal. From the viewpoint of the enlarged mentality, "shared culture" or "the sharing out of cultures" enriches all of its components, not in the flat, demagogic sense of a mere respect for "folklore" or "local artisanship," but in the more profound sense of the construction of a world that is at once diverse and held in common. This means that the notion of singularity can and must be directly attached to the ideal of that enlarged thought: when I broaden the scope of my experiences, I become singular, both because I surpass the particularity of my individual condition and because I accede, if not to universality, at least to an awareness that continually becomes more inclusive of, and richer in, the potentialities that are those of all humanity.

This also permits us to look at the enigmatic plurality of philosophical responses to the question of the good life in a new way, beyond skepticism and beyond dogmatism. That plurality, as we know, has usually been greeted with skepticism, which seemed justified by the mere existence of multiple responses. The argument goes roughly like this: Since the dawn of time, various philosophies have vied with one another without ever achieving unity. Being irreducible, that very plurality stands as proof of the inability of the philosophical tradition to attain a truth that, by definition, should be unified. Given that there are several visions of the world and that they cannot be brought into agreement, we have to admit that none of them has a more serious claim to hold the real answer than any of the others; hence all philosophy is futile. Dogmatism of course defines itself as an inverse language: admittedly, there are several visions of the world, but mine is obviously superior and truer than the others. The history of philosophy could easily show us examples of sweeping attempts at synthesis, some falling to the side of skepticism (eclecticism furnishes a model here), others to the side of dogmatism (the Hegelian claim to reconcile all positions within one system offers the most grandiose version here). The contemporary democratic spirit, weary of these old debates, imbued with relativism, and made to feel guilty by the memory of its own imperialism, seems willing to settle for compromise positions that all too often take refuge (in the name of a praiseworthy interest in "respecting differences") in vague concepts such as "tolerance," "dialogue," or "concern for others," which are often hard to define.

The notion of an enlarged mentality or a broadened thought suggests another path that, in the context of globalization and the debates regarding cultural identities that globalization elicits might turn out to be extraordinarily fertile. This broader view—without demagoguery and without renouncing its own convictions—attempts to identify wherever possible what might be right about a grand vision of the world that is not its own, and by what means that vision could be understood or even embraced. To proceed in this manner is to hold that all great philosophy summarizes in the form of thought a fundamental experience of humankind, just as all great art and literature translates human attitudes into their most sensible forms. Respect for others does not exclude personal choice; quite to the contrary, it is its first condition. This whole book has attempted to offer the reader the possibility of appropriating the great responses to the question of the good life, presenting those responses as *singularities* so as to enable the reader to make personal choices in an enlightened fashion. Hence the friendly debate that the present volume has maintained with both materialism and religions, with both ancient wisdom traditions and contemporary deconstructions. But the book has also taken as its point of departure the conviction that in order to understand the other, in order to evaluate what separates us from

that other but also what permits us to think about ourselves, we need not resort to self-renunciation. Acceptance of diversity is not the same as rever-
ence for diversity, just as respect for others is not relativism.

This is another reason—and a second trait of a contemporary spirituality—why we must adopt the Nietzschean criterion of intensity. If there is
any truth in what Nietzsche calls the "grand style," it is this: the most enlarged life is also the most singular, the richest, and the most intense. Nietzsche sees it as the life that brings together in harmony the greatest possible
diversity of experiences that enrich our view of humanity. Authentic happiness—or, more modestly, life's greatest joys—cannot be found solely in
the absence of trouble or passion. If that were the case, we would be easily
contented, and the oyster (provided it encounters no squeeze of lemon or
dash of vinegar) would provide the model of a good life. To paraphrase a
well-known passage in Kant's *Foundations of the Metaphysics of Morals*, if
providence had wanted us to be content with that sort of happiness, it
would have given us neither liberty nor intelligence, both of which spoil
most attempts on the part of human beings to be satisfied with seeking
only the soul's repose. If we must discover the human world, enrich our experience, broaden our views—thus constantly encounter a diversity of cultures and beings—it is because we possess (unlike the oyster) the curious
faculty of detachment from the particularities of origin. It is a talent that,
in spite of the anxiety it arouses, keeps encouraging us to perfect ourselves,
to enrich our lives—and to travel, to borrow Naipaul's image—rather than
to remain clinging to the rock we grew up on. The genius of Nietzsche's
notion of the grand style is that it presents us with the idea of repose and
harmonious serenity, not as a point of departure or an original given, but
rather as a point of arrival, a conquest that supposes both knowledge of
others (diversity) and mastery of the self (harmony).

To continue our pursuit of the thread of singularity to which the idea of
the enlarged mentality has led us, the harmonious intensity to which Nietzsche invites us must be supplemented by the exigency of love. Love alone
gives ultimate value and meaning to the entire process of "enlargement"
that can and must guide human experience. One might well ask what relation this has to the notion of singularity that has just been discussed. A
fragment from Pascal's *Pensées* will help, where Pascal wonders about the
precise nature of the objects of our affections and also about the identity of
the self:

> What is the Ego? Suppose a man puts himself at a window to see
> those who pass by. If I pass by, can I say that he placed himself there

to see me? No: for he does not think of me in particular. But does he who loves someone on account of beauty really love that person? No: for the small-pox, which will kill beauty without killing the person, will cause him to love her no more. And if one loves me for my judgment, memory, he does not love *me*, for I can lose these qualities without losing myself. Where, then, is this Ego, if it be neither in the body nor in the soul? And how love the body or the soul, except for these qualities which do not constitute *me*, since they are perishable? For it is impossible and would be unjust to love the soul of a person in the abstract, and whatever qualities might be therein. We never, then, love a person, but only qualities. Let us, then, jeer no more at those who are honoured on account of rank and office; for we love a person only on account of borrowed qualities.[7]

The conclusion that is usually drawn from this text is that the "I," the "Ego," which is already known to be hateful, is not a plausible object of love. It seems, at least initially, that I am mainly attached to particularities, to the intimate qualities of the person that I claim to love: his or her beauty, intelligence, and the like. Since those attributes are eminently perishable, however, I must expect to stop loving that person someday. As Pascal notes in another fragment, even the most banal experience suffices to confirm such cessation: "He no longer loves the person whom he loved ten years ago. I quite believe it. She is no longer the same, nor is he. He was young, and she also; she is quite different. He would perhaps love her yet, if she were what she was then."[8] Far from having loved in the other what he took to be her most essential "particularity," he had become attached to abstract qualities that can be found in any other person: beauty, intelligence, courage, or forcefulness are not inherent to one person or another; they are in no way intimately or particularly connected to the "substance" of a being but are instead, in a manner of speaking, interchangeable. Probably the lover in Pascal's fragment—if he really thinks in these terms—will divorce the former object of his affections and seek out a younger and more beautiful woman who resembles the one he married ten years earlier. Here Pascal discovers, well before Hegel, that the particular and the abstract universal, far from opposing one another, "pass one into the other" and are in reality one. I may think that I seize the very heart, the most intimate intimacy, of a person by loving that person for his or her qualities, but in reality the situation is quite different: I have seized only attributes that are as anonymous as a professional title or a military decoration, and nothing more. In other words, the particular was not the *singular*. Only singularity, which surpasses both the particular and the universal, can be the object of love. If one keeps to particular/general qualities alone, one never loves anyone, and in this light Pascal is correct when he says that we must not deride vain people who prize honors. The thing that makes someone likable, that gives us the feeling of being able to choose that person among all others, and to continue to love him or her even if disfigured by illness, is of course the very thing that makes that person irreplaceable as he or she is and not otherwise. What we love in someone (or what someone loves in us, as the case may be), and what we must consequently seek to develop for others as in ourselves, is not mere particularity or abstract qualities (the universal), but the singularity that distinguishes that person and makes him or her unlike anyone else. One might say affectionately to the person one loves, "Thank you for existing," but also, with Montaigne, "because it was he; because it was me," rather than "because he was handsome, strong, intelligent, courageous," and so forth.

Still following the thread of the enlarged mentality and of singularity as we have defined it, we can also return to the Greek ideal of the "eternal instant," the present that by its very singularity—because we hold it to be irreplaceable, and we evaluate its consistency instead of eliminating it in the name of what preceded or followed it—frees itself from both nostalgia and hope, from both past and future. It is that ideal, as we have seen, that constitutes the true object of love in Spinoza's view of love or in Nietzsche's *amor fati*. In the terms of nonmetaphysical humanism (or of the enlarged mentality), we can reformulate that same idea in new terms: if the process of forcible detachment from the particular and an opening to the universal form a singular experience, if this dual process simultaneously singularizes our own lives and gives us access to the singularity of the life of others, it also offers us both the means for enlarging our thought and the possibility of putting that thought into contact with unique moments—moments of grace—that are irreplaceable because they themselves are singular. It is at this point that lay spirituality rejoins soteriology, the doctrine of salvation that ideally permits us to conquer our fears, beginning, naturally, with the fear of death. Only contact with what escapes time or at least seems to abolish it, contact with the irreplaceable, succeeds in dealing with death— if not eliminating it, at least deemphasizing it.

What is the use of growing old? It serves precisely to achieve that aim, and nothing else. To enlarge one's view: to love the singular and once in a while to experience the abolition of time that the presence of the singular permits us. Victor Hugo understood this well, and he is one of the few who has hazarded a response to that ultimate question in one of his finest poems:

Booz était bon maître et fidèle parent;
Il était généreux quoiqu'il fût économe;
Les femmes regardaient Booz plus qu'un jeune homme,
Car le jeune homme est beau, mais le vieillard est grand.

Le vieillard, qui revient vers la source première,
Entre aux jours éternels et sort des jours changeants;
Et l'on voit de la flamme aux yeux des jeunes gens,
Mais dans l'oeil du vieillard on voit de la lumière.

Boaz was a kind lord and loyal relative,
Generous to everyone, though prudent every time.
Women looked at Boaz more than all the young men.
For the young man is handsome, but the old is sublime.

Old men, returning to the source of life, forego
The changing days and enter changelessness again.
And though you see a fire in the eyes of young men,
In the eyes of an old man you can see a glow.[9]

What, then, is the good life? Perhaps it is simply a life that reveals to one's fellows something of the grandeur and the light that Victor Hugo evokes. A fragile happiness? Probably. It may seem slight in comparison with the promises of religion, but viewed through the lens of humanism, I believe, it will look like happiness indeed.

P R O L O G U E

1. Sigmund Freud, "Creative Writers and Day-Dreaming," in *The Standard Edition of the Complete Psychological Works of Sigmund Freud,* translated under the general editorship of James Strachey in collaboration with Anna Freud, assisted by Alix Strachey and Alan Tyson (London: Hogarth Press and the Institute of Psycho-Analysis, 1959), vol. 9, pp. 143–53, quotation p. 148. In French translation by Marie Bonaparte and Mme E. Marty as "La création littéraire et le rêve éveillé," in *Essais de psychanalse appliqué,* Coll. Idées (Paris: Gallimard, 1933, 1971), 75.

2. See Jean de La Fontaine, "La laitière et le pot au lait," *Fables* (Paris: Garnier, 1960), X, Livre VII, pp. 165–66.

3. This expression is borrowed from Alain Ehrenberg, *Le culte de la performance* (Paris: Calmann-Lévy, 1991).

4. I am quoting Rousseau's formula (which I do not think is an exact quotation) from Pierre Manent, who comments on it in his *Cours familier de philosophie politique* (Paris: Fayard, 2001).

5. La Fontaine, "Le Renard et les raisins," *Fables,* XI, Livre III, p. 80.

6. *France Nouvelle,* 14 March 1953, p. 1. The front page of *France Nouvelle* for this date is reproduced in Michel-Antoine Burnier, *Histoire illustrée du socialisme (1830–1981),* rev. ed. (Paris: Janninck, 1981), 81.

7. We need to assume the following: it is a fact that Europe, at one time a continent of Christian nations, has become the continent of secularity par excellence and, in a manner of speaking, the laboratory of a world that seeks its references beyond religion. This is also why the question of the good life is posed in new terms in Europe. This should in no way prevent us—quite the contrary—from taking into account extra-European traditions. These will be mentioned frequently in the present volume.

8. The term "will to power" has a special sense in Nietzsche that cannot be reduced to a simple desire to hold power, as we shall see below.

9. René Descartes, *Discourse on the Method and Meditations on First Philosophy,* ed. David Weissman (New Haven and London: Yale University Press, 1996), pt.5, p. 38.

10. This is why, in a manner that may at first sight seems somewhat enigmatic, Heidegger insists that "profound boredom . . . reveals beings as a whole." Martin Heidegger, "What is Metaphysics?" in *Basic Writings from Being and Time (1927) to the Task of Thinking (1964),* rev. ed., ed. with introds. by David Farrell Krell (San Francisco: HarperSanFrancisco, 1977, 1993), 89–110, quotation p. 98; in French translation by Henry Corbin as Qu'est-ce que la métaphysique?" in Heigegger, *Questions: I, Qu'est-ce que la métaphysique . . .* (Paris: Gallimard, 1968), 56. On the metaphysical and religious dimension of ennui as an experience of

nothingness, see also Pascal, *Pensées,* in the Brunschvicg edition, frag. 131: "*Weariness. —* Nothing is so insufferable to man as to be completely at rest, without passions, without business, without diversion, without study. He then feels his nothingness, his forlornness, his insufficiency, his dependence, his weakness, his emptiness. There will immediately arise from the depth of his heart weariness, gloom, sadness, fretfulness, vexation, despair"; quoted from Blaise Pascal, *Pensées; The Provincial Letters,* trans. W. F. Trotter (New York: Random House, 1941), 47.

11. On this important but neglected theme, see Jean-Pierre Dupuy, *Le sacrifice et l'envie: Le libéralisme aux prises avec la justice sociale* (Paris: Calmann-Lévy, 1992). See also the profound thoughts on envy in Pascal Bruckner, *L'euphorie perpétuelle: Essai sur le devoir de bonheur* (Paris: Grasset, 2000).

PART I

The translation of the second epigraph on the part title page to part 1 is drawn from *Correspondence / Immanuel Kant,* trans. and ed. Arnulf Zweig (Cambridge and New York: Cambridge University Press, 1992), 197.

CHAPTER I

1. Simon Leys, *L'ange et le cachalot,* quoted from *The Angel and the Octopus: Collected Essays, 1983–1998* (Sydney: Duffy & Snellgrove, 1999), 36–37.

2. I shall return at greater length to this difficult question in part 5 of the present work.

3. André Comte-Sponville and Luc Ferry, *La sagesse des Modernes: Dix questions pour notre temps* (Paris: Robert Laffont, 1998), 15.

4. Except in special cases, I make no distinction between ethics and morality.

5. See *Restoring Faith in Reason, with a New Translation of the Encyclical Letter "Faith and Reason" of Pope John Paul II,* ed. Laurence Paul Hemming and Susan Frank Parsons (London: SCM Press, 2002).

CHAPTER 2

1. The Sophists and the Epicureans are probably exceptions to this rule, although, among the latter, ethics was also rooted in a certain conception of nature. We shall return to these distinctions in the chapters devoted to the "cosmologico-ethical."

2. For an excellent analysis of these "wisdom exercises" and "spiritual exercises," see Pierre Hadot, *Qu'est-ce que la philosophie antique?* (Paris: Gallimard, 1995); in English translation by Michael Chase as *What is Ancient Philosophy?* (Cambridge, MA: Belknap Press of Harvard University Press, 2002). I shall return to the significance of these exercises.

3. Epictetus, *Discourses,* III, xxvi, quoted from *The Discourses as Reported by Arrian, The Manual, and Fragments,* trans. W. A. Oldfather, Loeb Classical Library (Cambridge, MA: Harvard University Press, 1989), vol. 2, pp. 39–41; in French in *Les Stoïciens, Textes,* ed. Pierre Maxime Schuhl and Emile Bréhier, Bibliothèque de la Pléiade (Paris: Gallimard, 1962), 1039, 1039.

4. Friedrich Nietzsche, *La volonté de puissance,* trans. Geneviève Bianquis, text estab-

lished by Friedrich Würzbach, Coll. Tel (Paris: Gallimard, 1995), vol. 2, IV. This is the edition to which I usually refer in these notes, with the exception of certain passages that I have translated into French from the Schlechta edition (see chap. 5, n. 32).

CHAPTER 3

1. On this point, see Luc Ferry and Alain Renaut, eds., *Pourquoi nous ne sommes pas nietzschéens* (Paris: Grasset, 1991); in English translation by Robert de Loaiza as *Why We Are Not Nietzscheans*, (Chicago: University of Chicago Press, 1997).

2. As we shall see, the term "materialism" is legitimate here. It designates a thought whose main axis is a radical refusal of all figures of transcendence. Thus it applies to Nietzsche more than to any other philosopher. This is one reason why certain Marxist philosophers have found his philosophy so attractive. On this point, see the works of Yvon Quiniou.

3. Friedrich Nietzsche, *Thus Spoke Zarathustra*, in *The Portable Nietzsche*, comp., trans., and ed. Walter Kaufmann (New York: Viking Penguin, 1982), "Zarathustra's Prologue," no. 3, p. 125; in French translation by Geneviève Bianquis as *Ainsi parlait Zarathoustra*, in Nietzsche, *OEuvres* (Paris: Flammarion, 2000).

4. Friedrich Nietzsche, *The Will to Power*, trans. Walter Kaufmann and R. J. Hollingdale, ed. Walter Kaufmann (New York: Random House, 1967), III, no. 12, pp. 12–13; in French translation by Geneviève Bianquis as *La volonté de puissance*, text established by Friedrich Würzbach, Coll. Tel (Paris: Gallimard, 1995), vol. 2, III, no. 111.

5. Nietzsche, *Will to Power*, no. 1067, pp. 549–50; *Volonté de puissance*, trans. Bianquis, vol. 1, II, no. 61.

6. "The sciences, pursued without any restraint and in a spirit of the blindest *laissez faire*, are shattering and dissolving all firmly held belief." Friedrich Nietzsche, *Untimely Meditations*, trans. R. J. Hollingdale, ed. Daniel Breazeale (Cambridge: Cambridge University Press, 1997), 148; in French translation as *Considérations inactuelles*, III, no. 4.

7. Friedrich Nietzsche, *Joyful Wisdom*, trans. Thomas Common, introd. Kurt F. Reinhardt (New York: Frederick Ungar, 1960), no. 374, p. 34.

8. Nietzsche, *Will to Power*, I, no. 12, pp. 13–14; *Volonté de puissance*, trans. Bianquis, vol. 2, III, no. 3.

9. On the origin of the theme of the death of God, see Rémi Brague, *La sagesse du monde: Histoire de l'expérience humaine de l'univers* (Paris: Fayard, 1999), 219ff., in English translation by Teresa Lavender Fagan as *The Wisdom of the World: The Human Experience of the Universe in Western Thought* (Chicago: University of Chicago Press, 2003), 191–93.

10. Nietzsche, *Joyful Wisdom*, no. 343, p. 275.

11. Gilles Deleuze, *Nietzsche*, "Philosophes" no. 17 (Paris: Presses Universitaires de France, 1999), 18.

12. Ibid., 15.

13. Friedrich Nietzsche, *Ecce homo*, Preface to Part III, quoted from *On the Genealogy of Morals; Ecce Homo*, trans. Walter Kaufmann and R. H. Hollingdale, ed. Walter Kaufmann (New York: Vintage Books, 1989), 218, 284.

14. Friedrich Nietzsche, *The Antichrist*, in *The Portable Nietzsche*, no. 43, p. 619.

15. Friedrich Nietzsche, *Beyond Good and Evil: Prelude to a Philosophy of the Future*, trans. and ed. Walter Kaufmann (New York: Vintage Books, 1989), no. 203, p. 117.

16. Deleuze, *Nietzsche*, 26.

17. See Michel Foucault, "En intervju med Michel Foucault," interviewer, I. Lindung, in

Bonniers Litteräre Magasin (Stockholm), 37, no. 3 (March 1968), 203–11; in French translation in Michel Foucault, *Dits et écrits: 1954–1988* (Paris: Gallimard, 1994), vol. 2, no. 54, pp. 651ff.

18. Nietzsche, *Will to Power*, II, no. 303, p. 169, a fragment dated Spring 1888; *Werke in drei Bänden*, ed. Karl Schlecta, 4 vols. (Munich: Carl Hanser, 1954–65), vol. 3, IV, 428.

19. Nietzsche, *Will to Power*, II, no. 260, p. 150; *Volonté de puissance*, trans. Bianquis, vol. 2, III, no. 121.

20. *Volonté de puissance*, trans. Bianquis, vol. 2, III, no. 403.

21. Nietzsche, *Will to Power*, III, no. 616, p. 330; *Volonté de puissance*, trans. Bianquis, vol. 1, II, no. 134.

22. *Will to Power*, I, no. 55, p. 37; *Volonté de puissance*, trans. Bianquis, II, Introd., no. 8.

23. I am quite aware that it is inappropriate to apply the term "system," at least in its modern sense, to the works of Nietzsche. I use the word here in its older, etymological meaning of that which is posited and holds together coherently and firmly.

CHAPTER 4

1. Friedrich Nietzsche, *Ecce homo*, Preface, in *On the Genealogy of Morals; Ecce Homo*, trans. Walter Kaufmann and R. H. Hollingdale, ed. Walter Kaufmann (New York: Vintage Books, 1989), 217–18.

2. See Friedrich Nietzsche, *La volonté de puissance*, trans. Geneviève Bianquis, text established by Friedrich Würzbach, Coll. Tel (Paris: Gallimard, 1995), vol. 1, II, no. 41: "Life . . . is for us the best-known form of being." Ibid., no. 8; "Being—we have no idea of it apart from the idea of living." Nietzsche, *The Will to Power*, trans. Walter Kaufmann and R. J. Hollingdale, ed. Walter Kaufmann (New York: Random House, 1967), III, no. 582, p. 312. That life should be thought of as will to power is one of Nietzsche's most consistent themes: he says, for example, "Life itself is the will to power." *Will to Power*, I, no. 55, p. 37; *Volonté de puissance*, II, 246. If one admits the equivalence he posits (Being = Life = will to power), then the will to power appears as "the innermost essence of being." *Will to Power*, III, no. 693, p. 369: *Volonté de puissance*, II, no. 54. On this connection, see Luc Ferry and Alain Renaut, *68/86: Itinéraires de l'individu* (Paris: Gallimard, 1986), 83ff. I shall return to the exact meaning of the concept of the will to power.

3. Friedrich Nietzsche, *Twilight of the Idols*, "'Reason' in Philosophy," section 1, in *The Portable Nietzsche*, comp., trans., and ed. Walter Kaufmann (New York: Viking Penguin, 1982), p. 480.

4. Ibid., "The Problem of Socrates," sections 3, 5, in *The Portable Nietzsche*, 474–76.

5. Ibid., sections 7, 4, in *The Portable Nietzsche*, 476, 475.

6. Ibid., section 2, in *The Portable Nietzsche*, 474.

7. Friedrich Nietzsche, *Joyful Wisdom*, trans. Thomas Common, introd. Kurt F. Reinhardt (New York: Frederick Ungar, 1960), no. 357, p. 306.

8. An aphorism in *The Will to Power* states: "The subject: this is the term for our belief in a unity underlying all the different impulses of the highest feeling of reality; we understand this belief as the *effect* of one cause": Nietzsche, *Will to Power*, III, no. 485, pp. 268–69; *Werke in drei Bänden*, ed. Karl Schlechta, 3 vols. (Munich: Carl Hanser, 1954–56), III, 627. It is by that hypostasis of identity that we reach the erroneous conclusion that the "I" is an ultimate substratum of our representations. The Cartesian *cogito* turns out to be nothing but an effect of what Nietzsche considers a play on words and "a formulation of our grammatical custom." *Will to Power*, III, no. 484, p. 268; ed. Schlechta, III, 577. In reality, "'the subject' is the fiction

that many similar states in us are the effect of one substratum, but it is we who first created the 'similarity' of these states." *Will to Power*, III, no. 485, p. 269; ed. Schlechta, III, 627.

9. Nietzsche, *Will to Power*, III, no. 556, p. 302; ed. Schlechta, 487.

10. Friedrich Nietzsche, *Beyond Good and Evil: Prelude to a Philosophy of the Future*, trans., with commentary, by Walter Kaufmann (New York: Vintage Books, 1989), no. 21, p. 28.

11. Ibid., no. 17, p. 24.

12. As is known, this formula elicited joy and admiration in Claude Barrès, who hailed it as the long-awaited sign of a deconstruction of the individualist ideology emerging out of the French Revolution and the Enlightenment and the proof that finally a thinker worthy of the name could value the supremacy of traditional legacies, beginning with that of the nation, over the modern claim to "free will." The same line of thought appears later in the work of Jacques Lacan.

13. Nietzsche, *Will to Power*, III, no. 556, pp. 301–2; *Werke*, ed. Schlechta, III, 487.

14. Nietzsche, *Twilight of the Idols*, "The Problem of Socrates," 2, p. 474.

15. Nietzsche, *Will to Power*, II, no. 259, p. 149; III, no. 473, p. 263; *Werke*, ed. Schlechta, III, no. 441, 503.

16. This is the greatest difference between Nietzsche's perspectivism and that of Leibniz. In many ways, Hegel simply carried it to its highest point.

17. Nietzsche, *Will to Power*, no. 590, p. 323; ed. Schlechta, III, 503.

18. Which a psychoanalyst might also be. There are, in fact, many Nietzschean interpretations of psychoanalysis, beginning, of course, with that of Lacan.

19. We shall see in the chapter 5 how the idea of truth was reintroduced into Nietzsche's thought, paradoxically by the intermediary of art rather than science.

20. Nietzsche, *Twilight of the Idols*, in *The Portable Nietzsche*, "Morality as Anti-Nature," 5, p. 490.

21. Nietzsche, *Joyful Wisdom*, no. 374, pp. 340–41.

22. Michel Foucault, "Nietzsche, la généalogie, l'histoire," quoted from "Nietzsche, Genealogy, History," in *Foucault, Language, Counter-Memory, Practice: Selected Essays and Interviews*, ed. and introd. Donald F. Bouchard, trans. Donald F. Bouchard and Sherry Simon (Ithaca: Cornell University Press, 1977), 139–64, esp. p. 144.

23. Nietzsche, *Beyond Good and Evil*, no. 289, p. 229.

CHAPTER 5

1. Admittedly, Nietzsche himself fostered this notion: "And occasionally even foolishness is the mask for an unblessed all-too-certain knowledge." Friedrich Nietzsche, *Beyond Good and Evil: Prelude to a Philosophy of the Future*, trans. and ed. Walter Kaufmann (New York: Vintage Books, 1989), no. 270, p. 221.

2. One can be a great thinker without being a philosopher. One cannot be a philosopher without confronting, at one time or another, the questions raised in these three domains.

3. Friedrich Nietzsche, *Ecce Homo*, in *On the Genealogy of Morals; Ecce Homo*, trans.. Walter Kaufmann and R. H. Hollingdale, ed. Walter Kaufmann (New York: Vintage Books, 1989), "Nietzsche's Preface," no. 3, pp. 218–19.

4. Friedrich Nietzsche, *The Will to Power*, trans. Walter Kaufmann and R. J. Hollingdale, ed. Walter Kaufmann (New York: Random House, 1967), III, no. 853, p. 453; III, no. 693, p. 369.

5. See Friedrich Nietzsche, *The Birth of Tragedy*, trans. and ed. Douglas Smith (Oxford: Oxford University Press, 2000).

6. Friedrich Nietzsche, *Twilight of the Idols*, in *The Portable Nietzsche*, comp., trans., and ed. Walter Kaufmann (New York: Viking Penguin, 1982), "How the 'True World' Finally Became a Fable," no. 5, pp. 485–86.

7. Ibid., 486.

8. Gilles Deleuze, *Nietzsche*, "Philosophes" no. 17 (Paris: Presses Universitaires de France, 1999), I, 425, 482.

9. Gilles Deleuze, *Nietzsche et la philosophie* (Paris: Presses Universitaires de France, 1983), 117; quoted from *Nietzsche and Philosophy*, trans. Hugh Tomlinson (New York: Columbia University Press, 1983), 102.

10. Deleuze, *Nietzche and Philosophy*, 31.; *Nietzsche et la philosophie*, 35.

11. Friedrich Nietzsche, "Morality as Anti-Nature," *Twilight of the Idols*, in *The Portable Nietzsche*, nos. 5 and 6, p. 491.

12. Friedrich Nietzsche, *The Will to Power*, II, no. 246, p. 142; in French translation by Henri Albert as *La volonté de puissance*, Livre de Poche (Paris: Librairie générale française, 1991), 166.

13. Nietzsche, *Twilight of the Idols*, "Skirmishes of an Untimely Man," no. 36, in *The Portable Nietzsche*, p. 536.

14. On this aspect of Nietzsche's personality, see Daniel Halévy, *Nietzsche*, Coll. Pluriel (Paris: Livre de Poche, 1986), 489ff.

15. André Comte-Sponville, in *Pourquoi nous ne sommes pas nietzschéens*, ed. Luc Ferry and Alain Renaut (Paris: Grasset, 1991), 1; quoted from *Why We Are Not Nietzscheans*, ed. Luc Ferry and Alain Renaut, trans. Robert de Loaiza (Chicago: University of Chicago Press, 1997), 31.

16. Nietzsche, "Skirmishes of an Untimely Man," no. 34, in *The Portable Nietzsche*, p. 534.

17. Nietzsche, *Will to Power*, III, no. 800, p. 421, no. 815, p. 432.

18. Friedrich Nietzsche, *Human, All Too Human: A Book for Free Spirits*, trans. R. J. Hollingdale, introd. Erich Heller (Cambridge: Cambridge University Press, 1986), no. 276, p. 130.

19. Nietzsche, *Will to Power*, III, no. 842, pp. 443–44, in French translation by Geneviève Bianquis as *La volonté de puissance*, text established by Friedrich Würzbach, Coll. Tel (Paris: Gallimard, 1995), II, p. 338.

20. Friedrich Nietzsche, "Morality as Anti-Nature," no. 1, in *The Portable Nietzsche*, p. 486.

21. Ibid., no. 3, p. 488.

22. In *Will to Power*, II, no. 361, p. 197 (*Volonté de puissance*, trans. Albert, no. 409), Nietzsche states: "I have declared war on the anemic Christian ideal (together with what is closely related to it), not with the aim of destroying it but only of putting an end to its tyranny.... The continuance of the Christian ideal is one of the most desirable things there are—even for the sake of the ideals that want to stand beside it and perhaps above it—they must have opponents, strong opponents, if they are to become *strong*.—Thus we immoralists require the power of morality: our drive of self-preservation wants our *opponents* to retain their strength—it only wants to become *master over them*."

23. Nietzsche, *Will to Power*, III, no. 800, p. 420; *Volonté de puissance*, trans. Albert, II, 152.

24. My analysis here owes much to Jacques Rivelaygue, my late teacher.

25. Nietzsche, *Will to Power*, III, no. 847, p. 446; no. 848, p. 446, no. 800, p. 420; *Volonté de puissance*, trans. Albert, II, 139, 168, 152.

26. Nietzsche, *Will to Power*, III, 850, p. 448; no. 849, p. 447 (translation modified); *Volonté de puissance*, trans. Albert, II, 172, 170.

27. Nietzsche, *La volonté de puissance*, trans. Bianquis, II, 337.

28. Nietzche, *Will to Power,* I, no. 55, p. 37; *Volonté de puissance,* trans. Bianquis, Introd., no. 8.

29. Friedrich Nietzsche, *The Antichrist*, nos.7 and 18, in *The Portable Nietzsche*, pp. 573–74, 585.

30. See Nietzsche's note to Franz Overbeck of 30 July 1881: "I am utterly amazed, utterly enchanted. I have a *precursor,* and what a precursor! I hardly knew Spinoza. . . . My lonesomeness . . . is now at least a twosomeness. Strange"; *The Portable Nietzsche,* p. 92. On the meaning of Nietzsche's quest for beatitude, see Henri Birault, "De la béatitude chez Nietzsche," in *Nietzsche,* Actes du Colloque de Royaumont (Paris: Minuit, 1967).

31. On these notions, see Birault, "De la béatitude chez Nietzsche."

32. Friedrich Nietzsche, *Werke in drei Bänden,* ed. Karl Schlechta (Munich: Carl Hanser, 1954–56), II, 1128; III, 560; for the second quotation, Nietzsche, *Will to Power,* II, no. 462, p. 255.

33. Nietzsche, *Will to Power,* IV, no. 1041, p. 536; *Werke,* ed. Schlechta, III, 834.

34. Nietzsche, *Volonté de puissance,* trans. Blanquis, IV, 2442–44. In the same sense, see also *Joyful Wisdom,* trans. Thomas Common, introd. Kurt F. Reinhardt (New York: Frederick Ungar, 1960), IV, no. 341, pp. 270–71; *Le gai savoir,* IV, no. 341, and the famous passages in *Thus Spoke Zarathustra* in which Nietzsche comments on his own formula that "all joy [*Lust*] wants eternity."

35. Friedrich Nietzsche, *Thus Spoke Zarathustra,* pt. III, "The Seven Seals," in *The Portable Nietzsche,* 343.

36. This thought is well expressed in Pierre Hadot, *La citadelle intérieure: Introduction aux "Pensées" de Marc Aurèle* (Paris: Fayard, 1992), 161ff.; in English translation by Michael Chase as *The Inner Citadel: The Meditations of Marcus Aurelius* (Cambridge, MA: Harvard University Press, 1998), 144–45.

37. Nietzsche, *Ecce Homo,* "Why I Am So Clever," no. 10, p. 258 (translation modified).

38. Nietzsche, *Will to Power,* IV, no. 1041, p. 536; *Volonté de puissance,* trans. Bianquis, II, Introd., no. 14.

39. Nietzsche, *Volonté de puissance,* trans. Bianquis, III, no. 382.

40. Nietzsche, *Will to Power,* III, no. 765, pp. 402–3; *Volonté de puissance,* trans. Bianquis, no. 458.

CHAPTER 6

1. Even poetry, although it uses ordinary language, treats words not as concepts but as materials: for poetry, words are not simply means: in some fashion they are ends in themselves.

2. I have analyzed this history of the secularization of art on another occasion: see Luc Ferry, *Le sens du beau: Aux origines de la culture contemporaine* (Paris: Cercle d'Art, 1998).

3. Tzvetan Todorov, *Eloge du quotidien: Essai sur la peinture hollandaise du XVIIe siècle* (Paris: Adam Biro, 1998), 10.

4. Ibid., 17, 180.

5. Georg Wilhelm Friedrich Hegel, *Aesthetics: Lectures on Fine Art,* trans. T. M. Knox, 2 vols. (Oxford and New York: Clarendon Press, 1975), 2: 885, 887 (translation modified); in French translation as *Cours d'esthéthique* (Paris: Aubier, 1995–97), vol. 3, pp. 117, 119.

6. Todorov, *Eloge du quotidien,* 181.

7. Pascal Bruckner, *L'euphorie perpétuelle: Essai sur le devoir de bonheur* (Paris: Grasset, 2000), 103.

8. Ibid., 97.

9. What follows summarizes the main thesis developed in Ferry, *Le sens du beau.*

10. Pierre Clastres, *La Société contre l'Etat* (Paris: Minuit, 1974), available in English translation by Robert Hurley in collaboration with Abe Stein as *Society Against the State: Essays in Political Anthropology* (New York: Zone Books, 1987).

11. See Gilles Lipovetsky, *L'empire de l'éphémère* (Paris: Gallimard, 1991), available in English translation by Catherine Porter as *The Empire of Fashion: Dressing Modern Democracy,* foreword by Richard Sennett (Princeton: Princeton University Press, 1994).

12. Henri Murger, *Scènes de la vie de Bohème* (Paris: Gallimard, 1998), available in English translation as *The Bohemians of the Latin Quarter (Scènes de la vie de Bohème)* (Paris, London, and New York: Société des Beaux-Arts, 19–).

13. Murger, "Original Preface," *The Bohemians,* xxxvi.

14. Although it is impossible to date the emergence of a concept with absolute precision, see Donald D. Egbert, "The Idea of 'Avant-garde' in Art and Politics," *American Historical Review,* 73, no. 2 (December 1967): 339–66, esp. p. 343. On the historical background of the concept, see Renato Poggioli, *The Theory of the Avant-Garde,* trans. Gerald Fitgerald (Cambridge, MA: Belknap Press of Harvard University Press, 1968), originally published as *Teoria dell'arte d'avanguardia* (Bologna: Il Mulino, 1962); and Peter Bürger, *Theory of the Avant-Garde,* trans. Michael Shaw, foreword by Jochen Schulte-Sasse (Minneapolis: University of Minnesota Press, 1984), originally published as *Theorie der Avantgarde* (Frankfurt am Main: Suhrkamp, 1974).

15. On this strange movement, which was more symptomatic than truly innovative, see *Encyclopédie des farces et attrapes et des mystifications,* ed. François Caradec and Noël Arnaud (Paris: Pauvert, 1964). See also Daniel Grojnowski, "Une avant-garde sans avancée: Les 'arts incohérents,' 1882–1889," *Actes de la recherche en sciences sociales,* no. 40 (1981): 73–86, from which I have borrowed some of the remarks that follow.

16. Wassily Kandinsky, *Du spirituel dans l'art et dans la peinture en particulier* (1912), trans. Pierre Volboudt (Paris: Denoël, 1981), 43.

17. See Guillaume Apollinaire, *Méditations esthétiques: Les peintres cubistes,* ed. L. C. Breunig and J.-Cl. Chevalier (Paris: Hermann, 1965), 52.

18. Bruckner, *L'euphorie perpétuelle,* 88.

19. On this point, see Daniel Halévy's fine biography, *Nietzsche,* Coll. Pluriel (Paris: Livre de Poche, 1986).

20. Murger, *The Bohemians,* xxxviii; *Scènes de la vie de Bohème,* 36. For what follows, see Murger, *The Bohemians,* xxxvi, xl.

21. Murger, *The Bohemians,* xliii; *Scènes de la vie de Bohème,* 41. For what follows, see Murger, *The Bohemians,* xlii.

22. Kandinsky, *Du spirituel dans l'art,* 31.

23. Wassily Kandinsky, letter to Schönberg, 18 January 1911. On the Kandinsky-Schönberg correspondence, see the special issue of *Contrechamps,* no. 2 (April 1984).

24. As Dan Franck notes, in terms that provide a comment on Murger's statements on the two bohemias: "Before the First World War, although Picasso had already become rich, most of his companions lived in utter poverty. After 1918, by contrast, they could buy themselves Bugattis and private homes. The era of the inspired but starving artist was coming to an end." See Dan Franck, *Bohèmes* (Paris: Calmann-Lévy, 1998), 11, quoted from *Bohemian Paris: Picasso, Modigliani, Matisse, and the Birth of Modern Art,* trans. Cynthia Hope Liebow (New York: Grove, 2001), xiii.

25. Karl Marx and Friedrich Engels, *Manifesto of the Communist Party* (Chicago: Charles H. Kerr, 1906), 17. For a Marxist analysis of avant-garde movements, see Daniel Bell, *The Cultural Contradictions of Capitalism* (New York: Basic Books, 1996).

26. On this topic, see Pierre Bourdieu, "Flaubert et l'invention de la vie d'artiste," *Actes de la recherche en sciences sociales*, no. 2 (March 1975): 67–93.

27. Murger, *The Bohemians*, xxxiii–iv; *Scènes de la vie de Bohème*, 32.

28. This theme is explicitly developed by Nietzsche in *Twilight of the Idols*, particularly in "The Problem of Socrates."

29. On this point, see Paul-Laurent Assoun, *Freud, la philosophie et les philosophes* (Paris: Presses Universitaires de France, 1976).

30. See Sigmund Freud, *The Future of an Illusion*, trans. W. D. Robson-Scott (New York: Liveright, 1949), 76; in French translation as *L'avenir d'une illusion* (Paris: Presses Universitaires de France, 1995), 61–62.

31. Freud, *Future of an Illusion*, 52; *L'avenir d'une illusion*, 44–45.

32. See Freud, *L'avenir d'une illusion*, 61–62.

33. Sigmund Freud, *Civilization and Its Discontents*, trans. Joan Riviere (London: Hogarth Press and The Institute of Psycho-Analysis, 1949), 42; in French translation as *Malaise dans la civilisation* (Paris: Presses Universitaires de France, 1986), 31.

34. Sigmund Freud, *The Complete Introductory Lectures on Psychoanalysis*, trans. and ed. James Strachey (New York: Norton, 1966), 632; in French translation as *Nouvelles conférences sur la psychanalyse* (Paris: Gallimard, 1981), 228.

35. Freud, *Civilization and Its Discontents*, 42; *Malaise dans la civilisation*, 31.

36. Bruno Bettelheim, "The Three Little Pigs," in his *The Uses of Enchantment: The Meaning and Importance of Fairy Tales* (New York: Knopf, 1976), 41–44.

37. Sigmund Freud, *The General Introduction to Psychoanalysis*, trans. Joan Riviere, preface by Ernest Jones and G. Stanley Hall (Garden City, N.Y.: Garden City Publishing, 1938), 298–99; in French translation as *Introduction à la psychanalyse* (Paris: Payot, 1998), 321.

CHAPTER 7

1. I make no pretense to originality in this approach: Martin Heidegger, Leo Strauss, Alexandre Koyré, Michel Villey, and, more recently, Rémi Brague and Pierre Hadot invite us to read the Ancients, not as our contemporaries, but rather as authors who belong to a "lost world" and *as such* offer us many lessons.

2. I reiterate here an opinion well argued in Pierre Hadot, *Qu'est-ce que la philosophie antique?* (Paris: Gallimard, 1995), available in English translation by Michael Chase as *What is Ancient Philosophy?* (Cambridge, MA: Belknap Press of Harvard University Press, 2002). For a contradictory (and in my eyes unpersuasive) viewpoint, see Monique Canto-Sperber, *L'inquiétude morale et la vie humaine* (Paris: Presses Universitaires de France, 2001), 191ff.

3. It has often been noted, in this regard, that the Sophists and the Epicureans were "not Greeks" but were already "modern," in that they explicitly reject the idea of an organized cosmos within which each individual can and must find his place and his salvation.

4. This is a topic that I have discussed in André Comte-Sponville and Luc Ferry, *La sagesse des Modernes: Dix questions pour notre temps* (Paris: Laffont, 1998), chap. 10. It will be the subject of a work in preparation on Kant.

5. This is an objection raised by André Comte-Sponville in Comte-Sponville and Ferry, *La sagesse des Modernes*, 54.

6. Jean-Pierre Vernant and Pierre Vidal-Naquet, *La Grèce ancienne, 1: Du mythe à la raison*, Coll. Points (Paris: Seuil, 1990), 198.

7. Cicero, *De natura deorum*, in *De natura deorum; Academica*, II, xxiv–xxv, trans. H. Rackham, Loeb Classical Library (London: William Heinemann; New York: G. P. Putnam's Sons, 1933), 183–85.

8. It is in this perspective that I sketched out the idea of a close connection between the birth of modern philosophy and the secularization of religion, especially Protestant religion, in Germany. See Comte-Sponville and Ferry, *La sagesse des Modernes*, chap. 10.

9. Vernant and Vidal-Naquet, *La Grèce ancienne*, 202.

10. Ibid., 205.

11. Ibid. For what follows, see ibid., 233.

12. Ibid., 211. For what follows, see ibid., 214–15.

13. Hannah Arendt, "The Concept of History, Ancient and Modern," in Arendt, *Between Past and Future: Eight Exercises in Political Thought* (New York: Viking, 1968), 41–90, esp. p. 43; in French translation as "Le concept d'histoire," in *La crise de la culture: Huit exercices de pensée philosophique*, trans. under the direction of Patrick Lévy (Paris: Gallimard, 1989), 60ff.

14. Epictetus is quoted from *The Discourses as Reported by Arrian, The Manual, and Fragments*, trans. W. A. Oldfather, Loeb Classical Library (Cambridge, MA: Harvard University Press, 1989), III, xxiv, vol. 2, pp. 91–95; in French translation in *Les Stoïciens: Textes*, ed. Pierre Maxime Schuhl and Emile Bréher, Bibliothèque de la Pléiade (Paris: Gallimard, 1962), 1030.

15. Marcus Aurelius Antoninus, *The Meditations*, trans. and introd. G. M. A. Grube (Indianapolis: Hackett, 1983), IV, 14, p. 28.

16. Epictetus, *Discourses*, Loeb, II, viii, 28, 1:267; *Les Stoïciens*, 900.

17. Cicero, *De natura deorum*, II, 24, Loeb, p. 183.

18. Plato, *Timaeus*, 90 b—c, in *Plato*, vol. 9, *Timaeus, Critias, Cleitophon, Menexenus, Epistles*, trans. R. G. Bury, Loeb Classical Library (Cambridge, MA: Harvard University Press; London: G. W. Heinemann, 1975), 245–47.

19. Plato, Theaetetus, 176b, in *Plato*, vol. 2, *Theaetetus, Sophist*, trans. H. N. Fowler, Loeb Classical Library (London: William Heinemann; New York: G. P. Putnam's Sons, 1921), 129.

20. Aristotle, *Nicomachean Ethics*, X, vii, 8, trans. H. Rackham, Loeb Classical Library (Cambridge, MA: Harvard University Press; London: G. W. Heinemann, 1975), X, vii, 8, p. 617. The question of knowing how to understand this "immortality" (Is it personal or not?) remains very difficult to resolve in Aristotle, as is that of knowing whether his famous "so far as possible" points, as Pierre Aubenque believes, to an "ideal regulator." In this context that notion seems an anachronism, and in my opinion Aubenque is closer to Aristotle when he connects it instead to the idea that the human being is "the being of mediation." See Pierre Aubenque, *La prudence chez Aristote* (Paris: Presses Universitaires de France, 1963).

21. Aubenque, *La prudence chez Aristote*, 169.

CHAPTER 8

1. It is of course this vision of nature as a locus of perpetual conflict that certain ecologists attempt to erase, often by evoking the Greek concept of cosmic harmony.

2. Rémi Brague, *La sagesse du monde: Histoire de l'expérience humaine de l'univers* (Paris: Fayard, 1999), 137; quoted from *The Wisdom of the World: The Human Experience of the Universe in Western Thought*, trans. Teresa Lavender Fagan (Chicago: University of Chicago Press, 2003), 115.

3. See Brague, *Wisdom of the World,* 115.

4. Brague, *Wisdom of the World,* 115, 121; *Sagesse du monde,* 137–43. See also the development of this theme in *La sagesse du monde,* 153ff. It is truly difficult to understand why some otherwise estimable commentators, perhaps under the influence of certain Anglo-Saxon currents of thought, should ignore or deny this manifest and highly interesting specificity of the Greek world. See, in this connection, Monique Canto-Sperber, *L'inquiétude morale et la vie humaine* (Paris: Presses Universitaires de France, 2001), for example at p. 79: "It goes without saying that in these three philosophies [those of Plato, Aristotle, and the Stoics] one sees not the slightest trace of the thesis according to which the ends of man or moral ideas are given by nature." "It goes without saying"; "not the slightest trace"! These peremptory statements are directly contradicted, as we shall see below, by tens, if not hundreds, of essential texts that emerged from those three traditions and that clearly and firmly assert the contrary. That the relationship of ethics to cosmology is not one of simple "deduction" is one thing (and, incidentally, the point is so obvious that using it as an argument is like smashing through an open door). To assert that the notion of the "cosmologico-ethical" or, as Brague puts it, the "wisdom of the world" has little sense or is not characteristic of this sort of Greek philosophy, or to claim that the question of wisdom is only marginal (see Canto-Sperber, *L'inquiétude morale,* 191ff.), is to miss what gives ancient philosophy its deepest meaning and to retain only its least interesting and least specific aspects, which are just as easily found, for example, in contemporary American moral philosophy.

5. Seneca, "On the Happy Life," in *Moral Essays,* trans. John W. Basore, Loeb Classical Library (London: William Heinemann; New York: G. P. Putnam's Sons, 1932), III, 3, p. 107; in French translation as "De la vie heureuse," in *Les Stoïciens: Textes,* ed. Pierre Maxime Schuhl and Émile Bréhier, Bibliothèque de la Pléiade (Paris: Gallimard, 1962), 1030, 726.

6. Cicero, *De natura deorum,* in *De natura deorum; Academica,* trans. H. Rackham, Loeb Classical Library (London: William Heinemann; New York: G. P. Putnam's Sons, 1933), II, xiv, 37, p. 159; *De la nature des dieux,* in *Les Stoïciens,* 422.

7. Plato, *The Republic,* 6, 500c, in *The Republic of Plato,* trans. and ed. Allan Bloom (New York and London: Basic Books, 1968), 179–80; *La sagesse du monde,* 154.

8. Cicero, *De natura deorum,* II, vi, 16, Loeb edition, p. 139; *De la nature des dieux,* in *Les Stoïciens,* 415.

9. Cicero, *De natura deorum,* II, xvii, 16, Loeb edition, p. 167; *De la nature des* dieux, in *Les Stoïciens,* I, 425.

10. See Jacques Brunschwig, *Le savoir grec: Dictionnaire critique* (Paris: Flammarion, 1996), 1053; quoted below from *Greek Thought: A Guide to Classical Knowledge,* ed. Jacques Brunschwig and Geoffrey E. R. Lloyd, with the collaboration of Pierre Pellegrin; trans. under the direction of Catherine Porter (Cambridge, MA: Belknap Press of Harvard University Press, 2000), 989. Brunschwig states: "The skein of attributes of the Stoic world is so closely woven that it comes all together no matter on which strand one tugs: this world is a totality, not a simple sum; it is one, finite, spherical, geocentric, full, continuous, ordered, organized. The events that take place in this world are not mutually independent; this world's temporal and causal unity is summed up in the notion of fate, an orderly and inviolable arrangement of causes, a notion to which the Stoics held no less than to that of moral responsibility, which the notion of fate seemed to put at risk."

11. Marcus Aurelius Antoninus, *The Meditations,* trans. and introd. G. M. A. Grube (Indianapolis: Hackett, 1983), IV, 40, 45; pp. 34, 35; *Les Stoïciens,* 1166. It should be noted that in the Stoics the conviction of a continuous interconnection among things is the basis for an almost "rational" conception of the art of divination, something that today's science views as

superstition pure and simple. If in fact everything is connected, it is hard to see why, by connecting the dots, so to speak, that define the present, one could not arrive at a partial knowledge of the future.

12. Brunschwig, *Greek Thought,* 989; *Le savoir grec,* 1053.

13. Marcus Aurelius, *Meditations,* IV, 10, Grube translation, p. 27; *Les Soïciens,* 1166.

14. Aristotle, *The Metaphysics,* G, 5, 1010 a, 21–22, trans. Hugh Tredennick, Loeb Classical Library (Cambridge, MA: Harvard University Press; London: William Heinemann, 1956), 191.

15. Brague, *Wisdom of the World,* 108; *Sagesse du monde,* 129–30.

16. On this point, see Brague, *Wisdom of the World,* 130–31; *Sagesse du monde,* 153–54.

17. Cicero *De finibus bonorum et malorum,* III, xxii, 73, trans. H. Rackham, Loeb Classical Library (Cambridge, MA: Harvard University Press; London: William Heinemann, 1983), 293.

18. Cicero, *De natura deorum,* II, xxxii, 82, 81, Loeb edition, pp. 203, 201.

19. With the exception of Spinoza, the "most ancient of the Moderns" according to Leo Strauss.

20. This is one of the fundamental theses of Rémi Brague's *Wisdom of the World.* He states: "According to this view, there are not, on the one hand, a physical world devoid of 'values' and on the other, 'values' without roots in perceptible reality. . . . For [ancient and medieval thinking] the being is good at the outset and therefore has no need to receive that quality elsewhere than from itself. The interconvertibility of the Being and the Good not only governs metaphysics, in the doctrine of transcendentals; it has a cosmological version. It allows itself to be seen in the very structure of the world. This situation has ethical consequences: it asks for nothing less than a determined specific way to define human moral action. Good is not something that must be injected from outside into a neutral receptacle; it is already there, indeed, it imposes itself with brio into reality. This does not lead to any form of quietism. Ethics remain a task. But 'to do' good consists less of *producing* than of *reproducing,* than of transporting from one domain to another that which is already there." *Wisdom of the World,* 120; *Sagesse du monde,* 142.

21. The domination of the cosmological model, thus of the various forms of the "wisdom of the world," "belongs to a delimited period in time, a period we can now envision as a whole. This period in the history of human thought, which, from the point of view of the link between cosmology and anthropology that I wanted to explore, if of very specific interest, extends from Late Antiquity to the end of the Middle Ages. . . . Over more than a millennium, scholarly thought was dominated by a cosmography that, on the one hand, was broadly shared by virtually all, and, on the other hand, could easily be connected to an ethics. It was indeed a period in time, for it had a beginning and an end. For that connection . . . did not always exist. Subsequently—that is, for the most part in the modern era—the cosmography that could be agreed on was no longer associated with ethical concerns, either negative or positive. The modern cosmos is ethically indifferent. The image of the world that emerges from physics after Copernicus, Galileo, and Newton is of a confluence of blind forces, where there is no place for consideration of the Good." Brague, *Wisdom of the World,* 185; *Sagesse du monde,* 213.

22. Epictetus, *Discourses,* IV, vii, 20, quoted from *The Discourses as Reported by Arrian, The Manual, and Fragments,* trans. W. A. Oldfather, Loeb Classical Library (Cambridge, MA: Harvard University Press, 1989), vol. 2, p. 367; for what follows, see ibid., IV, vii, 7, Loeb edition, vol. 2, p. 363.

23. Ibid., II, xvii, 45–47, Loeb edition, vol. 1, p.327. For what follows, see ibid., II, xiv, 7–8, Loeb edition, vol. 1, pp. 299–301.

24. Pierre Hadot, *Qu'est-ce que la philosophie antique?* (Paris: Gallimard, 1995), 207, quoted from *What Is Ancient Philosophy*, trans. Michael Chase (Cambridge, MA: Belknap Press of Harvard University Press, 2002), 133. See also Pierre Hadot, *La citadelle intérieure: Introduction aux "Pensées" de Marc Aurèle* (Paris: Fayard, 1992), 122, 123, 180, etc.; in English translation by Michael Chase as *The Inner Citadel: The Meditations of Marcus Aurelius* (Cambridge, MA: Belknap Press of Harvard University Press, 1998).

25. Jacques Brunschwig states: "Stoicism takes to the logically coherent extreme one of the two great world views that characterized ancient thought, the other being perfectly represented by atomistic and mechanistic Epicureanism." *Greek Thought,* 989; *Le savoir* grec, 1053. This does not mean that the other tradition of Greek thought, that of the atomism of Democritus and the Epicureans, should not enter into our reflection on the good life. Quite to the contrary, and I shall return to the matter at greater length in the part 5 of the present work. As Brunschwig warns, however, we should be careful not to put the two currents of thought on the same plane, since one of them is explicitly backed up by a cosmological construction and the other by what we today might call "deconstruction." Rémi Brague proposes the same division, designating the atomist tradition—quite rightly in my opinion—that of "the other Greece." In the same sense, see Hadot, *Qu'est-ce que la philosophie antique?* 201.

CHAPTER 9

1. According to Simplicius, the title *Manual,* or *Handbook,* was given to this work because the maxims of Epictetus ought to be at all times "at hand" for those who wanted to live well, just as a dagger should be always "in the fist" of those who want to fight well.

2. *The Encheiridion of Epictetus,* in *The Discourses as Reported by Arrian, The Manual, and Fragments,* trans. W. A. Oldfather, Loeb Classical Library (Cambridge, MA: Harvard University Press, 1989), vol. 1, p. 483.

3. Pierre Hadot, *Qu'est-ce que la philosophie antique?* (Paris: Gallimard, 1995), 198; quoted from *What is Ancient Philosophy?* trans. Michael Chase (Cambridge, MA: Belknap Press of Harvard University Press, 2002), 127.

4. See Pierre Hadot, *La citadelle intérieure: Introduction aux "Pensées" de Marc Aurèle* (Paris: Fayard, 1992); in English translation by Michael Chase as *The Inner Citadel: The Meditations of Marcus Aurelius* (Cambridge, MA: Belknap Press of Harvard University Press, 1998).

5. Seneca, *Ad Lucilium Epistulae Morales,* CVII, 11, trans. Richard M. Gummere, Loeb Classical Library (London: William Heinemann; Cambridge, MA: Harvard University Press, 1953), vol. 1, p. 229.

6. It is evident that Stoics and Epicureans radically differ on this point. As Pierre Hadot notes about the latter: "Although bodies consist of aggregates of atoms, they do not form a true unity, and the universe is merely a juxtaposition of elements which do not blend together. Each being is an individuality—as it were atomized and isolated with regard to the others. Everything is external to everything else, and everything happens by chance; within the infinite void, an infinity of worlds is formed," and these worlds are also ruled by chance. "For the Stoics, on the contrary, everything is within everything else, bodies are organic wholes, and everything happens by organic necessity. Within infinite time, there is only one cosmos, which repeats itself endlessly." Hadot, *What is Ancient Philosophy?* 129; *Qu'est-ce que la philosophie antique?* 201.

7. Cicero, *De natura deorum,* II, xi, 30, in *De natura deorum; Academica,* trans. H. Rack-

ham, Loeb Classical Library (London: William Heinemann; New York: G. P. Putnam's Sons, 1933), 153.

8. See Plutarch, "On Stoic Self-Contradictions," 1043, 23, in *Plutarch's Moralia*, vol. 13, pt. 2, trans. Harold Cherniss, Loeb Classical Library (Cambridge, MA: Harvard University Press; London: William Heinemann, 1976), 23, p. 509.

9. Hadot, *What is Ancient Philosophy?* 130; *Qu'est-ce que la philosophie antique?* 203.

10. Plutarch, "On Stoic Self-Contradictions," 1045, 23; Loeb ed., pp. 509–10.

11. It is precisely this exception to the inviolable rule of general determinism that Plutarch sees as the principal contradiction of the Stoics.

12. Epictetus, *Discourses*, I, xii, 17; Loeb ed., vol. 1, p. 93.

13. Marcus Aurelius Antoninus, *The Meditations*, trans. and introd. G. M. A. Grube (Indianapolis: Hackett, 1983), VIII, 34, p. 79.

14. Plutarch discerns a major contradiction in Stoic thought here, because this process of "liberation" supposes that we can at least choose the path of reason rather than that of ignorance.

15. Hadot, *What is Ancient Philosophy?* 131; *Qu'est-ce que la philosophie antique?* 204.

16. Plutarch, 'On Stoic Self-Contradictions," 1056, 47; Loeb ed., pp. 593–95.

17. Ibid., p. 597.

18. Friedrich Nietzsche, *Beyond Good and Evil: Prelude to a Philosophy of the Future,* trans. and ed. Walter Kaufmann (New York: Vintage Books, 1989), no. 9, p. 15.

19. Epictetus, *Discourses,* II, xix, 21–25; Loeb ed., vol. 1, p. 367.

20. Seneca, *Ad Lucilium Epistulae Morales,* I, 1, pp. 3–5

21. Marcus Aurelius, *Meditations,* XII, 1, trans. Grube, 122.

22. Ibid., VIII, 36, trans. Grube, 80.

23. Seneca, *Letter to Lucilius.* See Pierre Hadot, *La citadelle intérieure,* 115–16, where Hadot cites this passage and gives an incisive commentary on it. Seneca is quoted here from Hadot, *The Inner Citadel,* 115.

24. Hadot, *What is Ancient Philosophy?* 191; *Qu'est-ce que la philosophie antique?* 293. On the same theme, see also Hadot, *La citadelle intérieure,* 130–31; *The Inner Citadel,* 112–13.

25. Epictetus, *Discourses,* III, 84–85, 86, 88; Loeb edition, 2: 211–13.

26. Marcus Aurelius, *Meditations,* XII, 3, trans. Grube, 123.

27. Marcus Aurelius, *Meditations,* II, 5; quoted from Hadot, *The Inner Citadel,* 135; *Citadelle intérieure,* 152.

28. Hadot, *What is Ancient Philosophy?,* 222; *Qu'est-ce que la philosophie antique?* 337.

29. Marcus Aurelius, *Meditations,* XI, 1, trans. Grube, p. 110.

30. Epictetus, *Discourses,* III, xxiv, 104–7; Loeb ed., vol. 2, pp. 217–19.

31. Notably, but not exclusively, in the materialist tradition, to which we shall return at the end of the present work

32. Marcus Aurelius, *Meditations,* IV, 4, trans. Grube, 26.

CHAPTER 10

1. Etienne Gilson, *La philosophie au Moyen Age, des origines patristiques à la fin du XIVe siècle,* 2nd ed. (Paris: Payot, 1986), 9.

2. All biblical quotations in this translation are drawn from *The New American Bible* (Chicago: Catholic Press, 1971).

3. See Augustine, *The City of God,* book X.

4. Gilson, *La philosophie au Moyen Age*, 11.

5. St. Justin Martyr, *Dialogue with Trypho*, trans. Thomas B. Falls, rev. and introd. Thomas P. Halton, ed. Michael Slusser (Washington, DC: Catholic University of America Press, 2003), 4; *Dialogue avec Tryphon*, in *La philosophie passe au Christ* (Paris: Editions de Paris), 120. The latter anthology also includes a translation of Justin's *Apologies*.

6. Augustine, "Of True Religion" (*De Vera Religione*), xxv, 46, in Augustine, *Earlier Writings*, trans. and ed. John H. S. Burleigh (Philadelphia: Westminster Press, 1979), 218–83, esp. p. 247.

7. Acts of the Apostles 17:18; for what follows, see ibid. 17:32.

8. The First Epistle of Paul to the Corinthians 1:20–25.

9. See, in particular, Augustine, *The City of God*, book X, chap. 28.

10. Etienne Gilson, *L'esprit de la philosophie médiévale* (Paris: Vrin, 1944), 18, quoted from *The Spirit of Medieval Philosophy*, trans. A. H. C. Downes (New York: Scribner's, 1936; repr. Notre Dame, IN: University of Notre Dame Press, 1991), 21.

11. Augustine, *Concerning The City of God Against the Pagans*, X, 29, trans. Henry Bettenson, introd. John O'Meara (London: Penguin, 1984), 417. For what follows, see ibid., book X, passim.

12. Porphyry, *Life of Plotinus*, 2, 25, trans. A. H. Armstrong, Loeb Classical Library (Cambridge, MA: Harvard University Press; London: William Heinemann, 1946), 7.

13. St. Justin Martyr, *First Apology*, no. 5, in *The First and Second Apologies*, Ancient Christian Writers, 56 (New York and Mahwah, NJ: Paulist Press, 1997), 26; in French translation as *Apologies*, in *La philosophie passe au Christ*, 35.

14. Justin, *Dialogue with Trypho*, 4, 10; *Dialogue avec Tryphon*, 121, 128.

15. Justin, *Dialogue with Trypho*, 12, 13; *Dialogue avec Tryphon*, 121, 128.

16. Augustine, "Of True Religion," iii, 3; trans. Burleigh, 226–27; *De la vraie religion*, in *Oeuvres de saint Augustin*, ser. 1, vol. 8, *La foi chrétienne* (Paris: Desclée de Brouwer, 1951), 27.

17. Augustine, *Confessions*, VII, 9.

18. Augustine, "Of True Religion," iii, 3; trans. Burleigh, 227; *De la vraie religion*, 25–27. Augustine asks: If a disciple of Plato had asked his master if he thought it possible that a man could persuade the mass of people of all the truths contained in Platonism, what would the philosopher have answered? His response is: "I believe Plato's answer would be: 'That could not be done by man, unless the very virtue and wisdom of God delivered him from natural environment, illumined him from his cradle not by human teaching but by personal illumination, honoured him with such grace, strengthened him with such firmness and exalted him with such majesty that he should be able to despise all that wicked men desire, to suffer all that they dread, to do all that they marvel at, and so with the greatest love and authority to convert the human race to so sound a faith.'" In other words, God's help would be needed, along with the incarnation of the *logos* in Christ, so that the truths that philosophy had already recognized could pass into fact and attain the universality among the people that is theirs in Christianity.

19. Augustine, "Of True Religion," iii, 3, 7; trans. Burleigh, 226, 229; *De la vraie religion*, 27, 33, 35.

20. See Augustine, *Confessions*, VII, xx and xxi, and, on the same point, Pascal, *Pensées*, fragments 556, 430, and especially 464 (Brunschvicg edition), where the opposition between a good that comes from the outside and a pseudo-good situated uniquely within us is common to both religion and philosophy: "Our instinct makes us feel that we must seek our happiness outside ourselves. . . . And thus the philosophers have said in vain, 'Retire within yourselves, and you will find your good there.' We do not believe them, and those who be-

lieve them are the most empty and the most foolish"; Blaise Pascal, *Pensées; The Provincial Letters*, trans. W. F. Trotter (New York: Random House, 1941), 153–54.

21. Augustine, *Confessions,* VII, ix; trans. Boulding, 169, 171.

22. Augustine, *The City of God,* X, 24; trans. Bettenson, 404–5.

23. Augustine, *Confessions,* VII, ix; trans Boulding, 171.

24. Augustine, *City of God,* X, 28; trans. Bettenson, 412, 414.

25. Ibid., X, 29; trans. Bettenson, 414.

26. Ibid., X, 29; trans. Bettenson, 414–16. Augustine further states: "You also say that in the celestial sphere there are immortal bodies of beings whose blessedness is immortal. Then what basis is there for your notion that escape from any kind of body is an essential condition for our happiness, a notion that makes you feel that you have rational justification for your rejection of Christianity?" Ibid.

27. See Luc Ferry, *L'Homme-Dieu ou le sens de la vie* (Paris: Grasset, 1996), 158ff.; in English translation by David Pellauer as *Man Made God: The Meaning of Life* (Chicago: University of Chicago Press, 2002).

28. Epictetus, *Discourses,* III, xxiv, 87–89, in *The Discourses as Reported by Arrian, The Manual, and Fragments,* trans. W. A. Oldfather, Loeb Classical Library (Cambridge, MA: Harvard University Press, 1989), 213.

29. Sogyal Rinpoché, *Le livre tibétain de la vie et de la mort* (Paris: Table Ronde, 1993), 63; in English translation as *The Tibetan Book of Living and Dying,* ed. Patrick Gaffney and Andrew Harvey (San Francisco: HarperSanFrancisco, 1992).

30. His Holiness, The Dalai Lama of Tibet, *The Way to Freedom,* ed. Donald S. Lopez Jr. (San Francisco: HarperSanFrancisco, 1994), 127; in French translation as *La voie de la liberté* (Paris: Calmann-Lévy, 1995), 68.

31. Rinpoché, *The Tibetan Book of Living and Dying,* 224; *Le livre tibétain,* 297.

32. André Comte-Sponville and Luc Ferry, *La sagesse des Modernes: Dix questions pour notre temps* (Paris: Robert Laffont, 1998), 438, 439.

33. Pascal, *Pensées,* 479; trans. Trotter, 157–58.

34. Augustine, "Of True Religion," xlv, 88; trans. Burleigh, 270–71, 276.

35. Ibid., xlv, 89; trans. Burleigh, 271.

36. Pascal, *Pensées,* 471; trans. Trotter, 155–56.

37. Augustine, *Confessions,* IV, xii, 18; trans. Boulding, 104.

38. Augustine, "Of True Religion," x, 19; trans. Burleigh, 234–35.

39. Augustine, *Confessions,* IV, vi, 11; viii, 13; ix, 14; x, 15, trans. Boulding, 99, 98, 100, 101, 102.

40. Ibid., IV, ix, 14; trans. Boulding, 101.

41. In this connection, see André Comte-Sponville, "L'amour selon Pascal," *Revue internationale de philosophie,* 1997, no. 1, special issue on "Pascal philosophe," ed. André Comte-Sponville, pp. 131–60.

42. Augustine, *Confessions,* IV, xii, 18; trans. Boulding, 103–4. For what follows, see ibid., IX, xii, 29; trans. Boulding, 231; IX, iii, 5; trans. Boulding, 212.

43. *Catechism of the Catholic Church,* c.1944 United States Catholic Conference, Inc.—Libreria Editrice Vaticana (Liguori, MO: Liguori Publications, 1944), no. 1015, 1017, p. 265.

44. Aurelius Augustine, *The Happy Life,* trans. and ed. Ludwig Schopp (St Louis, MO: B. Herder, 1939), 131–32; *La vie heureuse* (Paris: Rivages Poche, 2000), 103.

45. "The serpent asked the woman, 'Did God really tell you not to eat from any of the trees in the garden?'" (Genesis 3:1). In other words: Are you quite sure? Have you not the slightest doubt? The devil always tries to drive a wedge between man and God, because it is

eternal life that he deprives us of, and in order to do that, he uses the supreme weapon of doubt. On the theme of temptations, see Denis de Rougemont, *La part du diable* (New York: Brentano's, 1944; Paris: Gallimard, 1982), 35ff.; in English translation by Haakon Chevalier as *The Devil's Share* (New York: Pantheon, 1944).

CHAPTER 11

1. On the meaning of this expression and the context in which it was discussed, see Etienne Gilson, *Etudes de philosophie médiévale* (Strasbourg: Commission des publications de la Faculté des lettres; London: Oxford University Press, 1921), 30–31.

2. St. Thomas Aquinas, *The Summa Theologica Of Saint Thomas Aquinas,* translated by the Fathers of the English Dominican Province, revised by Daniel J. Sullivan (Chicago: Encyclopaedia Britannica, 1952), Q. I, Art 6, vol. 1, p. 6.

3. Gilson, *Etudes de philosophie médiévale,* 22.

4. In this second and resolutely antiphilosophic viewpoint, the ancillary role that Damian assigns to philosophy "and the comparisons that illustrate it do not by any means signify that theology can and must rely on philosophy for certain tasks, even inferior ones. They mean, to the contrary, that theology must have no confidence in philosophy and must maintain it, with suspicious prudence, in a state of strict servitude. . . . In the famous formula of St. Peter Damian, it is thus the idea of slavery that proves stronger—indeed, much stronger—than that of utilization." Ibid., 35.

5. The term "artists" of course designates the professors of the faculty of arts, who taught the seven liberal arts (music, geometry, arithmetic, astronomy, rhetoric, grammar, and dialectic).

6. See in particular, Pierre Hadot, *Qu'est-ce que la philosophie antique?* (Paris: Gallimard, 1995), 355–56; in English translation by Michael Chase as *What Is Ancient Philosophy?* (Cambridge, MA: Belknap Press of Harvard University Press, 2002).

7. Even the least attempt to emancipate oneself from the academic perspective arouses hostile reactions typical of the scholastic spirit of seriousness. See, for example, Monique Canto-Sperber, *L'inquiétude morale et la vie humaine* (Paris: Presses Universitaires de France, 2001), 192–93: "Do the philosophers deceive us when they claim to show us what constitutes the good life, the need for transcendence, and the virtues of the Moderns? . . . The object of this essay is to show that the philosophers have nothing to say to us on the wisdom of the Moderns or on contemporary forms of happiness, at least nothing that is philosophical, strictly speaking. . . . In antiquity, the task of philosophy was not to tell men how to live better, more easily, or more happily. Nor is this the case today." There is no doubt, at least where antiquity is concerned, that Monique Canto-Sperber is wrong—as is shown at length in the works of Pierre Hadot. As for the contemporary period, if Canto-Sperber's analysis were correct, it would constitute a radical condemnation of the very exercise of a philosophy reduced—and this in the best of cases—to an erudition "complemented " from time to time by an extremely modest supplement of soulful reflection.

8. Here, too, the works of Etienne Gilson and, more especially, Pierre Hadot offer decisive enlightenment.

9. On this dialogue, see not only the works of Alain de Libéra and Etienne Gilson, but also Roger Arnaldez, *A la croisée des trois monothéismes: Une communautée de pensée au Moyen Age* (Paris: Albin Michel, 1993). As Cyril Michon writes in his preface to the new edition of Thomas Aquinas, *Somme contre les Gentils:* (Paris: Garnier-Flammarion, 1999): "If the three

306 ~ NOTES TO PAGES 218–228

monotheisms were even in discussion, it was truly in the Middle Ages, and more precisely in the thirteenth century, when the three greatest readers of Aristotle in each tradition found, with the work of the latest in date among them, a means for debating the arguments. The religions debated and disputed thanks to philosophy."

10. The rediscovery of Aristotelianism in the Islamic world, and even in the Jewish world, clearly predates Averroës and Maimonides, however.

11. Averroës, *Commentaire de la physique d'Aristote*, trans. Salomon Munk, p. 441. For a more detailed commentary on this passage, see Maurice-Ruben Hayoun and Alain de Libéra, *Averroès et l'averroïsme*, Que sais-je? (Paris: Presses Universitaires de France, 1991).

12. On these texts and their like, and more generally on the reception of Aristotle by the three great monotheistic religions, see Alain de Libéra, *La philosophie médiévale*, Que sais-je? (Paris: Presses Universitaires de France, 2001), esp. pp. 164, 214.

13. Gilson, *Etudes de la philosophie médiévale*, 54.

14. On these condemnations, see, in particular, Alain de Libéra's excellent introduction to Thomas Aquinas, *L'unité de l'intellect contre les Averroïstes, Suivi des textes contre Averroès antérieurs à 1270*, ed. Alain de Libéra (Paris: GF-Flammarion, 1994), 22.

15. On this question, see, in particular, the works of Etienne Gilson (notably his *Etudes de philosophie médiévale*, which aims at showing how Thomism lies behind the rise of modern philosophy inasmuch as it permitted the liberalization of philosophy in general from its servile status), but also the analyses of Alain de Libéra, notably his introduction to Thomas Aquinas, *L'unité de l'intellect contre les Averroïstes*, and Libéra, *Penser au Moyen Age* (Paris: Seuil, 1991).

16. Alain de Libéra, following Gilson, has provided a brilliant demonstration of this thesis.

17. Ralph M. McInerny, *Aquinas Against the Averroists: On There Being Only One Intellect* (West Lafayette, IN: Purdue University Press, 1993), p. 212; for Thomas, see also Thomas Aquinas, *L'unité de l'intellect contre les Avveroïstes*, no. 123, pp. 196–97.

18. Averroës, *Le Livre du Discours décisif où l'on établit la connexion existant entre la Révélation et la philosophie*, trans. Marc Geoffroy, introd. Alain de Libéra (Paris: Garnier-Flammarion, 1996). The older French translation by Léon Gauthier (Paris: Vrin, 1909) gives a heavier but literal translation of the title: "Book of the decision of the question and of the establishment of what is between the religious law and philosophy in way of agreement."

19. Averroës, *The Book of the Decisive Treatise Determining the Connection Between the Law and Wisdom & Epistle Dedicatory*, trans., introd., and ed. Charles E. Butterworth (Provo, UT: Brigham Young University Press, 2001), I, 1, p. 1.

20. Ibid., II, 2, pp. 1–2; *Discours décisif*, no. 1.

21. Averroës, *The Book of the Decisive Treatise*, II, 6, 5, 9, pp. 4, 6.

22. Ibid., III, 11, pp. 8–9.

23. Thomas Aquinas, *Summa contra Gentiles*, book III, *Providence*, trans., introd., and ed. Vernon J. Bourke (Notre Dame, IN: University of Notre Dame Press, 1975), pt. 1, chap. 3, nos. 2, 3, pp. 63, 64; *Somme contre les Gentils*, trans. Cyrille Michon (Paris: Flammarion, 1999).

24. On this topic, see Cyrille Michon, introduction to Thomas Aquinas, *Somme contre les Gentils*, 60, 65.

25. See Thomas Aquinas, *Summa contra Gentiles*, II, 4, nos. 1, 4; IV, 1, no. 11.

26. See Thomas Aquinas, *Summa contra Gentiles*, book I, *God*, trans., introd., and ed. Anton C. Pegis, pt. 1, chap. 5.

27. See *John Paul II, Faith and Reason: Restoring Faith in Reason, with a New Translation of the Encyclical Letter of Pope John Paul II*, ed. Laurence Paul Hemming and Susan Frank Parsons (London: SCM Press, 2002).

28. Thomas Aquinas, *Summa contra Gentiles*, I, 7, no. 1; trans. Pegis, p. 74.

29. Ibid., III, pt.1, 48, no. 15; trans. Bourke, p. 167.

30. See Cyrille Michon introduction to Thomas Aquinas, *Somme contre les Gentils*, where he shows that this rationalistic reading of Thomas is not impossible.

31. On this crucial topic, see Pierre Hadot, *What is Ancient Philosophy?; Qu'est-ce que la philosophie antique?*

32. Latter-day disciples of Epicurus would probably insist, echoing Marx, that since the Master had never adhered to a cosmology but, to the contrary, had devoted his philosophic life to deconstructing the very principle of the atomist and materialist tradition (of which he was one of the most prestigious founding fathers), he is doing better today than anyone else. Things are not that simple, however. Epicurean morality was constructed on considerations of a physical order that have no more legitimacy today than those of his adversaries.

33. Among such works, see, in particular, Alexandre Koyré, *From the Closed World to the Infinite Universe* (Baltimore: Johns Hopkins University Press, 1957); in French translation by Raissa Tarr as *Du monde clos à l'univers infini* (Paris: Gallimard, 1962, 2000); but see also the many passages in Heidegger's works that contain useful reflections on this revolution in cosmology. The classic works of Ernst Cassirer and Etienne Gilson (notably the latter's *Etudes de philosophie médiévale*) remain highly pertinent, and Alain de Libéra's works have renewed medieval studies in France.

34. Koyré, *From the Closed World to the Infinite Universe*, 2; *Du monde clos à l'univers infini*, 11.

35. John Donne, "An Anatomie of the World ," quoted in Koyré, *From the Closed World to the Infinite Universe*, 21.

36. Pierre Hadot offers a similar diagnosis in an interview published in *Le Point* (17 August 2001), where he states: "I think that it is completely possible to separate the Stoic ethic from the cosmology that supports it. Stoic and Epicurean attitudes are still viable today; they are possible modes of life, but it is quite evident that the theories that were imagined to justify them are outdated. It is not life choices that depend on abstract theories; abstract theories are inspired by the mode of life."

37. Marcus Aurelius Antoninus, *The Meditations*, trans. and introd. G. M. A. Grube (Indianapolis: Hackett, 1983), III, 2, p. 19.

38. "Das Göttliche," quoted from "The Divine," in *Goethe: Selected Poems*, trans. John Whaley (Evanston, IL: Northwestern University Press, 1998), 45. On this poem of Goethe's, and more generally on the transition from the cosmologico-ethical to the neutral universe of the moderns, see Rémi Brague, *La sagesse du monde: Histoire de l'expérience humaine de l'univers* (Paris: Fayard, 1999), chapters 12, 13, and 14.

39. This is a theme that I have developed in Luc Ferry, *Le nouvel ordre écologique* (Paris: Grasset, 1992), in English translation by Carol Volk as *The New Ecological Order* (Chicago: University of Chicago Press, 1995), but also in Luc Ferry and Jean-Didier Vincent, *Qu'est-ce que l'homme? Sur les fondementaux de la biologie et de la philosophie* (Paris: Odile Jacob, 2000), where it is treated, in particular, in relation to the emergence of a new anthropology in Rousseau.

40. Etienne Gilson, *La philosophie au Moyen Age des origines patristiques à la fin du XIVe siècle*, 2nd ed. (Paris: Payot, 1986), 9–10.

41. Augustine, *The Confessions*, trans., introd., and notes by Maria Boulding, ed. John E. Rotelle (Hyde Park, NY: New City Press, 1990), X, xv, p. 247.

42. Ibid., XII, ii, 2, pp. 312–13.

43. Blaise Pascal, *Pensées*, Brunschvicg edition, nos. 793, 347; quoted from *Pensées; The Provincial Letters*, trans. W. F. Trotter (New York: Random House, 1941), pp. 278, 116.

44. Gilson, *La philosophie au Moyen Age,* 137.

45. Pope John Paul II, *Faith and Reason,* 57.

46. Ibid., 77.

47. Marcel Gauchet, *Le désenchantement du monde* (Paris: Gallimard, 1985), in English translation by Oscar Burge as *The Disenchantment of the World: A Political History of Religion* (Princeton: Princeton University Press, 1997).

CHAPTER 12

1. Jared Diamond, *The Third Chimpanzee: The Evolution and Future of the Human Animal* (New York: HarperCollins, 1992), in French translation as *Le troisième chimpanzé: Essai sur l'évolution et l'avenir de l'animal humain* (Paris: Gallimard, 2000).

2. André Comte-Sponville, "Baruch Spinoza, 1632–1677," in *Dictionnaire d'éthique et de philosophie morale,* ed. Monique Canto-Sperber, 2d ed. (Paris: Presses Universitaires de France, 1997), 1440–46.

3. Benedict Spinoza, *Ethics,* IV, 73, note, quoted from *On the Improvement of the Understanding; The Ethics; Correspondence,* trans. and introd. R. H. M. Elwes (New York: Dover, 1955), 236.

4. Benedict Spinoza, *Ethics,* III, 9–10; trans. Elwes, p. 5.

5. An analogous reasoning could be applied to the materialist doctrines, for we have seen how, since classical antiquity, they have relied on chance rather than necessity. Like the doctrines of necessity, the philosophies of radical contingency disqualify the idea of responsibility, for indeterminism is not to be confused with free will. Also like the necessity doctrines, their ultimate objective is to liberate us from time, to plant us firmly in the present as a means for achieving a human form of eternity. No one today believes in the theory of the *clinamen,* nor in the ontological argument that Spinoza uses as a base for his entire critique of free will, hence of morality (by showing that there can be no unrealized possibles). But this hardly matters: if its ultimate goal is not truth and lucidity but consolation, materialism accommodates itself equally well to a physics of chance and to one of necessity. Pierre Hadot rightly remarks: "As is shown with great force by Lucretius, it is the fear of death which is, in the last analysis, at the base of all the passions which make people unhappy. It was in order to free people from these terrors that Epicure proposed his theoretical discourse on physics. Above all, we must not imagine Epicurean physics as a scientific theory, intended to reply to objective, disinterested questions.... Indeed, philosophical theory is here merely the expression and consequence of the original choice of life, and a means of obtaining peace of mind and pure pleasure.... Research is carried out only to ensure peace of mind, either thanks to the fundamental dogmas which eliminate the fear of the gods and of death; or, in the case of secondary problems, thanks to one or more explanations which will suppress the mind's worries by showing that such phenomena are merely physical": Pierre Hadot, *Qu'est-ce que la philosophie antique?* (Paris: Gallimard, 1995), 184; quoted from *What Is Ancient Philosophy?* trans. Michael Chase (Cambridge, MA: Belknap Press of Harvard University Press, 2002), 117–19. Or, as Epicurus himself says in his *Capital Maxims* (11, 12): "There is no profit to be derived from the knowledge of celestial phenomena other than peace of mind and firm assurance, just as this is the goal of all other research"; Hadot, *What is Ancient Philosophy?* 118. Whether one attains that goal through Stoic determinism or Epicurean indeterminism is unimportant.

6. *Catechism of the Catholic Church,* United States Catholic Conference, Inc.—Libreria Editrice Vaticana (Liguori, MO.: Liguori Publications, 1994), nos. 156, 157, pp. 42, 43.

7. Blaise Pascal, *Pensées,* in *Pensées; The Provincial Letters,* trans. W. F. Trotter (New York: Random House, 1941), no. 430, p. 138.

8. *Catechism of the Catholic Church,* no. 88, p. 28.

9. See, for example, Paul Valadier, *Un christianisme d'avenir: Pour une nouvelle alliance entre raison et foi* (Paris: Seuil, 1999), 130ff. The criticisms that Valadier addresses to me are so offensive in their form and so lacking in substance that they largely discourage discussion—the more so because the indigestible gruel that the author laboriously concocts on the basis of Hannah Arendt's and Charles Taylor's works give one little desire to go further.

10. *Encyclical Letter of John Paul II, The Splendor of Truth: Veritatis Splendor* (Boston: Pauline Books & Media, 1993), no. 41, p. 54. For what follows, see ibid., pp. 56, 57.

11. Damien Le Guay, "Un nouveau théologien, Luc Ferry?" *Communio* (January—February, 2001).

12. Jean-Jacques Rousseau, "Discourse on the Origin and Foundations of Inequality among Men," in *Rousseau's Political Writings,* ed. Alan Ritter and Julia Conaway Bondanella, trans. Julia Conaway Bondanella (New York and London: W. W. Norton: 1988), 15.

13. Spinoza, *Ethics,* III, 9, note; trans. Elwes, p. 137.

CHAPTER 13

1. See, for example, Friedrich Nietzsche, *Beyond Good and Evil: Prelude to a Philosophy of the Future,* trans. and ed. Walter Kaufmann (New York: Vintage Books, 1989), no. 225, p. 154: "Whether it is hedonism or pessimism, utilitarianism or eudemonism—all of these ways of thinking that measure the value of things in accordance with *pleasure* and *pain,* which are mere epiphenomena and wholly secondary, are ways of thinking that stay in the foreground and naïvetés. . . . You want, if possible—and there is no more insane 'if possible'—*to abolish suffering.* And we? It really seems that *we* would rather have it higher and worse than ever. Well-being as you understand it—that is no goal, that seems to us an *end,* a state that soon makes man ridiculous and contemptible—that makes his destruction *desirable.* . . . The discipline of suffering, of *great* suffering—do you not know that only *this* discipline has created all enhancements of man so far?" This evocation in the grand style shows once again, incidentally, just how superficial and inadmissible the 1968 interpretation of Nietzsche as a hedonistic pleasure-seeker was.

2. Ulrich Beck, *Risk Society: Towards a New Modernity,* trans. Mark Ritter (London and Newbury Park, CA: Sage, 1992); in French translation as *La société du risque* (Paris: Calmann-Lévy, 2001).

3. See Rémi Brague, *La sagesse du monde: Histoire de l'expérience humaine de l'univers* (Paris: Fayard, 1999), 219ff., in English translation by Teresa Lavender Fagan as *The Wisdom of the World: The Human Experience of the Universe in Western Thought* (Chicago: University of Chicago Press, 2003), 52–56.

4. As Hannah Arendt rightly notes in "The Crisis in Culture: Its Social and Political Significance," in her *Between Past and Future: Six Exercises in Political Thought* (New York: Viking, 1968), 197–226, esp. 220.

5. V. S. Naipaul, "Two Worlds (the Nobel Lecture)," in Naipaul, *Literary Occasions: Essays,* introd. and ed. Pankaj Mishra (New York and Toronto: Alfred A. Knopf, 2003), 181–95, esp. p. 187.

6. Ibid., 193.

7. Blaise Pascal, *Pensées*, no. 323; quoted from *Pensées; The Provincial Letters*, trans. W. F. Trotter (New York: Random House, 1941), pp. 108–9.

8. Ibid, no. 123; trans. Trotter, p. 46.

9. Victor Hugo, "Booz endormi," quoted in English translation from "Boaz Asleep," in *Victor Hugo: Selected Poetry in French and English*, trans. and introd. Steven Monte (New York: Routledge, 2002), 219.

Abel, 12, 13
absolute, the, 20, 43, 52, 54, 137–38, 267
Adorno, Theodor, 100
Aesculapius, 148
age, 111, 166, 286–87
alienation, 103, 122
Althusser, Louis, 74
Ambrose, Saint (bishop of Milan), 192
Amiel, Henri-Frédéric, 109
amor fati, 99–100, 255, 256, 258; Nietzsche on, 93–102, 286
Anaximander, 140
animal nature and human nature, 250–53
Antipater of Tarsus, 165
Antoninus (Roman emperor), 193
anxiety, 33, 130, 147, 162, 229, 256
Apollinaire, Guillaume, 117
Arab writers, 216. *See also* Averroës
Arendt, Hannah, 146–47, 214, 279, 309n9
aristocracy, 12–13, 61, 63, 64, 136, 235
Aristotle: and Averroës, 218, 224, 225; on the cosmos, 31, 160, 219, 223, 239; on immortality, 33, 221, 226–27; and Maimonides, 219; *Nicomachean Ethics,* 153, 213; *Physics,* 218; and Plato, 149, 188, 219, 234; on providence, 189–90, 219; and reason, 213, 220–21, 228; rediscovery of, 194, 216, 217–18, 221, 223; and religion, 214, 216, 218, 220, 222, 223, 226; reputation of, 218, 219, 223; and science, 141, 223, 229–30, 241; and Thomas Aquinas, 136, 151, 193, 219, 222, 234, 238, 282
Arrian (Flavius Arrianus), 165
art, 39, 105–6, 119–20, 251, 253; aesthetics and, 82, 268; and culture, 281; ends of, 119–20; in Greek culture, 81, 106, 107, 110–11; Hegel on, 108, 137–38; humanization of, 105; imitation in, 111, 119; and the market, 111, 115, 119; Nietzsche on, 61, 64–65, 81–82, 111;

particularity, singularity in, 281, 282; sacred, 107, 108, 110–11
artist, 111, 114, 119, in ancient world, 110, 111; as bohemian, 105, 117–19, 120; as entrepreneur, 117, 122; as genius, 106, 115–16, 118, 138
arts, seven liberal, 305n5
atheism, atheists, 36, 37, 52, 55, 57–58
attachment, 175, 202–5, 207, 211, 253, 267; in Buddhism, 178, 180–81, 204; in Stoicism, 177–78, 179, 180–81
Aubenque, Pierre, 151, 298n20
Augustine, Saint (bishop of Hippo): *City of God,* 191, 192, 199, 200; *Confessions,* 191, 197, 198–99, 207–8; on Greek philosophy, 191, 192–93; on "heaven's heaven," 237–38; legacy of, 213, 214–18, 220, 227, 229; on love, attachment, 205, 206–9, 211; mentioned, 216, 219, 235, 237, 304n26; "Of True Religion" (*De vera religione*), 189, 197, 205; and Plato, Platonists, neoplatonists, 197–200, 217, 218, 219, 222, 226, 229, 237, 238, 239, 303n18
authority, 30, 265; arguments from, 27, 260–61
autonomy, 19, 36, 66–67, 259, 262–63, 270; in democratic ideology, 259, 263, 277; in Nietzsche, 67, 68, 73
avant-garde, 110, 114–15, 117, 118, 119, 145
Averroës, 218–29; "The Book of the Decisive Discourse" (*Decisive Treatise*), 223–24, 226

Bach, Johann Sebastian, 65, 111, 268, 282
Bachelard, Gaston, 62
Barrès, Claude, 293n12
Baudelaire, Charles, 65
beauty, 64, 82, 89, 263, 268
Beck, Ulrich, 274
Benjamin, Walter, 112
Bettelheim, Bruno, 124, 130
Bible, 143; Acts of the Apostles, 210; Epistle of

Bible (*continued*)
Paul to the Galatians, 206; Epistle of Paul to the Romans, 195, 200, 236; First Epistle of John, 188; First Epistle of Paul to the Corinthians, 191, 210; Genesis, 212, 219, 304n45; Gospel According to John, 43, 186, 188, 189,192, 202, 277; Psalms, 237
biology, 19, 39, 50, 251–52, 253
bohemia, bohemians, 42, 101, 103, 105, 110, 112–14, 115, 117, 118–20, 121, 122
Bonaventura, Saint, 216
Brague, Rémi, 155, 156, 297n1, 300nn20, 21, 301n25
Bruckner, Paascal, 109, 117
Brunschwig, Jacques, 299n10, 301n25
Buddhism, 31, 43, 78, 97, 98, 175, 176, 179, 203, 204–5, 206, 207, 208–9; and Stoicism, 33, 171, 175, 177, 178, 181, 202

Cain, 12, 13
Canto-Sperber, Monique, 299n4, 305n7
capitalism, 117, 120, 121
cause, causality, 168, 263–64
charity. *See* love, Christian (*agapè*)
choice, 170–71; freedom of, 173, 249–50, 256, 262. *See also* free will
Christianity, 26, 34, 35, 42, 43, 116, 137, 162, 254, 255, 262; and ancient cosmology, 235–36; and Aristotelianism, 214, 217–18; Augustine on, 197–98; fundamentalist, 170; hostility toward, 193; and humanism, 264–65; and Nietzsche, 3, 55, 84, 89, 90, 96, 294n22; Stoicism and, 33, 180, 181, 182, 185, 186
Christian philosophers, 36–37, 100, 108
Chrysippus of Soles, 155, 158, 164, 168
church, Roman Catholic, 34, 108, 220, 250; catechism of, 260–61; and science, 239–41, and Vatican II, 262; and World Youth Days, 26, 27
church fathers, 188, 191, 216, 225, 236, 238
Cicero, 140–41, 148–49, 156; *De finibus bonorum et malorum,* 160–61; on Stoicism, 158, 160–61, 164, 168, 172
civilization, 10, 275
classicism, 92, 93
Clastres, Pierre, 111, 243
Cleanthes of Assus, 164
Coelho, Paul, 27
communism, 36, 53, 244–45, 250
communitarianism, 103, 139, 144, 259, 268

community, 110, 132, 181–82, 244, 245; religious, 35–36, 244, 260
Comte, Auguste, 260
Comte-Sponville, André, 21, 85, 204, 254, 257
consciousness, 69–70, 73, 162–63, 258, 261
Constant, Benjamin, 52
consumerism, 12, 20, 38
Copernicus, Nicolaus: 230, 231, 300n21; *De revolutionibus orbium coelestium,* 230
Corneille, Pierre, 92–93
Cornford, Francis Macdonald, 140, 141, 142
cosmological moment, 30–34
cosmological principles, responses, 6, 38, 42–43, 103
cosmologico-ethical, 144, 146, 147, 153–63, 232, 272, 299n4
cosmologico-political, 144
cosmologies, 30, 37; 38, ancient, 34, 43, 50, 51–52, 54, 55
cosmology, 36, 162, 176; ancient Greek, 9, 26, 140, 143, 230–33, 235–38, 239, 269, 272; Nietzsche on, 52, 53
cosmos, ancient: 7, 30–31, 34–35, 41, 51, 54, 98, 116, 169, 174, 229–30, 277–81; as beautiful, 31, 157; contemplation of the, 31, 84, 152, 155, 156, 273; as determined, 168; as divine, 32, 144, 148, 149, 156, 157, 158, 162, 168, 187, 192; as eternal, 171, 190, 219; as good, 157, 159, 160, 162, 169, 180; as harmonious, 6, 32, 106, 110, 145, 152, 155, 158–59, 162, 169, 180, 187, 189, 192, 271, 272; as hierarchical, 152; as just, 158–59; as living, 153, 158–59, 161; as meaningful, 152, 155, 156; as moral, 152, 155, 160; as ordered, 6, 31, 35, 153, 159, 168, 169, 187; as perfect, 160, 172, 189; as rational, 168, 171, 187; in Stoicism, 32, 168–69; as transcendent, 137, 158; as uncreated, 238–39, as virtuous, 156
cosmos, from natural, to human, 277–78
Crates of Thebes, 32
Crescens, 194
culture, 116, 252, 253, 281
cultures, 282, 283, 279
Cynics, 32, 113, 194

daily life, 42, 103, 105, 108, 109, 110, 112; in art, 106, 113; and the avant-garde, 114; and bohemian life, 110, 120, 121, 122; and life of enterprise, 120
Damian, Peter, Saint, 189, 214, 216, 229, 305n4

Darwin, Charles, 239, 250
daydreams, 8, 12, 13, 103–6
death, 7, 34, 37, 122, 143, 166, 179; degrees of, 142,
146–48, 149, 150, 151–52, 211; fear of, 33, 40,
142, 146–47, 148, 151, 152, 171, 179, 180, 181, 190,
202–3, 204, 211, 241, 272, 273, 286; in Greek
philosophy, 33, 137, 139, 140; as passage, 147–
48, 190; vanquishing, 122, 146–47, 151, 152, 175,
179, 185, 190, 196, 203, 210, 211
Debussy, Claude, 64
Declaration of the Rights of Man and Citizen,
13, 26
deconstruction, 18, 37, 39, 258, 263, 283
Deleuze, Gilles, 54–55, 56, 82–83, 95, 120–21,
151–52
democracy, democratic, 11, 234, 243, 245, 259, 265,
275, 276, 277; envy, 13; ethic, 22; in Greece,
136, 144; ideal, 22; ideology, 27, 249, 261, 263;
law, 26; societies, 13, 23, 45; truth, 65
Democritus, 136, 301n25
Descartes, René, 9, 64, 69–70, 121, 137, 165, 251,
267; Cartesian coordinates, 232; Cartesian
tradition, 27, 28, 65–70, 261, 262, 292n8; on
"masters and possessors," 9, 274; Principia
philosophiae, 230
destiny, 173, 174, 180, 189, 195, 196, 232
determinism, 99, 250, 262, 267; in Spinoza, 257,
258, 267; in Stoicism, 167–69, 173–74, 189
devil, 34, 211–12, 227, 304n45
Diamond, Jared, 251
Diderot, Denis, 242
Dilthey, Wilhelm, 269
Diogenes of Babylon, 165
Diogenes the Cynic, 32
Diogenes Laertius, 164
disenchantment, 39, 49, 58; of the world, 8, 37, 38,
41, 42, 104, 132, 140, 143, 213, 230, 249, 265, 266
divine, divinity, 41, 106, 110, 111, 116, 241; in Greek
thought, 31, 33–34, 150, 192. See also cosmos,
ancient, as divine
Donne, John, 231, 232
doubt, 211–12, 227, 256, 258, 261
Douw, Gerrit, 107

Eastern thought, wisdom of, 21, 31, 43, 254
ecologists, 10, 31, 43, 276–77, 298n1
economics, 264; globalized, 10–11, 101; market,
119, 272
education, 252, 253, 267–68

ego, 69–70, 130, 284–85, 268
egocentrism, egotism, 3, 155, 234, 268, 279, 280
Ehrenberg, Alain, 289n4
Elinga, Pieter Jannens, 107
elite, elitism, 115, 120, 145
Empedocles, 179
ends, 10, 11–12, 155–56, 161, 278
Enlightenment, 10, 52, 53, 121, 276
ennui, 11–12, 289n10
enterprise, entrepreneurs, 42, 103, 117, 120, 122
envy, 11–14
Epictetus: on acceptance, reconciliation with
cosmos, 149, 162, 169, 175, 256; and Aristotle,
151; on death, 33, 147, 148, 150; on detachment, 178, 203; Discourses, 162, 165, 175;
Manual (Encheiridion, or Handbook), 165;
and Stoicism, 100, 165
Epicurus, Epicureans, 168, 290n1, 297n3, 307n32,
308n5; and Stoicism, 158, 168, 301n6, 301n25
equality, 104, 144, 243, 244, 275
eternity, 35, 142, 146–50; as the eternal, 40, 123,
258; Nietzsche on, 20, 94, 97; in present
moment, 97, 99, 179
ethics, 14, 24, 84, 169, 214, 233, 252, 253, 254, 264,
268, 278, 290n4; in ancient thought, 154, 155,
157, 160–61, 164, 167, 229–30; in Nietzsche,
63. See also cosmologico-ethical; morality
Europe, 26, 153, 187, 242, 289n7
evil, 159, 160, 267
evolution, theory of, 250–51

faith, 19, 26, 187, 213–22, 242, 245, 255, 262, 264; as
gift of God, 28, 261, 262, 263; and knowledge,
227, 261; in Nietzsche, 96; and reason, 188,
192, 195, 201, 215, 216, 223, 227, 240
fantasies, 2–4, 12
fate, 159, 162, 220; as Nietzsche amor fati, 94, 97–
98; in Stoicism, 167–73, 232,
Faust, 19
fears, 162, 171, 172, 180. See also death, fear of
Fellini, Federico, 5
fetishism, 80, 263
Feuerbach, Ludwig Andreas, 242
finality, 38–39, 161
finitude, 18, 33, 34, 35, 139, 140, 142, 146, 149, 150,
203, 211, 229; in Buddhism, 33; in Christianity, 35, 186, 196; in Stoicism, 33. See also
death
Fleiss, Wilhelm, 122

form, 66–67
Foucault, Michel, 57, 76
France, 86, 242, 244
Franck, Dan, 296n24
free will, 99, 101, 234–35, 236–37, 256, 258, 265, 267; in Greek thought, 31, 169, 173, 174, 195, 196; in Nietzsche, 96; in Spinoza, 171, 257
Freud, Sigmund, 73–74, 91–92, 122–31; on daydreams, 1–3; on death, 122–23; on happiness, success, 123–24; *Introduction to Psychoanalysis*, 125; on the libido, 125–29; mentioned, 4, 266, 271; and Nietzsche, 52, 73, 79, 88, 91–92, 121, 122, 131; on religion, 122–23, 242; and science, 79
future, 1–2, 176–78, 179, 243; expectation of, 244, 245, 255, 256; worry about, 175; future anterior tense, 181, 286

Gaia, 140
Galilei, Galileo, 137, 300n21
Gauchet, Marcel, 108, 242, 243, 245, 259; *Disenchantment of the World*, 242
Gautier, Théophile, 112
genealogy. *See under* Nietsche, Friedrich
genius, 64, 105, 111–12, 115, 116, 145; and art, 106, 110, 115, 116, 118, 119; and insanity, 78, 115, 293n1
Gilson, Etienne, on Christianity, 185–86, 238–39; on philosophy and religion, 188, 191, 220, 236–37
globalization, 10–11, 101, 275, 276, 283
God, 6, 28, 34, 40, 41, 168, 219, 240, 267; catechism on, 260–61; death of, 13–14, 37, 51, 52, 53, 56, 57, 58, 103, 109, 117, 266; existence of, 28, 226, 229; in Judaism, 191, 192; personal, 34, 35, 43, 189; salvation by grace of, 193, 196, 209; in Spinoza, 258; as transcendence, 7, 54
gods, Greek, 31, 137, 140–41, 143, 144, 152
Goethe, Johann Wolfgang von, 233, 281
Gorgias, 65
Gospels, 94, 122–23, 138, 215, 261
grace, 237, 262; moments of, 255–56. *See also* God, salvation by grace of
Greece, ancient, 31, 135, 136; art in, 106, 107, 108, 110, 113; Nietzsche on "great Hellenes," classicism, 90–91, 92, 93; philosophy in, 18, 30–32, 42, 136
Gregory VII (pope), 214
Gregory IX (pope), 216, 220

Guareschi, Giovanni, 7
guilt, 54, 55, 57, 98, 99, 256, 258

Habermas, Jürgen, 279
Hades, 140
Hadot, Pierre: on Epictetus, 165–66; on Greek philosophy, 163, 217, 297n1, 305n7, 308n5; on Stoicism, 168, 171, 178, 179, 301n5, 307n36
happiness, 9, 10, 121, 123–24, 176, 179, 203, 271–85 passim; in Greek thought, 151, 161–62, 167, 170–71, 172, in materialism, 40, 256, 257
heaven, Augustine on, 237–38, 240
Hegel, Georg William Friedrich: on art, 106, 138; on ethics, 22; on history, 8, 44; mentioned, 45, 165, 285, 293n16; on rationality, 138, 228; on religion, 108, 116, 137–38, 226, 229; tradition of, 283
Heidegger, Martin, 121, 138, 253, 266, 267, 289n10; on Greek philosophy, 136, 297n1; on technology, 8–9, 120; on will to power, 8, 120
here and now. *See* present
hero, 3, 7, 92
Hesiod, 140
heteronomy, 19, 28, 73, 243, 259, 260, 262–63, 264, 270, 277
Hipparchia, 32
historicity, 146–47, 196, 252, 253
history, 75, 101, 259, 277; in Hegel, 44; in Nietzsche, 80
Hobbes, Thomas, 271
homeland, 7, 41, 95, 116, 267
Homer, 282
Hooch, Pieter de, 107
hope, 40, 162, 172, 175–76, 178, 180, 245, 254–55, 286
Houellebecq, Michel, 96
Hugo, Victor, 92, 112, 287
human, humans, 104, 250–51, 252; and animal, 250–52, 267–68; divinization of the, 266–67
humanism, 41, 51, 156, 235, 278; authentic, 263, 264, 265–66; of the man-god, 39–42, 132, 247, 265, 270; materialist, 39–42; modern, 22–23, 36, 37, 136, 213, 245, 248, 249; Nietzsche and, 53, 54, 55, 57, 104; nonmetaphysical, 270, 286; and theology, 259
humanity, 30, 36–37, 95
humanization, 106, 109; of the good life, 29, 30, 43, 213–45
Hume, David, 52

humility, 28, 188, 191–92, 197, 198, 199–200, 201, 211, 212, 240, 261
Husserl, Edmund, 100, 267, 269

"I," 69–71, 104, 111, 130, 180, 261, 285. See also ego
idols, 40, 41, 121. See also under Nietzsche, Friedrich
immanence, 34, 39, 100–101, 265; philosophies of, 42; and transcendence, 34–35, 36, 108, 267
immortality, 185; in Aristotle, Aristotelianism, 151, 219–20, 221, 298n20; in Christian thought, 94, 186, 190, 208–9, 210, 211, 221, 226–27, 229; Cicero on, 149; imaginary of, 122; in Judaism, 196; in nature, 146–47; in Plato, Platonism, 149, 150, 199, 210, 226–27; in Stoic thought, 33, 147, 190
incarnation of the divine Word (logos) in Christ, 186, 187, 189, 192, 194, 211, 227; Augustine and, 192, 198, 199, 200, 201
Incohérents, 114
individual, 36–37, 178, 244, 248, 272, 282
individualism, 19, 103, 115–16, 119, 259, 260
innovation, 105, 109, 110–11, 113, 119, 120, 243, 259
insanity, 4, 115, 125, 129–31, 293n1
instant. See present
instincts, 90–91
intellect, 149, 151, 215, 221, 222
intelligence, 172, 174–75, 201, 284
intelligible, the, 62, 64, 65, 80, 91
intensity, 38, 42, 59, 281, 284. See also under Nietzsche, Friedrich
interest, interests, 272–73, 278
Islam, 26, 186, 217, 218, 222, 224, 225, 306n10

Jesus Christ: humility of, 199–200; as incarnation of the logos, 186–87, 189–90, 192, 194, 198, 211, 218; on love, 201, 202, 204–5; mentioned, 194, 227; parables of, 138, 198, 215; resurrection of, 210; resurrections by, 190, 202; as revealed truth, 239, 240; views of, by non-Christians, 191, 192, 200
Jews, Judaism, 35, 202, 210; and Aristotle, 216, 217, 218, 219, 222, 306n10; and Christianity, 190–92, 193, 194, 198, 200, 211; philosophy and religion for, 186
John the Evangelist, Saint, 186, 187–88, 190, 191, 194, 195. See also under Bible
John XXI (pope), 220
John XXII (pope), 222

John Paul II (pope), 27, 228, 240, 262–63; Fides et ratio (Faith and Reason), 27, 228, 240; Splendor of Truth, 262–63
Jonas, Hans, 152
judgment, 75, 100, 122, 163
justice, 95, 144, 261, 263, 268
Justin Martyr, Saint, 189, 191, 193–97, 219, 235; Dialogue with Trypho, 189, 194

Kandinsky, Wassily, 114–15, 119
Kant, Immanuel, 22, 23, 217, 256, 278–79; Critique of Judgment, 279; Foundations of the Metaphysics of Morals, 284; and free will, 256, 267; on happiness, 271, 273, 284; on reason and nature, 166–67; and Stoicism, 165, 174
Kierkegaard, Søren Aabye, 36
Kilwardby, Robert (archbishop of Canterbury), 222
knowledge, 9, 216, 254, 270, 278; of cosmos, 237; and faith, 227, 261; for Nietzsche, 75, 78; and science, 264, 274; self-, 237
Koran, 224, 225, 226
Koyré, Alexandre, 231, 232, 297n1

labor, 235
Lacan, Jacques, 136, 293n12, 293n18
La Fontaine, Jean de, 2, 5, 12, 22
language, 65, 139, 251, 253
Lanzky, Paul, 85
law, laws, 24, 68, 139, 260, 263, 268, 278; and democracy, 26; in Greek thought, 144; as heteronomy, 243; human origin of, 244; in Judaism, 191; the Law in Avveroës, 224, 225; and nature, 154, 234; in primitive societies, 259; and religion, 26, 34, 259, 262
Lazarus, 190, 202
Le Guay, Damien, 264
Leibniz, Gottfried Wilhelm, 69, 293n16
Leroux, Gaston, 3
Lessing, Gotthold Ephraim, 226, 229
Leys, Simon, 17
Leyster, Judith, 107
Libéra, Alain de, 224
liberty, 10, 39, 174–75, 235, 266, 271, 274, 277; in Buddhism, 203; in Christianity, 196, 261, 262, 263; determination and, 19, 173–74; excess of, 267; Kant on, 284; of others, 22, 280; in Stoicism, 167, 169–72, 203; and utopias, 38. See also free will

libido, 125–29, 264, 268; figure, 128

logic, 18, 24, 31, 73–74, 157, 164, 227, 282

logos: Jesus Christ as incarnation of, 186, 187, 189, 192, 198, 200, 201, 211, 218; Saint John's use of, 186, 187, 188, 190–91; Justin on, 194–95; in Stoicism, 168, 189

love, 97, 263, 281, 284; and attachment, 203–6, 207, 209; Christian (*agapē*), 201, 202, 204, 205, 207; in Christianity, 201, 202, 203, 204–5, 211, 255; "in" God, 186, 190, 206, 209, 297–98; of God, 186, 201, 202, 206–7, 211; of human beings, 206; in humans and animals, 253, 267; logic of, 24; of neighbor, 201, 202; as *philia*, 202, 267; of self, 106–7, 285; singularity and, 285–86; wisdom of, 257–58

lucidity, 121, 122, 123, 132, 254, 258, 270

Lucretius, 52

madness. *See* insanity

Maimonides (Moses ben Maimon), 218, 219, 222, 223, 226

man, 7, 57, 58, 104; death of, 53, 57

Manet, Claude, 64

Marcus Aurelius Antoninus, 159, 165, 170, 182; on death, 148; and Justin, 193–96; on living in the present, 176–77; *Meditations*, 148, 159, 176; wisdom exercises in, 178, 180

marginality, cult of, 105, 112, 120

Marquet, Auguste, 112

Márquez, Gabriel García, 282

Marx, Karl, 37, 73–75, 104, 120, 136, 271, 275; and Nietzsche, 71, 73, 79, 291n2; and religion, 242, 266

materialism, 7, 19, 39–42, 99–101, 214, 241, 245, 249–59, 283, 291n2, 308n5; and Eastern wisdom, 43; in the Enlightenment, 52; of humanism, 38–42; of Nietzsche, 40, 57, 58, 60–77, 96, 101; and religion, 55, 100, 253–54, 258, 264; spirituality of, 40, 253, 255–56, 302n31; and Stoicism, 13; and transcendence, 6–7, 19, 54, 60, 73, 263, 265, 268

meaning, 8–11, 50, 51, 100, 101, 122, 241; absence of, 58; in cosmos, 152, 155, 156, 171; logic of, 11, 50, 51

mentality, enlarged, 279–80, 281, 282, 283, 284, 286

Mephistopheles, 19

metaphysics, 18, 103, 138, 233, 251; idols of, 37–38, 39; illusions of, 121, 122–23, 124, 138, 257; materialism and, 254, 256; and philosophy, 39, 122, 141; and religion, 25, 138, 141, 258

Metsu, Gabriel, 107

Michon, Curil, 305n9

modernity, 274–77

Mohammed, 218

Molière, 282

monotheisms, 55, 96, 123, 269; and Aristotle, 217, 218, 221, 223; and Greek philosophy, 34, 158, 185. *See also* Christianity; Islam; Jews, Judaism

Montaigne, Michel de, 286

morality, 57, 58, 139, 150, 161, 251, 254, 264, 278; Arendt on, 146–47; "beyond morality," 21–25; in Christianity, 261, 263; and the cosmos, 152, 153; in Greek thought, 90–91, 144, 161, 195–96, 278; insufficiency of, 22–23, 24; materialism and, 254, 268; and nature, 154, 233–34, 252, 278; Nietzsche on, 68, 78–79; as secular, 53; and values, 22, 161, 267

Moses, 218

Mozart, Wolfgang Amadeus, 93

Murger, Henri, 112–20, 296n24

Muslims, 162, 219, 224. *See also* Islam

Musonius Rufus, 165

myth, mythology, 138, 140, 142, 143

Naipaul, V. S., 279–80, 284

narration, 252–53

nation-state, 275, 276, 277

nature, 21, 80, 111, 143, 144, 146–47, 167, 278; characteristics of, 144, 154, 155, 156, 160, 168, 235; in Christian thought, 35, 195, 215, 226, 240–41; domination of, 9–10, 232; and hierarchy, 12–13; human and animal, 250–52, 267; living according to, 32, 174; as living being, 9, 143, 144, 152; modern view of, 231–35, 274, 275; in Stoicism, 168, 174; and values, 41, 153, 154, 278. *See also* cosmos, ancient

Nero (emperor of Rome), 165

Nerval, Gérard de, 112

neurosis, 4, 127, 128, 129, 130

New Testament, 142, 277. *See also* Bible

Newton, Sir Isaac, 64, 137, 141, 153, 230, 300n21; *Principia mathematica*, 230

Nietzsche, Friedrich: *amor fati* in, 93–102, 286; as anarchist, 86, 88; on art: 61, 63–64, 80–81, 82–83, 84, 87, 99; on classicism, 92–93; on consciousness, 68, 69–70, 72, 73; on death of God, 43, 49–59, 94, 96, 249, 266; on death of man, 49–59; on democracy, 49, 56, 61, 63–64, 65; eternal recurrence in, 19, 20, 93–102, 103, 142; eternity in the instant in, 78, 93–102;

ethics in, 87, 90, 93; on no facts, 44, 68, 72, 75; on fetishism, 71, 72; on forces, active, 61–66, 86, 87, 88; on forces, reactive, 55, 61–66, 74, 79, 80, 86, 87, 88–89, 90, 130; on forces, vital, 70, 75, 84, 86, 87–88, 89, 92, 93, 98, 99, 121; on free will, 70, 174; genealogy of, 39, 50, 52, 73–76, 104; as genius, 37, 49, 78; grand style in, 78, 84–93, 94, 96, 98, 99, 116, 130–31, 284; on happiness, 271, 273, 309n1; on idols, 37–38, 58, 60–61, 67, 73, 78, 79; immanence in, 66–67; immoralism of, 79, 84, 93; as insane, 49, 78; intensity in, 38, 58, 59, 78, 84–93, 98, 99, 116, 284; interpretations in, 71, 72, 75, 76; on judgment, 67–68, 70–71, 72; and knowledge, 79–84; as materialist, 39, 50, 60–77, 73, 80, 241; mentioned, 8, 40, 105, 115, 117, 121, 122, 138, 142, 165, 174, 176, 198, 295n30; morality in, 84–85, 86, 87–88, 89, 90, 93, 95; nihilism in, 93, 116, 242, 245; object in, 71, 72, 73, 75, 80; on passions, 87, 88, 90, 92; philosophizing with a hammer, 49–51, 52–59; 73–76; *praxis* in, 84–93; on the real, reality, 51, 60, 61–66; and religion, 20, 49, 52, 53, 54, 55–56, 96, 122–23; salvation in, 93–102; and science, 49, 55, 63, 74, 291n6; on the self ("I," ego), 69–71; on the senses, 63; on sexual mores, 86, 87, 92; skepticism of, 76–77, 79; soteriology in, 93–102; spiritualization of impulses in, 84–93; subject in, 68–71, 72, 73, 75; *theōria* in, 79–84; on thinking, 71; transcendence, illusions of, 49–59, 60, 66–67, 68, 71, 94–95, 99; on truth, 79–83, 84, 96; on twilight of the idols, 49–59; on ugliness, 63–64, 65, 90; unconscious in, 68–71; and values, 49, 55, 59, 72, 93, 96; will to power in, 38, 58, 80, 93, 101, 120, 121, 292n2, 298n8; "will to truth" in, 49, 61, 63, 64, 66, 74, 79–84, 93; wisdom of, 59, 77, 78–102, 217; world, end of the, in, 49–59
Nietzsche, Friedrich, works of: *Beyond Good and Evil,* 56, 70–71, 174; *Birth of Tragedy,* 81; *Ecce Homo,* 60–61, 78, 79, 97, 104; *Human, All Too Human,* 87; *Joyful Wisdom,* 68–69, 75–76; *Thus Spake Zarathustra,* 50, 94; *Twilight of the Idols,* 63–64, 72, 75, 81, 84–85, 86, 90, 91; *Will to Power,* 72, 80, 92, 97, 99
nihilism, 37, 54, 55, 56–57, 91, 100, 103
nostalgia, 175, 178, 276. *See also* past

object, objectivity, 74, 76–77, 110
Old Testament, 236. *See also* Bible

ontotheology, 258, 264, 265
originality, 105, 109, 110, 112, 113

painting, Dutch, 105, 106–8, 120
Paris, 112, 113; University of, 216, 220, 222, 226
particularity, 281–83, 286–86
Pascal, Blaise: on the ego or "I," 261, 284–85; on the firmament, 238; on the good, 3, 303n20; on the libertine and space, 137, 231; on love, 204–9, 211, 258, 285–86; on man but a reed, 238; *Pensées,* 205, 284, 290n10; and Stoicism, 165; on weariness, 290n10; wager of, 196
passions, 92, 150, 172, 178, 202, 203, 205, 276
past, 1–2, 177, 243, 244, 277; attachment to, 175, 177–78, nostalgia for, 175, 179, 255, 286
Pasteur, Louis, 241
Paul, Saint, 190–91, 194, 195, 196, 206, 239, 255. *See also under* Bible
Peckham, John (archbishop of Canterbury), 222
Pelagius, 237
Penaetius of Rhodes, 165
performance, cult of, 8–11
perspectivism, 80, 293n12
Peter, Saint, 194
phenomenology, 100, 269, 270
philosopher, philosophers, 20, 106, 226, 278, 293n1; Greek, 31, 144–45, 217
philosophy, 18, 84, 136, 139, 157, 163, 194, 198, 200, 220, 228, 241, 278; Arabic, 194, 224; Christian thinkers and, 194, 211–12, 215, 216–17, 236, 240; contemporary, 18, 21, 217; Greek, 18, 32–33, 65, 131, 143, 145, 152, 164, 211, 236; Jewish, 194; lay, 213–45; modern, 76, 137; in Nietzsche, 61, 62, 79, 83, 84, 97; and religion, 19, 27, 32–33, 43, 136–37, 138–39, 140–41, 142–46, 147, 152, 163, 185, 212, 213, 216, 217, 221–23, 239; and salvation, 19, 32–33, 43, 137, 139, 150, 185, 217; and science, 21, 141, 143, 215, 232; and theology, 18, 141, 151, 186, 216, 221, 223, 241; as theology's "handmaid," 186, 189, 191, 195, 212, 214, 216, 229
physics, 159; ethics in, 156, 157, 160–61, 230; form in, 66, 67; Greek, 18, 31, 157, 164, 167, 230, 241; "material elements" as, 140–41, 143, 144; modern, 9, 137, 153, 158
Piaget, Jean, 125
Picasso, Pablo, 296n24
Plato, Platonists, 31, 156, 187, 230, 238–39; on art, 81–82, 83, 105; Augustine and, 192, 197–99, 200, 201, 217–19, 222, 229, 237, 238, 303n18;

Plato, Platonists (*continued*)
and Christianity, 188, 197, 198, 237; consciousness in, 69–70; dialogues of, 61–62, 63; and immortality, 33, 210, 226–27; and intelligible world, 81, 223, 227, 237, 239; Justin and, 189, 193, 194, 195, 196; labor in, 235; mentioned, 136, 143, 151, 219, 225, 282; neoplatonism, 197, 218; and Nietzsche, 80, 81, 90; *Republic*, 157, 210, 237; *Timaeus*, 149–50, 151, 153, 234; and University of Paris, 226
pleasure principle, 124
Plotinus, 193
Plutarch, 164, 168, 171, 173–74, 302n11, 302n14; "On Stoic Self-Contradictions," 173
Poe, Edgar Allen, 175
poets, poetry, 65, 144, 145, 295n1
politics: 21, 37, 139, 104, 116, 252, 260, 278; fundamentalist, 39–40; messianic, 39, 50, 58; morality and, 24–25; in primitive societies, 259; prophetic, 39; religion and, 36, 53, 245; in utopias, 245
Porphyry, 193, 196, 199, 200–201; *On the Life of Plotinus*, 193
Poseidon, 140
Posidonius of Apamea, 165
positivism, 68, 144, 274
praxis, 31–33, 78, 79, 84, 194, 195–96, 211, 235, 277–78
present, 1–2, 95, 98, 105; as eternal instant, 97, 98, 179, 286; living in, here and now, 105, 175, 176–77, 179, 255; and past, future, 99, 175
pride, 28, 192, 193, 198, 199, 201; philosophical, 188, 197, 199, 200, 215, 241; of reason, 200, 212, 216
progress, 10, 53, 54, 104, 119, 274–75, 276, 277; "progressivism," 55–56, 57–58
Protagoras, 65
providence, 159, 162; in Christian thought, 180, 186, 189–90, 196, 237; in Greek thought, 195, 219, 221, 232, 233
psychoanalysis, 19, 39, 68, 74–75, 101–2, 122, 124, 125, 129–31, 175, 277, 293n18
Ptolemy, 64
Puccini, Giacomo, 112
Puech, Aymé, 188
Pythagoras, Pythagorism, 193, 196

quotidian, the, 105, 108–10, 113, 116, 121

Rameau, Jean-Philippe, 282
rationalism, 9, 73–74, 140, 141, 144, 212, 214, 217, 223, 240, 241

rationality, 27, 32, 51, 138, 168
Rawls, John, 279
real, the, 101, 160, 256, 265
reality, 30–31, 39, 40, 173, 258; adapting to, 123, 125; in art, 82; reality principle, 124
reason, 10, 157, 212, 278; in Averroës, 225; in Christian thought, 187, 188, 193, 195, 198, 213–16, 218–19, 240, 241, 260–61; in cosmic order, 160, 171, 172; in Descartes, 9; in Greek thought, 187, 192, 193, 201; instrumental, 10, 157; and nature, 166–67; in Stoicism, 167, 168, 171, 178–79; in Thomas Aquinas, 220–21, 223, 226–27, 228–29, 240; as universal Reason, 171; and virtue, 171
religion, 9, 35, 36, 38, 42–43, 103, 241–45, 248, 259, 260, 274, 283; and art, 138; critique of, 52; decline of, 25–28, 30, 50, 103, 266; of earthly salvation, 241; Freud on, 121, 122, 123, 124; fundamentalism in, 39–40; in Greece, 140–41; Hegel on, 116, 138; materialism and, 39–40, 39, 254, 259; metaphysics and, 25, 254; modernizing, 259–70; Nietzsche on, 37–38, 55–56, 122–23; as "onto-theology," 264; and philosophy, 18, 19, 25, 43, 137, 138–39, 140–41, 142–46, 185–212, 213, 216–18, 222; and science, 230; of terrestrial salvation, 53, 54
republic, republicans, republican idea, 21, 23, 40, 56, 104, 268; neorepublicans, 276
Rembrandt (Rembrandt Harmensz van Rijn), 64
resurrection, 190, 208–11, 220, 227
revelation, 27, 34, 157, 188, 221–22, 226, 261; and Aristotle, 219, 220; and Augustine, 197, 198; and Averroës, 224, 226; and Justin, 195; natural, and "true Revelation," 220; reason and, 220, 228; Thomas Aquinas on, 227, 228
revolution, 7, 40, 95, 116, 243, 267
Revolution, French, 13
revolutionary ideals, ideology, 6–7, 54, 104, 116, 119, 171
rights: equal, 244, 275; of man, 22–23, 39, 50, 104, 154, 156, 275
Rimbaud, Arthur, 65
romanticism, 10, 78, 105, 110, 114, 234, 276, 281; Nietzsche on, 87, 90, 92, 93
Rome, ancient, 193, 194
Rosset, Clément, 100
Rousseau, Jean-Jacques, 4, 255, 267

sacrifice, 253, 266–67
Saint-Simon, Henri, comte de, 114

salvation 6, 35, 43, 55–56, 146, 150, 152, 201, 211, 241, 259; Christian doctrine of, 185, 186–87, 189, 191–92, 196, 199–200, 202, 209, 210, 214, 217, 220–21, 236–37; by God, 34; in Greek thought, 185, 186–97, 272; humanism doctrine of, 281; of humanity, 36–37; in Judaism, 191; in materialism, 6–7, 43, 254; by oneself, 18–19, 32–33, 37, 98, 137; by an other, 37, 192, 241; and philosophy, 18, 32–33, 43, 137, 139, 142, 143, 145; secularization and 135, 146; in Stoicism, 32–33; terrestrial, 36; 53, 241; by *theōria*, 33; in utopias, 36, 245. *See also* soteriology

Samuel ibn Tibbon, 219

Sand, George, 112

Sartre, Jean-Paul, 116, 267

Satan, 227

Saturn, 140–41

Schönberg, Arnold, 115, 119

Schopenhauer, Arthur, 58

Schubert, Franz, 95

Schumann, Robert, 93

science, 8–9, 74, 65, 116, 139, 239, 250, 276, 282; and church today, 240–41; early, 136; empirical, 223; Freud and, 73–74; in Greek thought, 141, 143, 144, 273–74; laws of, 275; Marx and, 73–74; materialism and, 250, 254; in Middle Ages, 223; modern, 9, 66, 161, 229–30, 232, 238, 240–41, 274; and modernity, 274–77; natural, 154; Nietzsche on, 51, 53, 61–64, 68, 71, 79, 80, 83, 291n6; of observation, 31; positive, 21, 153, 264; rationality of, 27; and Thomas Aquinas, 215

scientific revolution, 214, 230, 231, 232, 235, 239, 274, 275

scientism, 36, 53, 54, 253

Scripture, 195, 201–2, 228. *See also* Bible; New Testament; Old Testament

secularization, 37, 42–43, 113, 221, 223, 229, 266; and art, 106, 110; and disenchantment with the world, 104–6; and "modern humanism," 36; of religion, 137–40, 141, 142, 144; of salvation, 135, 146; of society, 106, 110, 213

self. *See* ego

self-reflection, 274, 276–77, 279

Seneca, 156, 165, 170, 175, 176, 177

senses, 62, 106; realm of the, 64, 80, 81, 82, 160, 223

Shakespeare, William, 282

Siger de Brabant, 221, 222

Simplicius of Cilicia, 301n1

singularity, 281–86

Smith, Adam, 52

society, 276, 277; democratic, 132, 136; hierarchy in, 12–13, 132; historical 242; modern, 120, 132, 242, 275; primitive, 259; religious, 132, 242, 243–44; roles in, 275; secular, 242; traditional, 110–11, 120, 242–44

sociology, 19, 39, 74

Socrates, 61–66, 90–93, 113, 157, 194, 237

solitude, 105, 115, 119, 203–4

Sophists, Sophism, 65, 91, 136, 158, 290n1, 297n3

soteriology, 93–102, 190–91, 273, 278, 281, 286; Augustine on, 199; in Christianity, 202, 210, 211; in Greek thought, 33–34, 194, 196, 272; of materialism, 254; and philosophy, 43, 79, 151, 152

space, 231, 232, 233

Spinoza, Baruch (Benedictus de), 22, 100, 256, 257–58, 268, 300n19; determinism, free will in, 168, 169, 171, 174, 267, 308n5; *Ethics*, 151–52, 257; and Greek philosophy, 149, 151–52; and love, 286; as materialist, 19, 39, 249, 254, 255; and religion, 40, 94, 142, 151–52, 258

spirituality: and death of God, 53; in Greek thought, 33, 185; lay, 132, 135, 181, 281, 284, 286; materialism and, 55, 249, 253, 254, 255; new forms of, 50, 132, 240; spiritual exercises, 173, 177–78, 179–80

Stalin, Josef, 7

Steen, Jan, 107

Stoics, Stoicism, 32, 51, 100, 193, 194, 203, 232–33, 236, 255, 258, 299nn10, 11, 301n6, 301n25; and acceptance of life, 32, 162, 247; Cicero on, 158, 160–61; as "cosmodicy," 233; and cosmos, 155–56, 230, 232; critiques of, 172–75; destiny in, 189, 232; fate for, 232; fear of death in, 33, 190, 202; as ideal type of ancient wisdom, 164–82; immortality in, 190; and liberty, 167; on *logos*, 187; on love and attachment, 202, 205, 206, 207, 209, 255; and materialism, 43, 256; nature for, 144, 155, 232–33; present for, 97, 98, 176; providence for, 189, 190, 232; salvation for, 32–33, 190; school, 153, 155, 164–65, 202; theory for, 32; well-lived life for, 31

Strauss, Leo, 297n1, 300n19

subject, 74–75, 101, 292n8. *See also* ego

subjectivity, 71, 74, 76–77, 110

success, 4–6, 8, 11, 12, 19, 122; in bohemia, 177, 119; degrees in, 150; for Freud, 121, 123–34; models of, 29–30; of others, 13–14; in philosophy, 103, 148, 150

Taylor, Charles, 309n9
technology, 8–12, 101, 117, 120, 121, 131, 230–31, 251, 274, 275
Teilhard de Chardin, Pierre, 251
Tempier, Etienne (bishop of Paris), 220, 222
Ter Borch, Gerard, 107
theologians, 191, 193
theologico-ethical, 146
theologico-political, 26, 132
theology, 34–36, 53, 54, 55, 223, 263; Christian, 189, 193, 195; and cosmology, 176; humanist, 259; illusion in, 122; and law, 26; and philosophy, 18, 151, 186, 213, 217; and science, 230
"theo-nomy," theonomy, 262, 263
theôria, 31, 33, 78, 79–84, 149, 156–57, 158, 187, 194–95, 211, 235, 273–77
Thomas Aquinas, Saint, Thomism, 27, 188, 214–30, 235, 237, 239–40, 241; *Summa contra Gentiles*, 228
time, 141, 177, 180
Tocqueville, Alexis de, 12, 136, 275
Todorov, Tzvetan, 106–7, 108–9
transcendence, 6–7, 30–36, 42, 43, 94, 103, 104, 108, 245, 259, 263, 269–70; in art, 106, 109; Christian, 34–35, 236, 237, 238, 264; criticism of, 36–37, 39, 73, 122; decline, eclipse of, 6–8, 13, 30, 37–39, 116; figures of, 41, 51, 54, 250; in Greek cosmos, 158, 238, 269; of the human, 32; illusions of, 49–59, 60, 249; of law, 244, 259; in materialism, 19, 40, 60, 250; in modern humanism, 36, 41, 239, 264, 265; new, 37, 41, 100, 265–70; phenomenological, 269; in philosophy, 145, 137; rejection of, 42; supernatural in, 100
truth, 62, 64, 65, 75, 80, 228, 265; in art, 80, 81–82; double, 218, 220–22, 227, 228; in Freud and Marx, 73–74; in modern philosophy, 76; Nietzsche on, 74; 81; psychoanalysis and, 74–75; revealed, 240, 260–61; scientific, 62, 64, 268; in Socrates, 62, 65
Trypho, 194

unconscious, 19, 68–69, 73, 75, 101, 104, 121, 127, 129
universal, the, 40, 51, 268, 282, 285, 286
universality, 63, 64, 139, 282, 285
universe, 62, 159, 227, 230, 239, 277; created or eternal, 219, 221, 238–39; disenchanted, 231; in Greek thought, 147–48, 150; modern, 152, 154; natural, 215; in Pascal, 231. *See also* cosmos, ancient

utilitarianism, 23, 271, 272–73
utopias, 8, 25, 30, 36–37, 38, 41; messianic, 21, 36, 50; modern, 244–45, 254; secular, 36

Valadier, Paul, 309n9
values, 6, 11–12, 232, 263, 264, 273, 274; changing, 84; Cicero on, 161; discovery of, 41, 43–44; as divine, 41; as human creation, 263; in humanity, 41–42; in materialism, 39, 263, 268; modern, 153, 154; in natural order, 161, 235; as respect for others, 22; transcendent, 49–59, 104, 263, 265, 266, 268, 270; in utopias, 245
Vermeer, Jan, 107, 109, 281
Vernant, Jean-Pierre, 140–45
Verne, Jules, 36
Villey, Michel, 297n1
virtue, 234, 235; for moderns, 234; in Stoicism, 166–67, 169, 172–75
Voltaire, 204, 242

Wagner, Richard, 98
Weber, Max, 13, 266, 273–74
well-being, 271, 272, 273, 274
Wiesel, Elie, 17
will, 121, 163, 169; will to power, 8, 38, 43, 117, 120–21, 292n2; "will to will," 121. *See also under* Nietzsche, Friedrich
wisdom, 35, 139, 163, 164–82, 253; ancient, 42, 43, 44, 97, 133, 136, 164–82, 187, 202, 206, 207, 230, 232, 255, 273, 283; Buddhist, 97; Eastern, 44, 204, 240; exercises, 31–32, 217; Greek, 78, 135, 202, 214; Hellenic, 204; of the "I," 179; of love, 257–58; materialist, 253, 254, 255; modern, 132; philosophical, 147; of the present moment, 175; of providence, 162; of radical immanence, 39–40; Stoic, 97, 164–82; theoretical, 148, 150; third type of, 254, 256, 270; of the world, 103, 156, 172–75, 179, 203, 299n4
Word, 186–87, 191–92. See also *logos*
world, the, 51, 57, 159, 277–78, 281; closed, 230, 232; common, 252, 253; end of, 52, 58; as *kosmos*, 277; as neutral, 233; order in, 30–31, 32, 34, 35; origins of, 140, 143; re-enchantment of, 266. *See also* cosmos, ancient

Zarathustra, 81
Zeus, 140
Zeno of Citium, 32, 100, 164